Old Parents and Purple Tulips

Family Outing to Spirit Lake, Mount St. Helens.
Left-right: Author, brother Rolf, father & mother, Author's aunt

Old Parents and Purple Tulips

Navigating The Maze Of Care-giving, Dementia, Sibling Conflict, And Guns

Betty Alder

Hansville Press

For information
Hansville Press
info@oldparentsandurpletulips.com

Published 2015

ISBN-13: 9780986190803
ISBN: 0986190802
Library of Congress Control Number: 2015937463
Hansville Press, Hansville, Washington

Printed in the United States of America

To my parents who provided years of positive parental nurturing and love in our family structure. Their support helped me persevere in my adulthood when I undertook to become a parental figure to them.

To Don, for his unwavering support and unconditional love in keeping me grounded in my family life and in Christian principles.

To my children Nick and El for their love and devotion to our family and for their effort to be mature beyond their years through some very rough times.

Acknowledgments

CAROLYN MADDUX, THANK *you for your belief in me that I had a story to tell which was worthy of sharing and would be helpful to others. Thank you for your pedagogical mastery that allowed me to feel confident that I was a writer capable and deserving of becoming an author.*

Thank you to my fellow members of Checkers Writing Critique Group – Dave Kragen, Ruth Schuler, and Jim Wise – for your knowledge, wisdom, and tenacity to weather through two-plus years of providing almost weekly constructive criticism and encouragement.

Frannie Nightingale, although you have departed this earth, you were a dear friend who listened and encouraged and loved me during our family retreats to Decatur Island. You relentlessly told me this story needed to be told. You graciously consented to do a first reading of the manuscript. I so wish you were here now to see the book finally published.

Jane Smith, you are a friend who eagerly agreed to be a first reader of the manuscript. You employed your editorial expertise and provided constructive comments as well as giving encouragement to continue and complete the project.

Trudy Catterfeld, thank you for your enthusiasm and encouragement for this project and for your incredible ability and patience in guiding this first-time author daring to master the steep learning-curve necessary to achieve publication in this age of technology.

Lucy Pullen Warner, thank you for your continued interest and encouragement in this arduous task of telling my family story. Thank you for believing in it, that it would be helpful and encouraging to others. Thank you for your friendship over 50 years, a friendship which was a wonderful part of my childhood, a friendship which I value even more now in our less-than-youthful stage of life.

And finally, thank you, dear Aunt Mavis, my mother's younger sister and the one person in our extended family who went to extraordinary lengths to be supportive, understanding, comforting, fair, and loving to us all in this strange saga. I love you!

CHAPTER 1

The Good Life

FREQUENTLY I STILL awaken, squint toward the blurry numerals on the bedside clock, and recoil under my pillow at the glow of 5-1-6. If it's earlier than 5:16 AM, I wait until I'm sure the clock hands have passed that combination. If it's later, I indulge in a leisurely wake-up. I sense this same eeriness when I receive $5.16 change at the grocery store, when I note 5-1-6 on a license plate, or when it's five hundred sixteen miles to a location on a map; and I can't help wondering if other people working in the kitchen have five minutes and sixteen seconds remaining on the timer as often as I do. I don't know if it's guilt, shame, some form of a divine visit, or a psychological fixation.

I grew up in a little white frame house where the mailman walked up to the front porch and deposited the mail in a small flat metal box attached to the wall near the front door opening. Above the mailbox and visible for easy identification were large black numerals, 5-1-6. The wrought-iron of the numerals matched the little wicket opening in the solid wooden front door. The house numbers were removed each time the house was painted every five or six years and carefully replaced to stand out against the whiteness of the front porch. That's how Mama wanted it, and that's how Daddy did it. After all, he built the house for her, every board, every shingle. He built it himself with only a little help on the wiring and plumbing.

It was a good house in which to raise a family. Family and home ownership were dreams being fulfilled by many Americans at the end of WWII. Bad times, fears, loss of life were over. Hope, family, and prosperity were imminent throughout the country, and for Mama and Daddy, too.

Years passed at 516. Spindly laurel twigs became a hedge on either side of the two adjoining fifty foot city lots. Front yard "Victory Gardens" producing vegetables for our family in war years became a lush lawn and a foundation landscape of rhododendrons, azaleas, and camellias. At the back of the property and parallel to the alley, rabbit hutches and chicken coops that housed animals providing meat for ourselves and others in our neighborhood in war time became a border of more than a hundred rose bushes. Each bush produced abundantly in response to well-aged rabbit deposits and fish innards routinely separated out from successful catches of salmon or

Author and brother Rolf play with rabbits raised for food exchanged with neighbors for chickens during WWII, c.1944

steelhead and carefully cultivated between the roots of each bush. These floral soldiers matured meshing their outstretched arms to guard two grape arbors, several kinds of berries, and a small orchard of apple, pear, plum, and cherry trees, and to discourage youthful alley invaders from helping themselves to the profits of a hardworking man's labor. Eventually allegiance to an unwritten "Good Fence/Good Neighbor Creed" resulted in installation of a cyclone fence, its metallic harshness softened by a palisade of colorful hollyhocks towering over the roses. More flower beds and a large vegetable garden took up the interior of the lot next to the house, enriched through the years by nurturing from Mama and Daddy, and as often as could be persuaded, or required, the additional attention and energy of two growing children.

In this setting Mama, Daddy, my brother Rolf, and I flourished. I would say we were a normal, happy family. I felt loved, supported, secure. I aspired to someday attain my own dreams, my own family, my own white frame house, but with less garden and fewer fruit trees.

Yes, years at 516 were good. In due time education, career, marriage, and children took me away from this home, but the positive impact of strong family support continued. The nurturing once given to verdant landscape focused on Don and me and our children, especially the children. Mama and Daddy became Grandma

Author on log in Toutle River, WA

and Grandpa Malfait, and they were wonderful grandparents with all the appropriate spoiling, pride, and special attention showered on their grandchildren. Trips to 516 were fun and exciting for all of us and supportive to our hopes and dreams for a bright future for ourselves and our children.

My mind often wanders back to the comfort of those years, but just as often my thoughts get hung up on the summer of 1983...

Don and I are in our new home. We both enjoy jobs in education, love our colleagues, and have only a five minute drive to work. We refinance our house at a very attractive low interest rate, and pay off *all* our debts. We pay cash for new furniture for the house, and we purchase a new 4-wheel drive truck to haul our "new-used" 19 1/2-ft. Bellboy with the 185 OMC engine and a brand new Evinrude 9.4 kicker engine. We still have a savings account of several thousand dollars, and that's a novelty since we haven't had one at all for twenty-two years of marriage.

We anticipate a superb summer vacation, if only the salmon fishing will measure up. Our children finished a great school year, with Nick being fifteen and completing 9th grade. He survived a year of football, the advent of facial hair and more hair, and the hormonal mentality that goes with it. El completed grade six and turned twelve years in age, which in her view is closer to age eighteen or twenty. She's broken several sixth-grade male hearts, is an enthusiastic soccer/softball kid, a first-rate participant in band and chorus, and strikingly beautiful. Both kids are neat people. Their years and hormones do make living with them stressful at times, but life is good then, too.

As usual Grandma and Grandpa Malfait have invited them for a summer visit, and they're both excited for that. Grandma thinks two weeks would be wonderful. We think one week would be better. Grandma doesn't always realize her energy level isn't quite as high as theirs. Besides, despite the good times with their grandparents in Ridgeview, Nick and El don't want to miss any time in the San Juan Islands and anticipated fun on the "new" boat. No matter how the timing turns out, we all anticipate a perfect summer 1983. For Don and me even one relaxing childless week will allow us to celebrate and enjoy our 22nd anniversary. Life is indeed so good!

CHAPTER 2

My World Falls Apart

OUR TRIP TO Ridgeview to drop the children off with Grandma and Grandpa Malfait is routine, three hours and fifteen minutes. We arrive in the early afternoon. After brief, boisterous greetings all around, we move to a shady spot under the cherry trees in the back yard to enjoy a picnic celebration honoring Mother and me, as we both have July birthdays. My brother Rolf stops by in time to join us for birthday cake, help us do a fairly recognizable version of "Happy Birthday," and share some good laughs as we relate experiences since we last saw one another.

Later in the cool of the evening we all walk the two blocks to a nearby lakeside park to take in the Fourth of July fireworks. Afterwards, Rolf departs for his home in Newcastle, as he has an early morning log-hauling job. Don and I stay overnight in Ridgeview and leave the next morning after breakfast, our list in hand of all the things we want to accomplish during our child-free week. Three hours and fifteen minutes of our return trip to our home flits by as we savor two-party conversation minus teenage banter.

Two days later Mother calls in the evening, "How are you and Don doing?"

"We're having a very relaxing time. The real question is, how are you and Dad doing?"

"Oh, we're doing pretty well. But I do need to tell you one of my pearl earrings which Grandpa gave me for my birthday is missing. I can't find it anywhere. El and the little girl from next door were playing in the front bedroom where my jewelry box is, and I thought maybe the girls got into it. I've grilled everyone but I can't get anything out of either one of the kids."

"Let me speak to Nick and El, Mom. Maybe I can help."

Nick is first on the phone. "Hi, Mom. Grandpa and me are loading the car with newspapers. We're going to the dump after lunch."

"But, Nick, Grandma tells me she's lost an earring. Do you know anything about that?"

"No, not really. I helped look for it, but we didn't find it. Grandma says it was in her jewelry box in the front bedroom. I wasn't even playing with the girls in that room. I told Grandma, but I'm not sure she believes me. She keeps talking about the missing earring."

"Have you both tried really hard to find it?"

"Yeah, I looked, but I don't even know for sure what I'm looking for. Here's El. You wanna talk to her?"

There's a shuffle as the phone is exchanged. "Hi, Mom."

"Hi, El. How are things going down there?"

"Fine."

"Tell me what all this earring stuff is about."

"Well, you know Grandpa gave Grandma those pearl earrings for her birthday, and one of them is gone."

"Did you help Grandma look for it?"

"Yeah, but she said she's sure she put it away in her jewelry box."

"But it's not there now?"

"No, and I don't know where else to look."

"Does Grandma have one of the earrings?"

"I don't know. Mom, she thinks Julie and I got into her jewelry box and played with her stuff. But we didn't."

"Were you in the front bedroom?"

"Yes, but Grandma said we could play there. We were playing with my dolls, and we didn't touch any of Grandma's things."

"Was Nick playing in there, too?"

"No. Well, he came in, but he wanted us to play tetherball, and we didn't want to go outside. He said dolls were girl-junk, so we kicked him out and shut the door."

"Has Julie been back over to play?"

"No, Grandma's going to go over and talk to her mom, but they're gone someplace now. They won't be back until the weekend."

"Well, the missing earring is important. It was special to Grandma. Will you continue to help look for it?"

"Yes, but Mom, Nick and I have both helped look." El's voice cracks, "We looked last night---and we looked---again this morning. I don't have it."

"El, are you okay?"

"Yes."

"Do you need Dad and me to come down there?"

"No."

"Are you sure? We'll come tonight if you want us to."

"No, don't do that, Mom."

"Okay, but you call if you need to. Okay?"

In the next couple of days there are no other calls. Don and I determine the earring must have been found.

Late in the week we learn how wrong we have been when I answer a phone call from Mother. All social amenities are devoid as Mother barks, "Betty, I tell you this week has not been a very good week. I never did find my earring, and that's not the only thing missing. Dad had $500.00 cash in a leather pouch in his room. Over $400.00 of his money is missing. We haven't been able to do anything or go anyplace all week because we had no spending money. Neither Nick nor El will admit to having anything to do with the missing items. Betty, other than Dad and me, they're the only ones to have been in and out of either one of those bedrooms."

"Let me talk to the kids, Mom I'm sure we can get to the bottom of this."

I hear Mother open the back door and call the kids to the phone. I grip the phone tighter and press it hard against my ear. Silence. No one is saying anything at Grandma and Grandpa's. I wish I could be there and look directly at them when we talk about this, whatever *this* is. El must be hanging back. I only hear Nick scrambling up the back steps and slamming the screen door. And, Grandma scolding, as usual, as she hands him the phone.

"Yeah, hi, Mom. Grandma said she was going to call you. She said El and me needed to talk to you."

"Yes, Nick, why don't you tell me why we need to talk."

"You know what, Mom, she thinks El and me took her stuff."

"Does she say that?"

"No. She doesn't really accuse us, but she talks about that earring and some missing money every day. I don't really know what she is talking about, but I know she thinks El and me know more than we're telling her."

"Do you know any more than you're telling, Nick?"

"No, Mom, I don't."

"What does Grandpa think of all this?"

"Grandpa doesn't think like that at all. He just tries to keep Grandma quiet. He tells her the earring is somewhere in this house and to leave El and me alone about the earring or anything else."

"Have you all gone to the beach or to the county fair this week?"

"No, 'cause I guess they don't have any money for that. Grandma says the vacation money got stolen."

"Have you done anything fun?"

"Oh yeah, we've had fun around here, especially with Rolf's dog, Taco. And Grandpa put up a tether ball pole in the back yard. We've all played with that, Grandma and Grandpa, too. Taco even tries to join in and grab the ball. We've been to the playground down by the lake, too. And we've been out to eat a bunch of times. I guess they have enough money to eat out. We just can't go anyplace."

"Nick, do you want us to come get you guys today?"

"No, don't do that; we're fine. Neither one of us likes Grandma to think we did things we really didn't do, but Grandpa keeps her hushed up pretty good. You're coming tomorrow though, aren't you?"

"Oh, yes, for sure. Is El nearby?"

"I don't see her. She was riding one of their bikes up and down the alley. Do you want me to run out back and look?"

"No, you tell her Dad and I want you both to behave yourselves, and we'll see you tomorrow. I love you, Nick. Goodbye."

"I love you, too, Mom. Bye."

The next day Don and I meet Grandma and Grandpa and the kids at a local park in Pleasanton, a town about half-way between our two homes. This town has been more than worthy of its name in past times when we've picked the kids up after vacation breaks. Today is a cloudless day with blue sky and bright sunshine, a day for sun glasses, tank tops and shorts. I feel the warmth on my arms and legs, but I am not comforted. River water babbles in the background in quiet irritation. Don and I have arrived early. As we sit at a big wooden picnic table, I feel as if the table is sitting on me.

Mother and Dad arrive. Our hugs and kisses are perfunctory. Nick and El rush off to toss a ball with Taco. Mother asks Dad to bring the picnic chest to the table, where she and I seat ourselves.

"Mom, tell me about this missing earring and this stolen money. What happened?"

"Now, Betty, I don't want you talking to these kids any more right now about our little incident this week. We're all okay at the moment. There are things we don't know, and we'll talk about this another time."

"Huh? Mother, we ought to air this thing out while we're all together."

"No, no, I don't want to do that. Let's enjoy this nice day and the picnic. The children may need some time to think about this past week."

"Mother, why did you and Dad have that much cash lying around the house? I want to believe Nick and El didn't do anything bad. But they are kids, and it may have been too great a temptation for kids."

"We were going to use that money to pay our taxes and to do some special things with the kids this week like going to the beach and the county fair. The only money taken out of that pouch was $50.00 to help Rolf buy a tire for his truck."

"Well, I think the amount of missing money makes the situation a felony. You should probably report it to the Ridgeview Police."

"Oh my God, Betty, we're not about to do something like that."

Dad clunks the ancient red cooler onto the table, sits down next to Mother, and begins lifting the lids on food containers. "Now, kid, let's forget this whole thing. Things are fine right now. You and Mom need to hush up. Enough's been said. "

"But, you guys, we can't leave things like they are with everyone in turmoil and under a cloud of suspicion. This whole thing could just be a big mistake."

Dad and Mother have filled their plates and are well into their lunch. Mother tosses the remains of a fried chicken wing into the garbage sack at the end of the table. "Betty, I don't see how you could say something like this is just a big mistake."

"Mother, I know you said the girls were playing in the front bedroom where your earring went missing and both Nick and El had been in the back bedroom where the money pouches were; but the kids weren't the only ones in that back bedroom. Last week when we were down, Rolf was there, too. In fact, he *was* in Dad's old bedroom. Maybe he got into Dad's leather pouch instead of his own. Both Dad and Rolf have those leather pouches, and they look similar. I don't know why Rolf keeps letting mail come to your house anyway. He's had an address at his house in Newcastle for over two years."

"Betty, I'll tell you right now, Rolf would not make a mistake like that. Dad and I know exactly what we had in our pouch and what we spent. Neither one of us is forgetful, and we're definitely not senile!"

"My, God, Mother, I didn't say anything about forgetful or senile. I merely suggested Rolf could have made a mistake. You bought both Dad and Rolf leather pouches to keep their mail and important stuff in, and those pouches look almost exactly alike. Anyway, Rolf was there when Don and I came down to drop off the children."

"Well, he wasn't in the house. He was only in the back yard for our picnic."

"No, Mother, that is not correct. I distinctly remember he was in the house, because I ran in for a bathroom break after our picnic and I had to sit and wait in the living room. I thought Rolf was in the bathroom. Finally I yelled at him to hurry up and get out of there. When he came out, it wasn't from the bathroom. He had been changing his clothes in Dad's bedroom. In all the fuss and hurry he could have made a mistake and gotten into the wrong pouch."

"Well, I doubt he made any such mistake, but I'll ask him."

Conversation slips to mundane chatter, and Mother and Dad and the children finish lunch. Most of Don's and my lunch goes in the garbage can. None of us is interested in taking the river walk today. Fun and light-heartedness are long gone. Mother and Dad want to get an early start home so they can drive in the daylight hours. We all depart Pleasanton on a less than pleasant note.

Once we're in our car and onto the freeway, I turn to Nick and El, "I want you guys to tell me everything you can remember about your week. Dad and I need to know what really happened. Grandma's messages are sort of confusing. You were both there. You know. You've got to help us solve this problem, if you know anything. If somehow one of you did something, or both of you, or the little girl next door---and if you don't tell us everything, Grandma and Grandpa might think Dad and I don't care whether our children do things like that, or they may even think *we* took their things."

El speaks up, "Mom, Grandma already thinks that. She said she and Grandpa didn't really know Dad very well when you married him, and that Dad has *all kinds of people* in his family. I asked her what *all kinds of people* meant, and she told me not to get sassy. But, Mom, I really didn't know what she meant."

Nick breaks in, "Yeah, but, Mom, *I* knew what she meant, and I explained it to El. That really pissed Grandma off!"

"And what did you tell El? And where did all this go on?"

El took over the story again. "We were riding in the car coming back from Jo-Jo's chicken place, and Nick whispered to me, 'She's talking about Dad's brother, Uncle Sonny---the one who got fired for stealing from the cash register. She's saying Dad's just like him or worse.' Right then, Mom, I told Grandma our Dad isn't anything like Uncle Sonny and he never would be."

Nick adds to El's defense of Don, "Yeah, and I told her if she said our dad was like that, then she was a liar!"

"Oh God, Nick! Then what happened?"

"Well, we were home by then. Grandma was so mad she could hardly get the key in the front door to let us in the house. Taco, Rolf's big Siberian Husky, was at the door jumping and barking, trying to get Grandma's left-over chicken bag, but she went straight to the kitchen and grabbed a yard stick from off the top of the refrigerator. By then she's yelling really loud. She says, 'Nick, you're just not going to call your old Grandma a liar and get away with it. I don't care what your mom and dad might think, I'm going to give you a spanking'!"

I am turned almost completely around in my seat. My neck is killing me. My mouth gapes wider at each sentence as Nick and El blurt out alternate volleys of details of events of the week at Grandma and Grandpa's. Don concentrates on his driving but shakes his head in agreement with my disbelief at Grandma's attempt to *spank* a fifteen-year-old boy who is almost six feet tall. I unbuckle my seatbelt and turn all the way around to face the two of them. "What in the world happened then?"

Nick snickers and El jumps back into the story, "Yeah, Mom, that part was really funny. She swung that yard stick at Nick's butt and it hit Taco instead. The yard stick broke, and Taco yelped and ran under the table. Right then Grandpa came running into the kitchen."

Nick grabs the story line. "Oh, yeah, Mom, that was even better. He says, 'Jesus Christ, Mama, what are you doing here? You're acting like a bumble bee stung you in the ass end! You put that stick away! You kids go to your rooms! You need to be in bed anyway'."

I clinch the back of the car seat, "Oh my God, and did you mind Grandpa?"

Nick continues, "Oh sure. We ran all the way through the house and upstairs to our bedrooms, but we could still hear them arguing downstairs in the kitchen. We couldn't make out what they were saying. We just went ahead and got ready for bed."

El picks up the story. "But this morning, Mom, it was kinda weird. Grandma acted like nothing at all had happened. But it did, Mom. And Grandma's a liar saying that stuff about Dad."

"Now, guys, let's not resort to name-calling. That's what Grandma did and look where that got her. I know she was desperate and trying to get to the bottom of a very sticky issue, and I'm sure she didn't really mean those nasty things she said about Dad. She was frustrated and angry; and when people get that angry, they become irrational. I'm frustrated, too. I don't know what to do about any of this. This whole mess is crazy. Maybe we all need to just cool down. I'm sure Grandma will be more reasonable when she's not so upset. Let's all talk about something else for a while."

I turn around in my seat and refasten my seatbelt. My own mind is anything but cool. I cannot remember my mother ever telling one of us, or anyone else, a lie. I cannot remember telling her a lie since I was about six or eight years old and spilled pop sickle juice on my new Easter suit she had made for me and which she had sent to the laundry for pressing. I swore to her I had not taken the suit out of the protective cover and I had not tried it on. I learned then for sure lying was not acceptable, and that was to the tune of a cherry limb from the backyard tree, a limb which did not break as easily as a yardstick. I know my children have told their fair share of stories--especially on one another--but they haven't done things like that for a long time. I'd like to think they're beyond that kind of behavior. Don and I have both emphasized honesty in their entire upbringing. Nick is fifteen years old and El is twelve. Their spontaneous account of what happened in Ridgeview makes me feel the training sunk in, and they didn't do any of the things of which they have been accused!

Once we arrive at our home we all busy ourselves doing the washing and packing necessary for our departure the next day to Decatur Island.

Our three-week vacation in the San Juans fulfills our dreams and expectations for relaxation and fun, and even some fishing success. Thefts, spankings, earrings--and anything else irrational--is all but forgotten.

The evening we return from our vacation Mother calls, "Did you have a good time at Decatur?

"Yes, we did. We even caught--"

"You should have had a good time. I'd have had a good time, too, if I had several hundred extra dollars."

"Now, wait a minute, Mother--"

"Betty, I've confronted Rolf about the missing money. He's prepared to kick ass royally of anyone who even suggests he would steal from us."

"That's not what I suggested. I asked you to see if he had made a mistake with those leather pouches."

"There were no mistakes made. The thief has to be someone in the family. As far as I'm concerned I don't want to speak to Don ever again in my lifetime!"

"Mother, this whole thing is unreal. You can't think Don or I either one would do such a deed. It didn't happen! This conversation isn't happening!" I break into heaving sobs.

Mother ignores my sobbing. "Well, no matter how much crying you do, I can tell you right now I'll not be talking to Don again."

"Mother, is Dad there? May I please talk to him?"

Dad gets on the phone and I ask, "Do you agree with Mother's evaluation?"

"Well now, kid, I just don't know. The money's gone and it does seem like it has to be someone in the family."

"But, Dad, do you believe it's Don?"

There is an extended silence.

"Dad, do you also never want to speak to Don again?"

"Now, kid, some day we'll all meet at the Judgment Bar, and then we'll know what this is all about."

"Oh, Dad, I think that's too long to wait."

I mumble my goodbye and weep bitterly.

A couple of days later Rolf awakens us with a call about 1:00 AM from a noisy bar or restaurant. "Yeah, I just got back from a big log-hauling job up north. I was talking to Mom about this money deal. What in the hell are you thinking telling her that *I* stole their money?"

"That's not what I said. You were in Dad's bedroom the day we dropped the children off with them. You made me wait forever to go to the bathroom. I almost wet my pants. That I have not forgotten. When you came into the living room, it wasn't from the bathroom at all. You had been in Dad's bedroom changing your clothes. Isn't it possible you mixed up those two leather pouches and got into the wrong one thinking you were taking your own money?"

"You know, Sis, Mom and Dad are pretty sharp. They don't make mistakes when it comes to money. I'd say the likelihood of someone making a mistake with money would be someone closer to you. In fact, I think over the years there's been several little instances in which someone *right* close to you may have latched onto to some other things that didn't belong to them."

"Do you mean Don or the kids?"

"I for one don't think that highly of Don's integrity, and I think any normal person who'd been around him much would agree. But he's not the only one. I'd like to have a few minutes with anyone else close to you, regardless of their ages. I'd kick some sense into anyone who got away with such thievery preying upon old people on limited incomes."

"Rolf, Rolf, hold it a minute! I suggest you not be quite so high and mighty. Your remarks are both slanderous and threatening violence to me and my family."

"Well, Sis, you do get my point! If I had any one of them here, I'd kick the shit out of 'em, and we'd get to the bottom of this!"

"Rolf, let me remind you, your threats are assault according to the law. And if you dare to actually lay a hand, or a foot, on either Don or my children, that would be battery. I would call the police immediately, and eventually I would sue your ass right up to your ear-lobes!"

"Little sister, you're obviously too close to the situation to fairly evaluate all the facts. If you ever really want to understand, I'll meet with you and explain it."

"Rolf, you're wrong in what you think and what you want to do. None of this makes any sense, but it doesn't matter. I don't think I even have parents any more. Mom and Dad don't care to have any further communication with us."

The next day Dad calls. "Now, kid, I want you to know you still have parents. I love you very much."

"Thank you, Dad. I love you, too, and I'm glad you called, but that doesn't solve the problem. Do you really believe Don or the kids stole money from you?"

"I just don't know who stole what."

"But, Dad, you and Don have shared so many experiences over the years. It seems to me you would *know* and have faith in Don's integrity. We've all been together for holidays, vacations, birth of children and childcare afterward--fishing trips, and even automobile trips clear across the United States to West Virginia to visit relatives. Dad, don't you *know* Don couldn't have done anything like that?"

"It's like I said, kid, some things we'll find out on Judgment Day."

The phone call ends. I still have parents, but I don't know how to feel toward them. They *have* to know none of us would steal from them or anyone else. Time will heal this. The thief will confess. Even if that doesn't happen, Mom and Dad will come to their senses and realize they have caused a hurtful and preposterous predicament because of their own frustration and hurt.

Fall passes. The children receive occasional notes from Grandma with massive amounts of tape on them but only mundane messages about where she and Dad have been to eat out or Taco's misbehavior. I talk to her a few times on the phone, but our conversation is usually about the weather or how much work they have been doing around the house.

Old Parents and Purple Tulips

Fall evolves into winter, and Christmas is particularly strange. For the first time in my forty-five years we don't get together to celebrate. Don and I send Mom and Dad Malfait gift certificates to Chuck's Wagon, a restaurant near their home. Mother calls to say they enjoy using them and thanks *me* very much for them. A package arrives at our house addressed to El containing wrapped Christmas presents for El and boxes of unwrapped microwave cookware with *my* name written across each box in bold permanent black ink. Grandma calls and asks to speak to Nick. She says she will send him a check, because she couldn't find the color of soccer socks she wanted to get for him. Besides, it's been so cold she hasn't been able to get out to finish her shopping. She also tells him she had her phone number changed, but she doesn't give him the new number.

I try to call Malfaits' phone number of the past forty years, but the monotone voice tells me, 'This number is no longer in service.' I try for operator help, but their new number is unlisted. A few weeks later when Mother calls, she gives me the new number but tells me only five people have it and I am not to give it out.

In retrospect the year 1983 was anything but perfection. If one believes in a total cosmic plan, an omnipotent plan of God, then *maybe* it *was* perfect. Our vacation to Decatur Island, our new experiences as a boating family, the joys of school achievements and activities, and all else occurs under the jaded gloom of an unsettled problem with Grandma and Grandpa. My Christmas letter to Aunt Mavis, my mother's younger sister who lives in West Virginia, reveals the poignant paradox between joy and pain in living our lives.

Dear Aunt Mavis, I've debated a long time whether to tell anyone about a problem we're having in our family, but someone else in the family needs to know what's going on. I am having the most frustrating, bizarre, painful experience of my life with Mom and Dad. It's bigger than I can handle. I know there's nothing you can do, especially from so far away, but I just want it to be a matter of record with you, because since my earliest childhood I've known you love us all very much. I'm not asking you to believe any particular person's viewpoint, but I need to be heard by someone else in our family.

Aunt Mavis, I know Don did not steal their money. This is a lovely man whom I have truly *shared* the last twenty-two years of my life with in a loving relationship. This is a man whom I have never mistrusted one single time in those years. He is trusted by his friends, colleagues, students, administrators, and church people---he always figures restaurant bills and tells of errors whether they're in his favor or not---he has spent hours emptying little church envelopes and trying to figure out a scrawled signature in order to credit the right account with some trivial amount---he doesn't cheat on his income tax. One of the ironies of this whole thing is that we refinanced our house last summer, and while being criticized and ridiculed as possible thieves, we had several thousand dollars in our savings account while we tried to figure how to best put it to use. Oh, Aunt Mavis, I don't understand any of this. Maybe Granddad's position of we'll all find out on Judgment Day is the only plausible one. Anything else is beyond my comprehension.

As I said earlier, I'm not asking you to believe any particular person's viewpoint. I just needed to express my thinking to someone else in our family. I don't think you can be of any help, but thank you for listening. Here's to the New Year---1984! May we all find greater peace and joy.
Love, Betty

CHAPTER 3

──❈──

Continued Agony

THE MONTHS OF 1984 roll by with little communication with Malfaits. Dad never was one to write or call. Mother writes Nick and El occasional notes, usually with innuendoes about guilty parties such as kids going down the alley and stealing their apples or some orneriness Taco has been into. She talks to me if I happen to answer the phone. But she has almost nothing to say other than a weather report, where they went shopping, or what they had for dinner. Don is totally ignored, not mentioned to the children nor to me. Mother is obsessed with humiliating and punishing the assumed thieving culprit of the past crime. If it's not Nick nor El, then it must be Don. Her weapon of choice is excommunication from the family.

I wish I could be more cognizant of the total picture of what is happening in my family. I battle my own obsessions. I spend far too much time questioning, asking why, flailing in futility. Each letter or phone call from Mother is like adding cedar kindling to dying embers. I smolder. I flame. I burn. I die out.

Some days I feel as if I'm walking along untroubled, almost happy. With no forewarning I step into a hole. I fall and fall, a swirling glob sucked down into a dark, bottomless crevasse. Abruptly I crash against a cold, steely surface. I am squeezed in a vise-like grip. I'm breathless. My entire being is limp, empty. I'm never sure I'll come up again.

Maybe all of this is a forging process, each heating and cooling venture shaping and strengthening my very soul for yet another plunge into uncharted emotional depths.

Dear God, am I crazy?

I am forty-five years old. I feel as insecure as a run-away teenager. *I* would like to run away--from my family.

No. I am a strong person. I *am* compassionate. I *can* understand. There's no prescribed manner for how to handle this family situation, but I *will* figure it out.

My academic background in education, psychology, and science offers no solution to my conflict. I read. I intellectualize. I see a therapist. These attempts provide no relief for me. Religious faith is on hold. I'm angry with God.

God, why? Why me? God, what have I ever done to warrant this family disaster? I have always placed family as a top priority. I can't think of any time I have not honored my parents. God, I'm not perfect, but I always try to live by the guides You have given. Why is this all falling apart?

Even though my raging at God is useless, I become more prayerful than ever in my lifetime, if what I'm muttering when I close my eyes and shut myself off from daily life is indeed prayer. Gradually the angry venting turns to pleading for guidance within God's will. I ask that I might be able to let go of the turmoil and pain this is causing me. From my inept prayerful prattle, it becomes apparent that the only way for Don and me to have any sense of peace is to concentrate on preserving and nurturing our own family relationships.

At the expense of relinquishing twenty-plus years of positive interaction and fun times we've enjoyed with my mother and father, I make a conscious and deliberate choice: I choose allegiance to my husband and my own family over my birth family! I share my perception with Don. He is supportive of what is basically to be a divorce from my family. He writes to them.

Dear Mr. and Mrs. Malfait, I hope you will take time to read this letter since I have no other way to communicate with you. I cannot understand why you have become so bitter about people and life! It seems to me if people really care for and love each other, they will not act as you have to Betty and me.

I have always had highest respect and love for you both. I would not do anything to cause you pain. I guess on your part a mutual consideration must not be there. Perhaps you have hidden your dislikes for years, but I want you to know I have *never* taken anything from you or anyone else. I'm sure Betty, Nick, and El did not take anything either. I do not like being accused nor having my family members accused of things they didn't do. If you need to find scapegoats for thefts, I suggest you look elsewhere.

May *both* of you have a wonderful and blessed life. If we do not see each other again in this life, at Judgment Day we *will* meet and you will realize you have made a great blunder!

Farewell, Mr. and Mrs. Malfait, and may God bless and be with you the rest of your days here on Earth. My Love to *Both* of you and thanks for the good things that have taken place in the past,

As Ever,

Don

Despite this letter deriving from a mutual decision to protect our own family structure, I hate the fact that I have placed my father in a tenuous position between believing Mother or me. And I bear painful awkwardness in regard to other people in my life whom I also love--my brother, aunts, uncles, cousins, family friends, and neighbors.

Spring 1984 passes into summer, and summer into fall.

The phone is quieter. Letters to the children are fewer. Our family life progresses positively for the most part but with no amends in broken relationships. Long weekends, birthdays, and holidays bring painful reminders of where happy, loving times have been spent in the past. This year we attend a Thanksgiving gathering of Don's side of the family which we have never done before. For Christmas we plan to be in our own home. We'll take the kids skiing at least once, since Santa is bringing ski equipment. The rest of the vacation days we'll be sure to have a supply of good movies on hand.

The day before Christmas break the telephone rings. I almost don't recognize the cordial voice, "Hi, how are you all doing?"

"Fine--?"

"What did you do for Thanksgiving?"

"We went across the water to be with Don's brother and family."

"We stayed right here and Rolf came by. I cooked a twenty-five pound turkey. Dad and Rolf really stuffed themselves."

"And you didn't, right?"

"Well, I guess I did, too. It was so good. Listen, Dad and I would like to have the family come to Ridgeview and be with us the day after Christmas this year."

"Uh--well, we've made some plans, but I'll see if we can change them."

"I know with the kids and all, you have too much to haul around to come down Christmas Day, but we'd like you to come the day after, if that's all right."

"Mom, Don will be home in a few minutes. Let me check with him, and I'll call you right back."

"That's fine. We'll be right here."

I flop onto a kitchen stool. My shaking hand is still grasping the silent phone when Don walks in. "What's wrong? Are you okay?"

"You aren't going to believe who just called?"

"It has to be your mom, your dad, or Rolf."

"It was Mother. She invited the family to Ridgeview for the day after Christmas."

"Does that mean me, too?"

"Gee, I didn't ask her specifically, but to me you're part of *the family*. I felt like the whole phone call was an attempt to return to old times, but I'm not sure. I don't know if we just erased our family problem or what."

"Well, if she meant all of us, I think we should go."

"Yeah, I guess you're right. I hate to imagine how such a visit might go or what other motives there might be, but we did say we would not deny any overtures with a potential for healing and restoration. I guess that call was an overture."

I wipe my sweaty hand on the dish towel I am still clutching in my other hand, get a fresh grip on the phone, and dial. Mother answers immediately.

"Well, Mom, we've already altered our vacation plans so we can come down the day after Christmas. But did you mean *all* of us? I mean--does that mean Don, too?"

"Well, of course, that means Don! Why wouldn't that include Don?"

"Uh--yes--okay. We accept your invitation. We'll look forward to seeing you all."

The first days of Christmas break throw us all into a frantic rush. Shopping. House-cleaning. Shopping. The tree. Shopping. Menu-planning. Shopping. Baking. Shopping. And wrapping, wrapping, wrapping.

Our family enjoys a beautiful Christmas Eve candle-light service at church.

The next morning, Christmas Day starts early with two teenagers giggling and tittering their way up the stairs. Having assumed the personae of their much younger years, they attack the stockings which they had hung over the fireplace the night before in hopes that Saint Nick would be as good or better than in all the previous years. They grab the stockings for Don and me, too, and clatter their way into the master bedroom to deliver them. We all enjoy our stocking stuffers and indulge in a few of the peppermints and chocolates, before we make our way to the kitchen where the coffee pot gets turned on, the cinnamon rolls get put in the oven, and we pace ourselves alternating gift-opening and breakfast munching.

Finally skis and ski boots get unstrapped. Long underwear and assorted clothing, books, and games get sorted and delivered to each person's room. The recycled paper gets separated from the garbage. And dinner preparations get underway with each of us doing some special part. There's no denying that the progression of the day seems a bit odd. Still, it's a joyous occasion. In the evening we pack for our trip to Ridgeview to visit Grandma and Grandpa Malfait, each of us hoping this venture will continue to be a happy time.

I awaken early the day after Christmas. I roll out of a cozy warm bed to find the house unusually cold. I pull open the bedroom curtain and squint my sleepy, near-sighted eyes at the stark brightness of the canyon behind our house covered in a massive, puffy white comforter of snow. Fir and cedar branches are weighted to the ground by a foot or more of white fluff. No one is driving anywhere, regardless of plans for the day after Christmas. The bedside clock radio sputters forth through the chilly darkness, "Highway 105--currently closed--ice--fallen trees--heavy snowfall--delay crews from--Please limit your travel if at all possible. Forecast--more snow--today--no let-up predicted--three days. Now we return you to--."

I'm sure it's not Biblical prayer modeling, but I squeeze my eyes tight and whisper into the softness of the green silk drapery panel, "Thank you, Jesus. Let it snow, snow, snow!" I feel a warm rush as I turn and pick up the phone to call Mother and let her know we can't come.

Later in the morning Don bakes home-made bread. I man the washing machine and dryer for wet sledding clothes. Don and I alternate laundry routine with our own excursions outdoors for sled rides with our kids. The pantry is well supplied. And best of all, we are not carrying any guilt for not being someplace else for the holidays.

Snow confinement continues throughout the entire Christmas break. We awaken each morning to a few inches of new snow. It's a very unusual winter.

A couple of days before the end of vacation break the shrillness of the telephone interrupts my attempt to grab a few more winks of sleep. I am again surprised by my mother's friendly voice.

"Hi, I suppose you're still snowed in up there?"

"Well, sort of, but not today. For the past two weeks the ground has remained frozen and we've had new snow every day, except yesterday and today. Things are thawing out pretty fast now. It's almost melting too fast. Now we'll have to listen for reports of mud-slides and soft roadways. Around here that affects the school buses and schedules as much as the snow does. I don't ever remember a winter like this. The kids have had a great time though, but as far as I know we go back to school tomorrow as scheduled. How are you guys doing?"

"We still have snow on the ground, but it's melting fast here, too. Today is the first day we've been able to get the car off the driveway. They've told people here in town to stay home, unless it was an emergency. You better believe we did a big grocery shopping this morning. Dad has been able to walk down to the little store on the corner to get us a few things, but I'm telling you, our cupboards were bare! Dad's worked awfully hard shoveling snow off the sidewalks all week. He's had to shovel every day. Every night it snowed us in again. We're okay now though, since we can get around with the car.

"Dad and I have been talking, and we'd still like to get together for some kind of Christmas celebration. We have our gifts to give to the children and such. We thought maybe we could all meet at that nice restaurant by the waterfall in Pleasanton. We could have lunch, give the kids their gifts, and do our celebrating that way. Does that sound like a good idea?"

"That would be nice. Are you sure you want to drive that far?"

"Oh, driving's not a problem. Rolf says he'll drive us up. He's been all over the countryside this week, and he says the roads

Author and Rolf in front of the "house That Daddy Built" – c. 1946

are pretty clear everywhere except right here in town." "That's nice of him, but we could drive down and have lunch some place there in Ridgeview. Then you and Dad wouldn't have to drive at all."

"No, we don't want you all to come down here right now. We've got a broken toilet to fix, and we can't be having the plumber out until after payday. That's this Friday. We'll have him out one day next week. Besides, it would be nice for us to get out for a drive. We've been stuck in this house for so long. We like that restaurant by the falls, and we haven't been there for a long time. They have good food, and Dad really wants to do that. Rolf already said he'd drive."

"Okay, if you're sure you don't mind being on the road."

As I hang up the phone, I mutter aloud, "Why is their toilet broken? Why can't they get a plumber until after pay day? Why do they wait for something so urgent? Why would they spend money to take a trip and eat in a fancy restaurant? They have two pretty good retirement incomes. They shouldn't have to wait with a broken toilet."

I leave the bedroom shaking my head and emoting to the family pictures along the hallway on the way to the kitchen, "That's another phone call that didn't make much sense. Malfaits' behaviors don't make sense. That toilet thing is ridiculous. How do they go to the bathroom? Oh well, most of our conversations for the last year and a half have included more than enough fecal matter. I don't need to be worrying about their plumbing problems nor their finances!"

Our two families meet in Pleasanton as planned. It's awkward after our long separation but *sort* of like old times. The entry area of the restaurant is crowded with about a twenty minute wait, which gives me confidence it's still a great place to eat. As we chat, pleasant whiffs tease our olfactory senses each time busy waiters hurry past. Grandma and Grandpa marvel at how much the children have grown. Rolf is present and has done the driving, but he says nothing to anyone. After a few minutes in the crowded restaurant he announces to no one in particular, "Let's get the hell out of here. There's too many people and the wait is gonna to be too long."

Mother barks back at him, "We've waited this long. It can't be much more."

The two of them move closer together and continue to bicker for several minutes. The rest of us are mute statues. Rolf is loud and domineering. Mother matches his tone. Finally, I'm not sure by whose decision, we all file out of the restaurant, load back into our cars, and go to a pancake house nearby. It turns out Mom, Dad, and Rolf were in the area earlier and ate breakfast in this same pancake house.

A hostess shows us to a table near the back. Before we can seat ourselves, Rolf makes a hasty retreat to the restroom. Mother and the children settle themselves amidst renewed loud affectionate teasing and giggling. Mother is repeating her remarks about how much they have grown, how hungry she is. She wonders if they're hungry.

Dad says to Don, "Well, let's you and I get in here, Don. I'll sit by you, so we won't have a divided house."

My father has never been one to make sarcastic, hurtful remarks. I wonder if he knows how much his remark stings. Dad and Don visit clumsily, while Nick, El, and Grandma banter across the table--loudly from them because they are, and loudly from her because she can't hear. Rolf returns to the table, moves his chair out in the aisle, sits down, crosses his arms and stares into space. Don and Dad finally pull him into a conversation, and he tells of his trips to California riding with his friend Mike in his semi.

"Yeah, it wouldn't take too much to convert my logging truck to a flatbed. Then I could haul independent freight. That's what Mike does, and he makes a darn good livin' at it. Anyway, since Mom and Dad wanted to come up this way, we just come up earlier this morning and I stopped in a couple of places that do conversion jobs like that. In both shops the guys said about the same thing. To rebuild trucks like I want mine done wouldn't be too difficult. I'm gonna think seriously about doin' it."

Rolf continues talking to Dad and Don, but he has nothing to say to me nor the children. He doesn't even look at us. He seems angry even as he talks about his plans for his truck. He is a stranger at the table--well, sort of at the table.

Mother has forgotten to bring El's Christmas gifts, but she tells her all about her present, a pink leather purse with fringe on it and a fuzzy pull-over sweater of the same color. She gives Nick a ten dollar bill and tells him she didn't know what size shirt to get for him. While putting her billfold back, she discovers she has less money than she thought. Since it's about time to order, Don suggests we treat them. That idea is not well received. I'm sure they would eat nothing rather than accept Don's offer. Finally Mother and Rolf argue it out, and she remembers she paid cash for a gas fill-up earlier. I nudge Nick under the table.

"Huh? What?"

I point to the ten dollar bill which Nick is still holding and roll my eyes in Grandma's direction.

Nick immediately pushes the bill across the table. "Here, Grandma, you take this back. You need it for gas money."

"No, no, Nick, that's your Christmas money."

"Yeah, but Grandma, I can get a shirt another time, or you could mail me the ten bucks. Okay?"

"Well, okay. Thank you, Nick."

The storm dissipates as the waitress arrives at our table. Everyone orders sandwiches except Rolf who orders a blueberry sundae. That's weird.

I notice Dad has failed a lot. His left hand, which he injured last fall while helping the garbage man load pruning brush into the truck, is pretty weak. I am more concerned with how both his hands quiver. His hands have always been steady--aiming at a deer, using a table saw, giving me driving lessons, even walking me down the aisle. Today they shake constantly. He is even confused making choices from the menu. But such a task is more difficult with two other people telling you what you want, as both Mother and Rolf do.

The food arrives. Rolf uncrosses his arms, moves near the table and attacks the whip cream mound on his sundae. The rest of us choke down our food. The hour passes.

In our parting after lunch I am discomforted by Dad who gets teary-eyed. His voice cracks when he speaks, "I don't know when we'll get to see you again, kid." I feel his tears on my cheek as he kisses me good-bye. I feel the tremor of his hands through my winter coat as he hugs me.

Mother reaches out to Don and kisses him on the cheek. "I'm glad we could all get together."

Hugs for Don, yes. Kisses? Never in all these years.

Rolf stands, silent, arms crossed, scowling.

I speak to him anyway, "Rolf, thanks for driving them up. It would have been too hard for them to come by themselves. I'm really glad you could all come."

"Yeah, yeah, yeah."

I guess we are going to ignore that we have a family conflict or pretend it never happened. Maybe that's better than accusations, but it doesn't relieve the frustration and hurt of what happened on those dreadful days so long ago when someone I love made a terrible mistake, and it has never been acknowledged nor forgiven. Everyone must live in doubt and mistrust.

In the new year, 1985, our extended family relationships continue with renewed occasional inane phone calls, mostly weather and gardening reports. However, good things are happening in our immediate family. The children are growing and developing, active in several school activities, and being excellent students. Our bonds are strong in our immediate family, despite the ominous cloud over our larger family.

In late February Mother calls with a special request. "I want to know if the kids will be coming down during spring vacation. Dad and I want them to."

"Mother, I don't think so."

"Well, I'd like to know why not. Why won't you let them come?"

"It's not that I'm not *letting* them come. We are going to do some other things."

"Well, you'd be pretty much of a heel if you don't let them come down here."

"Now, Mom, I told you it's not that I'm not *letting* them come down there."

"Well, there sure wouldn't be any other reason they wouldn't come."

"Mom, it's not like that. We've decided to use spring break to take a family trip. We just feel like we need to do something different."

"Family trip--shit! That's a crummy thing for you and Don to concoct--plan some trip, so the kids can't come down here."

"Mother, it's not like that--"

"Betty, I can see how your planning is going. I'd like some better reason than a dumb trip for the children to not have a visit with their grandparents."

My usual instant guilt trip is slow to well up. I struggle to be calm but firm as I tell her, "Mother, the kids are hesitant to return to Ridgeview in light of their past experience. They feel the accusations against them and their father summer before last were unfair, and the problem doesn't seem settled to them. Actually, Don and I feel that way, as well."

"Well, no one down here ever made any accusations. Any such notions the children have about something like that is water under the bridge."

"Mother, the kids don't feel good about being down there by themselves. They're afraid they won't get along, or they'll get blamed for something. It just won't work. They don't feel comfortable coming down. So they will *not* be coming to Ridgeview for spring break. We will be taking a family trip of our own."

"Well, I'll tell you there's one thing that has always ticked me off, and that's the six half-gallons of grape juice that are missing from the upstairs of this house. We all have to stand in front of the Judgment Bar someday! Goodbye."

"Huh?"

I stand mouth agape staring at the silent phone mouthpiece. I do remember Don drinking unsweetened canned grape juice with Dad. It was like some sort of macho social thing they did in the name of good health. The potency of Dad's home-canned grape juice was the nearest thing to a glass of wine Mother would allow in the house. Mother did send some jars home with us--eight quarts, not half-gallons. Don didn't drink it by himself; and no one else in our family would dare touch it. It's still in our can cupboard.

I close my eyes and blink as Mother's inferences of thievery sear into me. The tears flow. "I can't handle this! I'm going crazy! She's crazier! They're both crazy! They're my parents, but they're crazy! I have to *do* something!"

I call Aunt Mavis and sob my way through this recent call from Mother.

"You know, Betty, your Uncle Malcom and I have been talking about maybe now is a good time to come for a visit out there."

"Oh, Mavis, I hope that's true--for them especially, but I need you also! I need someone to help me understand what is happening with them."

In my head, as well as my heart, I know the likelihood of Mavis and Malcom making the trip is about nil. Mavis--maybe. Malcom--forget it. He's my favorite uncle and I love him dearly, but he has promised to come for a visit many times over the years and then not carried through. In fact, it's so often that any kind of canceled trip among our family members is described with, 'Well, we'll have to do an "Uncle Malcom" on that. I'd like to do an "Uncle Malcom" with my parents--agree to come down and never go--or go, but not go there--or just run away all together. Everything with them is so confusing. They probably wouldn't even notice whether I showed up or not.

Weeks later, a letter arrives from Grandma, addressed to El, sealed securely and double taped along all the edges. El scowls as she reads. "Mom, I don't know what Grandma's talking about--they're having the bathroom redone and the toilet repaired. Why would she write me stuff about their toilet? I hope she doesn't think I broke her toilet. I haven't been there for years. Mom, read this; she blames people for things even when they haven't been there."

El, we had to have the septic-rooter man come and plunge our sewer pipes. He had to tear the toilet off the floor and take it outside. Then he used special equipment to clear the line from the house all the way to the alley. He found some kind of an odd object stuck in the line. We're very unhappy about that. Sometimes the water would back up and overflow the toilet. The man couldn't tell us what the object was, and it would have been too costly to dig the whole line up. But I sure would like to have known what it was. If I had it to do over I'd have him dig the whole thing up and remove the object. This job did not come cheap, that's for sure. At least your old granny doesn't have to go to the "back 40" anymore and search for a place like Taco does! During all this time we did a busy business out here at the Texaco Station, too. I went there so many times I felt like putting on a mask for part of my stops! I guess there's no chance seeing you and Nick for Spring Vacation according to your mom on the phone the other day. That's okay, El--Just you and Nick remember Grandpa and Grandma love you.

I don't know what all this means any better than El does. A broken toilet for months? Going to the bathroom in her garden? I feel guilty, because I know they need help. Spring break is next week. The kids don't want to go for a visit. We don't want them to go. None of us wants to place ourselves in a position of jeopardy. Our own family dialogue is agonizing, but the process draws us closer together as we reassure one another of our own loving care. No one is going to Ridgeview, and Grandma and Grandpa's new plumbing job should last forever!

CHAPTER 4

Please Don't Say Alzheimer's

IF THE WEIRD lunch at the pancake restaurant after Christmas was supposed to solve our family problem, it didn't. We no longer go to Malfaits' home in Ridgeview, as none of us wants to be accused of anything. The children will not go by themselves. And Don and I support their choice, despite the abusive flak I inevitably take from my mother regarding this. We invite Malfaits to our home for weekends or holidays and to Decatur Island with us for summer vacation and salmon fishing. They always decline.

As 1985 progresses we do have occasional outings at our half-way spot in Pleasanton. We eat at their favorite restaurant by the falls, regardless of the size of the waiting crowd. Or we picnic at the nearby park. Rolf does not come with them. There is some happiness in these times, but no one speaks of the ever-present undercurrent of accusation and hurt. Each of us is shackled behind an invisible wall in chains of unforgiveness.

Letters from Aunt Mavis share bits of information about Mom and Dad. Mavis feels like we do about Mother's obsession with people taking things, but she is determined to come for a visit and take her chances with her sister's accusations. Of course, Uncle Malcom is "doing a Malcom" for such a trip.

> Betty, I know you probably think I shouldn't stay at their house, but since Malcom isn't coming with me and they have three extra bedrooms, I'm going to risk it. Their accusations of thievery remind me about when I used to stop by and visit my Aunt Maggie, who was your granddad's twin sister. When she was 62

or 63 she behaved somewhat like your mother in that she said the neighbors were trying to take some of her land and her garden produce, and they were always spying on her. She had a big high fence built around the garden because of her fear of people taking things. Eventually she wouldn't go out of her house at all. Her son and his wife had to do all her grocery shopping and other errands. I used to occasionally stay overnight with Aunt Maggie, but when I became aware of these peculiar behaviors I stopped staying overnight and would just visit for a couple hours or so. With either Aunt Maggie or your mother I don't know if it's a case of hardening of arteries or what. I would hope it is by no means akin to something I read recently about a condition called Alzheimer's Disease. Please do not mention to your folks that I used the word Alzheimer's or disease at all!

Mavis' letter strikes me like a foul ball smashed into the bleachers and hitting me right between the eyes! I've never heard of Alzheimer's Disease. What is it? Mother has long accused "Nosy Bill," her next-door neighbor, of stealing berries, cherries and flowers. She accused another neighbor of doing some needlework for her, then shorting her in delivery of the finished pieces. She accused a nephew visiting from Texas of all kinds of felonious behavior, both in her house where he had been invited to stay while attending college in Ridgeview, and even some crimes in the larger community. Mother's accusations of her neighbor taking fruit or flowers may be true, but Malfaits' property is laden with produce and flowers almost year round, and everything they touch grows lavishly. They're always giving away things from their garden—to the lady who runs the corner store, their doctor, their minister, and sometimes people just walking by the house. It's not as if they would even miss small amounts. I wonder if they give other items away and then forget they did.

As to her suspicions of her nephew, I myself saw a sawed-off shotgun under his bed in her house—only because one of my children was playing in that area, discovered the weapon, and told about it before picking it up. That was a scary incident, but we figured it was a piece from Rolf's gun collection, although I think it's an illegal alteration of a shotgun. Or, was it actually the nephew's weapon used in local crimes as Mother had accused? Who knows?

There might be validity to some of Mother's judgments. There's so much I don't know. But accusations of theft against Nick, El or Don will never be acceptable regardless of other probable judgments. The rift goes on. Our family relationship resembles a chronically-picked scab on a skinned knee.

The parallel between Aunt Maggie and Mother is scary genetically. Red flags wave ominously through my mental fog. I search in our school library for reading material on this mental condition called Alzheimer's. There's not much there. El becomes interested as a result of our family discussions and decides to use it as a topic for her sophomore English research paper. We both make a trip to the city library. There's not much on the subject there either, but the librarian helps El achieve her required six references despite the brevity and lack of definitiveness in the available information. But our family shares and discusses any material as we come across it.

Aunt Mavis arrives in Ridgeview in the fall. She doesn't say so, but I think she wants to see things firsthand, perhaps even be a peace-maker for all of us. I'm sure she would like to bring Rolf and me to a realization of a problem far greater than the misunderstandings and hurt feelings we have been harboring.

With Mavis' arrival Mother's phone calls to us resume a frequent schedule, sometimes more than once a day—happy, excited, somewhat repetitious.

"Hi, Betty. Well, we tried again to make a hookup with Rolf today. Mavis really wants to see him. He's driving all over the place right now. We missed him yesterday, and he didn't call in the evening. He just works too hard.

"Today though we did catch him for about ten minutes. We drove out and just waited at the gas station where Dad said he would have to stop for fuel."

"How long did you have to wait for him to show up?"

"Oh it wasn't too long. But, like I said, he only had a few minutes to be with us. We had to do our talking while he gassed the truck."

"That wasn't much of a visit, was it?"

"Well, no, but he said he'd be off on Sunday. Mavis invited him to breakfast for Sunday morning. You know Rolf—he wouldn't pass up a free breakfast."

Sunday evening I get an update on the breakfast. "Well, Betty, we finally made a connection with Rolf. We all got to sit down together and have a bite."

"Where did you go for breakfast?"

"Oh, there's a nice little place out near where Rolf parks the logging truck. It's called the Woodchuck Barn."

"Did you have a good visit?"

"Oh, yes, but it was a little bit rushed. Rolf had to go out once to move his truck. I don't think it was blocking anything, but another driver he knew came in and asked him to move it to a different spot. When he went out to do that, he noticed one of his tires was going flat. He came back in and finished his breakfast, but then he had to hurry off to go get that tire fixed."

"Did he just drive away on a flat tire?"

"I guess so. It's got so many wheels on the thing, maybe they all don't have to be full of air. Anyway, he said he thought he could get it down to the tire shop before it went completely flat."

"It sounds like that was sort of a short visit, too."

"Yes, it was, but we're doing so many other things, it didn't really matter. We went on to Oregon after breakfast and looked up a woman Mavis worked with when she lived with Dad and me about twenty-five years ago. We stopped and had dinner at The Crab Pot on the way home. We're all having so much fun, Betty. But we're all a little tired of the confines of the car with all this tripping. We went to Long Beach the day before, too. Dad does get a little tired driving."

"I'm not surprised you're all tired. That's a lot of miles for three or four days."

"Oh, we're not done. We want to get up to see you, too."

"I wondered if we'd be scheduled for one of your trips?"

"Of course, you're on the schedule. Could we do that this coming Saturday? Mavis has to fly out on Sunday."

"Sure, we'd love to have her come up for a visit."

"Well, we wouldn't really have time to come all the way to your house? Could we meet at Pleasanton and just have one of our picnics together?"

"Yes, if that's what you'd like to do."

"That would be wonderful. If you'll make one of your good potato salads and a pound cake, I'll fry up some chicken and we'll bring fresh raspberries from our garden. I'll bring the rest—you know, pickles, chips, things the kids like."

On picnic day we arrive shortly before noon at Pleasanton. The day reflects all the amenities of the town's name. Blue skies. Not even a hint of a cloud. Temperature in the upper seventies with an expected high of eighty. We stake claim to one of the big wooden picnic tables under a

Family trip to Mount St. Helens with Dog's Head in backgrouond

sprawling maple tree. We have a spectacular view of the river and the waterfalls. A slight breeze teases the checkered paper table cloth I have spread and touches us gently with a hint of cooling river mist.

Malfaits and Mavis arrive soon after us. Greetings all around are as warm and hospitable as the weather. I feel as if I have regressed several years. I am immersed in the love and nurturing of my family. Is that possible?

Taco has come with them. He's friendly and excited as usual, especially with the kids who are more than happy to take him for a run. A luscious picnic spread evolves on the table with each trip Dad and Don make to their car. Nick and El cruise by the table snatching potato chips for themselves and for Taco. Stories of the week are shared. Laughter ripples in tandem with the water falls. And sometimes loud giggles even evoke smiles from nearby picnickers. Appetites are whetted to new heights as soon as the lid comes off the still warm pot of fried chicken. Grandpa begins his own food foraging, but Grandma nails him when he hoists a huge golden chicken breast from the pot.

"My God, Dad, you're worse than the kids and Taco put together! Don't you dare give any of that chicken to Taco. Hurry up and say grace for us, before you eat it all up and there's nothing left for the rest of us."

I don't ever remember saying grace at picnics. Oh well—

Food intake is vigorous. Conversation is warm, animated, exciting. Compliments to family chefs are plentiful. And there's even real whip cream for the dessert.

We're just finishing the pound cake and raspberries when Mother announces, "Well, we need to get all this picnic stuff packed up. We have to get back on the road right away. We want to take Mavis to visit our cousins in Hazelwood."

"Huh?" My plastic fork stops short of my mouth. My last bite of raspberries and pound cake dribbles down the front of my white tank top. "Mother, you and Dad haven't visited those people for years, have you?"

"No, we haven't been there in a long time, but they're still our cousins."

"Do they know you're coming?"

"No, they don't know we're coming. They'll really be surprised and happy to see Mavis arrive with us."

"Yes, I'm sure they'll be surprised to see you all." I dip a clean paper towel in my ice water and lean over my shirt speaking to the red splotches. "And they'll be about as happy as I am trying to smear the raspberry goop off my white shirt."

Old Parents and Purple Tulips

A few weeks later Mavis writes:

> I'm still recuperating. I came out there for the visit and not to
> be on the go all the time to tourist places and visiting shirt-tail
> relatives I don't even remember being related to. I couldn't stop
> either one of them. I can tell you for sure it is no pleasure to
> be the car with Francine yelling and directing Roger's driving.
> Her memory is atrocious. Half the time she tells him to turn in
> the wrong places anyway. She purchases double food items, loses
> clothing, keys, her purse—you name it. I fear she'll have a stroke
> one of these days during one of her yelling and shouting sprees.
> You can't imagine how bad it gets. I really think there is a medi-
> cal problem. I told your dad I thought she should have a medical
> check-up. He said he's tried to get her to go to the doctor and she
> won't, so I guess there's nothing any of us can do.

After Mavis' visit Mother's calls revert to an infrequent schedule with
mundane news about the weather, the garden, or the ongoing sequence
of automotive failures in their old cars. In one call she tells me the bathroom sink is still off the wall, and all their hand-washing is being done at
the bath-tub or the kitchen sink.

"When did all this sink stuff start, Mom?"

"Oh, you know Dad. He started a little sink repair job to stop a fau-
cet drip the night before Mavis arrived, and he hasn't had time to finish
it."

"You mean you didn't have a sink in the bathroom the whole time
Mavis was there? And you still don't?"

"Mavis had to do just like we have to do. She had to wash her hands
in the bath tub or she had to go to the kitchen."

"Does Dad need some help to get the sink back up, or do you need
a plumber?"

"No, we don't need any help, and we sure don't need a plumber. Dad
just hasn't had time to finish the job. We did fine when Mavis was here,

and you don't need to be worrying about things that are none of your concern. We'll get that sink taken care of."

I decide not to ask any further details lest she suggest the problem with the sink was somehow related to me or my children.

Aunt Mavis doesn't think money is the issue with the Malfaits. I don't think so either. With their combined pensions and Social Security, they should be able to manage. They have no real bills or debts. Their house is paid for. Rolf is working steadily and seems recovered from loss of log hauling work due to the Mount St. Helens eruption. They have only themselves. They should be okay. They eat out often, and that may be a big item. But if they spend $30.00 per day at Chuck's Wagon, which is their favorite way of eating out, they'd only spend about $900.00 per month. That's not half of their combined income.

It's peculiar that Dad handles the bill-paying now. Mother did that as long as I can remember. Like many survivors of the Great Depression, Malfaits absolutely believe in paying their bills in cash. Mother's forgetfulness may have caused some difficulties in this regard. Maybe that's why Dad took over the task.

I only hear inadvertent comments in phone conversations, "Oh, Ruthie drove me downtown to pay a late light bill today. She said they'd turn the electricity off again if we didn't get it paid today." I don't dare ask about *again*. I think Dad is aware that Mother has a problem but refuses to acknowledge it for what it is. But who knows what *it* is? Why do they wait for things, especially necessary things like the sink? Why do they endure unhealthy, unsanitary conditions? Why don't they buy a decent, dependable car or truck? What do they do with their money?

Communications from Malfaits have become a steady irrational repetitious litany. My ears are accustomed to the drone of illogical actions and events. It's not really a surprise when Mother forgets Mavis visited just a few weeks ago. She insists Mavis drove herself out from West Virginia and they had not picked her up at the Portland airport. Why should I argue with her? Why should I make her angry over such a petty point?

Old Parents and Purple Tulips

Mavis *did* drive out once from West Virginia to visit, but it was years ago. What difference does it make when? My brain disengages. It's less stressful. Less painful.

I need a break. I need a break from Malfaits.

Don and I and the children begin to consider making a trip down South. Another summer is fast approaching, and none of us is eager for a battle with Malfaits over why the children will not be coming to Ridgeview during vacation.

A call to Aunt Mavis inquiring about a potential visit gets the word out to a string of cousins, initiating a flurry of letter-writing, phone calls, and invitations from relatives enthusiastically anticipating a visit from their Western family.

Nick is a senior with all the usual symptoms of "senioritis." The prom, the sneak, annual signing, and sometimes even homework. He has a summer job, and his college arrangements are in order for fall. El is completing ninth grade, which entails its own degree of folderol such as her first floor-length formal and a first real date. He's a tough-looking football player with a huge mop of hair, and he wears a gargantuan onyx ring that looks as if he might use it like brass knuckles if Dad and I say she can't go. We relax somewhat when the young man's mother comes to our house unannounced to *interview* the family of her son's potential first date.

Interspersed in such routine events, we plan our summer trip with the hope that a trip to West Virginia may at least show our children there is an extended family who cares for them and loves them sight unseen. In some small way this may help make up for the failure of interaction between them and their grandparents and with their Uncle Rolf. We will not invite Grandma and Grandpa to accompany us, nor will we discuss our intentions with them ahead of time, though in years past we have made this same trip with them by automobile.

The only hitch to our plan comes when Nick astounds us during graduation week with news that he has signed up for a United States

Marine Reserve Program. Don and I are speechless. Nick wants to help pay for his college expenses, and military educational benefits seem desirable and logical to him. He figures he can complete basic training in the summer and still be at university for fall quarter. We are sure it won't work that way, but the decision is final and it is Nick's, even if it was made in his eighteenth year while in the throes of "senioritis."

Grandma's reaction to Nick's independent decision-making is another form of "senioritis." Following a phone conversation with Nick, *I* receive a scathing seven page letter written in *red* ink and capital letters, which I have come to recognize as an indication of her anger. In part she tells me, "WHAT IN THE WORLD WERE YOU THINKING? WHY DID NICK JOIN THE MARINES? WHOEVER ENCOURAGED HIM TO DO THAT I WISH THEY HAD TO TAKE HIS PLACE! AND I COULD SAY A LOT MORE TO YOU ABOUT THIS!"

I don't want to call, but I feel as if I should respond to her red ink epistle. I clinch the phone, take a deep breath and dial. Dad answers.

"Hey, Dad. I got Mother's letter today. I want you both to know Don and I didn't even know Nick signed up for this Marine thing. He talked to some other guys in his class and they were signing up for the military to help with college expenses. He thought that was a good idea. He talked to the local recruiter. He made a decision. And he signed on the dotted line. He didn't talk to either one of us about it. He's eighteen and feeling like he can make his own decisions now. I guess he can, but this was a huge shock to both Don and me."

"Well, Mama and me were sort of surprised, but don't you be worried about it. The Marines will be a good experience for Nick. He'll sure think better the next time. And I'll bet there'll be no re-upping. You can bet on that."

"I know Dad, but I'm sorry this is causing you both any frustration or anger or whatever it is Mother was trying to say in her letter."

"Oh, hell, Betty; I'm not mad at Nick, or you or anyone else. Your mom gets too excited and bent out of shape sometimes. I'm real proud of

Nick. Don't you worry. He'll be fine in the Marines. I'm sure he can hold his own. I want to get up there for his graduation, if we can work it out."

"I hope both you and Mother will come for graduation, even if she is angry about the Marine thing."

"Ah, you don't be worrying about Mom. I want to see Nick graduate whether she comes with me or not."

"Really, Dad? Nick would love for you to be here. We all would."

"Well, he's my only grandson, and I really want to see him graduate. I've already told Francine I want to get up there for that, but she's not budging. Your mom doesn't want to make the trip. She says I can't drive good enough, and I can't come up by myself. She doesn't want to leave the place for that long. She can be pretty stubborn, you know."

I sense his tears welling up. "Dad, is she there now? Let me talk to her."

Mother and I chat about the usual nothing with no mention of the red ink letter. "Our garden has really put out this year, and Dad has been making jelly at all hours of the night."

"Mother, we're pretty busy up here too with the end of the school year and Nick's graduating and all. It's such a happy time, and we're so proud of him. We want you and Dad to come up and share in that with us. Nick is so excited, and he wants you both to be here, too."

"We can't possibly do that."

"But, Mom, this is a once in a lifetime thing. Nick has done a wonderful job through high school. There's over two hundred fifty in his class. He's on the honor roll. He's been admitted to university, and he's going on to college.

"Mom, I'll even be marching in the ceremony with all the faculty. We'll be in full cap and gown regalia with color cords and collars representing all our various universities and colleges. It's really a beautiful ceremony. Oh, Mom, we all want you and Dad to be here with us for this event. Please—"

"Dad and I are real proud of Nick, too, and we'd like to see him graduate."

"So you'll come then?"

"No, Betty, I told Dad and I'm telling you, I can't possibly do that."

"Not even for one day—just one overnight?"

"No, it's like I told Dad, I can't leave this place and all the animals and Rolf. You never know who would do what. Dad can go if he wants to, but he can't drive himself up there. You'll have to come and pick him up."

Amid a busy end-of-the-year teaching schedule for Don and me and graduation practices and school checkouts for Nick, we make the three hour and fifteen minute trip to Ridgeview to pick up Grandpa. When we arrive, Nick and I run up to their front door step and ring the bell. Don stays in the car.

We hear Grandma's voice through the door wicket, "They're here! They're here! Dad, hurry up. Have you got everything? They can't wait all day."

The door opens and Grandma greets us, "Hi, Nick. Congratulations on your graduation." No hugs. No kisses. No acknowledgement that I'm present. Grandma continues, "Dad's all ready." She reaches back and pulls him through the entryway onto the doorstep. Get on out here, Dad. They're waiting."

It's been a hot day. The living room shades are pulled. Mother is blocking the doorway, but it's cool and dark behind her. Shadowy shapes hulk in the blackness making it seem crowded. An unpleasant odor is even less welcoming than the darkness. I'm curious, but I can't really see into the living room. I don't have time for seeing anything more anyway.

Dad is standing on the sidewalk with a small suitcase in hand, but he extends his free hand to Nick for a hearty handshake and a one-armed hug. "Congratulations, Nick. I'm real proud of you, son."

Nick returns the handshake and hug, then blinks and steps back. "Wow, Grandpa, you look great!"

Dad is decked out in one of his favorite Sunday suits, a soft tan gabardine, and a white shirt with French cuffs showing off jade cuff links, each with a small gold nugget in the center. A subtle paisley patterned silk tie is secured to the shirt by a jade tie tac which matches the cuff links but with a larger gold nugget in the middle.

"Nice shoes too, Grandpa. That's a Marine shine."

We all look down to Grandpa's brown, recently shined, wing-tip Florsheims.

Dad smiles and nudges Nick's arm. "We all have to look good for the big occasion, don't we? Let's get this shindig on the road!"

Nick and I back off the walkway as Grandpa brushes past us with his suitcase and heads toward the car parked by the street curb. Grandma pulls the heavy front door closed and hurries off the steps jostling past Nick and me.

"Come on, you two. Let's get Dad loaded into your car."

We move in a rushed cluster down the sidewalk toward the street. We bump into Mother when she stops suddenly half-way to the car and yells out to her neighbor, Nosy Bill, a noisy description of our visit and Nick's graduation. Nosy Bill puts down the rugs she has been pretending to shake from her front porch and comes over to offer her congratulations to Nick and engage him in conversation about his future plans.

Amid noise and confusion, mostly Grandma alternately bragging to Nosy Bill about Nick and leaning into the car to remind Grandpa to behave himself, we all buckle up and pull away for our three hour and fifteen minute return trip.

Grandpa is happy as he speaks from the back seat, "I sure do thank you, Don, for driving down to pick me up. Mama was awful stubborn on this deal. She just wouldn't come with me. Sometimes I just don't know what's the matter with her. She didn't want me to ride the bus or the train, and she sure wouldn't hear of me driving myself up to your house. Hell, I know I could of made it up there. But I'm real glad you came down, and I thank you for doing that for me, Don."

Grandpa turns to Nick and elbows him gently, "Congratulations again, Nick. I'm real proud of you, son."

Grandpa is obviously elated and he has always been quite a talker, but his prattle in the car is constant the entire three hour and fifteen minute trip, mostly joking with Nick. Later in the evening he talks *all* through dinner and *all* through the movie afterward. He even chatters to himself after he is in his room in bed with the lights off. Early the next morning he appears at the breakfast table completely dressed in the same impeccable attire, and the motor-mouth activity resumes and continues throughout the whole day—and the entire lengthy graduation ceremony in the evening, as is attested to by Don's brother and his wife with whom he is seated.

After the buses crammed with jubilant whooping graduates pull out of the parking lot headed for their all-night party, Don and I load ourselves and Dad back in our car and begin our own all-night party—the return trip to Ridgeview. Dad's vocal barrage continues nonstop for the three hour and fifteen minute return trip. He has not lost his sense of humor and mostly keeps Don and me laughing. But there is definitely a problem!

We arrive in front of 516 well after 1:00 AM. Dad gets out of the car immediately, turns and leans back in the back door, "Thank you both for coming down to get me and for bringing me home. I'm really glad I got to see Nick graduate. Thank you for all the nice meals, too. You drive careful now. Goodnight." He closes the car door, turns, and ambles up the walk to the front door. Mother opens the door for him as if she has been waiting for him to arrive at this very minute. He turns and waves, then disappears into the blackness of their house.

Mother scurries out to the car in her nightgown and leans toward my open window. "Thanks for taking Dad. You guys be careful. You have a long drive home."

She asks no questions about the trip nor the graduation. We aren't invited in. She hurries back up the walkway and disappears into her own darkness.

Grandpa's being at the graduation of his only grandson is a confusing but treasured triumph, especially important to Nick.

CHAPTER 5

---⟨∞⟩---

The Trip, and Then Another Trip

OUR WEST VIRGINIA trip date arrives. We get off on schedule. The flight is five-and-a-half long, cramped hours, but the reception from Uncle Malcom and one of my cousins at the airport in Atlanta is exuberant. Our cramps disappear. Tiredness is forgotten. And a joyous, loving mood prevails throughout a two-hour drive into the mountains where many of our relatives live.

It feels as if it has been only a short drive when my cousin makes an abrupt turn off the main road and pulls the big maroon Lincoln town car up a short winding gravel lane, lined on each side by a row of cottonwoods, and stops in front of his home. It's early afternoon. Bright sunlight comes down over the cottonwoods and strikes the front of the house, enhancing the stark whiteness of the entryway and a veranda which stretches the entire length of the house. Six huge tall white pillars stand at attention along the front of the veranda contrasting the red brick of the two story home. I feel as if we have stepped into a scene from "Gone with the Wind."

Uncle Malcom doesn't need to remind us of the weather, but he does anyway. "Well, I guess you all can tell today's been a pretty hot one."

I'm still taking in the beauty of this impressive, very southern home and silently hoping my deodorant has been successful against the sweaty moistness I feel in more places than my armpits as I respond, "Wow. We sure didn't feel this when we were cruising along in your air-conditioned town car."

We all move to the back of the car and begin to unload the trunk when Uncle Malcom swings an arm down toward the road. "Well, looka there."

Betty Alder

A well-kept older model black Ford pickup cruises slowly by, stops in the middle of the county road, backs up, and eases off onto the shoulder. Uncle Ed, Granddad's older brother, climbs out and waving a big straw hat in our direction smiles a smile that warms the sticky southern afternoon even more. He scrambles up a steep bank and steps through a border of young sourwood trees along the front of the property. As he comes across the lawn, Nick's and El's eyes widen to the size of fifty-cent pieces. Together they blurt out, "Mom, it's *Grandpa!*" The likeness is remarkable. Uncle Ed, who has never met them, sweeps both teenagers into a bear-hug they will never forget.

Nick marvels, "Mom, he's just like Grandpa, only fatter."

El joins in, "He hugs like Grandpa, too. He about crushes your bones."

As we laugh and get better acquainted with Uncle Ed, I feel such elation. I would have made this trip solely for these last few moments.

Later in the afternoon at a family picnic, Aunt Elsa, Grandpa's older sister, enthralls the kids with stories of her and Granddad's childhood. "Why, I remember one time when we was all teenagers, Ed, your daddy, me, and our little brother, George, had us a big time scarin' the daylights out of Mother Malfait. She was *our* momma, you know. She'd be *your* great grandma. Ever'one called her Mother Malfait though, even youn-guns that wasn't her children.

"Now, Roger, that'd be your grand-daddy, was workin' that summer up on Bell Mountain where they was buildin' the new highway. And he brought home some dynamite so's he could get rid of a big old stump in the upper field and make plowin' through the corn rows there a might easier. That Sunday evenin' me and the boys all sneaked up on the hillside above the road where Mother Malfait would be walkin' home after her evenin' church meetin'. We all had to go to church with her of a Sunday mornin', but we didn't go to evenin' meetin', unless it was a special singin' or somethin' such as that. We was supposed to be gettin' chores done and be all ready for school the next day. Anyways, we thought it'd be funny to set off this dynamite under that big old stump right about when she was walkin' by. We figured she'd think it was the 'second comin' just like she'd probably been hearin' at preachin' that evenin'. You know, them preachers down to her church, why they're just gettin' wound up good at the end of morning church. They really bring on the hell-fire and brimstone at night services."

Nick and El giggled at their own perception of hell-fire and brimstone, and Nick leaned across the picnic table and asked, "Aunt Elsa, tell us some more about growing up with Grandpa."

El scooted over closer to her and echoed, "Oh, please, please do."

Aunt Elsa grinned her appreciation and continued, "Well, you know, there was seven of us kids. Your daddy and your Uncle Fred was the oldest. Then came us girls: me and Carrie, then Verna, then, and last was the baby, Claudine. We was all pretty good children. Of course, Mother Malfait would never believe *any* of her children would do orneriness of any importance—you know—no real bad stuff. Maybe little things to each other—but never to her. If she did suspicion any little thing goin' on with any of us, you know, why your daddy and my other brothers would tell some little story to cover for us, especially for me. I was the only girl that'd go up there with 'em on that dyamite deal though. My sisters wasn't about to go out in that field in the daylight much less in the even' with dark comin' on. I guess I was kinda the tomboy of the group."

Aunt Elsa paused for a sip of her sweetened ice tea, and Nick took advantage, "But, Aunt Elsa, did it go off? Did Grandpa really set that dynamite off?"

"Oh my yes! It was so loud and blew so much dirt and tree bark up in the air, I believe all of *us* thought for a minute it *was* the second comin'!"

Aunt Elsa's teasing nature and her beautiful face very much resemble Grandpa. And her story verifies his rendition of an event he had once shared with Nick and El. As the afternoon progresses, other aunts, uncles, and cousins arrive, share stories, add to the already plentiful array of picnic food, sample each other's latest recipes, and profusely express to us the family camaraderie and love we have all sorely missed the past four years.

A few days later Don and I and the children leave my cousin's place and travel to a more remote area in the mountains to visit a long-time family friend. While we are there Aunt Mavis calls, "Your mom called me this morning and told me Roger had a light stroke. She said it's by no means major. It's just a light one and you are not to worry but she wanted you to know."

"Mavis, do we need to get back to your house and get on our way home?"

"No, your mom was worried you might want to do something like that. She was emphatic that Roger is in the hospital and he's okay. He's being well taken care of, and in no way do they want you and your family to cut your vacation short and return home. She said your help is not needed. Everything is being taken care of in the hospital."

"Mavis, I don't know how accurate Mother's reports might be."

"Well, all I can tell you is she was *very* clear about not wanting to bother you people. In fact, at first she didn't even want me to call you. Then she decided I should tell you but she doesn't want you to come home early. She did say if you have time, give them a call in a couple of days."

"When did all this happen, Mavis?"

"She said the stroke was earlier this week, and she and Rolf took him to the hospital. She had found him passed out in the floor between the bathroom and the little hallway to the bedroom. When she got him awake enough to talk, he told her his legs wouldn't hold him up. She rolled him over and partly lifted and partly dragged him to the bed. I myself am concerned about that part, because it doesn't sound like a *little stroke*. But she said Rolf was there, so I have to trust he has better sense than her."

"I don't know, Mavis. She probably just told you what she wanted you to hear. Are you sure about the time frame?"

"No, I'm really not sure. She was unclear about the time from when she found him to when Rolf took him to the hospital. For all I know it may have been a day or two later when Rolf got there, but she said in the same conversation Rolf was *there* when it happened. Betty, I just don't know. I tried to write down as much as I could, but I see here in my notes I have it written two different ways."

"Aunt Mavis, all communication with Malfaits in recent years has been confusing, and I certainly don't hold you responsible for gathering precise details. Mother has a way of making you think the information is precise, but later you'll be scratching your head. I know the feeling."

We return to Aunt Mavis' the next morning, and I call Mother.

"Oh, I'm so happy to hear from you. I'm sure Mavis has already told you, but I want to tell you right off Dad and I don't want you to worry or be planning to come home early. Things are fine here. Everything possible is being done in the hospital. Dad's getting good care, and there's nothing any of us can do. His doctor is a prissy little thing named Dr. Kettlesman, or Kettlestone, or something like that. Everyone just says Dr. K this or Dr. K that—and oh, yes, that Dr. K's the best of the best."

"Is that a man or a woman?"

"Oh, he's an arrogant little man, but I guess he knows his business when it comes to stroke victims. I don't like him much though. Anyway, Dad is doing fine right now, and so am I. I walk to the hospital every day to help feed him, and he eats like a logger. You wouldn't believe it. He's really progressing well."

Mother convinces me all is well. She convinces Mavis, and she convinces her brother Malcom. After the three of us discuss our various perspectives, we conclude all really is well with Dad's situation and he's in good hands.

My family and I leave the next morning for a week in Florida to visit to Disney World and Epcot Center. I call Mavis daily, and she reports continued positive progress. I call Ridgeview and get Mother's firsthand reports. Dad is complaining about the hospital food, the service, and his roommate. He is sitting up, walking a little, and still eating like a logger. I usually get a recitation of the full menu, as well. It sounds like a person on the mend. Mother herself seems fine, almost like she's thriving on her new responsibilities.

Arriving back at Mavis' at the end of the week, I call Mother again and am surprised to find she has taken Dad home. "Oh, Betty, I'm so pleased with his progress. He has no drawing at all in his face like happens to so many stroke victims. I'm so thankful for that, and he can use his hands and move both legs. I've been giving him alcohol baths. I rub it on his legs and massage his back with it regularly."

"Did the doctor tell you to do *alcohol* baths? That sounds so cold."

"Oh, Dad likes them. I just rub that alcohol on, and I know it's helping."

Her words lure me into a comfort zone. I want so badly to hear he's doing well. "I guess the rubbing is good for him. I don't know about the alcohol part. Did the doctor prescribe any kind of regular therapy or exercise?"

"Well, yes, I guess he did. One day we had some know-it-all expert from the hospital come here to the house trying to explain exercises for him. Some fat-assed therapist she was! She didn't know any more about rubbing a stroke patient than I do."

"Is she the one who told you to do alcohol baths?"

"Hell, no, I didn't even let *her* in the house."

"Oh, Mother, I think you should have let her in. She's trained to know how to help Dad."

"She was just a fat, slobby old bitch who didn't know shit! I'm sure she was sent out to the house by that asshole of a doctor, little Dr. K."

I move the telephone away from my ear and give my head a vigorous shake. The profuse expletives are a bit much for Mother who never tolerated even *damn* from Rolf and me in our growing up years. I try to ignore the words and accept stress as the cause of her crude barrage.

"Mom, I know you said you didn't care much for Dr. K at the hospital, but the hospital personnel are not against you. They want Dad to get well, whether they like him, or like you, or whatever. Making people well is their business. They're highly trained in the latest techniques. You need to listen to them for Dad's sake."

"Well, I don't know where that shitty little Dr. K learned his bedside manner. He actually told Dad there wasn't a thing wrong with him. He was just an ornery old man and that's how come he had a stroke. Now that was the crowning blow! No one should say that to a man who has been as near death's door as Dad. We were both furious over that. Dad wanted to get the hell out of there and come home immediately. I wanted to bring him home. And I did!"

In some bizarre way bringing Dad home equates with wellness to Mother, but I'm thinking all is *not* as well as Mother would like us to believe. Despite her convincing telephone demeanor, I have a weighty ball in the pit of my stomach.

Through the week Mother continues the glowing reports to Mavis and me, but each time the news rings more hollow. "Oh, Betty, you wouldn't know he'd been so sick. He gets stronger every day. I can see it right before my eyes."

My own equally hollow voice echoes, "I'm really happy to hear that." I shake my head and heave a sigh across the kitchen table at Aunt Mavis as she and I are finishing our morning coffee. "How are *you* getting along, Mom?"

"Oh, I'm a little tired. I've got an awful lot to do around here. In fact, well—er—now I don't want you to come home early or anything, but do you think maybe when you do get home you could come down here for a little bit?"

I press the phone more firmly against my ear, "You want *me* to come down *there* and stay for a while and help?"

"Well, I could use a little help, but don't you come home early from your trip or anything. We're fine for right now."

"Yes, I would like to help you and Dad. If I were there, I'm sure I could at least help with the housework and laundry, right?"

"Oh no, you could just be with Dad. I'm taking care of the laundry. I've been going down to the corner laundromat. That's been a God-send.

I put in the wash and then I have a nice lunch at Sally's lunch counter next door while it's drying. Then I take Dad a hot lunch back to the house."

"Is it okay to leave Dad like that?"

"Oh yes, he takes long naps. He sleeps all the time I'm gone, but when I walk in that door with a hamburger and milkshake, he wakes up pronto."

"Oh, Mom, I wish I was there now. I know this is hard for you."

"Well, I could use a little help, but don't you come home early. When you do get back though, would you come down then?"

"Of course I will."

"Thank you. I think I do need a little help."

"Okay. We'll be home in a couple days, and I'll come down then."

Later that same day, we all go to Uncle Malcom's home for a farewell supper. While we are there, Mother calls and informs her brother Malcom, "I have no idea where Don and Betty are. They're running around all over the country. Betty has not called here all during her whole vacation."

Uncle Malcom holds the phone away from his ear and shakes his head. "Listen, Francine, do you want to speak to Betty? She's right here."

"No, I guess she'll call when she gets good and ready. Good-bye."

"Wait, Francine. Wait..."

Mother's voice was loud enough that I heard most of her conversation. I think she cut Uncle Malcom short and hung up to avoid talking to me. I stare at my supper plate and watch my very favorite southern supper of juicy fried chicken, crispy okra and fresh slices of red ripe Early Girls meld into blurry, moist streaks of indefinable modern art. The tears spill over. "Uncle Malcom, you know better. I've made several phone calls from right here at your house!"

"Lord, child, don't you worry yourself sick until *you* have a stroke. Confusion *is* reality for your mother. Mavis and I are both here with you. We've both heard the calls from Francine. We can't all be crazy."

Old Parents and Purple Tulips

We all try to accept Uncle Malcom's thought that we can't all be crazy, and my family leaves the next morning at an early hour and heads for Atlanta for our flight home. We arrive at Portland Airport at 5:30 P.M. It's been a month since our departure from this airport. Despite floating in jet lag, within an hour I unpack, repack, and get on my way to Ridgeview. I decide not to call Mother before setting out for their house. She would probably tell me everything is fine and not to come. I have not been to Ridgeview nor in their home in over four years, unless I count the few minutes in the entryway when we picked up Dad to bring him to our house for Nick's graduation. Potential thief or not, I am going to go stay with them for a while. And I am going to arrive at their home after midnight.

The three hour and fifteen minute drive passes in a surreal blur of headlights, tail-lights, road signs, small towns, rest stops, and the sarcasm of a late-night radio commentator who doesn't care any more than his listeners what he says on the air. If verbal shock helps keep himself and the listeners awake, all is well.

Not fully cognizant of time nor travel details, I find myself standing on the doorstep of 516 in pitch blackness. I ring the doorbell several times, lulled momentarily by each four-tone melodious sequence pealing into the cool night air. I lean close and further announce my presence by calling through the closed wrought iron wicket. There are many guns in the house, and I don't want to get shot. Mother knows nothing about using them, but what if she tries?

The little metal wicket snaps open. "Well, my God, look who's here! Oh, Betty, I'm so happy you've come."

"Hi, Mom. I'm sorry to arrive so late. I didn't mean to frighten you."

"Oh, I'm not frightened. Are you okay?"

"Yes, yes, I'm fine."

"Did you have a good trip?"

"Yeah, it was great."

"How are Mavis and Malcom getting along?"

"Mom, they're fine, but could we visit inside instead of through the door wicket?"

She fumbles with the deadbolt several times, and then returns to the wicket, "I don't know why this thing won't cooperate. It usually pops right open."

"Come on, Mom, give it another try."

She returns to the lock. I hear a tiny click and the heavy door yields. Mother steps back into the living room. No hug. No other greeting. "Well, get on in here and speak to your Dad."

I follow her ragged flannel nightgown as she shuffles through the dimly lit living room into the front bedroom. Some place in those few steps I drop my heavy overnight bag with a vague thought, How will I stay in this house? And where? A more than unpleasant odor permeates the thick air in the living room and bedroom, and indistinguishable crowded shadows press in from the darkness all around me.

In the front bedroom 40 watt rays from a bedside lamp dull the happiness of the pink and white roses on the wallpaper of my childhood room. From the puffiness of pillows and comforter struggling pale blue eyes flicker in fuzzy wakefulness. I lean over and kiss the bony cheek of an emaciated likeness of my father. From shaky hand motions extended in my direction, I know he knows I am here. His speech is impossible to understand, but his hand grip and repeated irregular squeezes of my hand convey his happiness. I make out enough of his guttural sounds to know he wants to be sure I haven't cut short my vacation. I assure him I haven't, and he is pleased.

The hour is late. Mother's pathetic disheveled figure is silhouetted in the bedroom doorway clutching an armful of bedding. "Here, make yourself a bed out here in the living room on the couch." She hands me a sheet, a quilt and a pillow. With no further word she passes in front of me and gets into bed beside my father.

There are two bedrooms upstairs and another back bedroom downstairs. Why does she want me to sleep on the couch? I go back into the living room with my bedding, which is stiff and cold and smells of something other than having been stored too long. I turn on the ceiling lights in the living room and survey the big old curved three-piece sectional nestled almost half way around the once cozy knotty pine walls. The pine boards are much darker than I remember. A dinginess engulfs the whole room—and me, too. Harsh light from three bare overhead light bulbs glares off dirty ceiling tiles. Broken pieces of the ceiling lamp shade have been cast haphazardly onto the coffee table atop stacks of newspapers and piles of unopened mail and magazines. I wonder how the light shade got broken. The unpleasant aroma which I had detected earlier pinches into my nasal tissue, causing my eyes to water and my throat to itch. Boxes of clothes, guns, newspapers, books, flowerpots, afghans, unemptied kitty litter, automotive parts and heavy chains squelch any semblance of coziness. Most of the debris appears to be Rolf's. I feel diminutive, overwhelmed by a sick aura in this room—in this whole house.

Mother's house-keeping has never been meticulous but the house has always been comfortably cluttered, warm and inviting. At this moment judging from articles I can recognize, it looks as if Rolf has moved all of his Newcastle house and dumped it in their living room. I wrestle with the junk covering the couch—some boxed, some just thrown. It's difficult to find places to restack anything as all the chairs, tables, TV, and floor are already piled out of sight. As I work I become acutely aware that the unpleasant, ill-defined stench I noted earlier pervades everything. It makes my skin crawl and my nose run. My body prepares for an impending allergy war.

I tell myself my feelings and emotions are exaggerated. Mom and Dad have survived here. I can too. I squeeze myself into my crude bed on one and a half sections of the couch and use my overnight bag to form an incline between the hard arm of the couch and the sagging cushion. I slip into exhausted sleep, calmed only by a feeling that I have made Dad happy, even if it is momentary, garbled elation, possibly mine as much as his.

The night absorbs my exhaustion, but when I awaken in the morning it's apparent Mother needs *lots* of help. The stench is real, the sources too numerous to narrow down to a single offending place or item. I begin a total sanitation assault—first the kitchen and whatever items I can *find*. Haphazard stacking takes on a whole new meaning, and it's all embedded in layers of grease and grime with many items stuck together or stuck to the counter top. I work with driven ferocity. I need hot soapy water, but I can't even get that until I get rid of the moldy vegetable peels clogging the drain-catch and clinging to dishes and pans in the sink. There's no garbage disposal and no rubber gloves, but I am blessed with various brands of dishwasher soap and a gallon of bleach long forgotten under the sink. I launch my assault bare-handed. I uncover more dishes with leftover food on them on the table, on top of the freezer, and on the refrigerator. After reclaiming the stove top and one end of the table, I open the refrigerator and find a whole new world of mold, most of which I place directly into plastic bags for the garbage dumpster in the alley. I sweep up the debris from my kitchen combat along with the fall-out of years of lost battles for cleanliness, and then I mop the floor with a strong bleach solution. When I finally pause to rest and get a drink of water and a cup of tea, I find I must wash all the dishes and glasses in the cupboard and the teapot. I even wipe off the tea package with my damp bleach cloth before opening it.

The only rescued refrigerator items are milk and eggs, which I hope are fairly recent purchases. There's bread in a plastic sealed container on the table. It's enough to make breakfast.

Dad is awake, and I hear Mother helping him to the bathroom. Afterwards he is loud and fussy, making it known through faltering speech and hand motions he wants to come to the table.

"Dad, you need to get yourself back to bed. I'll bring you some breakfast."

"Now—Mama—I want—to go—to—table."

"Well I can't carry you out there."

"Betty's—here—I want—to have—breakfast—with her."

When I approach the two of them, Dad reaches out and takes a shaky grip on my arm and makes a faltering step toward me giving me a rubbery smile of victory. He will have it no other way. He has to have considerable support, but he shuffles his frail body a few inches at a time and squeezes my arm repeatedly as he changes his less than secure grip from one pile of Rolf's junk to the next until we finally get to the kitchen table. He drops onto a chair, almost falling off the other side. I lift his legs and move them under the table.

He is hungry and attacks his plate as soon as it is placed before him. He feeds himself and eats remarkably well, despite shaky spills and sometimes missing his mouth. It's no place close to eating like a logger, unless it's one who has been flattened by a tree and can only see in blurred tunnel vision straight in front of himself.

Breakfast and another bathroom trip tire Dad out. I help him shuffle back to bed where he is confused and disoriented in simple things like how to sit down on the edge of the bed, how far and which way to scoot back, and how to get his head on the pillow. On his first attempt his body slumps to a prone kitty-cornered position far away from the pillow. I hold his hand and help him try again. It's the third attempt before he successfully flops onto the pillow. I tell him how proud I am of his hard work, but his eyes are already closed. His lips move, but no audible sound comes forth. Still holding his hand, I ease down onto the edge of the bedside chair. As I glance about the room I feel my hand being squeezed sporadically in death's grip both literally and figuratively with all the appropriate ugliness. The bedroom is as filthy as the other areas of the house I have been in, both from human use, clutter, and the household cats. The bed sheets which are supposed to be white are a dull gray. The once beautiful hand-pieced quilts tucked under Dad's chin smell of urine. A large coffee can which has been used as a urinal sits on the far corner of the bed in its red Folgers alertness. Paper towels used for whatever purpose have been tossed against the wall. The kitty litter tub beside the bed is in dire need!

I feel physically ill. I utter no critical remarks as I release my hand from Dad's and move back into the living room where Mother is seated on top of my couch-bed. She is almost unnoticeable in the general appearance of the room—tired, broken, disheveled, unkempt.

"Betty, I'm awful glad you've come. Can you stay a few days?"

"Of course, I'll stay however long you need me."

"I'm so glad. I just need a little help to catch up."

My insides are fighting back a biological urge to throw up. In this house one will *never* catch up! "Mom, I'll be happy to help in any way I can, and I'll stay as long as you need me. Where shall we start?"

She points to a pile of clothes in the center of the room, "I've gathered all the wash. We can go to the laundomat at the corner store now while Dad's sleeping. He usually sleeps four hours or more in the morning."

There seems to be no alternative but to leave Dad by himself. Mother and I stuff the dirty laundry into her wire push-cart and walk down the block to the corner store. We do a short shopping at the grocery store next door while the laundry runs. When we return to the house, Dad is still asleep. My first task is to change the kitty litter. The noise, the sweeping, and the crinkling of newspaper has no influence on Dad's slumber, and neither does Mother's loud objections to my rearrangement of the litter pans.

"I don't care what you think, Betty, we need those litter pans to be right there close beside the bed."

"But, Mom, they're so dirty and they're right in the way of getting Dad in and out of bed. They'd be in your way, too, if you get up in the night."

"I've got to have those pans where I can keep an eye on the kitties."

I brush the two scraggly, emaciated cats away from me as they tussle to see which one gets to use the fresh litter pan first. "Geez, Mom, your cats look about as skinny as Dad. They sure aren't eating like loggers."

"Those kitties are fine. You'll probably be skinny, too, when you're as old as they are. You leave their pans and dishes right there. Dad likes watching the kitties when he's awake, and that's where I feed them. Sometimes they crawl right up there beside Dad and curl around his head. They know he's not well."

I place the litter pans where Mother wants them, and Dad finally stirs and mutters, "Francine—feed—kitties."

"You don't worry about these damned cats. I need to get you to the bathroom."

While the two of them do their wobbly walk to the bathroom, I strip the sheets and clean up around the bed as best I can. Dad stays up for lunch, and to my surprise he again eats well. I don't want to be overly confident, but maybe there is some hope for this once wiry, tough, agile man who is now so frightfully thin. But it will surely take more than a few good meals. I offer to help Dad bathe, but he says he is too tired. He does agree to put on some clean sleep wear without a bath.

Finding clean clothing is another challenging chore. I can't even get the door open to the back bedroom where his bureau and closet are. There are too many boxes wedged behind the door, piled all over the bed and the floor space. I return to the living room and find a box of folded laundry on the couch and help him into clean long underwear, underwear that's well past a Salvation Army standard of acceptance.

Once he's down for his nap, Mother says, "Dad's long overdue for some new underwear. He's lost so much weight, none of his clothes fit."

"Mom, I'll go downtown sometime and get some new sets."

Mother locates her heavy black purse from the laundry push-cart and extracts her zipper purse. "Well, he needs it today. I'm ashamed of those rags he wearing. Here, here's five dollars. You go downtown to Penney's right now while he's sleeping and get two new sets of underwear. Get it in smaller sizes."

It may be more my own desire for temporary escape than solving the underwear problem, but I take the five dollar bill and leave. As I pull away from the curb I roll down all the car windows and let the sunshine and fresh air bathe my face and hair and my bleached hands and arms.

Upon my return, Mother happily receives the bag and immediately takes out the underwear packages along with the receipt which shows the total price for the purchase to be five times the amount she had given me. "Oh, my God, that's outrageous. Well, maybe it's been longer than I think since Dad has had any new underwear. Here, let me pay you for the rest." She hands me another five dollar bill. "Will that cover it?"

"You don't need to do that, Mom."

"Is that enough, Betty? I don't want you buying Dad's underwear."

"That's fine, Mom."

I don't want to tell her the total is a more than a little short. I wonder how they shop and pay for simple things. I have no time to think
about finances now. As I continue to clean and work in their house,
I feel increasing anger toward my brother Rolf for coming into their
home and literally dumping his belongings. A normal person would
have a difficult time navigating through the pathway to the kitchen,
much less a recuperating stroke victim trying to achieve such a precari-
ous obstacle course.

The sink in the bathroom has been reconnected crudely and allows a
small trickle of cold water. Any real hand-washing has to be done in the
kitchen sink. This was a problem last fall when Mavis was here! It's almost fall again. Behind the closed shower curtain I discover the bathtub
is full of filthy underwear and towels from Mother's previous *cleanings*.
There's at least two whole loads which didn't make it to the laundromat
with us earlier. For sure no bathing has been done in this tub by either of
them for a long time.

Amid the stench and my frustration I continue my rescue mission.
The dining room looks like a public recycling bin. I make a trip to
the local liquor store and get heavy boxes with lids and pack up Rolf's
magazines—over a hundred current issues of gun magazines plus
years of copies of <u>Gun Digest</u>, <u>Boy Hunters Digest</u>, <u>Guns Illustrated</u>,
<u>Shooters Bible</u>, and others. The entire table is stacked two feet high
or more with magazines. When I get them all boxed, I am surprised
to find Rolf's Siberian Husky, Taco, has claims on the area under the
dining room table.

"Mother, what's with this dog? He won't move out from under the
table?"

"That's where he stays most of the time."

"You mean under the dining room table is his dog house?"

"Well, he needs some place. You leave him alone. That's his space."

Old Parents and Purple Tulips

Great Christopher! In this same dining room there are two corner cabinets full of 'Old Salem' Spode china and Fostoria crystal. Actually there's service for twelve in each pattern, and teapots and coffee pots and other serving pieces. This is a dining room with a solid maple table which is still covered by a hand-crocheted tablecloth underneath all these present day stacks. This was the center of past family celebrations, bridal showers and baby showers for friends, dinners for visiting preachers, and other social gatherings. *Now* it's Taco's doghouse? I give no argument. I complete rearrangement of the dining room doghouse by hoisting Rolf's huge burl coffee table upside down atop the boxes of books and other clutter in the middle of the once beautiful maple table. At least the stacks are more stable and there is a path from bedroom to bathroom to kitchen with places for Dad to hang on as he negotiates his way through the house.

I retire to the living room and plop down atop my quilt-bed next to Mother who is reading the newspaper. I scan the room and decide there is no time for a rest. There is mail everywhere! "Geez, I guess you guys are behind on your mail, huh?"

Mother glances my way, "Oh, that's all Dad's junk mail."

"Wow! He must have an obsession with sweepstakes contests."

There are several envelopes, sheets of selection stickers, crudely scrawled notes inquiring about his winnings, and partially filled out orders for magazines. Interspersed with the contest mail are bills and business notices, personal cards and letters. I get a couple of my liquor store boxes and begin retrieving mail—from the coffee table, lamp tables, TV, on the floor, under couch cushions, and under the furniture. I end up with two full boxes of mail. With a black Sharpie I mark one box for Mom and Dad and one box for Rolf. Rolf's are mostly unopened bills.

"Mom, I've made a box for you and Dad and a separate box for Rolf. There's a lot of unpaid bills here."

"Oh, yes, those are Rolf's. He needs to get on the stick and take care of his business."

"Yes, but Mother, some of the unpaid bills are for you and Dad."

"Well, I don't see how that can be. I just paid bills a few days ago."

I show the mail to Mother. She claims not to know about a lot of things, including most of the bills. It is difficult for me to tell if she knows and doesn't want me to know something, or if she hasn't had anything to do with bills for a while. Among my finds is an unpaid water bill only a couple of days from shut-off date, an overdue PUD bill, a health insurance bill, and a statement from Fibex Credit Union showing an overdue payment for $468.90 on a loan that has a balance of $22,604.39.

"Mother, we'll do something tomorrow about most of these, but there's one here I don't understand at all."

"What's that?"

"It's from Fibex Credit Union."

"Oh, that's Rolf's bill."

"Yeah, I saw notices like that in his box, but there's a whole bunch of late notices addressed to you and Dad. Rolf's are unopened, but so are the ones to you and Dad."

"That's Rolf's business. Dad and Rolf took out a loan together. You need to just leave all that stuff for Rolf."

I don't think I approve, but having not been in their home for over four years, it's strange enough to be sorting their personal mail. I have never handled any of their bills nor mail previously, much less read it. I dare not pry.

The next day, Mother and I take care of regular bill-paying. As we return to the house the mailman is delivering a bundle of letters, including fresh notices from the collection department of Fibex Credit Union for the elusive bill.

Mother worked for Fibex Company for thirty-five years, and Malfaits have always had excellent credit. This can't possibly be their collection notice. It can't be their bill. They must just receive copies, and it's Rolf's debt. I add the additional notices to each of their boxes. I'm not so sure about Rolf's credit. His box is full of all kinds of pieces of mail marked 'Urgent' and 'Past Due.'

In the afternoon Rolf drops by, and I mention the Fibex bill to him. He takes the bill in hand, squints and readjusts the paper as he studies it.

"Yeah, yeah, that's just some over-zealous bookkeeper's mistake. That's been paid. I'll run out to the credit union and clear it up." He takes the paper with him and drives off. He comes back a short while later but says nothing more about the bill. I guess he took care of it. I ready myself to go home to my own family.

I have a feeling these last few days are just the beginning of my second trip of the summer, an itinerary marked by bits and pieces of information depicting fragmented, unattractive scenes as far as Rolf is concerned— and even more dismal pictures of Malfaits compared to how they could and should be living.

CHAPTER 6

The First Follow-Up Appointment,

A Saga in Senility

BEFORE SUMMER ENDS my family and I again escape for two weeks to Decatur Island, our favorite spot in the San Juans. It's relaxing to be in the midst of such beauty punctuated daily by tides and ever-changing intertidal zones. Our highest priorities are salmon fishing and beach-combing. Any day a salmon catch is a prize, and from beach walks our most desired treasures are agates, unique remnants of geologic time. Days without scoring an agate, we settle for finds of flotsam and jetsam from careless boaters or endangered storm-tossed ships. An array of birds chirp, coo, or scream as their needs demand. At nighttime the vastness of the Milky Way and falling stars can be seen more clearly from these northern latitudes. I am able to regroup and recognize my own importance as a person, and at the same time feel my insignificance in the universe and the endless span of time and space. I release my parental concerns into this larger perspective.

With such renewed spiritual reference, I return to Ridgeview to take Dad to his first doctor's appointment after his stroke. Since Grandma and Grandpa have wanted Nick and El to visit, they accompany me for their first time back to this house in over four years.

We arrive about 9:00 AM. Mother is shocked to see us.

"My God, Betty, what are you doing here?"

"Mother, this is Dad's doctor appointment day. It's on your calendar."

"Why, I don't think I've got that on the calendar for today."

"Maybe you forgot to read the calendar. I called you last night."

"Why, you didn't do any such thing. My God, Dad, look who's here. Nick and El have come to visit us. Oh, I'm so happy you're all here." Grandma embraces each of us, then turns and shakes her finger at Nick and El. "You two shouldn't scare your old grandma like this. You should call me before you show up on the doorstep."

"Mom, maybe we better not waste time arguing and scolding. We barely have enough time to get Dad ready for his appointment."

"Now, Betty, I've got an awful lot to do today. I don't have time to get Dad ready to go anyplace. I've got to go to the laundromat."

"Huh? Don't you think getting him to his doctor's appointment is a higher priority than going to the laundromat? He hasn't been seen since he had the stroke."

"Well, that may be, but you can see from the looks of this living room I need to get the washing done."

A quick scan of the room makes me feel as if I never worked in this room at all in any kind of clean-up effort. "Mom, we'll help you with that later. Right now, we need to get Dad ready."

"Okay, but I have to run down to the corner store and get a few things. We haven't had our morning coffee yet. We can't go anywhere without eating. My old legs hurt so bad I don't really want to walk down there."

I drive Mother the two blocks to the store. Once we're there she can't remember what she needs. She buys a quart of milk, one can of cat food, and a can of Spam. We hurry back to the house where El is already cooking eggs and oatmeal. She adds Spam and toast to the menu, and Dad, who never liked Spam, eats ravenously with no complaints and has seconds on everything including oatmeal and Spam.

Before he can ask for more, Mother gets him up from the table and hustles him off to the bedroom to get ready. As El and I clean up the kitchen, Nick gathers the garbage. We can easily hear Grandma in the other end of the house 'helping' Grandpa get dressed.

"Here, Roger, hurry up and get these on."

"Mama, I want my brown dress pants."

"You've lost so much weight, they don't fit you right. You don't have time to get all dressed up. Here, take these."

"Mama, those are dirty! I wore those to work in the garden. I'm going for my doctor appointment, and I want my brown dress pants."

"You take these and get them on right now. They're brown."

"They're not brown either. You need glasses."

"Well they're brown-checkered. Brown is brown."

"Mama, those are my work pants. I want—"

"You get these on! Betty is ready to go, and you're already late. You ought to have a bath, but we don't have time for that either."

As the kids and I finish our cleanup work in the kitchen and move into the living room, we hear Dad submit to Mother's choice of clothing. "Well, okay, give me those old pants, Francine. I sure don't have time for a bath."

He finally emerges from the bedroom with Mother following, lamenting all the while his not having any clothes that fit nor any time for a bath. It seems as if her talking about a bath is the same as actually doing it. She gives him a sharp nudge toward the front door, "You're plenty clean, Roger. You look fine. Now let's get going."

We're almost through the door when the phone rings, and Mother runs back to answer it. In her best convincing voice she extols Dad's miraculous progress and gives details of his eating habits to her cousin who lives in a nearby town. I am reminded of phone calls with her when we were on vacation.

Nick, El, and I guide and cajole Granddad out of the house and into the car. I hurry back to the front porch, and though the door is locked, through the wicket I can hear Mother's positive phone chatter still feeding her cousin's inquisitiveness. It's already 10:30 AM, Dad's appointment time. I run back and jump in the car.

"Dad, I think we better get going without her. We're already late."

"Hold on there a minute, Betty. Here comes Mama now."

Mother ambles out, gets in the car, and slams the door.

I can see Nick and El in the rearview mirror rolling their eyes at one another knowing they couldn't get by with slamming the car door like that. I say nothing and strive for self-control as I back slowly out onto the street. "Okay, guys, we're already late. Tell me how to get to your doctor."

Dad speaks up and motions shakily, "Take a right down here at the corner and let's go to Oregon. I get my cheese and day-old bread there."

Nick and El giggle as Granddad winks at them. Mother snaps, "Don't pay any attention to that old fool. He's had a stroke, and he doesn't know where he is half the time. The doctor's office is someplace over behind the YMCA."

"Someplace? Mother, your directions are about as useful as his."

My comment sets off a skirmish of loud bickering between them. I stop at the first phone booth I see and escape into the confines of the smelly little compartment to collect my senses and try to recall phone calls during vacation at Aunt Mavis' and the name of the doctor with whom they had been so angry. Whatever his name is, they just called him Dr. K. There is only one listing under 'K', a Dr. Kettle. It registers as slightly familiar, so I take my chances and jot down his address and hurry back to the vehicle.

We arrive at the appointment twenty minutes late. I give Nick and El quick instructions on how to follow the hiking trail along by the lake, and they leave to walk back to Malfaits' home. Mother and I steady Dad as he shuffles into the doctor's office. My phone book search was successful. The lady at the appointment desk has his name on the day's roster. It doesn't matter that we're late, as it's another forty minutes before we are admitted to a patient room.

A nurse arrives shortly with a clipboard and pen, "Good morning, Mr. Malfait. I need to get a little introductory information from you as a new patient.

Mother speaks up, "You don't need any introductory information. Dad is not a new patient here. Dr. K has been Dad's doctor for years."

The nurse drops her chin, narrows her eyes, and looks toward the voice. "We have no record of Dr. Kettle having seen Mr. Malfait before at this office, so we'll need to complete these forms."

Mother insists, "Well, I don't know how that could be. He most certainly has been seen here."

"Uhhh—okay." The nurse clasps her clipboard to her bosom and looks directly at Mother, "Tell me what he was seen for, Mrs. Malfait."

Mother returns the direct eye contact. "Well, I can't remember what ailment he had, but he certainly has been seen here."

The nurse rearranges her clipboard calmly. "Okay—tell me, Mrs. Malfait, does Mr. Malfait smoke?"

"Yes."

I straighten up in my chair, where I have been trying to occupy Dad's hands to keep them out of the doctor's trays of supplies. "When, Mom? When did Dad smoke?"

The nurse ignores me and maintains her official questioning directed to Mother, "Has he smoked recently?"

Mother is prompt again, "Yes."

"Has it been in the last ten years?"

"Yes."

I know I have been away for several years, and I didn't know who his doctor was this morning, but some things about my father I know for sure. He has *never* been a smoker. I strive to be gentle. "Mother, Dad has not smoked during my forty-nine years on the scene. If he smoked before that, that's not really recent."

Mother glares disapprovingly at my interruption and then faces the nurse, "Well, it's been about twenty years then!"

The nurse is getting the picture, but I am getting it less and less! She pokes the unused pen into the slot at the top of the clipboard, smoothes the blank pages as if sweeping the invisible introductory information away, and leaves the room.

Presently Dr. Kettle comes in with a friendly greeting and proceeds with his examination listening to Dad's heart and having him do 'nose-to-finger visual tests.' Dad does not do well with the tests, especially with his left hand.

"That's okay, Mr. Malfait. You sit back here and just breathe deeply for me." The doctor continues moving the stethoscope from place to place on Dad's back, while he turns toward Mother and me. "Mr. Malfait had a massive stroke in the right lobe of his brain, and there will be some permanent loss of vision and coordination. His actions and reactions this morning are not at all unusual for this stage in his recovery."

Mother interjects, "Yes, Dad is doing so well. It's just a miracle how much improvement he has made and how well he is eating. He's made amazing progress considering the man had a little stroke."

The doctor's brow wrinkles as he stares at Mother, but he goes on with his explanation about the location of the blood clots which came from Dad's irregular and aging heart, and how they moved from the heart to his head and burst there. "Yes, he is doing well and the hemorrhaging has stopped and healed well." The doctor takes the stethoscope ear pieces from his ears. "However, Mrs. Malfait, you are going to *have* to accept that your husband is never going to be exactly the same, even when he is fully recuperated."

"Well, Dad is doing well right *now*, and he keeps improving all the time."

Both the doctor and I are sensing more of Malfaits' total health picture, and the problem is not all with *Mr.* Malfait. Dr. Kettle is busy writing notes. I ask if before he finishes his examination I may see the medical reports.

The doctor looks up from his writing. "Mrs. Malfait, can you get Mr. Malfait dressed now? I'd like to speak to your daughter for a moment in my office and get some further paperwork for her."

When we are in the privacy of the doctor's office, I express some of my concerns about both my parents, my general observations about their living conditions, and a brief explanation as to why I have not been in proximity to them for several years. The doctor tells me based on his current observations, he understands my concerns. He has known them both to be fiercely independent, and they are not very receptive nor cooperative. If I want to pursue the issue further and go through court hearings to gain a guardianship for them both, he will immediately write the necessary letters indicating their incompetence to live independently and care for one another properly.

I don't know exactly what a guardianship is, but I am shocked at Dr. K's directness and tell him I am not ready to do something that drastic. I can't accept it fully myself, and I need to consult other family members before making such a decision.

Dr. K proceeds to go over the medical reports indicating certain permanent limitations, mainly in sight and judgment. These characteristics will not only be limiting to Dad, but really to both of them. He tells me he is obligated by law to inform them Mr. Malfait will not be driving again because his impairments are permanent, and he is going back into the patient room and do that today. He will hold off on any other judgments until I have had time to discuss the situation with other family members.

The doctor and I return to the patient room. Dad is dressed now and sitting on the examination table staring at the wall. Mother is seated on a chair and staring at the same wall. Dr. K thumbs through the papers on his clipboard and adds some notes. "Mr. Malfait, you're doing well in your recovery, but you have some permanent damage in your brain affecting your thought processes and your eyesight. I am obligated by law to inform you that you will not be driving again because this impairment is permanent."

Mother snaps to attention, "I don't know why you would say a thing like that. We've got to get around. Dad is a good driver. He hasn't had any tickets for years."

Dad's driving record is questionable in my mind, but I say nothing.

The doctor continues, "You and Mr. Malfait should sell your cars. The city bus runs right by your house, and you should use it—or use a taxi—or the Kiwanis bus for senior citizens. There are plenty of ways to get around."

Mother declares, "Well, I drive!"

The doctor locks stares momentarily with Mother. "Mrs. Malfait, I'm not so confident in your judgment that you should be driving either."

Mother gasps, "Why, whatever do you base that on? I have never had *any* tickets, and I have always passed my driving test at the time of renewal."

The doctor remains low-key. "Mrs. Malfait, the last time I saw you I was not sure your visual judgment was good enough for you to be driving. It would be most unfortunate if a small child ran out into the street and you hit the child because either you did not see him or you could not react fast enough."

Mother's face flushes crimson. Her brown eyes, solid ebony orbs, emit a barrage of silent, stinging invisible messages to the doctor. She sucks in a noisy gasp of air and juts her chin out. Her voice is steady but at a higher than usual volume. "I don't have any awareness of my poor driving ability, and I don't remember being seen by you!"

The doctor scribbles a few more notes on his clipboard pages and looks up, engaging the ebony orbs directly. He responds in a low, smooth professional tone. "I'm not going to get into an argument with you, Mrs. Malfait. The cars should go, and you both should depend on other transportation for your own health and safety, as well as that of others." There is an awkward silence interrupted only by the doctor's resumed scribbling. "I would like to see Mr. Malfait in a month."

Rolling his eyes and giving me a futile glance, Dr. Kettle leaves the room. Dad leans heavily on both Mother and me as we negotiate the halls and doorways to get him outside and into the car. He is obviously tired and wobbly. Mother and I go back into the office to make his appointment, and she seems calm and cooperative as she places her big black leather purse on the counter and leans over to quietly speak to the receptionist. "Be sure to make Roger's appointment late in the afternoon on a Friday to give Betty time to drive down to help me get him here. She shouldn't miss any more school than necessary."

"How about September 18th at 4:30 PM? Is that late enough, Mrs. Malfait?"

"Yes, thank you. That will be fine." Mother crams the appointment card into her already overstuffed bag and snaps it shut with an air of command over any and all kinds of overstuffing. She turns and takes my arm with a firm grip. I'm not sure which one of us is doing the guiding out of the office as she seems to be moving under renewed power.

When we get out onto the sidewalk, Mother erupts viciously, "Well, I can tell you one thing—that little Dr. K gets the 'Asshole of the Year Award' in my book for such stupid remarks about our driving. I told you what he was like. How'd he ever get to be a doctor anyway?"

"Mother, it was really Dad's appointment, and the doctor's comments were mostly in regard to Dad. It's his job to inform Dad about the limitation to driving. He said he had to do that as a legal responsibility."

"What else did that little shit say to you during that whole hour you two spent cozied up in his office?"

"I wasn't in his office for a whole hour for one thing, and we weren't cozied up. He made copies of the hospital reports and went over them with me. Then he went over the driving limitation factor. Maybe he didn't want to belabor the idea of Dad's permanent impairments in front of Dad. He simply said he was going to go back in and inform you both of the driving restriction."

Mother lurches to a stop in the middle of the sidewalk. Freeing her arm from mine, she steps in front of me. Facing me, clutching the big black purse in one hand and waving her free hand back in the direction of Dr. K's office she shouts, "Betty, you certainly don't need to defend the little bastard."

Passers-by glare and look away in embarrassment.

I strive for low volume and some degree of civility. "Mother, let's get in the car. Dad is waiting, and he's very tired."

Mother is not deterred. Volume still on high, she attacks, "You're being just as shitty as Dr. K! You two must be in this together!"

I move around her, step off the curb, and get into the car on the driver's side. Mother stands alone on the sidewalk. She looks one way and then the other, as if trying to assimilate my disappearance. She squints back toward Dr. K's door. An older couple goes around her and continues toward another doctor's office. She says nothing but glances all around again.

Inside the car I clutch the steering wheel, my life-saver ring in a raging silent sea.

Dad breaks the silence. "What's Mama doing out there, Betty? Why doesn't she get in this car? My doctor's appointment is over."

Mother squints toward the windshield of the car for several seconds before she hobbles toward the passenger door holding onto the car as she edges along. She gets in and slams the door.

The abuse to the door is her signal to re-establish her ranting at high volume. I try to ignore her. I am a desperate swimmer clawing at my life-saver ring bobbing in the roar of a thunderous sea. The drive to their home only takes a few minutes. Dad has not spoken, but when we are almost there he erupts in a halting staccato voice matching Mother's volume, "Mama—hush! That doctor—doesn't know—everything! I'm going—to be—fine! I need—to get home—and—get a shave. El is going—to—help me shave. I should have—shaved—before—I went—to the doctor. I'm going—to be driving—again! Right now—I need a shave!"

We become an instant frozen trio. I am fearful Dad will, or is, having another stroke. We pull into their driveway and progress into the house in silent rage and confusion. Mother goes to the kitchen where she corners Nick and unloads another explosive volley about Dr. K and the driving issue. El and I escape with Dad to the bathroom and ready him for his shave.

A while later as we are cleaning up the shaving tools and towels, Mother bursts through the bathroom door and screeches to a halt, "Oh, my God, look at you!" Her voice suddenly softens, "You are sooo handsome! Why, you look as good as the day we met. Well, maybe not that good—but you look the best you've looked in years!"

We all move back to the living room and Mother exclaims to Nick, "Doesn't he look just wonderful? He is so handsome! Ooooh, yes!"

She turns back to me, "Now, Betty, let's all get ready right away and get to Chuck's Wagon. We need to celebrate how good Dad looks and how great he is doing."

Nick and El roll their eyes in silent desperation. "Gosh, Mom, that's really nice, but we're not that hungry, and we're not dressed to go out to dinner."

"Chuck's Wagon is no place special. You don't need to dress up. We're all hungry. I know Dad and I are very hungry."

On cue Dad joins in, "I—am—hungry. Let's go—right now!"

None of us can resist Dad. We load back into the car, and proceed to the restaurant. El sits with Grandpa at a table while I fix their trays. Nick assists Grandma. After everyone is seated at the table, a quietness settles over us as we begin to eat. Glancing at my watch I note it's late afternoon. No wonder everyone is hungry. Nick, El and I have not eaten for over nine hours. As our meal progresses, despite spills and slurps, greasy hands, and conversation through chunks and strings of food, the trauma of the doctor's appointment seems never to have occurred.

The ride home is pleasant enough, and when we get into the house, Mother takes Dad to the bathroom while I make his bed. The sheets and pillow cases are greasy gray again. I dig all kinds of old wadded up paper towels from the space between the bed and the wall. Mother must use paper towels to wash and dry his hands and then throws them over near his 'pee can'.

Which is better, this kind of crude nursing by a loved one or some more professional level of care? What about the possibility of a fire if the discarded paper towels fall down on the wallboard heaters? I may as well give up thinking about it, because I know I won't get to first base suggesting any professional service to help them. Besides, no one with any kind of professional standards would come into this situation. And the likelihood of Mom and Dad going any place else is *less than nil!*

Dad is behind me in the bedroom grumbling about not being able to find his glasses. He says he lost them in bed, but I didn't find them when I made the bed. I try to look again as I help him lie down, but there's so much piled all over the room and on the bed itself that I haven't been able to make the bed very well, much less find a pair of glasses. I give up looking and tuck him in as best I can.

He is pleased with his 'clean' bed, "You're—so good to me—kid. You do—so many—wonderful things. I promise you—I'll go—right to sleep."

Dad rolls over and continues babbling quietly to no one in particular. I loosen my hand from his and ease off the edge of the bed. There's no break in the garbled muttering. I edge my way between the bed and the kitty litter basins and out to the living room, where Mother is seated on the sofa with her arms crossed.

"Mother, we can go to the laundromat now. I see you've got it all gathered up, and they're still open down there."

"I don't want to go to the laundromat."

"Well, do you want to go to the grocery store and do the shopping?"

"No, I don't want to go shopping. I don't need anything."

"You and El made a grocery list this morning. You must need those things."

"Let me see that list." El hands her the paper. "I don't want to go to the store for these few items. I'll go down here to the little corner store later."

"Mother, this morning you bought one can of cat food, and you said you needed to buy a case later. It's time to feed the cats again, and we've used the one can."

"I don't care. I don't want to go shopping."

"Well, if you don't want us to do any chores or go shopping or work on anything around here, I guess we ought to get on our way home."

"I don't see any work that we need to do around here. What work would we do?"

"El could vacuum. You and I could do the laundry and the shopping. Nick could take Taco for a long run around the lake."

No matter how needed, how helpful, how logical, Mother doesn't want to do anything, and she doesn't want us to do any work. The children and I make an awkward departure, each of us aware of the unspoken raging undertow. I guess her refusal of our help now is her way of saying she can do anything necessary around here, perhaps even driving.

The children and I travel the three hours and fifteen minutes to our home. It's 10:00 PM when we walk through the front door. We are startled by the ringing of the telephone.

Mother inquires, "How was your trip home?"

"Fine—"

"You probably got caught up in all the commuter traffic, huh?"

"Well, no, it wasn't too—"

"I want you to tell me what that doctor talked about privately in his office."

"Mother, it was like I said before, he ran copies of the medical reports and—

"In my book he's just an A-number-1 asshole!"

"Mother, he just went over the re—"

"I don't care what he went over. Dad and I ought to sue him. He ought to be run out of town!"

"Mother, do you want to know what those medical reports said or not?"

"Dad and I are just going to have to change doctors. You must be in cahoots with that crazy asshole."

I yell into the phone, "I'm not in cahoots!"

Mother outshouts me, "You've just signed Dad's death certificate by canceling his driving privileges! He's terribly depressed. He says he doesn't want to live any more. And that's all your fault!"

I grit my teeth and suck air through flared nostrils. In simulated calmness I respond, "Mother, I will not take responsibility for Dad's depression nor whether he wants to live any more! His limitations are the result of his stroke. And that's not my fault!"

"You may as well have cut off his hands your very own self. That's how bad it is for both of us. Furthermore, I'll tell you one thing, if I ever get sick, you'll be the very last person to be called or to see me. When you see me, I'll be a corpse! This is all your fault for siding with that asshole doctor! You've destroyed your father! I wish you had never come to help at all!"

"Okay, I won't help you anymore, but at least can I come to visit Dad?"

"That's all I have to say to you—EVER!"

The slamming of the phone sends a hurricane pounding against my eardrum. I am numb. This isn't real. Whatever the cause of dementia—strokes, breathing dirty kitty litter fumes, genetics, or eating at Chuck's Wagon—it's contagious. I feel as confused and inept as they are.

I decide to call Aunt Mavis. Despite the wretched feeling in my stomach, I make myself wait until 11:00 PM to make my call. I want to be considerate of the three hour time difference. In my own stress-induced dementia, I thoroughly astound Mavis when I awaken her shortly after 2:00 AM.

"Oh, Aunt Mavis, I'm so sorry to wake you up. Oh, God, I really screwed up. I figured the time difference *backwards!* I feel as if I'm doing almost everything backwards lately. I've taken steps 1,2,3, or more myself toward old age senility, or whatever it is!"

"Oh, don't worry about waking me," Mavis drawls sleepily. "You have a lot to think about these days."

"Mavis, I feel all the times I've gone to Ridgeview I've been as helpful as I can possibly be. I've worked hard, but it doesn't show very much. I get things half-way clean, and the next time I go it's dirtier than before. It's repulsive. I feel sick to my stomach half the time. I don't think I can go back. In fact, Mother was pretty clear tonight that she doesn't want my help ever again, and she hung up on me while I was trying to ask if she would let me come back just to visit Dad. It's so bizarre down there, I actually have some fear she may pick up one of those rifles leaned up in the corners of the living room or the hallway and threaten me—or shoot it off accidentally. She was totally out of control today. I have never in my whole life seen such rage. Actually, I've thought several times Rolf may be more dangerous than either of them, because he knows how to use the guns. He seems as crazy as they are! After today I'm not sure which one of them will shoot me first."

Old Parents and Purple Tulips

"Betty, I think you're just tired."

I begin to sob. "Oh, God, Mavis, I know that. Where are any of the people I used to know? Am I crazy? Are they? What is crazy?"

"No, you're not crazy. I understand your predicament. Maybe you should just sit still until the anger subsides over the driving issue. I'll let the dust settle some too, and then I'll give them a call. You're doing fine, Betty. I really do appreciate the phone call. Never mind the late hour."

A few days later Mavis follows up with a supportive letter to me after Mother called her with her version of Dad's medical appointment. In her letter Mavis tells me she told Mother she was confident I had done my best to be of help, and she wondered where Rolf was that he couldn't help? She also said the next time she comes out to visit she fully intends to have a good talk with Rolf and set some things straight, and he better stop that logging truck long enough to talk to her.

I myself need to have a good talk with Brother Rolf and set some things straight. On several occasions I've tried to talk to him, but the result has been passive tolerance of my venting and avoidance of any dialogue about our parental problems..

Several more days pass before I receive an early morning phone call with a deep booming voice barking at me during a mid-oatmeal bite, "Yeah, what's happenin'?"

I grasp my opportunity, "Rolf, I'm glad you called. We need to talk. We have some real problems the two of us need to discuss, particularly Dad's recent medical evaluation. Mom and Dad need your help. *I* need your help!"

"Yeah, yeah, yeah. You know half the problem with both of 'em is the smell of that damn cat piss. Breathin' that stuff causes a lot of health problems. If I was around there very much, I'd find a way to lose a couple of cats, if you know what I mean."

"Rolf, I'm not sure that's the answer. Mother doesn't much want my help, but I'm going to be down next weekend whether she wants my help or not. Couldn't you please come by the house so we could discuss these matters?"

"Yeah, sure. I'll probably see you Sunday afternoon."

Later the same day my next phone call is from Mother. I know she's talked to Aunt Mavis because she's calmer, but she gives no acknowledgment of her previous tirade. I guess she forgot that's all she had to say to me—EVER!

"It's been so nasty and rainy down here I don't know when we'll ever get any work done in the garden or the lawn either. I'll tell you one thing I would just really like to understand is what that doctor said to you when he took you into his office."

"Mother, it's like I've told you already—he went over the reports from the hospital. He gave his interpretation of what had actually happened during Dad's stroke. Then he said what he believed the permanent impairment to be."

"Do you believe him?"

"There were three doctors' opinions in the medical report. I have no reason to doubt them."

"A lot of times people make full recovery, despite doctors' reports."

"Yes, that's true, and I hope that will happen for Dad."

"I still think Dr. K is an asshole, and we may change doctors anyway."

"You and Dad have to figure that out."

"The doctor should have talked to me, not you."

"I'm sure you're right, but I thought he had already spoken to you. It said in one of the reports the family had been informed of Mr. Malfait's condition and of some permanent impairment. Mom, I just wanted to read the medical reports for myself."

"I wasn't informed of any such permanent impairment in Dad's condition."

"You know, Mom, you're not the only one who is upset by all this doctor appointment information and misinformation. I was very upset by your phone call last weekend when you hung up on me. I thought you didn't want me to come down anymore, *ever*—not even to visit Dad."

"No. You can visit, but the doctor should have talked to me, not you. Dad is getting up by himself now, and he's coming to the table for all his meals. He went to the bathroom by himself today."

"That's great, Mom."

"Now tell me again what that doctor said to you while you were in his office. I have to get it straight so I can tell Mavis when she calls me."

I feel strange not acknowledging I have been in communication with Aunt Mavis, but I take yet another deep breath and begin, "He went over the medical reports with me and explained the permanent—"

Mother interrupts, "That's all I have to say. Goodbye!"

I guess that's all I have to say, too.

I have a couple days reprieve before another phone call from Mother. Her voice is calm but forlorn, "Dad's not doing so good. He's just not coming along like he should."

"I'm sorry, Mom. I want to help, but I don't know how."

"Well, he's still getting up by himself, coming to the table and going to the bathroom, but he's doing weird things."

"Like what, Mom?"

"He went out to the garage and got a shop light and brought it in and hooked it up in the dining room. Then he draped the cord across the chairs and the couch through the living room to where he likes to sit. I don't know what he's trying to do."

"Have you found his glasses yet?"

"No, he hasn't ask for any glasses. He says a man needs more *light* to read by, but I don't think he needs to use that damned extension cord light."

"Mom, at least he's trying to read, and since he can only see straight ahead, he probably thinks there's not enough light. The other day I saw his glasses in the living room on top of the television. See if they're still there. It would be great if he gets interested in reading again."

"Well, I need to take everything out of that front bedroom."

"Why do you need to do that?"

"Because I can't find his string of keys. He's lost them, too."

"You have all kinds of keys in your black purse. Maybe you've got his."

"I've looked there. I don't have them. I have mine but not his."

"Why is it so important to find Dad's keys?"

"Dad's string has the keys to the cars, and I've got to find them."

"Have you been driving since I was last down?"

"No, and it's because I can't find the keys."

I cover the mouthpiece, suck in a breath and squeeze my eyes shut, *Dear God, please don't let her think I have her keys. Please don't let her find the keys! Please don't let either one of them drive!*

I try to change the subject. "Have you been able to get all the groceries and kitty supplies you need?"

"Yes, we've been going to the little neighborhood store down at the corner. Besides, Rolf came in when I didn't know anything about it, and you know that little cupboard above the sink—he's filled it with all kinds of canned goods. He either came in the night or he came when Dad was up and Dad forgot to tell me."

"Is Dad often up when you're not?"

"Lately I've been so tired I go to bed and leave him sitting out there with the newspaper and that damned extension cord. He tells me he'll be along in a minute."

"That's normal in the past, Mother, but I'm not sure it's a good idea now for him to be up rambling about while you're sleeping. Do you need help keeping track of him?"

"No, and I'm not trying to restrict you from seeing Dad. I don't need *anything* right now."

"I have some time off next week. Would a visit be okay then?"

"Yes, but you be sure and call before you come."

"Have you been sorting the mail into those boxes I labeled?"

"Yes. Rolf has only gotten one letter."

"Has he done anything about that unpaid mortgage payment?"

"He must have been by. That kitchen cupboard is completely filled with cans of soup. You can have some when you come down."

"Mother, did he say anything about the Fibex mortgage, the one for $468.90 a month? It's way overdue. Fibex keeps sending letters to each of you, and that last one said the payment had to be taken care of, or they would have to take legal steps since Dad was a co-signer."

"No, Fibex hasn't said anything to Dad or me. That's Rolf's business, and Rolf can't do anything right now because he's in California. He's with his friend Mike. The company sent them down there with a load, and they can't come back until they have a full haul for the return trip." Mother continues with more detailed information about long-haul trucking, more than I want to know, but at least her voice is not so gloomy. I let her ramble with little comment.

CHAPTER 7

~oxxo~

A Second Visit With Dr. K, "I
Need My Medicine, Kid"

ON THE MORNING of Dad's second follow-up appointment I call Mother before leaving for Ridgeview.

"You're coming down now? What for?"

"Mother, look at the calendar on the wall right behind you. What does it say?"

There's a pause. I hear her rummaging for her glasses. "Let's see, the 18th...Dad...Dr. K...4:30 PM. Well, I have news for you. We're just now leaving the house to walk down town to see a lady about some business. I don't know if we'll be back in time for any appointment."

"Well, this is the appointment for the second checkup since his stroke. You're the one who made it for this day."

"Okay, you come on down. We may be back in time. If we're not here, you just wait for us on the driveway."

Three hours and fifteen minutes later I arrive at their house. They're home, and greetings are warm from both of them. Mother tells me, "We just got back from coffee. We walked down to Sally's Café down here at the corner store and had a nice breakfast."

Mother appears to be dressed and ready to go again, but Dad is dressed in dirty gardening clothes. I know garden work is impossible, but I gently inquire, "Have you been working outside, Dad?"

"Hell, no. I'm all cleaned up and ready for that there doctor's appointment. Let's get it done, kid."

Despite his unclean clean appearance, he speaks much more clearly than last time I was with them. I avoid any confrontation and take his arm and turn toward the door. Mother reminds me, "You ask his doctor about his medication. He lost it."

"How long has he been without it?"

"I don't know...maybe four or five days. He said he had it in the bathroom."

"We have a few minutes. Let's look for it now."

I barely begin my search of the bathroom medicine chest when I come across a ten year old prescription for Valium. Dad is watching over my shoulder.

"What's that one? Give that to me."

"Dad, I can't give you this. It's an old prescription, and I'm sure it's not for someone who has recently had a stroke."

"Give me that. I've got to have my medicine."

"Mother, help me make him understand this isn't the one."

Mother snatches the bottle from me and reads the label. "Why, you old fool, that'll kill you. That's some old Valium." Mother hands it back to me.

Dad clumsily claws at the bottle. "That's just what I do need! Give it here, kid!"

"No, no, Dad, I'll take it along with us and show the doctor. If he says you need this, then I'll give it to you, and he can tell you how much to take."

"Oh shit!"

Dad doesn't like my decision, but it seems to quell the storm. I get him out the door and into the car. Mother follows us to the car and abruptly announces, "I'm not going with you two, so don't forget to ask about his medicine." She turns back toward the house.

Dad jerks to attention. "Kid, you get her to come back and go with us. This is my doctor's appointment, and Mama needs to be with us. If she's not going, I'm not going." Dad unbuckles himself, opens the car door, and follows Mother toward the front steps in a fast shuffle. I sit in the car and watch them bicker on the front porch.

Nothing will budge Mother. She points toward the car, "You go get in that car. It's your appointment, not mine. Betty has come all the way down here to take *you* to the doctor, not *me!*"

Finally, Dad wheels on wobbly legs and swats both hands through the air, "Oh shit, Mama! You make me so damned mad!" He comes down the walk at what I could almost call fast and gets in the car by himself.

"Let's get going, kid."

When we get to the doctor's office, Dad grumbles all the way into the patient room. "Your mama ought not to do that way. We need her here with us."

Dr. K greets Dad with usual professional good cheer and gets directly to his tests. He has him run in place, which Dad does amazingly well, looking like a gangly teenager with flailing arms and flapping feet. Next the doctor has him balance on one foot then the other. It is difficult for Dad to understand the directions as to what the doctor wants him to do, but once he understands, he carries out the tasks pretty well. Balancing on his right leg is okay but his left leg crumbles under him. Dr. K has him do a hand strength test, gripping the doctor's fingers and pushing physically against him. Dad is particularly aggressive in this task, practically pushing Dr. K over.

"Whoa, Mr. Malfait, you've really gained strength."

"See there, young fella, I'm stronger than you are!"

"Very good, Mr. Malfait. Now tell me who the president is."

"I told you the last time I was in here the president is that Reagan fella. He isn't worth a damn, and why do you bother to ask me again?"

"We're just testing your memory, Mr. Malfait. How many presidents do you recall before Ronald Reagan?"

"Well, Jimmie Carter was one of the best ones we ever had, then came Ford and Nixon. Nixon was the worst son-of-a-bitch ever was. Then there was Johnson and then Kennedy. Kennedy was our first president, and a good one, even if he was a Catholic." Dad jerks his head in a nod of self-approval and turns and winks at me.

"Very good, Mr. Malfait. Your memory is improving. And, you're right, your strength is probably better than mine."

"I walk regular, and I work hard."

"You keep that up, Mr. Malfait. It's good for you."

I interject the information about the lost prescription. Dr. K says that's no problem, and he quickly writes out another one. Then I show him the 'found prescription', "Dad wants to know about taking this."

"What is this, Mr. Malfait?"

"That's my Valium, and I need that."

"I'm surprised you have a prescription for Valium. This one is very old. It's from Dr. Putnam. He retired several years ago. Why did he give it to you?"

"Dr. Putnam was a good man. He really helped me. I used to get leg cramps so bad they'd make me want to scream. I'd take just one of them Valiums and the cramps went away. I didn't use 'em much, but when I needed one, I *really* needed it!"

"That probably did you good then, but this drug would be dangerous for you now, since you're recovering from a stroke. I could give you something else that would be compatible with your heart medication in case you ever get those awful leg cramps."

"All right. That'd be good." The doctor steps out of the room to get more prescription blanks, and Dad leans toward me and whispers, "Give me the Valium, kid. Please."

The doctor's quick return saves me from an argument. "Here you go, Mr. Malfait." Dr. K turns away from Dad and says quietly to me, "I think your dad should be institutionalized. He is just too disoriented. This problem *will* become worse, and he will become more unmanageable. I suspect right now he is a good deal more of a problem than your mother can keep up with, and she doesn't seem to be in very good health either. Betty, you *have* to understand this situation is not going to get any better than what you observe today. It *will* get worse!"

I nod in response. I *do* understand the medical prognosis, but Dr. K doesn't know the total picture of the Malfait household. There is so much that falls within the realm of bizarre. Who *will* help them? Who has the *power* to make such decisions? Will Rolf *ever* converse with me on this subject? Should a man who walked two miles to town and two miles back this morning, and then did a great hopping routine for the doctor be placed in a nursing home? What about all the years of mistrusting me? How will Mother ever reach a point of trusting my judgment in this situation, especially when my judgment coincides with the "asshole doctor"?

After we leave the appointment, I am glad for the comfort of my car and Dad's quiet babbling, whatever it is he is talking about. We go to a nearby drugstore to get his prescription filled. After dropping off the prescription, I guide him back toward the front of the store where we find a display rack of reading glasses.

"Oh, Jesus, kid. This is just what I need." Dad begins trying on glasses regardless of numbers of magnification, colors or sizes of frames.

After a short while a female voice on the store intercom blares, "Mr. Malfait, your prescription is ready. Prescription for Mr. Malfait."

Dad drops the glasses he has been looking at to the floor and yells out, "We're coming, dearie, we're coming right now!"

I rescue the glasses from the floor and replace them on the rack, then run to catch up with him, "Dad, wait! Wait for me!" Just before the pharmacy window, I loop my arm through his and slow him down, "You're running like a man possessed, Dad!" Two older ladies waiting on a bench in front of the pharmacy window shake their heads and smile at us. The irony of my words stabs to my very soul.

We get the prescription and make our way back up front to the checkout stand. Dad pulls out his checkbook and scrawls a check for $2,245. "Dad, you better get a decimal point in there or this prescription will break your bank." He allows me to guide his hand to the correct spot. He makes a sizeable circle between the 2 and the 4 and scribbles the interior of his enlarged decimal. "There! Any fool can read that plain as day!"

"That's good, but you may want to write on the stub what the check is for."

"Oh shit, kid, don't worry about that. There's plenty of money in my bank account."

I glance in embarrassment at the long line of people which has formed behind us and decide I hope there *is* enough money in there. I feel sweaty, partly from my run through the store but more from stress and embarrassment. I take his arm in clammy despair and tug him gently toward the exit.

What can I do to help my parents regarding money, banking, checking? Does he always carry his checkbook in his front shirt pocket? Right now I can see several twenty and fifty dollar bills sticking out of his checkbook. Everyone else can see them, as well.

As we're leaving the parking lot, I spy the 'big golden arches' down the street. Since Dad needs to take his medication right away, I ask, "Would you like to stop and get a drink and have an ice cream, Dad?"

"No thanks, kid. I can't do that. Mama never gives me any money."

I refrain from pointing out his cash supply stuffed loosely in his check book. "That doesn't matter, Dad. Let me treat us both."

"No, I don't want any ice cream. I don't want to put you out. I really need to get on home and check on Mama."

I drive into the drive-through lane and order two strawberry sundaes and water. We pick up our order at the next window and ease into a nearby parking spot. Dad attacks his sundae. Then the pill. Then the whole glass of water. Then back to the sundae. He stops half-way through the ice-cream.

"I'm gonna save the rest for Mama."

"Come on, Dad, eat up. We'll get a fresh one and take it home to her."

"No, I'm gonna take this one to her."

Nothing will change his mind. He won't eat any more. The ice cream is melting. I put the lid back on mine. "I'll save her some of mine too."

I back out of the parking space and pull into the lane of traffic, hoping we'll get home before anything else melts. It's only a five minute drive. I pull onto the driveway and barely get the brake set when Dad is out of the vehicle and making a rushed shuffle up the sidewalk. Mother opens the front door just as he gets there. He shoves the sundae at her and quickly kisses her on the cheek.

"Well, my God, what's this? What are you doing?"

"I don't know what I'd do without you. I love you, Mama!"

Dad pushes past Mother into the house. Mother sits down on the front step, "Well, my God." She finishes off the half a sundae Dad brought her and with no question takes the half I offer. She makes short work of it too, not asking why there were two or why they were so small, or melted, or half-eaten. She abruptly gets up and goes into the house calling, "Dad, Dad—Did you get your medicine?"

"Yes. I took it already, and I put it away in a safe place. I'll show you."

Dad goes to the nightstand beside their bed and begins searching. He is immediately agitated. "I can't find a damn thing in this house! I don't know why people keep taking my medicine."

He returns to the living room where Mother and I are discussing his doctor's appointment. "What kind of a person would do a thing like that to a sick man? Mama, did you take my medicine?" He sits down on the couch and continues complaining in an irritated, monotonous babble, making occasional head and hand motions toward the stack of newspapers and mail on the coffee table. "Betty, you've got it. kid, please—give me my medicine!".

"Dad, I don't have it, but I'll go look for you." I go to the bedroom and look all about and in the top drawer of the nightstand. No prescription. I return to the living room and look in his shirt pockets. No medicine.

Dad bats my hand away, "I'm telling you, I put it in that drawer in there. I know what I done with my medicine!"

I go back to the nightstand and open the lower second drawer. *Voila!* There is the new prescription. Everyone is relieved. I sit down next to Dad and mark each bottle with black permanent ink, both on the front and on the top of the cap with pictures of a heart on one bottle and a leg on the other bottle. Dad likes the pictures and says they will help him know which one is for his heart and which is for his legs. He decides to carry his medicine in his shirt pocket so he won't lose it. He thanks me for marking them and stuffs both bottles in his shirt pocket behind his cash and his checkbook and an assortment of pens. I guess that's okay, as long as the pills don't go through the washer. Actually, the washer is a very unlikely place that any of their things will go.

Despite the new prescriptions in his pocket, Dad continues to sit slumped on the couch long after Mother and I go about other business. He dwells on the lost Valium. He babbles. He raises his voice. He shakes his head in disgust as he continues derogatory comments about people who deprive him of his medicine. His monologue continues until suppertime and even at the table during the meal. He finally has *both* Mother and me in tears because of his relentlessness and his lack of reasoning. We tell him how much we love him and want him to get well and to be safe in the process. We give him compliments for his progress to date. We explain a hundred times or more why he can't, and shouldn't, have the Valium.

Finally Mother removes his dinner plate with an angry jerk and tells him, "You just as well hush about that Valium. I flushed it down the toilet."

Dad's mouth falls open in speechless disbelief. He sits several minutes and stares blankly at his shoes. Finally he lurches from the table and goes into the living room and begins going through his junk mail. He takes letters out, reads aloud, talks to himself about his possibilities of winning the sweepstakes and about what he thinks he has already won. He folds letters back up and replaces them in envelopes randomly.

It's about two hours later when Mother tells him, "Roger, you need to put all your mail away now, because Betty has to sleep on that couch."

Dad continues to sit in the same spot and reread the same mail.

"My God, Roger, you've read us all that junk three times or more. Get that shit put away right now or I'm going to toss it all out. I told you

Betty has to sleep on that couch. You and I have to get to bed too. And I mean *now*! It's almost midnight."

"Oh shit, Mama!" Dad puts his mail stacks on the coffee table and wobbles off toward the bedroom.

Despite the filth and clutter which I had no time to work on today, I fall into my makeshift couch-bed and doze off. I awaken at 5:30 AM. I can hear Dad in the bathroom. By 6:00 AM I am fully awake and realize he's still in the bathroom. He's opening drawers and cupboards and mumbling about Valium.

I get up and go to the bathroom and rap on the closed door, "Dad, it's too early for you to be up. Come on, Dad, go back to bed." A drawer slams and the babbling continues. "Dad, I need to use the bathroom." More drawer slamming. More babbling.

Behind me in the darkened hallway comes another kind of babbling. "Dad, you old fool, get out of that bathroom! You're not the only one in this house. Betty has to use the toilet. You get out of there. *NOW!* I need to use it too! I can't wait any longer! If you don't want me to go right here on the floor, you'll get yourself out here right now!"

Dad fumbles with the door lock and finally comes out and heads down the hallway, mumbling about Valium each step of the way toward the bedroom.

Mother and I use the facilities and we each return to bed. I watch the first rays of dawn streak through the dirty Venetian blinds as I drift off again. In my pitiful calm I still hear the muffled ranting rhythm of the frustrated Valium seeker as he rolls and tosses in his bed in the front bedroom. As Dad becomes louder, Mother chimes in with her own ranting rhythm, establishing higher volume than his. Sleep is not to be.

By 7:30 AM Dad has had enough of his own frustration and Mother's antagonism. "Get out of my way, Honey, I'm getting out of this bed."

"What do you think you're doing, Roger?"

"I'm getting up and getting dressed."

I hear the shuffling and grumbling as Dad crawls over Mother and rummages for his clothes, "My God, Roger, what in the world are you getting up at this hour for?"

"I'm going to Oregon. I don't want to split up our home, Mama, but I can't live this way anymore with people taking my stuff right here in my own house."

"Why, you old fool, you get your butt back into this bed."

"I can't do that, Mama. You know I don't want to split up our home and our marriage, but I just can't stay. I'm going to run away. I need some money. You get up from there and get me some money."

"My God, what next?" I hear Mother climb out of bed and begin a search for her purse. I wonder if either of them knows what they are doing, or if they realize I am in the house.

"Dad, I can't find my purse, and I don't have any money anyway. You have all the money. No, no wait, here's my little change purse."

Dad opens the bedroom door and mumbles his way into the living room, "Well, hurry up and give me some money. I've got to get on my way." He stands barefoot staring back at the bedroom door, pants unzipped and dirty wool plaid shirt partly buttoned. Mother emerges from the bedroom with her little change purse and rips open the Velcro flaps. No one notices me 'asleep' on the couch. "Here, Roger, you can have all I have." She turns the little purse upside down and dumps a dime into Dad's shaky outstretched hand.

"Well, Jesus Christ, Mama! A man can't run away on a dime! That won't even buy a cup of coffee! You can damn well give me more than that to run away on."

"I'm telling you that's all the money I've got," Mother chuckles.

"Give me my checkbook then."

"That's all the money I have, and you're not going to run away on what little we've got in the checkbook. You've written ten or twelve checks on it anyway, and you didn't put down where you wrote them to or for how much. There's probably not enough left in that account for you to run away on."

"I got credit cards. I can use them."

"I'm not giving those to you either."

Dad starts toward the front door with Mother right behind him. They both stop and concentrate on the couch, seeming to notice me for the first time. Dad shakes the tightly clutched dime in my direction, "Your mom won't give me any more money to run away on." He turns away and begins to fumble with the deadbolt in the heavy door.

Mother shouts toward his back, "Betty's right here, and if you go out that door, she and I will call the cops!"

Dad doesn't look back. "Well, I don't give a good goddamn about that! Cops are my friends. Maybe they'll give me some money."

"If you open that door, I'm going to call Rolf."

I sit up and throw the covers back, "Mother, go ahead and call Rolf. I think that's a good idea. I approach Dad and pat him gently on the back. "Hey, Dad, wait a minute. Mother has a good idea. Would you stay here with us just until Rolf comes?"

Dad pauses in his struggle with the deadbolt, which he has not been able to manipulate, "Well, sure, I'll stay if he's gonna come. He'd probably take me to Oregon, and I can get on my way. From there I could take the bus, or I could walk."

I back away and both Dad and I move back into the living room.

Mother doesn't budge to make the call and maintains her previous volume, "You keep acting this way, and you're going to that nursing home! That shitty little Dr. K would put you there right now. And when Rolf gets here, he'll probably drive you right over there!"

I match Mother's volume, "Mother, you need to get out of here and get on with your phone call!"

She turns away and goes to the kitchen to make the call to the trucking company where Rolf and Mike are both employed. It's Mike's truck, but Rolf is his helper on the long-haul drives to California.

It's a fortunate phone call, as Rolf and Mike just checked in a few minutes earlier from their California haul. Mother is able to speak to Rolf immediately as he is still standing in the office.

She goes through the normal amenities of 'How was your trip? How's Mike? Did you two get a good load to haul back? Did you have good weather all the way?' She smiles at Dad and me who are now standing in the kitchen doorway, and she nods in amiable agreement with whatever Rolf is telling her. Her expression abruptly changes into a furrowed scowl and she barks into the phone, "Listen, Rolf, Dad is much worse lately. Betty's here, and he's giving both of us a bad time. Neither one of us can do a thing with him. He thinks he needs to run away to Oregon."

Dad jerks to attention and shuffles his bare feet across the kitchen, "Gimme that phone, Mama. I want to talk to Rolf."

"Hold on, Rolf. Here's Dad now."

Rolf shows off catch on family vacation to Horse Lake, Canada

Dad smiles and jerks his head in an appreciative nod toward me and winks. "Now we'll get somewhere. "Hello, Rolf...Oh, yeah, son, I'm fine...Things aren't too bad here...You know your mom; she just gets excited. I do need to talk to you though. Can you come on by the house when you leave from there?...Good. Here's Betty. She's as bad as your mama bullin' her way in here to the phone."

I have moved over close to Dad. I guess that could be perceived as bulling. Dad thrusts the phone at me. "Yeah, hi, Rolf...Hell no, things aren't like Dad's telling you. Mother can't manage him, and I can't manage either one of them. Dad wants to run away to Oregon this morning. And if he decides to walk out the door, he is plenty strong enough. I can't stop him. For that matter, I'm not even going to try."

"What set him off like that?"

"I'm not really sure it was any one thing. More like a whole sequence of events: the lost prescription, the doctor's appointment, the old out-of-date Valium prescription he found. Maybe even Mother and me trying to tell him what to do.

"He's been relentless about people taking his things. He's all bent out of shape over a long lost prescription for Valium, and he's set on running away. I can't reason with him at all in his present state of mind. But he says if you'll come home, he'll wait to run away until you get here. He needs to talk to you about his plan.

"Rolf, Dad's not the only one who needs to talk to you. I've been begging you to talk with me. We really *have* to talk! This time Mother and I both need some help, and Dad needs you too."

By the end of the call Dad seems satisfied Rolf is coming home. He and Mother both eat breakfast calmly, almost pleasantly as if nothing unusual had occurred. After breakfast he takes it as his personal responsibility to wait and not miss Rolf. He stakes himself out on the couch in the living room with his junk mail and waits peacefully for the next four hours.

As soon as the front doorknob and deadbolt rattle, signaling Rolf's arrival, Dad jumps up from his guard position amid the debris on the couch and begins a recitation of his woeful morning, the thievery of his medicine, and his need for some help to run away. Rolf walks over to face Dad squarely, listens for a few minutes, then takes hold of both of his shoulders and presses him down, firmly but gently, to a sitting position on the couch.

"You sit your ass right down here and listen to me."

"Now, son, I really need your help with this—"

"Just shut up and listen to me! I'm only going to say this once. You are not going anyplace. You are *not* running away. Running away is bullshit. Grown men don't run away. This Valium business is bullshit, too. You are not taking it. Mom and Betty were right in throwing it away. It may have served a purpose once, but you are never taking it again. It's a junkie's habit-forming drug, and it's dangerous for you to take, especially with your heart medication."

Dad looks like bread dough being punched down after the first rise. As he relaxes, Rolf releases his shoulders, straightens up, and stands before him with his arms crossed. "Now that I have your full attention, and you're not acting like some dumb dingbat, maybe I can take you out of here and on some short trips with me when you're feeling better. I can't take you to California, but I got some short hauls coming up that are close by, and you could go along with me. Would you like that?"

Dad's eyes show a spark of interest. "Well, sure, I'd like that."

"Then you get yourself straightened up, and I mean right now, because I ain't taking no junkie along with me. You're going to fly right!"

Dad looks up at me and nods as if all is well. "Kid, you and me got some shopping to do. I want to get to the grocery store before all the sales go off."

He pulls himself up off the couch and in the next few minutes is very cooperative about letting me straighten his shirt and pants and help him with his shoes and socks. He and I set off for Mark Down Groceries leaving Mother and Rolf in the kitchen, Rolf having his first warm meal in two days and Mother eating her second breakfast of the day.

At the store Dad is confused in regard to which doors to use to enter, and he is further disoriented inside. He clutches his grocery list and is persistent in trying to find all the things on it. I play to his cooperativeness and helpfulness. However, he insists certain items are located in certain places. He is extraordinarily strong despite his frail appearance, and I can't hold the cart back when he decides to push on to whatever certain place seems to match an item on his list.

A young mother is shopping on one of the aisles with her child, a little boy about five years old. The boy is pushing a small plastic children's cart with several cans of soup in it. She pauses to look at some canned goods and read labels. The boy pushes his cart a short ways down the aisle and mimics his mother's label-reading. He sounds like a 'little babbling granddad." She calls to him to come back and keep his cart near hers. He turns sharply to obey and spills all his soup cans in the middle of the aisle.

Dad and I are progressing down the aisle toward the little boy's spilled cart. I try to hold Dad's speed down to allow time for the mother and child to pick up things. Dad pushes harder. I plead, "Dad, there's a little kid in the middle of the aisle, and he's spilled his cart of cans all over. Let's stop a minute for him."

Dad gives the grocery cart a mighty thrust. "Let the little son-of-a-bitch get hit. He's got no business in the middle of the aisle!"

The mother looks up at us aghast, just as I manage to get Dad stopped. I mutter in her direction, "I'm sorry—really, really--so sorry. Oh, God--"

The shock in her eyes dissipates as she recognizes my embarrassment, which is flashing like a neon beer sign. "Oh, oh--I understand. It--it's okay." She moves the little boy from in front of Dad's cart just in time, as Dad gives another mighty heave freeing his cart from my grasp and propelling it through the spilled cans like a NASCAR driver on his winning lap. I don't have time to look back and see if he laid strips of rubber in the aisle nor to make any further apology. Dad's already at the end of the aisle elbowing another lady out of his way as he resumes searching shelves for the next item on his list.

Somehow we survive the Mark Down shopping, and I take several long breaths in the privacy of my car as we buckle up. However, Dad isn't finished. "Betty, I've got to make a stop at the Thrift Bakery."

"You have plenty of bread at the house, and you didn't have that on your list."

"I've got to stop there anyway. I've got a list in my head."

"What do you mean you've got a list in your head?"

"I need to get some bear claws, and the only good ones are at the Thrift Bakery."

"Dad, I don't know where the Thrift Bakery is."

"Oh, hell, kid, just take us down this street; we'll come to it. I walk there all the time to buy bread."

"Do you go by yourself?"

"Hell, yes, if I waited for Mama to go buy bread, I'd have to do without."

"Now, Dad, do you mean you walk there now or was that before you had the stroke and were in the hospital?"

101

"I walk there now. I was there yesterday."

Even though I know that wasn't possible, I humor him. "Okay, tell me which way to go."

"It's near Homer's Repair Shop and the old Builders' Hardware Store."

I remember the hardware store from my childhood, and that knowledge gets us on the right block. I spy the Thrift Bakery sign, and we pull up by the curb near the front door. It's really a loading zone, but before I can figure out where to legally park, Dad gets out of the car. "I'll just go in and get my bread and some of them bear claws."

"Wait, Dad, you don't have any money. Mother has your checkbook." I scramble to find some money from my purse.

Dad holds out his hand and takes the $5.00 I offer. "Oh shit, kid, I've got lots of money." He turns and stands a moment on the sidewalk, squints in each direction, and then walks into the plumbing shop next door to the bakery. I fumble with my emergency lights, jump out of the car, and run in after him. He is not the least bit concerned that he is in the wrong shop. I guide him back out onto the sidewalk and head him toward the bakery.

"Dad, if you wait a minute I'll park the car correctly and go in with you."

"No, no, I want to do this by myself."

He's already opening the door to the bakery. I guess I ought to let him try to do for himself. I fear what may happen in the store, but I resign myself to the more urgent problem of my improperly parked car. At least I can see him through the window.

He moves awkwardly from aisle to aisle. He gets the bread and rolls, pays, and comes out and gets back into the car.

"Now that wasn't too long a wait, was it, kid?"

"No, no it wasn't. You did fine, Dad."

"Well, I'll tell you something else, kid, this shopping wears a man out!"

"Yeah, I know, Dad. I know you're tired, and I'm pooped!"

We head for home, and as I pull in Malfaits' driveway, I note Rolf in the side yard playing with Taco. This may be my opportunity to speak with him privately. Dad and I carry in the groceries, and he and Mother begin snacking on bear claws immediately. I make my way around the house to where Rolf is wrestling with Taco.

"Hi, Rolf, how's it going?" I seat myself on the grass near him.

"Oh, I'm pretty beat. I've been working seven days a week here lately."

"Rolf, I'm glad you came by. There's a bunch of things we need to discuss."

"Yeah, yeah, I know. Things are totally out of control around here. It's worse than ever. Is that what you think?"

I share in detail with Rolf all of the points of the conferences with Dr. Kettle. Together we ponder the options available to us for dealing with our parents now and in the future, including some kind of more guided care and eventually the necessity of a nursing home, probably for both of them.

When I leave the yard, I feel Rolf is fully informed. He understands we have to make some changes. As children who have not grown up in conditions as they are now in the Malfait household, we can't ignore the situation. Mom and Dad need help. It's our responsibility to provide it.

In the days ahead I learn what a total disaster that trusting conversation was! After my departure, Rolf openly discusses all the details of our *confidential* discussion with *both* Mom and Dad. Mother no longer taunts Dad with, 'You better mind or you'll end up in that nursing home.' Now she gives him a constant barrage of, 'If you don't mind, *BETTY* will have you put away!' and 'Betty and that asshole doctor are just the ones to do it!'

My guts churn chronically with every phone call and in between. My emotions are threadbare! I cannot count on Rolf for any help or cooperation. His interest is only self-serving! How could he betray my confidence like that? How could he knowingly be so hurtful to them? What is he trying to accomplish? He had to know the turmoil he would cause by sharing details of our conversation with two people who are obviously mentally imbalanced. They *are* the ones who are sick, aren't they? Or is the sick one Rolf? Or, is it me? Where is the Rolf who is my brother?

CHAPTER 8

—◁◦▷—

The Third Dr. K Visit, "I Don't Want to Be Laid Out Under the Apple Tree Early"

A MONTH PASSES. I leave everything in Ridgeview on the back burner. Mother and I talk on the phone a few times but about nothing meaningful. I call to remind her about the October medical appointment.

Her response is, "Dad doesn't want to go to that doctor anymore. He says he hasn't helped him and he's not going. We both think Dr. K is an asshole."

"Fine, you either cancel the appointment or ignore it. Dad is probably doing as well as can be expected anyway. I'm not going to tell you what I think is best."

"No, he should be seen, but we haven't been able to pick out a new doctor yet. Maybe we'll just go to Portland."

I bite my tongue and pray they won't try to drive. "Mother, I don't have any way to help you find a new doctor. Do you want me to come down and help take him in for this next appointment or not?"

"Yes, I guess so. He needs to be seen, and he would enjoy seeing you for a visit. Yeah, come on down."

"Mother, turn around and read to me from that calendar on the wall. What does it say the appointment time is?:"

"It's this Friday at 4:15."

"That's tomorrow. I'll be down about an hour before the appointment time."

Betty Alder

The next day I arrive early, but Dad is not home. Mother says he is supposed to be pushing a grocery cart back to the Mark Down Grocery
Store, which is about a mile away. He has been doing this often lately,
and it's good exercise for him. She says he knows about the appointment
and he should be back in time.

Mother and I visit pleasantly and she shows me the back yard and
all the work they have been doing. The outside of the house looks good,
even though the lawn is still burned out from a hot summer followed by
an unusually warm September. The vines and berries have dried back,
and the trees have lost their leaves. As we stroll to the back of the property by the rows of raspberries, I spy a string of keys hanging on the
fence. They are Dad's long-lost car keys, and the dried berry canes have
allowed them to be exposed. Mother is as overjoyed as I am reluctant,
but I give her the keys.

Further time passes and Dad is not home. Mother and I go in my car
to look for him. We find him about two miles away walking along obliv-
ious to everything, talking to himself and gesticulating with both hands.
He's dressed in his usual dirty gardening clothes. I'm not sure they're not
the same clothes from the last time I was down two weeks ago. When
we pull up to the curb, Dad immediately comes over, opens the car door
and climbs in. He has no greeting to either of us. He brings a distinct
odor of urine, his or the cats', or both. He is calm enough but doesn't say
anything. He slams the car door and stares down at his feet.

Mother attacks, "Where have you been, you old fool, walking along
here like some crazy man talking to yourself?"

"Why, Honey, I've been down to check on my visual test."

"That's not possible. You did that two days ago."

"Well, now, I've got the paper right here in my pocket." He with-
draws a wrinkled paper from his shirt pocket and hands it to me. I read
silently, 'Vision - 20/80; Permanent impairment in peripheral vision,
reduced to 110 degrees'. An added note in a different color ink says,
'Decision-making judgments for driving are permanently impaired in all
major areas.'

Dad takes the paper back and replaces it in his overstuffed shirt pocket. As he pats the pocket, he nods at me, "Now, kid, I've got my visual paper, and I'm ready to go take my driving test."

"Dad, I think we better get on the way to your doctor's appointment first."

"Oh, hell, kid, that's just down the street. Let's get to it. I got my visual paper right here, and I'm going to set that bastard straight about my driving."

While he and Mother bicker about what he will and will not say to the doctor, I drive on. Lateness doesn't matter to Dad who has no idea what time it is, even though he is wearing three wrist watches. When we get to Dr. K's office, Mother refuses to go in with us, but she rolls down the car window and hollers after us, "Dad, you behave yourself while you're in there today! I can tell you if you don't, that asshole doctor will be the one to keep you from driving. He may just send you directly over to the nursing home anyway."

In the doctor's office lateness doesn't matter either. They are way behind schedule, as usual. Once we're in the patient room, we are pleased with good news from the nurse's routine checks. "Wow, Mr. Malfait, you've gained twenty pounds this past month, and your blood pressure is good. All that walking is doing you good. The Lanoxin is doing good things for you, too. Are you taking it daily?"

"Oh, yes, I'm taking my medicine real regular two times per day."

"Oh, you should be taking it just once per day."

"Yeah, I know. Don't you worry, dearie. I'm taking it *once* in the morning and *once* at night."

The nurse leaves shaking her head as Dr. Kettle comes in. "Well, Mr. Malfait, this looks really good--weight gain, exercise, regain of strength. Let me listen to your heart. Hmmm--There's a little bit of an irregularity. That's due to some deposits and clotting around your heart that still seems to be evident. You don't want to have another stroke, so you've got to be really faithful in taking your medicine. You shouldn't be off on long walks by yourself either."

I have said nothing to either the doctor or the nurse about walks or anything else this morning, but I'm sure they have received some kind of information preceding our arrival today from whomever Dad had consulted regarding the "visual paper" he picked up earlier. The doctor's remark is a reminder to me that Dad needs to have someone with him all the time--as in supervised nursing home care.

"Well, Mr. Malfait, is there anything else I can do for you today?"

"Yes, sir. I want you to know I've had my visual, and I'm improved. I want you to write me up, so I can get to driving. I'm not going to be walking these streets the rest of my life just because some people want to lay me out under the apple tree early."

"I certainly don't want to lay you out under the apple tree early. You're far from that state. All that walking has really been good for you."

"Doctor, I've got to get to driving."

"Mr. Malfait, in my best judgment, you have lost your peripheral vision permanently, and your judgments would not be adequate enough for you to drive safely. However, you don't seem to want to listen to me, nor to your daughter, about that. Would you like to see someone else for a second opinion?"

"Yes, sir, I think someone else might see it my way."

Dr. K writes three names of other doctors on a prescription blank and hands it to Dad. Dad lurches off the examining table and thrusts his hand shakily toward the doctor. "Now I don't want you to be mad at me because you're wrong about this."

"I'm not at all mad at you, Mr. Malfait. You come back and see me anytime. Your records will remain on file." The doctor turns to me, "He should be seen fairly regularly to keep track of the clots which have formed in his heart." To Dad he says, "Just a moment, Mr. Malfait, we better give you a flu shot today before you go."

Dad points a finger at Dr. K. "There you go again with something else you're wrong about. I don't need a flu shot today."

"Okay, we'll not force it on you, although it's recommended for people your age."

Dr. K again turns to go, and Dad speaks up, "I better have that flu shot."

"Okay, I'll send the nurse back in."

The nurse comes in, prepares, and gives the shot. Dad looks up from his arm, "Now, before you leave here, dearie, you give me that flu shot. Dr. K thinks I need it."

"I already gave it to you."

"You did? Well, thank you very much."

I take Dad's arm and we steer in wobbly tandem out of the doctor's office. We're both quiet, and we're both tired. Mother has been asleep in the car and continues to doze on the way home. We barely get in the front door though, when she becomes a verbal dinner bell, "Let's get Taco fed and then get ourselves down to Chuck's Wagon. We all need to have a good dinner."

"Mom, nobody's dressed or washed for any kind of dinner. Dad and I are tired."

After an hour's fussing and fuming nobody has changed clothes. Nobody has washed. The dog has not been fed. We are on our way to Chuck's Wagon. I don't know how that happened. I really don't care.

Dad insists on going through the line himself. He heaps large portions of food on his plate, sometimes missing the plate landing with a plop on the tray. He piles mashed potatoes on top of his salad. He puts peas on his cottage cheese and gravy on his roll, but he gets through the line all by himself. At the table, both Mom and Dad attack their food. They eat huge amounts of food ravenously, slovenly. Should I be glad they both have appetites like loggers? I nibble at my food and push it around until my tray looks about like theirs.

The trip home is quiet. Everyone is sated. Maybe we can have a peaceful evening. Once inside the door, Mother lies down in the front bedroom and Dad begins a frenzied search from room to room. He jerks open whatever drawer he is near. He shuffles through his contest mail, newspapers, and anything else nearby.

"Dad, what are you looking for?"

"The other day when I was downtown, I saw Allie, our old church secretary. She told me the building bonds had come due, and she had checks for me. She had tried to call us, but she couldn't get through. I went down to the church one day last week, but she couldn't give me one of the checks because it isn't made out to me. It's made out to you, Betty. I've got to find that payment booklet and prove I paid for those bonds, and I'm gonna need you to go with me to get that check for us."

In years past Malfaits were very active in their church and participated in the building of their new church by buying church bonds to help finance the project. I recall they took out one in Rolf's name and one in my name. "Okay, Dad, maybe I can help you. I do remember some kind of payment booklet for those bonds. We could look tomorrow, couldn't we?"

Dad returns to shuffling his mail. "I'm sure it's on this coffee table."

I pick up a stack of newspapers and join the search. "Geez, Dad, these papers are sticky. What is this? Oh yuk! It looks like the cat has crapped on your papers, and pissed on them too. They're all stuck together."

Mother bellows from the bedroom, "My God, Dad, can't you do anything right?" She is instantly out of bed, yanks the bedroom door open and kicks one of the cats out of the way as she lurches toward the table. "What do you mean the papers are all stuck together?" She grabs the offending fecal glue mess from me and rushes in her fastest wobbly gait to the kitchen garbage can. "Dad, that's your job to keep the cat shit picked up. Have you let Taco out for his night run yet? I suppose he'll shit next."

I busy myself pulling out the sectional pieces of the couch to look between and under them for the bond booklet, while Mom and Dad continue to roar at one another. I find a check for $407.00 from the credit union and a letter that states, 'Your check has been here over two weeks and you have not picked it up, so we are mailing it to you.' It was postmarked over a month ago.

"Mother, stop all the fussing for a minute and take a look at this."

"Is that the church booklet?"

"No, but I think you may be happy with this. It's a check for $407.00."
Mother yanks the check out of my hand. "Boy, can we ever use this.
I'm so glad you found it. I'm going back to bed now. I've got to get some
rest."

She takes the check with her and disappears into the front bedroom
without another word, leaving Dad and me to search for the bond booklet. Dad continues to claw through the mail and newspapers on the coffee table, scattering and restacking, talking to himself about the church
booklet and the bond.

I am tired and even more tired watching him. "Dad, I don't think I
can look anymore. I'll help you again tomorrow."

"That's fine, kid. You need to get some rest."

I push the sectional pieces back together and make up my usual bed
on the part not covered by Rolf's junk and crawl in. Rolf promised me he
would move his stuff when we had our big talk, but then he told me he
would do a number of things when he had his three-day break. He came
to the house, stayed an hour and did nothing! I can't do anything about
Mom and Dad and surely not about him. I drift in and out of restless,
exhausted sleep.

CHAPTER 9

—⚬⚬⚬—

Kid, You Do Need to Get Some Rest

ABOUT 11:00 PM I wake up gagging.

"Dad, Dad? Is that you? What on earth is going on?"

"I'm looking for my church booklet. I've got to find it."

"No, no, I don't mean that. My God, Dad, what is that smell? Where's Taco? Did you let him out?"

Our blurry-eyed, frantic conversation is interrupted by a mighty volley of oozy flatulence. I sit straight up in my make-shift bed. "Is that you, Dad?"

From the other end of the couch Dad shouts, "Taco, Taco--No!"

It's too late. Dad jerks himself up from his seat and wobbles toward Taco, stepping right into the oozy fecal piles. Taco has the runs, probably from eating table scraps, and he has made at least five wretched piles from the bathroom to the front door. Dad hits them all.

As I continue to gag, Dad lets the dog out and begins a cleaning effort using bathroom tissue. When he empties the toilet paper roll, he goes to the kitchen and gets paper napkins and paper towels. I pull the sheet over my face in hopes of filtering out some of the aroma, and I keep my head under the quilt. I have no shoes nearby and although I'm wearing socks, I can't bring myself to get out of my bed.

Taco whines at the front door, and Dad lets him back in. I hear Dad ripping apart paper towels and using them on the living room rug. "Oh, that's all right, Taco. I know you didn't mean to do this. Don't you worry; we're getting it cleaned up." Dad takes his soiled papers to the bathroom. The toilet flushes and makes rebellious gurgling noises as it bubbles into an overflow. "Oh, Jesus, Taco, look what you've done now."

113

I pull my head out from my quilted cave, "Dad, do you need help?"

The commotion awakens Mother, and that is no help at all! She crashes from the bedroom in a sleepy awkward motion, hanging onto the walls and the television for support as she moves toward the bathroom shouting at full volume, "My God, Roger, what have you and that dog done now? Get out of the way, Taco! Dad, let me in that bathroom!"

"Mama, you go back to bed. It's going down now. I've got this under control," Dad emerges from the bathroom and troops through the living room with what used to be a sponge mop dripping the liquid remains of 'other accidents' in a wiggly trail. "I told you, Francine, you get out of my way and go on back to bed." He begins scrubbing in irregular but vigorous motions, working the ooze into the shag carpet from the dining room to the bathroom.

Mother troops across the damp carpet and goes into the bathroom. I can hear her urinating. I call out, "Mother, you'd better not flush that. Dad, please wait with that mopping; let me find my shoes and help you."

"No, no, you go back to sleep. I've about got this done."

I give up all too easily and pull my head back into my quilt cave. Vague recollections of other plumbing problems in Malfaits' home flit through my sleep-deprived brain.

Mother returns to the living room, opens the front door, and fans the air with a cluster of newspapers. Several minutes later I hear the door close with a thud and the click of the deadbolt. Mother returns to her bed. Dad continues to scrub with the nasty mop. I stare into the darkness of my quilt cave.

Sleep is not to be.

When Dad is finally satisfied with his scrubbing work, he announces to no one in particular, "I've got to get to the store. We'll all need toilet paper in the morning."

I hear him fumbling with the deadbolt. I force myself to pull my head out of the pretend security of my cave, "Dad, it's the middle of the night."

"I know; but, kid, we don't have a single sheet of toilet paper."

"But where are you going?"

"If I can get this damned door open, I'm going to walk down to Safeway."

"Dad, it's after midnight. Stores are closed."

"No, no, Safeway's open all night."

"That's over two miles."

"Oh shit, kid, I'll be back before you need any toilet paper."

I hear the bolt give way and the door open. "Wait, wait, Dad." I struggle up from the couch. "I'll drive you. You can't be out walking around in the middle of the night. Just let me find my shoes."

I wrestle on a pair of jeans and a loose shirt over my pajamas and ram my feet into my untied tennis shoes. I catch Dad at the end of the sidewalk where he is standing trying to decide which direction to walk. He hears my keys rattle in my hand.

"Oh shit, kid, you didn't need to do that. You need to get your rest."

A few minutes later we pull into the Safeway parking lot, and I park in the space nearest the front door. The Handicapped sign peering into my windshield doesn't even come close to indicating the Malfait condition, sticker or no sticker. Dad opens the car door before I can get the brake set and the motor turned off.

"You just stay here in the car. I can get in there and get the paper and be right back." He moves in his fast shuffle into the store and disappears down the paper aisle. Shortly he is back at the check stand. It looks as if he has money and is paying for the toilet paper. I sit helplessly and watch him ask two different people where the exit is. By 1:00 AM we are back home. I kick off my tennis shoes and shed my travel garb and try to re-establish the false security of my quilt cave. Dad goes to bed, and I can hear Mother grumble as he crawls over her.

"I'm sorry to disturb you, Honey, but I have to find that church booklet. Oh, Lord, Mama, I worked so hard to pay that thing off. Allie will have to give us the check."

"You shut up and go to sleep, Dad. We'll go see her first thing in the morning."

"I've got to find the booklet. Betty will sign the release, and then we'll get our money. Mama, I know she'll sign it off for us."

"Dad, we may have to get the deacons to help us get the money. Are any of them men who worked with you when that church was being built? They'd know we paid for it. Maybe they could sign for us."

"Oh, Lord, Honey, I don't know what we'll do. Allie says we have to have the booklet. I found the damned thing the other day. I know it's on that table."

The desperate litany is repeated innumerable times. The clock hands read a little after 4:00 AM. I fall asleep--or perhaps more into stupefied exhaustion. Whatever it is, it isn't restful.

At 6:00 AM another repetitious, raw, rendition resumes about the church booklet, the money, the bond, my signature. Amid the havoc we all get up and agree to go out to breakfast, after which we will go by the church and check on the bond. I don't think anyone will be in on Saturday morning, but agreeing to go there has a calming affect.

Dad again searches through everything on the coffee table. Suddenly he is jubilant. "Praise God, people! I found it! Look here. I've got the payment booklet. Let's get the hell out of here and get down to that church!"

Mother snatches the booklet from him, "Well, you old fool, where was it?"

"It was right here tucked in the pages of the family Bible."

"Why did you put something that important there?"

"I put it there for safe keeping. I remember doing it now."

"Well, you old fool."

It's 9:00 AM when we arrive at the church. Allie does not work on Saturday, but a helpful associate pastor calls her at home. Allie explains what is necessary to pick up the check. Just as I thought, two church bonds had been taken out, one in my name and one in my brother Rolf's name. The redeemed value of each is $750.00. The one for 'Rolf V. Malfait' was picked up earlier. The pastor does not know whether it was signed by Rolf V. Malfait or Roger V. Malfait. The remaining check can only be claimed by me. I sign the form the pastor places on the counter, receive the check, and we leave headed for our next stop, the local Pancake House.

As I turn into the restaurant parking lot, Mother interrupts the relative calm, "Betty, take us to a bank so we can cash this check."

"Mom, you don't need to do that right this minute."

"Oh yes, we do. Get this car turned around."

Dad chimes in, "Oh, God, kid, we do need to do that right now."

"But, you guys, we're here at the restaurant now. Let's have breakfast."

Mother braces her right hand on the dashboard, as if we're about to crash, and pushes herself forward with her other hand which is behind Dad, who is sitting between us. "Breakfast, hell, you're the one with our money; we need to get to a bank. We need that money to pay our Whidbey Island land taxes."

"Look, you guys, I agree you need to pay the Whidbey Island taxes, and that's fine to do that with this check. However, cashing this check today will be impossible. It's Saturday. The bank is closed. Besides, you shouldn't be paying your taxes in cash."

Mother leans further forward and screams, "You get us to that bank, because that's what we're going to do with that money! That money is not yours, and you're not going to get your hands on it!"

"Mom, I'm not trying to get your money; but the check is in my name."

"Your father worked hard for that money, and we need it. It's not yours."

"I don't want your money, but where am I going to cash a check that size on a Saturday made out to me in my maiden name? I haven't lived in this town for thirty years! We all need to get in to this pancake place and have breakfast!" I ease the car into a parking place but take my frustration out on the brake. It's a good thing Mother is still braced in her potential crash position.

Not even that jolted stop deters Mother as she opens the door and gets out, all the while keeping up a barrage of derision directed toward me. "Just because that check has your name on it doesn't mean it's yours.

You don't need to be thinking you can just help yourself to that. We need every penny of that for taxes. You don't need to be planning another vacation with it!"

"Mother, I know you need the money. I'm not trying to take the check, and I'm most certainly not planning a vacation. It's after eleven o'clock. We've had a horrible night, and we all need to have a cup of coffee and something to eat."

Mother is relentless, "We *need* to get ourselves to a bank. That money is ours, and we need to get that check cashed."

Inside the restaurant there's a momentary stifling of the abuse. We get seated, and they each order ham and eggs with pancakes--eggs over easy. I'd like to turn them over--hard! My entire being is churning. I want to scream. The best I can manage is, "Coffee, please. Black. Dry toast. Wheat."

As if my order turned on an invisible switch, Mother renews her scathing attack, "How could you ever stoop so low?"

"Mother, I'm not stooping low. I can't cash a big check like that on a Saturday. I can't let you go around carrying that much cash pinned in your bra like you do your pension check money. Let's get a cashier's check made out for the amount of your Whidbey taxes, and I'll see that they get paid."

Mother's volume increases, "I never expected you to hump up like this and shit all over us and take what isn't yours!"

"Mother, turn your voice down. You don't know what you're saying. I don't want your check nor your cash! Here, you take the check!" I lay the check on the table near her. "It's just that you shouldn't pay your taxes in cash."

"Oh, yes, we are going to do just that. We're going to drive to Whidbey and find out the amount and pay them."

"Mother, the tax bill for those taxes is in your house. I saw it when I organized your mail. We can find the exact amount without driving to Whidbey Island and have a cashier's check written out for that amount on Monday. Then we can mail the payment. It doesn't have to be done in person nor in cash."

"We always pay in cash, and we pay in person."

"Yes, but we could both see that it gets done without that. I could come another day during the week and take care of it with you."

Dad chirps his own repetition regardless of what else is being said at the table. "Just sign the check, kid."

The waitress arrives with hot plates of food.

Mother does not decrease her volume, "Don put you up to this whole shitty scheme, didn't he? He's never been for shit! Did he get you to do this?"

Dad chirps, "Oh, kid, please sign the check. We need it so bad."

The waitress is embarrassed, "Errr--will there be anything else?"

Mother and Dad ignore the waitress and attack their food. They ignore me. They talk to each other with their mouths full, Dad in his monotonous plea and Mother venomously. "I'll tell you what, it takes a pretty shitty person to steal our grape juice. Now, here you both go trying to steal our money, too."

"Just sign the check, kid, please. We'll drive up to Whidbey and pay the taxes."

My face feels hotter than my coffee cup. Just embarrassment is a condition I could wish for. This is much more. I feel as if I am walking on a tightrope in a giant blender!

Mother glares across the table at me, shoves a large chunk of pancake in her mouth, and speaks, "Why do you come down here time after time to be a troublemaker? You're no help at all! You make everything worse, and I can tell you on Monday there'll be nothing for you to be *an executor of*! I wish you had never come down here at all!"

I understand the executor reference, as it is a directive in their wills. Their wills are about the furthest thought from my mind at the moment.

"Kid, she doesn't know what she's saying. Now, Mama, you hush! You don't know what you're talking about. Just sign the check, kid, please."

"You shut up and eat! And you, Betty, you don't need to stay around here and make any more trouble for us. You can go home, and I can tell you if I'm sick I don't need you to come running down here to see what kind of trouble you can cause. I'll be cold and in the ground before you'll even know about it!"

"Just sign the check, kid."

"Do you hate me that much? You want me to leave? You don't even want a ride home this morning?"

"No, you don't need to hang around here to give us any God-damned ride home. Get on out of here and put that tab for our breakfasts right down here on the table. I wouldn't want one thing ever from you or Don--and certainly not this breakfast! We'll go right back to the house and call Allie and get her to write this check out to Dad."

My brain is churning. It isn't real! It isn't real! I stagger outside and get into my vehicle. I grab hold of my steering wheel life-preserver with my quivering hands and squeeze until I am frozen to the wheel. Did they really say those things to me? Did all the people in the restaurant hear all that ranting and raving?'

A few minutes later Malfaits come out of the restaurant. An incoming patron stumbles, and they both stop quickly and reach out to help prevent his falling. Dad grabs the man by the arm and pulls him back upright, "Whoa there, partner, you're in a mighty hurry to get to breakfast. Are you okay?"

The man responds with thanks, and both Malfaits exchange friendly greetings with the stranger and wish him a good day. They proceed directly through the parking lot past six or seven cars and get into my car.

No one speaks. I start the motor and pull out into traffic. Shortly, I turn onto their street, and the derision and slanderous comments erupt anew from Mother. "I just don't know how you can do what you're doing. What makes you think that money from the church bond is yours?"

Dad accompanies, "Just sign the check--please, kid."

I say nothing, letting their demented repetitive duet play its course. I pull slowly onto their driveway and jam on the brakes, giving Mother another morning jolt. I lean in front of Dad and scream at Mother, "I can't take it any longer! I can't stay here and listen to this craziness! Give me your God-damned, fucking check! I'll sign it! I don't want your money or anything else. I care about *you,* and I want to help you, but I seem not to be able to do that." I sign the check in a flurry of furious motions and shove it into Dad's ever-overflowing shirt pocket. "There! Get out! Both of you!"

Mother gets out and Dad turns toward me, "Well, how am I going to cash this thing, kid?"

"You're probably not going to do that. Like I said, it's Saturday."

Mother is headed up the sidewalk toward the front door. She shouts back at the vehicle, "I'm going to call Allie right now and talk to her about this."

Dad slides out and comes around to the window on my side, "Now, kid, you've signed it for us. That's good. Now let's go downtown and get it cashed."

I heave a sigh and stare into his faded old blue eyes. "Dad, I doubt you'll cash a check like that on Saturday. And, even though I signed it over to you, it still may be a problem because it's made out to me--and in my maiden name. I don't think *I* could cash it. I just don't know, Dad. You do the best you can. You have to know that I don't want your money. I just want to help you and Mother."

"Now, kid, don't you worry about your mom. You don't worry about this whole thing." Dad leans into the window. "Let's forget this ever happened. Promise me you won't tell anyone about this."

"Dad, forget it. I love you. I just can't help you!"

Mother comes out the front door and crosses the lawn to my open window. "Allie says we can't do much about cashing this check. It's made out to Betty, and she has to sign it over to Dad."

"Mother, I did that already."

"Well, she thought you might have to cash it *with* us. We need that money, so let's just get downtown and get it cashed."

"Okay, I'll take the check and try to find a way to cash it."

Mother turns and commands, "Dad, get yourself back in that car. We're all going."

I lean out the window and match my mother's volume. "Like hell! I don't want your damned money, but if I'm going to cash the check, I'm going by myself!"

Dad leans over to the car window and holds the check in my direction. "That's fine, kid. I know you'll do that."

Mother gasps, "And you'll probably keep going! We'll never see you or the check again!"

I snatch the check from him, start the engine, and begin to roll down the driveway as I shout out the window, "I don't know how the hell you expect me to do this! It's impossible! I won't be able to cash a check this size, especially when it's written in my maiden name. I don't even have any identification that proves that's who I *was!*" My logic is lost in the screech of tires as I jam the car into gear and speed off, leaving them standing pathetically on the driveway.

Stops at Safeway and Mark Down Groceries get me negatives. It's against store policy. I'm sure that's going to be the story every place. The thought occurs to me maybe I can write personal checks at places like Penney's or Sears. I can use my credit cards for identification. I should be able to write fifteen $50.00 checks before closing time. I see the sign for the local Fred Meyer in the distance. "Okay, Betty, try one more time. If I get another 'no', I'll start writing my $50.00 checks here. Then I'll work my way across town and go on toward Portland."

As I cross the parking lot, I whisper a prayer.

Dear God, please help me. Please help me find enough places to cash checks so I can give them the money. You know I don't want their money. You know I only want to help them. Please.

The manager of the Fred Meyer in his most sympathetic voice responds to my request, "Lady, I *do* believe you. But it's also our store policy that we can't cash checks such as this. I have an idea though. I have a friend at a bank nearby, and she is working today on some catch-up work. Maybe she could help you."

I shall never know whether he had similar experience dealing with parental irrationality, or whether his decision was an answer to my muttered prayer as I came into the store, but I will be eternally grateful to that nameless man and to his nameless female friend who admitted me for a few miraculous moments to her bank!

After two of the longest hours of my life, I turn back onto Malfait's street. From the corner I can see both of them out on the curb like two expectant children looking at each passing car. I wonder if they've been doing that the past two hours. I pull into the driveway, put the car in park and set the emergency brake more gently than the last time. I surprise myself at my own harshness as I rip a piece of paper from my notebook and print, 'Betty cashed the First Emanuel Church bond check for $750.00 and gave the cash to Dad and Mom. Signed: Roger V. Malfait.' I draw a line for his signature.

They are both standing outside my car window. I roll down the window, "Here, Dad, sign this. It's a receipt showing I got your check cashed and I'm handing you $750.00 right now." I thrust the paper and the money toward him.

Dad leans against the hood of the car and signs the paper, pulls out a fifty-dollar bill and hands the receipt and the bill back to me. "Here, kid. I want you to take this for your gas money."

I shove the money back at him, "I don't want your money. Jesus Christ! Don't you understand at all? I just want to help you people."

Mother snatches the bill out of Dad's hand and shoves it in my face, "Go ahead and don't take it. You could cause him to have another heart attack right here by not accepting something he wants to give you. You just go ahead and be responsible for that, too!"

I close my quivering fingers around the money. "Thank you. It's worth the fifty bucks to shut you both up."

I release the brake and begin to let the vehicle move slowly back.

Dad grabs onto the mirror and looks pleadingly at me as he walks with the slow-moving vehicle, "I knew you wouldn't let me down. I knew you wouldn't steal anything from me. Thanks, kid." He waves the remaining clutched bills at me.

I stop and through my tears look into his old blue eyes, "I know you know that, Dad. Thank *you!*."

He leans closer in the open window, "Kid, just promise me you'll come if I ever call and ask you for help."

"Dad, I'll always try to help, whether you call or not."

"Kid, you help us a lot. Let's forget this morning. Let's forget all this check business. Please don't ever tell anyone about all this stuff today."

I could promise him most of it, except the last part. Mother stood off to the side, her looks speaking silently, 'I don't trust you for one minute.'

I stare through my blurred vision at one and then the other. "Both of you know, I am taking nothing from your house. I am not stealing anything from you--not your money--nothing. I never have, and I never will."

Dad continues to cling to the mirror, "I know, kid, I know. Please don't tell anyone about this. Let's just forget this."

Mother remains stone-faced.

"Dad, I just want to help you both to be healthy, to be organized and business-like in paying your bills, to not have the water or power shut off, to be able to get repairs done to your house. Look at it." I wave my hand up to the moss-encrusted roof and the peeling dingy white paint. I look back into his imploring eyes. "Dad, I love my family in the same way you have loved yours. And it isn't fair to have Mother, or either one of you, make slandering remarks about any of the people I love. I'm trying so hard to be helpful."

Mother sticks her chin out, and glares at me as she shouts toward the window, "I never said one thing slanderous about any of your family, nor you!"

"But, Mother, just today in the restaurant you said all those nasty things again about Don and the grape juice and your missing money. And you accused me of trying to steal the church bond money."

"I never *ever* said Don was a thief. I never said that to anyone! I never said *you* were a thief either! Her voice modulates but is emphatic, "Dad and I will see that the Whidbey Island taxes are paid, and we'll send you a photostatic copy of the receipt."

"That's not necessary. You didn't think my advice was any good about how to pay the taxes in the first place. You owe me no explanation for any of your business."

Old Parents and Purple Tulips

Failure, rejection, anger, whatever the churning ball in the pit of my stomach signifies, I begin to let the vehicle move again backwards down the driveway with Dad holding on and shuffling alongside.

"Kid, let's forget this whole thing. You've got to come if I call you. You're always welcome here."

"Let go, Dad."

His grip loosens and his arm drops to his side. His other hand still clutches the money. I back into the street. My heart is pulsing in my throat as I put the gear into first and move slowly forward. In the rear-view mirror, I see their piteous, woeful figures standing sadly by the driveway.

I am barely a block away when Ruthie, a long-time friend since my pre-kindergarten years approaches from the opposite direction in her car. She waves. No traffic is coming either way. We both stop our cars in the middle of the street. "Ruthie, do you have time for a cup of coffee?"

"Sure, I'd love that. Come on down."

I turn around and drive back to her house. I can see Mom and Dad still standing at the end of their driveway--watching nothing--watching time pass--who knows?

Whether from years of soap-opera viewing or because she senses something is wrong, Ruth hastily parks her car, runs out to the curb and jumps into my vehicle. Let's run down to the chicken place. You look as if you need something to eat. Let me take you to lunch."

I barely get to the end of the block. My body begins to shake all over. I pull over to the curb and blurt, "Oh, Ruthie, I just need *someone* to tell me they love me--someone to tell me I'm not demented. Please, Ruthie, I'm not crazy, am I?"

Ruth unbuckles her seatbelt and scoots over to me and sweeps me into her arms. "Betty Anne, I love you, and I never believed for one minute any of that junk about thievery and Don and Nick and El. I've told your mother a hundred times she's wrong, wrong, wrong!"

I can feel my body heaving, a massive pulsating glob. The logjam bursts. I sob uncontrollably. Poor Ruth. I try to protect her pink sweater from the steady stream of tears and my nasal drip. I practically rub my nose and face raw with the old left-over McDonald napkins within my grasp on the seat. I feel her arms holding me. I feel her soft pats and strokes on my back and my face. I hear her tender voice singing, "Oh, Betty, I love you. They're wrong. Betty, believe me. They're wrong, wrong, wrong."

I feel strength flow from this wonderful lady into my very being.

Somehow I find enough support from Ruthie's love and kindness to know I am okay. I truly am okay. When my tears dry up and I can see again, I decline the lunch invitation and turn around and take her home. Malfaits are not in sight.

I begin my three hour and fifteen minute drive to my home.

Ruthie's compassion has been only a temporary respite for me. Once on the freeway, it's as if I am on automatic pilot in a rainstorm at 70mph, but the storm is *inside* the car! I cannot live in their dementia. I cannot control it. They cannot live in my ordered, routine world with time lines and habits that suit my needs and my family's needs. They, in their dementia, are stronger than I. They outwit me at every turn. They misunderstand all of my practical advice and suggestions. I must give up these futile attempts! Trying to help them is insane!

No one is home when I arrive, and that's just as well. I shower until I feel I have scalded off the outside layer of my body. I wash all the clothes I took with me, whether I used them or not. I fall into bed.

Don and El get home a few minutes later and tiptoe in to ask how things went in Ridgeview. "Worse than my last trip. You really don't want to know." I drift off into an exhausted sleep that lasts until well after noon Sunday, some twelve hours later.

CHAPTER 10

Brotherly Help

THE SCHOOL YEAR '87-88 passes. Seasons change. My family problems do not. I go to Ridgeview less often. I hate to go. I hate not to go. My Christmas letter to Aunt Mavis expresses my anguish.

I appreciate your continued interest and support regarding Mom and Dad. Any resolution of their problems is <u>impossible</u>! I have decided my sanity is also a high priority, and I have been going down there less often. They tell me on the phone everything is fine. I know it isn't. Their living conditions and personal behavior are deplorable, but I can't get a handle on how I am supposed to be helpful. Rolf and I were not raised this way, and yet Mom and Dad exist doing, and not doing, things that were required of us in our childhood, especially in cleanliness. I feel guilty for not solving at least that part of the problem. Still, there is an indefatigable robustness about them and a kind of happiness, although I'm not sure "you old fool" is really a term of endearment. Rolf seems to be there more often, and I hope he's helping them, although I'm not certain about his cleanliness standards and personal behavior either.

A Monday morning 5:30 AM phone call from Mother in late spring the week before school is out is disturbing. My fumbling hands juggle the phone as I roll over and cram it against my ear. "Lo?"

An almost unrecognizable voice sobs, "I don't know--what to do-- Dad has--lost all his marbles! He's--totally unmanageable. Oh, Betty, what am I going to do?"

Mother has never been one to cry, not even when Dad had his stroke. I sit up in bed, eyes wide open, body instantly in emergency mode. "My God, Mother, what has Dad done?"

"He's just a crazy old fool." I hear her yank off a paper towel and blow her nose.

"But what does that mean, Mom? What has he done?"

Mother instantly bawls like she's being jabbed with a sharp instrument, crescendoing to a higher pitch with each repeated jab.

I yell into the mouthpiece, "Mother! Mother, What's he done? Mother?"

Another paper towel is ripped off. Then the nose-blowing. "Betty, he's just--lost all his marbles!"

"Mother, do you need me to come down there *right now?*"

A blast of nasal echo rattles through the phone. "No, but when is school out for you?"

"I have to work Thursday, but I could come early on Friday."

"Well, don't come now. I can manage. Dad's always been like this. I mean--well--he's been like this ever since his stroke. I don't know what I'm going to do, but I can manage until Friday."

"Okay, I'll be down early on Friday."

I give in too quickly to Mother's command not to come. I grumble to the silent cradled telephone, "I don't know what you're going to do either. I don't know how to help any of you whether I come today, or Friday, or ever."

Friday arrives, and the phone rings just as I am going out the door to make my trip to Ridgecrest. I rush back to answer.

There's no greeting in response to my hello, but a firm, controlled voice tells me, "Betty, everything is fine. You don't need to come down today. Dad is doing better and I'm fine. Everything is fine."

"But, Mother, I'm all packed and on my way out the door right now. I ran back just to answer the phone."

Her reply is emphatic, "No, don't come. It would be a waste of gas. Let's wait. Nick will be home soon from Basic Training. I want you all to come down then."

"Okay, if you're sure." Again I succumb to the easy way out and hang the phone up quickly before she changes her mind.

A week passes before Mother calls again, "Is Nick home yet?"

"No, Mother. Read the calendar on the wall right behind you."

"Uhh--Nick--the 29th of June. That's next week."

"That's right. How's everything going?"

"Pretty good. Dad is minding better. We walked out to the Ocean Espresso for morning coffee today. He seemed to enjoy that."

"How far is that?"

"It's about twelve blocks. We either go there for coffee in the morning, or we go down here to the corner and have hamburgers. The cafe next to the store is under new management. The little girl who does the cooking is so nice, and she makes a hamburger just the way Dad wants it, with extra thick slices of onions."

"I'm sure he likes that. Mom, I'm out of school now, and El hasn't started her summer job yet. Would you like us to come down today just for an afternoon visit?"

"No. Things are fine. I don't want any visitors today. I want to wait until Nick gets home and you all can come.

"Besides, you know, you and I both have birthdays coming up in July. Nick will be home then, and if you come down the Saturday in between our birthdays, we could celebrate both birthdays and Nick's homecoming at the same time. That would be nice for all of us."

"Oh, Mother, I don't want to celebrate my birthday."

"And I know why. It's the big five-O, right? Ha! Do you know how old I am?" Before I can answer, she announces, "I'm 74. Maybe I should skip celebrating mine, too? No, let's not skip. We have a lot to be celebrating, and Nick will be home by then.

"Now, Betty, in the meantime, Dad and I want you to find a blouse you like and put it on lay-away. You spend at least twenty dollars, because that's what Dad and I would like to give you for your birthday."

Mother gives me the instructions about the twenty dollars and the lay-away blouse at least three more times. I don't object. I know I won't be doing it, but it feels good to let her ramble on about the gift they want to give me. It feels good to have some sort of conversation that expresses caring and happiness. I refuse to hear the repetitiveness or the absurdity of the lay-away plan.

Nick arrives home from Basic Training as scheduled. But instead of a ten-day break, he has only three days before he must leave for his specialist school on the East Coast. His orders won't allow him to be home for the designated celebration weekend.

He and I decide to make a hasty trip to Ridgeview by ourselves. I call Malfaits and give them the change in plans. They are excited and want us to get there as soon as possible. Nick and I head out immediately. This trip is the most enjoyable three hours and fifteen minutes I have spent on this highway for years, as I catch up on Nick's experiences in Marine Basic Training. It's even better being chauffeured by him in his '65 Mustang.

It seems no time at all Nick and I find ourselves standing on the doorstep of 516, smiling at one another enjoying the familiar melodious tones of the doorbell. The pleasantry of the moment is interrupted as we hear Grandma struggle to open the deadbolt on the big heavy front door and Grandpa commanding, "Get on out of the way, Francine. Let me at that thing."

"Why, you old fool, you don't know any more about how to open this door than I do. Rolf's got so many boxes piled here by the door, it's a wonder either one of us can get in or out of this house. Get out of my way." The door flies open, and Grandma shrieks, "Oh, my God, Dad, look who's here! Betty, you need to call us before you come down here like this. Nick, give your old grandma a hug. Oh, my God, Nick, this is a surprise!"

"Jesus Christ, Mama," cries Dad, "you're stomping all over my feet! Well, hello there, Nick." Grandpa manages to squeeze by Mother for a handshake and a hug and then elbows Mother, "Well, get out of the way, Francine, and let 'em in the house."

Once inside, Nick and I are the ones to be surprised. Rolf is sprawled out on the couch, almost indistinguishable from the piles of laundry. More boxes than ever hide all the furniture and most of the floor. Rolf takes up the only available spot on big curved sofa where anyone could possibly sit. He and all his boxes have staked their claim and are exercising their squatters' rights.

Grandma gushes, "Oh, Nick, you're so handsome...but sort of skinny."

Grandpa squeezes Nick's bicep. "Skinny, hell, Mama, that's muscle. Right, Nick?"

Nick chuckles. "Well, Grandpa, I did have to work pretty hard to do the things the Marines require in boot camp. I lost fifty pounds. I guess that's skinny compared to before."

Rolf remains on the couch, arms folded across his chest. He doesn't get up. He doesn't shake hands. He doesn't speak. I guess this is Nick's greeting from his uncle whom he has not seen in several years. Rudeness is unnoticed in this world of the bizarre.

Grandma commands, "Let's get this skinny boy to the pizza parlor and get some food into him. Come on, Rolf, come with us."

"Naw, I gotta get goin'. I got a couple of errands to do." He hoists himself off the couch and edges around everyone toward the front door maintaining a scowl as if leaving a bad movie. I move aside so he can open the door. He nods in my direction, "I'll be back by here. I'll catch ya later."

Our celebration at the local pizza parlor is messy but fun. Grandma and Grandpa repeatedly express pride in Nick and his achievement in graduating from Basic Training. There is no mention of Grandma's objections, and certainly not about her red-letter hand-penned objections to Nick's decision to join the Marines.

Granddad asks, "Have you got yourself a car, son? Oh, God, where's *my* car? I don't see it anywhere out there."

Nick pats Granddad's arm. "I brought you. We came in *my* car. Remember, Granddad?"

"Oh, yeah. Sure, son. Which one is that?"

"It's the white Mustang right there outside the window."

"Oh, yeah. That's the one with the 350 engine. You know, a young fella usually can't get insurance on one of them. It's such a high-powered engine in a little car. You got insurance?"

"Yeah, Granddad, I've got insurance. It costs a fortune though."

"You know, you could really 'soup' that one up, son. I guess that's what you're interested in. The gear ratio in that big 350 gives you a lot of oomph." Granddad goes into a dissertation on gear ratios. It sounds authentic, and Nick seems to understand what he's talking about. Is this the same man who can't remember how he got to the pizza parlor and who has to have help buttoning his shirt and zipping his pants?

When pizza is finished, the doggy bag ready, and we are headed for the door, Granddad again becomes agitated. "Where's my car, son? God, where's my car?"

We all calm him as we load into the Mustang for the short drive back to Malfaits' house. Rolf is nowhere about. In the past I've thought his disappearing act was to get out of helping with the never-ending work around 516, but this time he did say he'd "catch us later." Besides, more recently he has been a "reappearing act." Ominous feelings stir within me, especially in light of all the new boxes in Malfaits' living room. By late afternoon he has not reappeared.

As Nick and I travel home I am disturbed about Rolf's rude behavior today and his not "catching us later." I haven't seen him for months, but he's definitely at their house more often. His reappearances have occurred in the past year when I haven't been to Ridgeview as much. I try to remember when I first noticed this. I conclude it's mostly from hearing him in the background in phone conversations. Nick has other things on his mind, so I try to not dwell on family problems. We turn our conversation to the hope that specialist school will not be more of the same routines and methods of Basic Training and what possibilities there may be for Nick's future.

CHAPTER 11

A Magical Cleaning Genie

AFTER MY TRIP to Ridgeview with Nick, I call Mother more often and listen more carefully. Several times I find she's in bed at a time of day when she should be up and about, and her speech is often slurred and evasive.

On one particular occasion I ask, "Are you sick?"

"No, I'm tired."

"Do you need some extra help?"

"No, I'm just tired. You don't need to come down here. I'm fine."

In the background I hear some kind of argument, and then cursing and swearing. "Mother, what's all that ruckus?"

"Oh, that's Rolf shooting off his mouth, but it's not as bad as it seems. He's not like this all the time."

There's a noisy skirmish and shuffling at the phone. "Is that Betty? Gimme that phone. I need to talk to her."

My silent brain chides, What for? I've been needing to talk to you for years! I wonder if I can do a disappearing act now, and *"I'll catch you later."*

"Sis, it's totally out of control down here! Everything smells like cat piss. You know that stuff makes everyone goofy, whether they've had a stroke or not."

"What do you think should be done, Rolf?"

"Well, for starters, these God-damned cats ought to be tossed out. Mom and Dad ought to be tossed in the bathtub. Then everything needs to be scrubbed down good with Lysol, or Pinesol--or something!"

"Are you working on that?"

"No. And I ain't gonna throw their cats out either. They worry more about them damn cats than anything or anyone else. If they'd pay half as much attention to how it smells around here, things would be a lot better."

"Do you have any constructive suggestions other than just bitching?"

"No, not really. It's just out of control, and something needs to be done. You need to get down here and see for yourself."

"I have been down there and seen for myself. I've had years of seeing for myself."

"Well, it's worse, and you need to get down here."

Our conversation is a monotonous dead-end litany. "Rolf, we're not solving anything here today on the telephone, and Mom doesn't want me to come down right now. I'll check my calendar and work out a later time. Maybe I'll see you then."

When I hang up the phone, I feel mean-spirited, childish, a fifty-year-old entangled in sibling rivalry. Rolf is there more often. Maybe he's doing some of the cleaning. Maybe he isn't disappearing as often. Maybe he is beginning to understand. Maybe he really is helping. *Maybe* now we *could* work together to help our parents. God knows someone needs to be doing something together in our family!

By the end of the week Nick is at his Marine specialist school. El is working. Don is recuperating from cataract surgery. *Maybe* it is *I* who should try harder at positive family relationships. Today's my birthday and Monday is Mother's. This weekend was supposed to be our birthday-family celebration. I could help make it a birthday celebration anyway and give Rolf a break, maybe even try to talk to him again. He seems to have a new perspective.

In the afternoon I bake a pound cake, a favorite of both Mom and Dad, and I bake a deliciously wicked thing called a Tunnel of Fudge. The next morning I buy deli sandwiches, watermelon, cantaloupes and other picnic trimmings and set out for Ridgeview. When I am well underway,

Old Parents and Purple Tulips

I stop at a road-side rest stop and call Malfaits. I ask if I may come down and bring a birthday lunch. Mother is delighted. She doesn't ask where I am or when I'll arrive. I tell her I'll be there shortly.

Arrival at their house is *déjà vu* into oblivion. Mother says I'll have to excuse the mess in the house because Rolf has been cleaning. I can see a pathway through to the kitchen, and it looks as if he has scrubbed the refrigerator. The table is stacked high, but the stacks appear to have been sorted.

Suddenly Rolf bursts through the back door, a magical cleaning genie dressed in logging attire: an old hickory shirt, jeans cut-off at mid-calf, heavy wool boot socks, Romeo slippers, and wide red suspenders. Beads of sweat glisten on his bald head and his brow. His bushy beard fans out from his face like bent, rusty wires. Despite the limited dimensions of the kitchen and lack of need for volume, he bellows, "Yeah, well, little sister, you caught us right in the middle of a little job, and there's a hell of a lot more to do around here!" Rolf hoists another box of 'garbage' to his shoulder as if he doesn't have a minute to spare and yanks the back door open with his free hand.

Mother screams, "Now there you go again with another box of my good canning jars! Dad, get in here and get these jars from him!"

Dad comes to the kitchen in his fast shuffle, "Rolf, Rolf, put those jars down! That's my good grape juice you got there. I won't have a thing to make jelly with. Mama and me need those."

Rolf turns back and slams the dirty box down on top of the resorted piles on the kitchen table, grabs one of the glass jars from the box, and wrenches the lid off. "Here, here, smell this!" He thrusts the open jar under each of their noses. "This is the good grape juice you value so highly." The smell of fermentation gone awry permeates the thick kitchen air. "You ain't gonna make nothin' out of this. It's gonna make you both sick." My nose is spared the close-up fermented jolt. Rolf turns and goes out the back door with the jars, juice, box and all.

As if nothing happened, Mother turns to me, "Let's clear off the end of this table and get ready for that birthday celebration."

I finish unpacking my picnic treats and sit down at the table with Mom and Dad. Rolf again bursts through the back door and without any further word—and without washing his hands—sits down with Mother, Dad, and me amidst the 'new level of cleanliness' for the birthday celebration. He reaches for the cantaloupe and begins eating with the same intensity he had been working. Mother eats cantaloupe, pound cake, and Tunnel of Fudge alternately, chanting between repeated helpings, "I just can't hold another bite."

Dad eats a deli ham sandwich and samples each of the other picnic goodies and proclaims, "Honey, I believe I'll have some more of that stew." Mother doesn't answer him. He gets up and shuffles to the kitchen stove and helps himself from a five-gallon canning pot of hearty looking beef stew on the back stove burner.

Rolf has definitely been cleaning and I guess cooking also. The overwhelming animal odor is considerably reduced, but Mom and Dad are disastrously unkempt. Rolf is no better.

Mother finishes off her third helping of cantaloupe and dumps the rinds and her dirty dishes into the already overloaded sink. "We need to get ready now and go over to Ocean Espresso for coffee."

Rolf lowers a thick wedge of Tunnel-of-Fudge he has been chomping on, "I told ya before, neither one of you are going to coffee or anywhere else until you've washed—and I mean via a trip to the bathtub!"

His words are harsh but definitely a warranted ultimatum. No one objects, and I assume that's a prearranged plan for today. "Rolf, while they're doing that, would you help me? I brought some tomato starter plants down for their garden. I need to get them to a cooler spot before the heat of the day."

"Yeah, sure. I'll put 'em around back."

He gets up and goes out to my vehicle, and I hurry to catch up. We carry the tomatoes to the garage. I can see he has been working there too. It's still full of junk, but the stacks have a "recent appearance."

"Geez, I haven't been in here for a while. What is all this stuff?" I tug at a pile of orange and white silk and tangled rope. "Hey, this is a parachute! That's hardly an activity Dad would ever have indulged in. *Whose* stuff is this?"

"Well—it's about half and half—theirs and mine."

"Ohhh, and is that the same story for *inside* the house?"

"Yeah, you could say that. But I'm going through every bit of the stuff."

I can see he's been working. I don't want to discourage him, so I bite my tongue. He's torn out the old kennel cage where Mom and Dad kept their collie dog years ago, and he's gotten rid of seven or eight wooden cat cages. Malfaits never could resist housing stray cats. Sometimes I think people left off their unwanted animals in the alley near their garage knowing Malfaits would adopt them.

"Man, Rolf, the garage looks a hundred percent better."

"It ought to. It took me damn near all one afternoon just to haul their newspapers to the recycling. They had 250 pounds. I can tell ya I was pissed when the guy only paid me a buck-twenty-five. Newspaper is only bringin' about a half-cent a pound now."

"That's not much different than last summer. I got $2.50, and I hauled 500 pounds. I'm ahead of you in volume, so you can haul the next 250 pounds."

"Yeah, yeah."

Rolf doesn't respond, and I feel guilty for my childish sibling barb. The work needs to be done, regardless of by whom. Rolf and I need to work together.

The garage door squeaks open. "You two come on. We need to get over to Ocean Espresso for our coffee."

"That's okay, Mother. I can't stay long. I need to get on the road and get home. Besides, there's plenty of left-over food here, and it's nice and cool in your backyard. We could picnic some more here if anyone's hungry."

July is always hot in Ridgeview, and the recent days have been record-breaking. Their back yard is pleasant and cool but a jungle. Malfaits planted a veritable farm on their two city lots. Everything grew and is now overgrown. The grape vines are especially aggressive climbing over the roof of the garage and the corner of the house. There must be over a thousand pounds of big lush Concords on those vines. In addition, cherries, apples and plums hang in heavy clusters from crowded trees at the back of the property. Red currants, blueberries, gooseberries, raspberries and loganberries fight for space with shrubbery and border flowers. The house and garage may be squeezed into destruction by these producers of sustenance and landscape decor.

Rolf does not disappear. We all settle into lawn chairs in the verdant coolness of the yard and visit like families usually do.

CHAPTER 12

Pizza Parlor Coffee Date

A SHORT WHILE later as Rolf makes his exit, he asks me to meet him at the local pizza parlor for coffee on my way out of town. I agree to do that.

It's after 3:00 P.M. before I am finally able to break away. I'm pretty sure Rolf will no longer be at the pizza parlor, but I stop by anyway. Surprise—there he sits at a table in the far corner of the almost vacant restaurant.

As I approach the table he begins shaking his head and speaking, "Betty, you just don't know how bad this thing is down here."

I slide onto a bench directly across from him. "Yes, I do know how bad it is. I've been coming down on weekends for *years!* In fact, I've come every other weekend for over four years, except this last winter when I haven't come as often. I just couldn't get anywhere with them."

"Sis, it's really, really bad. You can't know unless you've been here with them."

"Rolf, I'm telling you I *have* been here *with* them. What the hell do you think I've been doing for years? I tried to tell you. I begged you to talk with me."

"We've really gotta be open and frank about this whole mess."

"Rolf, the last time we talked openly and frankly, you went directly back and told them word for word everything Dr. K and I had said. He and I both became objects of their scorn and hatred!"

A young man in a cook's apron and red beret cruised up to our table. "How about a coffee refill, mister?"

"Yeah, sure."

"And you, ma'am? I brought an extra cup just in case?" He reached into the apron pocket and produced a cup and saucer.

"What can I say but yes. Thanks."

"No problem." Off he hustles toward the kitchen.

I take a sip of the dark, bitter brew. "Coffee is great, no matter what time of day."

"I agree, even if this is about my fifth cup in here." Rolf puts his cup down and leans toward me, "But, listen, Sis, I didn't realize how much guff you took as a result of that stuff about Dr. K and his medical reports. And I didn't realize what a hard time the folks gave you. I've been having my own hard times, you know."

"No, I know relatively little about you or your hard times, as you haven't really talked to me for a long time!"

"Things ain't been easy for none of us. I've been digging through everything around the place and trying to organize their bills."

I can't restrain a sarcastic smirk. "How do you manage that, you who don't have your own bills organized? Do you keep lists? Do you have a budget book?"

"Well, no, but they don't really owe that much."

"You're right there, but they do pay a humongous mortgage payment of $468.90 per month, which takes about a fourth of their monthly income. All I know is that it's somehow related to you, and it has been overdue repeatedly."

"Well, it's being paid."

"Yeah, I know, but why are *they* paying it?"

"Well, like I told you, things ain't been easy. I been in a very bad spot, and that loan was a consolidation of debts."

"Yes, but consolidation of *whose* debts? It wasn't *theirs*! I think it's wrong for you to use their income that way."

"Well, that's water under the bridge."

"I'm not so sure it's water under the bridge if they're still paying it. If they had to be in a rest home or any other type of care facility right now, they wouldn't have enough income to cover the costs. I don't know how much might be supplemented by Medicare/Medicaid, or whatever you call it. Probably none. For people who worked their fingers to the bone and paid handsomely to educate two children through university—that's *both of us*, Rolf—this isn't a very good way to be spending their retirement and their old age."

"Well, I'm managing for now. I've had a couple opportunities to do some long haul work, but I can't leave for very long at a time. Besides, I still have a lot of work to do here at the place."

I want to ask what he means by 'the place'. Isn't it *their* place? Is he now intending to help them? Or, is he helping himself? Has he gradually moved all of his belongings into their home? Does he *live* there now? Is it *his* place?

"You know, Sis, I really began to realize the seriousness of the situation here a while back when I asked Dad to pay an overload ticket for me."

"Why would you ask him to do that? Dad wouldn't realize overload from no-load? The man had a stroke, you know. His brain is permanently impaired!"

"Yeah, yeah," Rolf laughs, "so he didn't pay it. A little while after that I got stopped for having a light out on the truck and some snot-nosed cop nailed me for the previous unpaid citation."

A couple of kids holding hands come into the restaurant, order pizza at the check-out counter, and start toward our corner table.

I lean toward Rolf and ask, "What do you mean, you got nailed?"

"I mean I spent the night in a po-dunk jail in some little jerk-water town in Oregon."

I don't know if the kids suddenly notice us or if they hear the word jail, but they abruptly change directions and proceed to the opposite corner of the room. They scoot onto a bench, establish themselves in convenient kissing range, and begin to lock lips in the privacy of their opposing corner table.

I take a sip of my coffee. "It seems to me an overload ticket or having a light out on the truck are sort of minor offenses to warrant a night in jail, and you're kind of feisty and jovial about it now. How serious was your jail stay?"

"Ah, the next morning, the local tin-star who had me arrested seen the light, and he released me early."

"Rolf, it seems your loud-mouthed, know-it-all methods got you a night in jail, and those same methods aren't very constructive with Mother and Dad either. For that matter, I don't appreciate your tactics, and they're not healthy to your own existence."

"Probably not. Now about the folks...you know as well as I do Dad can't be running wherever and whenever he wants."

"I agree with you on that."

"Some woman brought him home a few days back. She picked him up out on the highway by the mill. He was standing in the middle of the road looking lost. The lady's a Ridgeview teacher. She got him to come over to her car, and he gave her his name. I guess he knew his phone number too. She called the house and brought him by and dropped him off. I talked to her for quite a while. She was real nice, a really good-hearted person."

"I guess we're all lucky she was a good-hearted person, but you can't depend on one of those every time Dad decides to take a walk."

The apron-clad waiter in the red beret ambles by with a small pizza and heads for the far corner.

"Yeah, that's for sure. There's all kinds of scum bags around this town. I've already decided to be tougher on his traveling by himself. One day here last week, Mom went down to Wilma's to visit. You know, she needs to get out sometimes. Right away Dad wondered where she was. I told him, and he said he was going to go down there and get her. I said no. Well, he wouldn't take no for an answer, and he started through the door. About the time he got on the first step down, I got hold of his jacket, and that sort of left him spinning his legs uselessly with me holding him by the collar. Actually, it was sort of funny."

"I'm not so sure of the humor in that, Rolf."

"Well, the old man's got a lot of piss in him, you know?"

Old Parents and Purple Tulips

The waiter passes by our table and smiles—maybe overhearing, maybe just appreciating anyone with a lot of piss in him.

Rolf continues, "Dad, he turns back on me and grabs me by the shirt and says, Let me go or I'm going to knock the shit out of you! Go ahead, I says, and I'm gonna hit you back. Well, the result was Dad did, and so did I. Now, mind you, it was a very light jab to the ribs, but Dad let go right away. He went back in the house whimpering I had hit him with one of them 'saguichi karati chops' and broke his ribs. In fact, if I recall, he said, Damn, Rolf, you've separated my ribs from my backbone!" Rolf chortles, "Well, I guess you know he didn't go to Wilma's."

I am appalled, but I make no response. I doubt Rolf really hit Dad, although he probably did have to hold his collar to keep him from leaving. How much of this is Rolf's embellishment? How much of it is part of the daily bizarre routine at Malfaits' house? Dad and Mother have often outmaneuvered me, both physically and verbally. Is Rolf experiencing the same thing? Does Dad really have to be restrained physically?

Rolf continues, "There was another time here about three weeks ago when Mom tried to stop him from going out, and he hit her."

"No way, Rolf! That never happened!"

"Well, you can believe me or not, but I'm tellin' ya, things are completely out of control down here!"

As Rolf drones on, my brain dredges up memory of the sobbing phone call in which Mother told me Dad had completely lost his marbles. Though their bickering at one another over the years has often been upsetting, they never in all their lives hit one another—nor even us, for that matter. I can only remember a couple of spankings for either one of us during our entire childhood. No wonder Mother was so non-communicative when she called. I'll bet Dad did hit her, and she was so upset she wasn't able to tell me. The timing of the episode coincides with her increased evasiveness and depression I've noted in phone calls. These physical rampages also match up with Rolf's presence in their home. His being there as a care-taker is not relieving the stress level. It's escalating it.

Besides the filth, boxes of junk, deplorable hygiene, and abuse by all of them to each other, I worry about guns. Rolf has been a collector since early teen years, but he has guns strewn all over their house now, as if guns are the same kind of clutter as newspapers, magazines, and junk mail.

I interrupt Rolf's complaints. "You know, Rolf, with all this craziness going on with Mom and Dad I think you need to get some of those guns out of sight—and out of their house. I noticed a couple of new ones in the hallway today. And what's that thing mounted on the tripod on their coffee table?"

"What thing? You can't even see their coffee table."

"You know very well what I mean. Under a couple of sheets of open newspaper there's a weird looking gun like a small caliber rifle with a scope mounted on it. It's on a tri-pod and pointed at the front door."

"Oh, that. Well, sometimes I sleep on the couch there in the living room, and I need some protection. All kinds of weirdoes roam up and down their street and sometimes come up to their door."

"Protection my foot! Who do you need protection from? Who cares about weirdoes? What if Mom or Dad picked that thing up?"

Rolf ignores my last question and smirks, "In this day and age people need guns for protection. It's not just a macho thing, you know. Women keep guns too.

"Yeah, Wilma's sister was out here from Oklahoma visiting last month, and she had a hand gun she kept right in her purse. She's gone home now, but she left her gun with Wilma. Of course, Wilma, she don't know nothin' about guns, and she don't want nothin' to do with 'em. Mom bought the gun from her."

"What? My God, Rolf, that's for sure something you and I both know Mother doesn't know zip about."

"Yeah, I know," Rolf sniggers. "I looked for the damned thing, but I can't find it. I guess it's loaded too."

"That's scary as hell, Rolf."

"Yeah, maybe, but it's not like it's really anything weird to have guns around. As for me, if I ever got the opportunity and was alone with the guy who caused all my problems over my log truck—actually he outright stole my truck, part by part—I'd like to have a gun—I'd kill him!"

"Oh geez, Rolf, you might get more than one night in a po-dunk jail for that."

Rolf enjoys his own laughter. "Well, it would have to be under the right circumstances and not traceable. I tell ya, it wouldn't be a problem. I could easily kill the son-of-a-bitch! But, you know I still have a shred of Christian values, and that's the only thing that holds me back from doin' the fucker in." Without even a pause for breath, Rolf continues, "You know, I'd give anything to find that money—you know, the money that was stolen from Mom and Dad—so we could settle this family problem once and for all."

Though his sudden lurch from ramblings on murderous vindication to the stolen money have no real connection, I make the leap with him. "Rolf, I know for sure I'm innocent of the deed, and I know Don didn't do it. And after years of watching Nick and El grow and mature, I'm sure they didn't do it either. However, you have shut yourself off totally from both of them by your accusations and tough-guy threatening demeanor. You wouldn't know if they're grown or mature or anything else about them."

"Now what do you mean by that?"

"Rolf, you've done so many disappearing acts I couldn't begin to count them. Most recently would be when Nick returned from Marine Boot Camp and the two of us came down here. You hadn't seen him for over four years. You sat on that couch all puffed up looking disgusted and angry and said nothing at all to him. Don't you think that was more than peculiar for an uncle's behavior?"

"Well now, as I remember, it was Nick who avoided me."

"Bullshit, Rolf! You sat there in the only seat available on the couch—the only spot in that whole junked up living room—and you crossed your arms and didn't say hi, kiss my ass, or anything else!"

"Now, now, I think it was Nick who acted kind of sneaky and guilty-like and didn't speak to me!"

"Rolf, how can you sit there and say that?"

"Well, you're just remembering it like you want to, little sister."

The waiter in the red beret is joined by two cohorts. This red beret team begins a scrub-down on all the tables. A fourth team member follows them with a broom and dust pan.

I glance at my watch. Our coffee date has been venting these strands of irrationality for over three hours. "Rolf, what do you want to do now? What are we both supposed to do?"

"Just hold as is for awhile. I still have plenty of work to do around the house, but I'm getting things done."

"Okay, next time I'm down I'll bring the truck and help you in any way I can. Maybe we could at least haul away those 55 tires piled in front of the garage doors. Maybe even haul a couple of those old cars away, especially that eyesore parked beside the driveway in the front yard."

I leave the restaurant with a shred of hope for sibling cooperation with our parents, but on my drive home ambivalence and doubt wrench at me. What's right? What's wrong? What is Rolf really doing? Why is he going through everything in their house? Is he living in their house? Is he helping *them*? Is he helping himself? Is he offering *me* brotherly help? Are Mom and Dad safe with their son? Is there danger to me personally coming to their home? Who can help? Can anyone?

CHAPTER 13

That Danged Rolf

AFTER MY COFFEE date with Rolf, I decide I need to be a better helper to my parents. I may be the only one who *can* help them. In his own way Rolf is trying, but I'm doubtful what he does is right or beneficial to them. I need to participate more.

I resume regular trips to Ridgeview, but I am mindful of Rolf's hard times and I am more considerate of his financial limitations. I tell him to call me collect any time he feels he needs to, from their house or when he's on the road. He appreciates my offer, and I feel better about his being with them more and about my re-dedicated efforts to try to help with their care and well-being.

It isn't long before Rolf makes one of those collect phone calls to tell me Malfaits' tax bill for their Whidbey Island property came. "Yeah, I told Mom they better pay them taxes or they'd lose that land, and they ought to take care of it right away. Well, actually that was a couple of months ago when I told 'em. I keep asking her about it, but she's real un-cooperative. She tells me those Whidbey taxes are none of my business, and I have enough to worry about to take care of my own bills. Once or twice she told me they already paid them, and then again she told me they're *going* to drive up there and do it. Hell, I don't know if they did or they didn't pay their taxes."

Mom and Dad's Whidbey property adjoins land Don and I own on the island, and I tell Rolf, "Well, we don't pay our taxes in person, and I don't really want to go up there, but I'll make a trip to the courthouse and check it out. I still have grades to turn in at school, but spring break is next week. I'll go on Monday, and I'll call and let you know what I find out."

On Monday morning of spring break my teaching friends are relaxing in various exotic locations: Mexico, Hawaii, and Disneyland. I'm on the Port Townsend-Keystone ferry headed for Whidbey Island. It's not exotic, but it is a gorgeous spring day. The Olympic Mountains are showing off their splendor against a crisp western blue sky, and in the east the Cascades Mountains are competing for the eye of the beholder. There have been times when this trip and this scenery were exciting and stimulating to our future dreams. One of those dreams for Don and me and Mom and Dad was to build our retirement homes on our adjoining acreages on this island. Present circumstances definitely obscure that dream.

At the historic Coupeville Courthouse I find my way to the Treasurer's counter where I introduce myself and describe the acreages for which I have questions. A pleasant lady on the other side of the counter smiles and tells me, "Oh, yes, I recognize your name. I've been recording your tax payments for over twenty years. I'm very happy to meet you in person."

"Oh, good, I wasn't sure I was even at the right counter to ask my questions."

"Well, I do have to say most people, even those who live on the island, don't pay their taxes in person, so I usually don't get to meet the people. It's always a special treat for me when I can match a face with a particular parcel of land. What may I do for you today?"

"Well, we've already paid our taxes, but my folks are Roger and Francine Malfait, who own the acreage adjoining ours to the south. My dad had a stroke a while back, and Mother has had her hands full trying to manage things. She doesn't know whether their taxes are paid or not. Would you be able to tell me that? I have their reminder notice with me with their land description."

"Oh, no problem." The lady types in the notice information and scowls at her computer. "Oh, goodness, I hate to tell you this, but Malfaits' taxes have not been paid this year—nor for two previous years. I know you didn't want to hear that."

My trip home is dreary, despite the natural beauty of the day.

Rolf is on a long-haul truck job, and it's two weeks later when I talk to him. His response to the information I gleaned is, "That can't be right! You know those secretarial types up there in Coupeville. Those girls at the counter are probably just college kids and somebody's daddy got 'em a job. I been thinking about that tax bill ever since we talked last time, and I'm pretty sure Mom and Dad paid them taxes. I think they even showed me the receipt."

"This is serious, Rolf. I went to the Treasurer's Office in person. The lady who waited on me was a long-time employee, not some college girl. She looked up the official tax record for Malfaits. The record shows their taxes have *not* been paid. I suppose Mom and Dad could have paid them in the last two weeks while you've been gone, but I doubt it."

"Nah, none of the cars look like they've been moved. I don't think they've been drivin' anyplace."

I take a long sip of my cold coffee. "Geez, I guess we should be thankful for that. Now I wonder if they've paid the taxes on their house and property there in Ridgeview. Do you know anything about that? I mean, if the Whidbey taxes are three years in arrears, I have to wonder about their house taxes. I would have to see receipts for myself to believe they paid taxes on either one of those properties."

I finish the cold brew in one shuddering gulp. "Rolf, you say you think you *saw* the receipt for the Whidbey taxes? When was that?"

"I don't *have* the thing, but I'm pretty certain they paid them. I remember when they got the bill, but I didn't open it. Hell, you know the hand-record-keeping in a place like Coupeville. They probably haven't recorded the payment. They never have their records up to date. I'm certain I seen that receipt."

Our phone conversation ends on an uneasy note.

There is so much I don't know, and I don't have a legal right to be involved in Malfaits' finances. I want to believe Rolf. He may even have driven them to Whidbey, since they were so insistent on paying in person when I gave them the cash from the church bond. If he did, why doesn't he say so? What if the taxes really haven't been paid? What happened to the $750.00 cash from the church bond I signed over to them? And what happened to the other church bond check made out to Rolf V. Malfait? Did Dad pick that one up and cash it, or did Rolf? Ross—Rolf? Who knows? Maybe that's why Rolf is so evasive. Maybe he picked up the check made out to him and cashed it, and they raised a fuss about needing that money to pay taxes. Maybe, maybe, maybe—I don't know. If Rolf did that, it really was *his* check. He probably needed the money as much as they did. None of this is any of my business, but I can't help wondering, What *do* Malfaits do with their income?

Another two weeks passes before my next trip to Ridgeview. Mother is anxious about bill-paying and asks, "Betty, will you get out to Fibex Credit Union and pay that bill. Rolf has been dragging his feet and hasn't got it paid again, and it's overdue. I'm just so tired. I don't feel like bill-paying."

"Sure, I'll do that."

She takes out a crumpled bank envelope from her big black purse and counts out five one hundred dollar bills. "There, that ought to cover it."

In the credit union I stand in the line of one of the clerks who has often waited on Mother and me. My turn comes up quickly. "Say, I've been coming in here paying this bill for my mom and dad for a long time now. Can you tell me what it's for?"

The clerk reaches a well manicured hand across the counter and rakes the stack of hundred dollar bills to her side. She counts them, writes a receipt, and shoves the receipt and $31.10 to my side.

Looking up she inquires, "And who are you?"

Old Parents and Purple Tulips

"I'm Francine and Roger Malfait's daughter. I'm trying to help my mom and dad get their affairs in order. I've been in here several times over the last few years with my mother paying this bill. I just wondered what it was for."

"I've seen you in here with your mother, but the loan is really theirs."

"But they've received so many letters from you people about late payments, and I don't seem to be able to get them to take care of the situation promptly by themselves. It's been especially difficult since Dad had a stroke, and they're neither one doing very well. A payment of $468.90 is a huge chunk of their monthly income, and there are many other things that need to be done around their place. It's overwhelming to them and to me, but if I'm going to be of any help I have to know what's coming in and what's going out, and for what."

"I appreciate what you're saying. I know from seeing you come in here with your mother that you're trying to help her. However, our rules are very firm. I cannot divulge the nature of Malfaits' loan to you. I can only tell you both of their names are on the paperwork, and the business of the loan is *theirs!*"

The same response is given to me wherever I make inquiries about Malfaits' business. However, a kinder, gentler voice from Mr. Tim, one of Mother's favorite helpers at her local bank says, "I know you're trying to help them, Betty. They're such sweet people, and I know how much your mother has been stressing since your dad had the stroke. But sometimes a loving son or daughter is more interested in their parents' business for reasons not stemming from love. I feel that's *not* your situation, and I believe you're trying hard to be helpful. But policies are written to protect the innocent, and often older folks *are* innocent--and vulnerable. Your work could be done more effectively if you had a legal right, either a *Durable Power of Attorney* or a *Guardianship*. Then you could gain access to their business affairs legally. It would officially allow you to help."

My tears spill over. Mr. Tim shoves a tissue box across the desk. "I'm sorry, Betty, but those are the only legal options to allow you to do what needs to be done."

"Oh, God, I don't want this whole thing to be so disastrous that I need legal paperwork through the *courts* to be a helpful daughter."

"Betty, the legal paperwork verifies that you *are* a helpful daughter. It would allow you to do the helpful things officially."

I wipe my eyes and blow my nose. "Well, if I need the paperwork, I need the paperwork. But I am not the only child of Malfaits. I'll need my brother's name on it, and he hasn't been all that cooperative in other aspects of helping our parents. I'll try to talk to him though."

Later that evening, Rolf stops by, and I attempt to discuss with him my experiences at the various places of business.

"Yeah, yeah, we need to do somethin'. We gotta be able to have a little money around here."

"Rolf, we can't be messing in their business without their permission, and they won't give permission to either one of us. Bills don't get paid. The lights have been shut off at least once that we know of. Threatening letters get sent. Wouldn't it be better to find out what we need and how we're supposed to go about this legally?"

"Yeah, yeah, I guess you're right."

"Well, we definitely need a lawyer to do that. Do you want me to try to find one? Both of us could go and see what it is that we need to do in our situation?"

"That sounds like a good idea."

"Okay. I'll investigate the lawyer thing and try to get names of two or three. We can check them out and see what other people around here think of them. You know more people here than I do, so you'd be better to do that part. Okay?"

"Yeah, yeah, go ahead and get the names for me. I'll call you next week and see who's on your list. That'll be the end of August. I got some free time then."

August passes into September with no call from Rolf. I plan for my next Ridgeview trip. I routinely mow Malfaits' lawn, but on this trip my goal is to cut the laurel hedge, which on windy days slaps at the second story window. I need power pruning equipment and a chain saw. I cannot do this kind of work by myself. Rolf is never around when I mow the lawn. I haven't been able to reach him to ask for his help with this. Don and I are both reluctant, but we decide he is the only available one who can help me.

When the weekend arrives, the two of us load the necessary tools in the pickup and set off, even though Don has not been on their property since the family rift years ago. Arriving in Ridgeview we stop at a local burger joint for a quick lunch. When we get to the house, we don't even go to the door. We unload the equipment from the truck and immediately begin our tasks.

Mom and Dad emerge after a few minutes to investigate the noise. They are delighted when they see what's going on. No one seems surprised by Don's presence nor asks why we didn't come in the house first. Everyone becomes engrossed in the frenzied outdoor labor. I mow grass. Don cuts hedge. I rake. Dad and Mom collect grass clippings and hedge trimmings into big plastic bags and drag them around back to the dumpster in the alley.

After several trips Mother wipes her brow and laments, "I wish we could get Rolf out here to help us. It would sure go faster."

"I know, Mom. He's never around when we need him."

"Why, he's sitting right in there in the living room watching TV."

"You mean to tell me we're out here sweating up a storm, and he's sitting on his butt in front of the TV?"

"He stayed overnight last night."

Instantly I am on the front door step simultaneously ringing the door bell and banging on the door. Everything is locked up as if it's maximum security. I yell through the wicket, "Hey, Rolf, get up from there! Come out here!"

After a few of my repetitions, Rolf opens the door in sleepy-eyed, silent response.

"We've been working on the hedge for almost two hours. Didn't you hear us?"

"Yeah, yeah."

"Well, come out and help! It's going great, but we could use another hand."

"Yeah, sure."

I turn and go back to work, feeling confident the new, cooperative Rolf will take a few minutes to wake up and then join us. Not so. Hours pass. Late in the day I can wait no longer. I make a bathroom break and confront him in the house. "Listen, lazy-bones, if you're not going to help us, could you please get off your haunches and run down to the gas station and get some more gas? Don's just finishing the hedge, and I'm coming down the stretch on the lawn. We're both about to run out of gas, and it's going to get dark on us. Couldn't you at least help us by running to the gas station?"

"Yeah, yeah, sure."

I give him money for the gas, and he leaves without further comment. He returns shortly, plunks the gas can down on the walkway near the front steps, and as I guide the lawnmower close to the steps, he extends his hand, "Here's your change--two bucks." He turns and goes into the house. The closing door cuts off the flickering TV.

It's dark when we finish the hedge and lawn. Everyone is pleased with our accomplishments, at least as much as we can admire by street light and porch light.

Mother interrupts our sweaty, green-stained admiration, "Let's get ourselves cleaned up and downtown for some dinner."

"Mother, no. No, please. We can't. We still have a long trip home, and we need to get going. Don and I will grab a bite somewhere on the way."

We're all tired, dirty, and hungry. I know there will be no "cleaning up" before dinner. Neither Don nor I want to go out for dinner, nor do we want to eat in their house. I feel it's barely acceptable for *me* to be in their house, and Don has not been on the premises for years. I did go inside today to use the bathroom. I didn't ask Don how he handled his need. Probably he visited Mother's 'garden facility.' Despite the good deeds of the day and appreciation of accomplishments, neither of us wants to jeopardize ourselves in Malfaits' distorted thinking.

Don leans close to my ear, "How about I make a quick burger run?"

"Good idea, but make it just for them. You and I can stop some place on the way home."

Don slips away and makes the trip downtown to a drive-in while Mom and Dad and I juggle conversation in continued bizarre mode. Are we going to Chuck's Wagon or the hamburger joint? The lawn and hedge are beautiful. That danged Rolf...he could have helped. You and Don should stay overnight here at the house. We'll all get cleaned up in just a minute. Man, the mosquitoes are bad this year. I promise next time I'm down, we'll get all spiffied up and I'll take you both to lunch at the inn by the river. I swear this is the best looking lawn on the block. My God, I'm tired!

Don returns with a bag of hamburgers, drinks and fries. Tantalizing greasy aromas mingle with the heavy sweetness of the freshly mowed grass. Without encouragement or invitation, Mom and Dad take the bags of food to the picnic table under the cherry tree in the backyard. They sink down in lawn chairs, slurp soft drinks, and squeeze their green-stained, dirt-encrusted fingers into the hamburger buns.

Don and I make our departure unnoticed.

We barely make it to the end of the block before a flood of venting bursts forth in the cab of the truck. "Oh, Don, I can't say it enough-- thank you! Thank you for all your hard work today."

"Thank *you* for all *your* hard work. I don't know how you do all you do for them, for our family, for me, for school--all that, and keep your sanity, too. You're amazing!"

"You're the amazing one--you're the cornerstone of my sanity. I couldn't do anything without you."

"I've never been called a cornerstone before, but it has a nice ring to it." We both laugh, and Don reaches over and squeezes my hand. "See those lights up ahead. It's only a fast food place, but this cornerstone needs a good scouring and then I'm going to be the first cornerstone ever with a massive appetite."

CHAPTER 14

⎯⎯∞⎯⎯

I Hate Myself This Day

On my first October trip to Ridgeview I keep my promise to take Mom and Dad to lunch at the inn by the river. Despite their less than appropriate appearance and their irritating bickering, cleaning up is not clean. Dressing may omit zippers. Wearing a checkered work shirt with checkered pants looks fine. Dirty clothes are clean enough. Dirty hands? Who's got dirty hands?

"Dad, your hands are filthy. You go wash them."

"Why, Mama, my hands are cleaner than yours will ever be."

"You old fool, don't tell me my hands are dirty. You get yourself into that bathroom and wash."

"I just washed my hands after I went to the bathroom."

"That was two hours ago." Mother shoves Dad none too gently toward the bathroom. "Do it again before we leave."

"Jesus Christ, Francine, I can get to the damned bathroom by myself."

Is this senile reality or real senility? Dad's? Mother's? *Mine?* The mood becomes a milder but happier delirium as the three of us load into the car and proceed on our outing.

We arrive at the inn, are seated, order our food, and eat without being noticeable or interruptive to other patrons in the restaurant. In fact, abusiveness and rudeness seem replaced by good manners and a demeanor familiar in years gone by. I feel as if I'm not with the same people who had gotten dressed to come on this luncheon date. We are served by a charming, attentive waitress who knows Malfaits and has missed seeing them. The food is good. The service is good. And the view is spectacular with lots of activity on the river.

As we are slipping out of the booth at the end of the meal, my hand slides into a pool of water around the buttons of the leather seat where Mother had been sitting. "Yuk!" I fold my napkin and blot up the moisture. Mother and Dad are almost to the restaurant door. The pleasant mingling of restaurant aromas does not disguise the identity of the liquid. I drop the wet napkin on the pile of dirty dishes and say nothing.

Having completed this lesson in humility, or humiliation, I return Malfaits to their house. Rolf is not there as he was supposed to be. It's time for our first appointment with the lawyer we selected from references given to us by Dad's doctor and from personal recommendations of family friends. I go to the preliminary appointment with the lawyer by myself.

The attorney listens to my personal descriptions of Malfaits and their living conditions, and I share quotes from Dad's doctor. He advises neither Mom nor Dad appears to be of a mental capacity to be granting a *Durable Power of Attorney*. They should have granted this legal power to one of us, or some other person of their choice, in their more cognizant years. He feels the only option for Rolf and me at this stage of their mental and physical functioning is a *Guardianship*. I leave his office in a lonely, blurry-eyed daze muttering to myself.

Dear God, where are You? I need help here. I'm such a gutless wonder! I should have told the lawyer right now to proceed with the paper work. I know this has to be done, but I want Rolf to be responsible and a leader. He's older. He should be the one doing this. God, I don't want to do this by myself. God, I don't want to do this at all. Is a formal legal process really necessary? Oh, God, please help me. Dad's not going to get any better. Mother is getting worse. I think Rolf is sick, too. I don't even know about my own sanity. I heard the words today, but I'm not at all sure I know what the hell a legal guardianship involves. I am so alone and inept. HELP!

A few days later when I call Ridgeview, Rolf answers. It is I who jumps in with no greeting, "How come you didn't call me like you said you would?"

"I've been pretty busy. I've had a couple of driving jobs."

"Did you forget we were supposed to meet with the lawyer together?"

"Nah, Nah, I didn't forget. I've just had a bunch of stuff to do."

Despite my irritation, I fill him in on the preliminary attorney visit. "I can't go any further by myself, Rolf. I need your input. Am I doing what we agreed to do?"

"Yeah, yeah, that's what we agreed on."

"What do you want to do next? Do you want to go in and meet this guy and see if you think we could both work with him?"

"Yeah, that would be good."

"Well--when do you want to do that?"

"I'll call you next week as soon as I know my hauling schedule. Then we can both see him. I do want to know more about this guardianship thing. I got a few questions for him. I'll call you next week."

There is no phone call from Rolf next week.

After three weeks, I call Mom for a pre-Thanksgiving chat, hoping to plan some kind of holiday celebration. Again, Rolf answers the phone.

I'm not at all interested in how he is. "Where the hell have you been? Three weeks isn't exactly *next week*?"

"Yeah, yeah, I've been really busy."

"Couldn't you have at least called?"

"I suppose I could have, but I've been working really hard. I've had a couple of trips on my own, too."

"Do you still want to pursue this guardianship thing? Do you want us both to go see the lawyer?"

"Yeah, yeah. Sure I do."

"Rolf, it's hard enough with them, but when you're so undependable, then I don't know what anyone wants or needs. You say you want me to pursue finding a lawyer, but then you don't show up for the appointment. I don't know if I can trust you to carry through on anything."

"Oh, I ain't that bad. I'll tell you what, comin' up pretty soon--in fact, next week--I got some days off. I *promise* I'll call you next Friday. We can meet at that little truck stop near Pleasanton and make some kind of plan on how to proceed."

"Tell me again *exactly* when, and I'll write it down right now on my calendar."

"Okay, I'm going to call you between one and three PM on Friday, November 24, 1989. How's that for being specific?"

"That's exactly what I put down--between one and three PM, Friday, November 24, 1989. Please don't let me down, Rolf. Now, are Mom and Dad around? I'd like to talk to them."

"They've gone to bed for the night."

"They *have*? It's only 4:30 in the afternoon."

"Well, they're both in bed, and they're sound asleep. That's all I can tell you."

November 24, 1989, I am home. I stay near the phone well before 1:00 PM and all day late into the evening. There is no call. Is Rolf just as nuts as they are? Does he really not want to see an attorney? I can't mess around in their business without the proper authority. I don't think what he is doing in regard to their business is right. I don't really think what he is doing in the name of care-taking is helpful either. This whole picture is dreadfully wrong.

I give my own thoughts some validation by making an appointment with Don's and my personal attorney, John Braden. I outline the situation with my parents, giving personal descriptions of Malfaits and their living conditions and sharing quotes from Dad's doctor.

John listens and scratches on a big yellow pad for several minutes while I sit quietly. Looking up from his notes he purses his lips and shakes his head. "Betty, I'm really sorry to hear of this situation with your parents. And, I hate to tell you this, but neither your mom nor your dad appear to be of a mental capacity to grant a *Durable Power of Attorney.*

"There are really two kinds of Power of Attorney. In one case a non-incapacitated person may grant Power of Attorney to a trusted person temporarily, as in a situation prior to surgery, an extended trip, service deployment, or other circumstances which might keep the person from taking care of their affairs as usual. The person who initiated the agreement can then revoke this agreement when things return to normal, or it can end at the time of death.

"However, in the second type of agreement, a *Durable Power of Attorney,* only a non-incapacitated person can enter into this type of agreement. This is an agreement that endures, even after the once non-incapacitated principal becomes incapacitated. In a Durable Power of Attorney, the non-incapacitated principal names another person to act on his or her behalf in the event that they become unable to manage their own affairs. The person named will then not have to petition a court formally to declare the principal incapacitated."

I fiddle with a pen in my hand, loosening and tightening the cap. I don't have any paper to write on. It doesn't matter. I know what incapacitated means. I feel incapacitated here in this office. I'm not a lawyer. I tell myself to focus--*focus.* I shift in my big padded leather chair and make eye contact with John, hoping I haven't missed anything. I lean forward and place the pen on his desk.

John glances at the pen but continues his explanation. "Of course, in our state the RCW uses words 'mentally incompetent' rather than incapacitated."

"God, that sounds even more serious than incapacitated."

"You may be right, but either way it means the person is unable to carry on their affairs. As you can see, the choice of that trusted person is not made casually. But, when the choice has been made, if the condition of the principal deteriorates, it will not be necessary for the family to seek formal guardianship--a process that takes time, often results in high legal fees and is more restrictive on the rights of the principal."

I myself feel incapacitated. I would like to pick the pen up again, but I refrain. I shift to the other side of the big padded chair. "So, John, neither type of a Power of Attorney is applicable to Malfaits. Right?"

"Right. Your parents really should have granted this legal power to one of you, or some other person of their choice, in their more cognizant years."

"Well, John, in their own way, I think they thought they took care of that when they named me as an Executor in their will, but that doesn't seem to apply in this current situation."

"No, it definitely does not. That doesn't carry any power to it as long as the person is living. An executor is just a designation for a person to clear up all the legal affairs after the loved one's death.

"My advice, based on what I've heard today, is that the only option for you and Rolf at this stage of your parents' mental and physical functioning is a *Guardianship*. And that legal procedure should be pursued in Ridgeview where your folks have lived for over fifty years."

"Okay, so now I know a little bit about a Durable Power of Attorney, and that is not appropriate at this time. I have to tell you I know even less about a Guardianship. What does that entail?"

"Well, they're a bit more complicated. A *Guardianship* is a legal relationship between an individual who is incapacitated, the ward, and a person who is given the right to act on their behalf, the guardian. Unless the court limits the guardianship relationship, the guardian will manage all of the ward's personal, legal and financial affairs. In a guardianship the ward may lose some basic rights such as the right to vote, hold a business license, marry or enter into contracts. Most of the restrictions are probably not relevant to your case, but it definitely would give you the right to do the financial management you need to do and which your parents seem to expect you to do."

"Oh, man, I don't know about the loss of voting rights, John. I'd bet they'd be very aware of that one--and they would be adamantly opposed to giving that up. Even in their current mental state they are opposed to giving up any power. Mother has expressed that specifically to her banker."

"Betty, that's sort of typical behavior on the part of the person who most needs the help. That's why it has to go through a court process."

"But, John, what if I feel I just can't go to court to do this?"

"If you feel you can't do this, and if the deterioration in both of your parents continues--and it most likely will--there may be a point in time when they come to the attention of the court anyway. It could be via law enforcement, public complaints, death of one or the other of them, or something else. For whatever reason, they may then become a ward of the court, and the court will have to appoint a guardian for them. After a family member, the courts next look to financial institutions and guardianship agencies when appointing a legal guardian. Most states have a provision for a public guardian when no one else is available or appropriate. Sometimes that may be Social Services, non-profit agencies, or volunteer programs."

"Oh, God, I wouldn't want that to happen to them....Somehow we've just got to get this guardianship thing done."

"Betty, I'm going to personalize for just a moment. For whatever reason Rolf seems to be resistant to following a legal pathway. You need to consider that you may have to pursue a guardianship on your own. I sincerely believe that based on your parents' mental and physical functioning as you've described today the only option is a *Guardianship*--and--Betty, if your brother won't cooperate with you, just know that it doesn't require both siblings to participate."

I leave another attorney's office in a lonely, teary-eyed quandary. I *know* this guardianship thing has to be done. I *know* it in my head, and I *know* it in my heart. I go directly home, pick up the telephone, and call the Ridgeview attorney. I ask him to send me the necessary paperwork. Brother or no brother, I am going to pursue gaining a guardianship for my parents. I am going to legally and publicly through the superior court system declare that my parents are "incompetent persons as defined by RCW 11.88.010 by reason of mental confusion and disorientation."

I hate myself this day!

I hate Rolf more!

CHAPTER 15

Procrastination

THE OFFICIAL PAPER work arrives a couple of days later. I practically wear the papers out reading and re-reading them, smudging them with my tears.

> *Dear God, where are You? I need You so. I can't do this by myself. I want Rolf to help me. I need to have him work with me. Dear God, I don't really hate him. I'm sorry I even thought that, but I'm so angry and frustrated with him. I've always loved him, and I love him now! But I'm having a hard time working with him as things presently exist. We are both Malfaits' children. He must want good care for them. He must want them to be safe and clean. He knows their living conditions are deplorable. They deserve better. Please, God!*

I escape into classroom responsibilities. I do my Christmas shopping. Don and I attend holiday parties and programs. I make sure our family celebrates another new year, and that we all recall the good of the past year and express hope for better in the coming year. I do everything possible to stay upbeat, to keep my social mask in place, and to keep my anguish and embarrassment hidden. I don't want anyone to know I come from such a dysfunctional family and from mentally incompetent parents.

All my efforts bring false security. There is no comfort. The guardianship application papers haunt me with all of their official specifics. They lie in a smudged manila envelope in the back bedroom under Christmas decorations and gift wrapping debris. I fall asleep and I awaken visualizing snakelike black letters slithering into word pictures. *Superior Court. Incompetent. Malfaits.* I leave the paperwork under the holiday clutter in the back bedroom through the month of January. I am miserable and empty behind my social, professional, and career masks.

CHAPTER 16

∞∞∞

Financial Fury & Frantic Phone Calls

THURSDAY, FEBRUARY 1ST, 6:15 AM shrill ringing of the phone shatters the last few minutes before my usual wake-up time. Rolf is calling. I must be dreaming. He launches into an agitated dissertation, "Man, it's awful down here! I can't get anything through their thick heads. I can't reason with either one of them."

"Geez, Rolf, it's 6:15 in the morning. You were supposed to call me two months ago. You promised! Is this your best time?"

"Yeah, yeah. Well, I've been busy. I figured you'd know I was busy."

"Other people get busy too, you know."

"Well, let me tell you something, little sister, I'm ready to bail out of here!"

I pull the comforter up against the harsh morning chill. "Well, I can tell *you* something. I figure promises are meant to be kept. I waited three hours for that phone call that never came on November 24, 1989, between 1:00 and 3:00 PM. It's really hard for me to be too sympathetic to your situation when you expect all the understanding to go your way--mine and theirs."

"Jesus, Betty, you just don't know how bad it is."

"I *do* know how bad it is, but what's so urgent today at this hour?"

"Well, I thought we were getting along okay there for a while. Dad's pretty spacey, but I thought I could at least talk to Mom. I thought she was coming around. She opened an account out at Fibex, and we were supposed to use it for emergencies and end-of-the-month food money. She put my name and hers on it. Well, a few days ago I got this notice of an unpaid traffic citation I got while I was long-haul

167

trucking. You know, it was no big deal. I just didn't have a medical card in the truck with me while I was driving. The card was headed south in my friend Mike's truck, but I was headed north. Anyway, this perfectionist road-warrior-cop gave me a citation, and it cost me $135.00. But it was Dad who screwed it up."

"And how, pray tell, could he screw up *your* traffic citation?"

"Well, you know how he's always screwing up the mail. He messed it up as usual, and I didn't receive the proper notice about this ticket. Now, I'll be damned if I'm gonna spend another night in jail like I did before, because Dad messed up handling the mail. So, I went down and wrote out a check for the amount of the ticket."

"You paid for *your* traffic citation on *their* bank account?"

"Yes, I did! You know, Mom said it was for *emergencies*, and that was damned well an emergency!"

"I'm not so sure of that, Rolf."

"I told Mom I was gonna be doin' that, but she says I didn't tell her any such thing. She says I didn't ask nobody nothin'. Then she goes down to the credit union and checks and finds out I took out a couple hundred bucks."

"I thought you said the ticket was for $135.00."

"Well, yeah, but I had some expenses to get the whole thing straightened out."

"So then what happened?"

"Well, Mom was mad as an old wet hen, and she goes back to the credit union and closes the account. She's been at me all week about the missing money from the checking account and other missing cash. You know what I mean? Anything that's missing she blames on me."

"Yes, I know that feeling. It sounds as if you're all getting on each others' nerves. Sometimes I think they're calmer and do better if they're by themselves. Couldn't you go some place for a while?"

"Yeah, I think I'm gonna make a little trip down to my place at Newcastle for a couple of days and let things quiet down. I can't go 'til next week though."

"I think that would be good for all of you. I've got to run and get to school."

A couple of days later I get another 6:15 AM wake-up call from Rolf. "You ain't gonna believe this. Mom and Dad went down to SeaFirst and closed out their bank account there, too."

"Did they tell you that?"

"Well, no, but I been makin' some inquiries, and I been havin' 'em show me their purses and their money. I'm tryin' to keep track of where the money goes. There was $100.00 missing, and Mom said they used it to open a new account at SeaFirst that didn't have my name on it."

"You know, Rolf, they can do whatever they want with their money and their checks. You don't have any right to demand to see their purses or anything else."

"Yeah, I know, so the guy at the bank tells me. But I gotta be able to keep track of things around here. And I'll tell you this, when Dad's pension check came, I just snagged it. At least that's $193.67 that I'll know where it is."

"You had better not cash that, Rolf. It's made out to Dad."

"You may be right, but when we run out around here, I'll damned well know where that much is."

The early morning gets later as Rolf vents. It's a good thing for me a snow storm had its own sort of fury during the night and school is on a late schedule.

Rolf continues, "Listen, do you think you could talk to Mom and help get this thing calmed down?"

"Do you want me to come down this weekend?" To myself I'm saying, *What's wrong with me? Why do I always give in to him?*

"That would be even better."

"I'm free this weekend. I could come tomorrow. But, Rolf, despite their confusion and disorientation, I understand their anger. I don't see how your traffic citation or possible arrest was their fault, and you have no right to hold back their checks. I'm not going to defend your action in something like that. *And*, you for sure had better not try to cash that check!"

"Well, Dad's goofy, but he ain't stupid. He understands how to save my mail.

"Rolf, I think for you to have your mail arrive at 516 is irresponsible on your part. You have your own place in Newcastle, or you could get a Ridgeview P.O. Box. Mom and Dad shouldn't have to sort your mail at all."

After I hang up the phone, I dress for school and check the snow reports for the weekend and driving conditions on the Interstate. The phone rings again.

"Betty, can you get down here right away? Rolf has taken all our money?"

"Mother, Mother--wait a minute. Are you all right?"

"Hell, no, I'm not all right! Can you get down here? Rolf has drawn out all of our savings. He's spent it all on himself."

"Mother, you must have misunderstood."

"I did not misunderstand. He took everything out of our bank."

"Where are you?"

"I'm at Ruth's. I can't make calls from home."

"Is he keeping you from the phone?"

"No, but he listens to everything. Anyway, I *had* to call from here. We can't make long distance calls from the house. The long distance service is turned off."

"Did you pay the phone bill? Or, did you forget how many times you've called your sisters and brother in Texas and Virginia and just run up a big bill?"

"I don't know what happened. I just know the phone service is shut off. I don't have any money, and Rolf has used it all up from our bank."

"Mother, that can't be. I'm sure we can work all this out. I'm getting ready to come down tomorrow. Are you okay until then?"

"Yes, I'm fine."

As I hang up the phone, I don't think anybody is fine. I don't know if anyone is even safe. I don't know if *all* their savings means the $200.00 Rolf told me about, or if it means *all their savings*. I don't even know if they have any savings.

CHAPTER 17

What's an Ad Litem Figure?

THE NEXT DAY in Ridgeview I meet Rolf at The Sterling Motel, where he has been staying. He says it's a temporary arrangement. I do not go into his room, but from the doorway it looks rather permanent to me, or at least long-term. After seeing his car, he may be living in it. It's stacked floor to ceiling with clothes, papers, books, ropes, and tools. The Sterling may be only now and then, but Rolf is very friendly with the man and woman who are the proprietors. They seem to know all about our family situation and have lots of sympathy for Rolf, and he is not at all hesitant to ask them to give me the same commercial rate they give him.

When they grant his request, I breathe a sigh of relief. I haven't been able to sleep in Malfaits' house since the "Taco experience," and I've had to pay regular rates at a nearby motel when I stay over in Ridgeview. The appearance and decor of my new weekend abode is considerably less than its namesake, but the price is right and the sheets are clean. Besides, there is comfort in knowing these less-than-sterling walls have experienced the whole gamut of life's intimacies. Whatever my experiences in the realm of bizarre have been, or will be, it will be nothing new in this place.

After I am settled in, Rolf and I drive out to one of his favorite local restaurants, The Whistlestop, where we plan to have dinner. We spend the next three and a half hours in my truck in the restaurant parking lot. We talk more than we have since the great family rift and the nasty accusations that were cast at my children and my husband all those years ago.

"Rolf, I don't agree with you at all in regard to this recent check-ticket thing. We both know Mother and Dad are difficult to help, or manage, or whatever it is we are trying to do. Despite their fierce independence, the fact is they're senile. However, I do believe their recent anger is justifiable, senile or not."

"Sis, none of this would have happened if they'd manage the mail the way I want them to. It *is* their fault, and *I* think they should pay!"

"Rolf, they shouldn't pay! Malfaits don't owe you shit!"

"What does that mean?"

"It means they *shouldn't* pay! It means over the years they have *helped* you far more than they were ever obligated to do as parents. I know you had bad luck with your finances and loss of your logging truck after the Mt. St. Helens eruption, but those things are not their fault and not their responsibility. You've been back to work in long-haul trucking for some time now. You need to quit feeling sorry for yourself and quit being such a taker. You need to get on with your life."

"Well, yeah maybe you're right, but it ain't that easy."

"I know that, Rolf, but you've done really well in the past, and you have a lot of varied skills. Over the years you've made good money working in the woods, in fishing, and on the Alaskan Pipeline. You've always been a hard worker. You can do it again.

"Yeah, well, I have been pretty busy with this long haul driving, but that doesn't help me get my truck back. I'm always doing for someone else."

"That's fine, but you are working, and it's my understanding that mortgage payment of $468.90 per month was for *your* debt consolidation. When you got back to work, you were to be responsible for it. You need to do that, and the time is long overdue. After Dad had the stroke both of them insisted you were *going* to do that. They say that *now*. They *believe* that! Rolf, you have to realize when they pay that debt for you, it takes over one-fourth of their monthly income. You have not upheld your end of the bargain. Malfaits, even in their senility, understand their house is the collateral for that loan. What they want most is to live as long as possible in their own house. It's not fair they must live month to month in fear of losing their home."

"Well, yeah, but I've had hard times, and I needed the help."

"Rolf, tickets, lawsuits, legal battles, financial debt consolidation--the list of what you consider *help* is endless. It's beyond help! Those things should be your responsibility *alone*! You've been working. You should be paying. If you can't pay, there is such a thing as bankruptcy, you know."

"Yeah, well I can tell you one thing, when I get my feet on the ground, I'll settle that Fibex debt once and for all if I die trying!"

For several moments Rolf's response hangs between us in hollow hypocrisy. I don't think either one of us believes his pledge will come to fruition. It will probably dissipate as easily as the steam on the truck windows.

"Rolf, time is running out. Mount St. Helens blew in 1980. That pretty well took out the timber industry in this state. I understand your disaster and your need for help, but that's over. It's been ten years. How long do you need to get on your feet?"

"Well, I'm gonna make it right by them. I'll tell you something else I'm gonna make right, and that's to find out who stole their money way back that summer."

"You've certainly said enough mean, derogatory things about my children and my husband that it's pretty obvious whom you think stole their money."

"I never said one word of anything mean or derogatory about you or your kids."

"Rolf, Rolf, how can you sit there and say that? What do you suppose caused the separation of our family from Grandma and Grandpa and a lack of communication over these past five years or more?"

"Hell, I don't know where you've been or why you've been away."

"*You* don't know why we've not been around Malfaits' house for all these years? I don't suppose you remember that long-ago telephone conversation you and I had in the middle of the night?"

"What long ago phone conversation in the middle of the night? What are you talking about?"

"I'm talking about the call *you* made to me after the theft incident. You called me one night at one o'clock in the morning and proceeded to tell me what you thought about who really stole Malfaits' money. Then you told me what *I* should be doing to find out who did the deed. You even said if *you* had my kids for a few minutes on your own, you would kick some of the shit right out of them, and you would get to the bottom of the disappearance of the money. And, if it wasn't their doing, you'd be looking to kick the shit out of whoever else had been near that room. You know I was sitting in the living room that day when you were in the bedroom. I sat there in pain waiting to go to the bathroom. You also know Don was in and out of the house that day. Rolf, you know damned well what you were implying, and so do I!" I cover my face with my hands and shake my head vigorously as if that might somehow shake some degree of clarity into my brain. I suck in a big breath and turn to face him, "Listen, Rolf, at the time I explained to you what you were saying about my children and what you were suggesting about me or my husband was assault--and if you *ever* dared actually lay a hand or a foot on them, or on any of us, that would be battery, and I would see your ass in court."

"Where do you get this stuff? I never called you at any such hour with any implications like that. I never said anything like that about you or anyone in your family."

"Rolf, Rolf--I've annotated those conversations. If you like, I can go back and look it up, and you can read it in my journals for yourself."

"I'm tellin' ya, I never said anything like that."

I want to rip open the truck door, wrench my notebook from behind the seat where I have been sitting, and force him to read it, but I simply comment, "Rolf, annotations don't lie. Journals or diaries are acceptable evidence in a court of law. My recall of events is in those journals. Furthermore, I intend in some way to annotate the experiences of this weekend, at least from my perspective. I've been doing annotations ever since, as you say, 'things began to get goofy around here'."

Rolf is quiet for a moment. "Well, that's probably good. Someone should be writing stuff down."

My journal annotations have taken Rolf by surprise, but he makes no admission of lying to me about the phone call, and he makes no promises in regard to being responsible for the huge debt. He simply says, "Well, we better call it a night here pretty soon." He opens the truck door and slips out. Leaning back in he tells me, "Oh, by the way, I made an appointment for the both of us to see that lawyer, Mr. Hinson. It's tomorrow at 3:30 in the afternoon. Is that okay with you?"

It's my turn to be surprised. "Yeah, sure."

With no comment and no dinner, I start the engine, turn on the defroster to remove at least some of the fog of the past hours. I ease the truck out of the parking lot and head back to The Sterling.

He made an appointment?

The next day I meet Rolf at the attorney's office. I don't see his old car, and there are no cars in the lot next to the building. I don't know how he got there, but he's standing on the sidewalk near the front door.

As I approach I am more aware than ever as to how different we are and how those differences alienate us from one another. It hasn't always been like this.

Rolf yanks open the door and goes in. I follow. We approach the counter, I in my classic sweater-slacks teacher attire and Rolf in his disheveled, filthy logger garb. His beard bushes out in gray, greasy irregular coils. Long, straggly wisps of hair form a dingy, yellowish-gray ring around his bald spot and hang over his shirt collar at the back of his head. He has no teeth in front, and when he speaks his other teeth further back in his mouth look dark and rotten. His clothes, or perhaps his body, give off unpleasant odorous wafts mixed with diesel and gas fumes. Two secretaries look up from their work, eyes widening until they look like twins wearing glasses without really having glasses on. They recover their professional demeanor quickly. One of them turns back to her paper work, and the other one offers us coffee.

Shortly Mr. Hinson steps into the waiting room and greets us. Before introductions are complete Rolf speaks, "Contrary to what my appearance might look like, I ain't no hippie. I ain't no drug addict. And I ain't no off-duty Santa Claus."

Mr. Hinson shakes hands with each of us and comments, "Razor blades are definitely expensive."

As we proceed into Mr. Hinson's office I remind him, "I received the guardianship paperwork you sent after I was in the last time, but I wanted Rolf to come in with me so we could both learn more about the guardianship process. Besides, Rolf wants to update you on some recent events that are pertinent to our problem, since he's been around Mom and Dad's house more often than I lately."

Instantly Rolf takes over the dialogue. "You know, just the other day was your real typical example of the kind of stuff that happens all the time. Dad went out to walk Taco--it's really my dog--he's a Siberian Husky. It was more like who was walkin' who, you know? Anyway, Taco got away from him, and Dad followed him down the street. He got down to the end of the block, and Taco ran on across the street. Dad, he hurries after him and missed the step down off the curb and fell out into the street. The man who lives across the way sees him fall, and he hurries over to help him up, but Dad thinks it's some guy trying to rob him, so he began to fight him. The old lady who lives in that corner house is watching these two old guys struggle, and she calls the cops." Rolf chuckles and takes a breath. "Oh, hell, I guess it wasn't really funny, you know? The police arrive, and they pull over where these two old geezers are still arguing. They got the red and blue lights flashing and the whole cop thing goin' on. They manage to get both old guys settled down and figure out what happened, you know? They send the one old man back across the street to his house. Taco, he comes back across the street to where all the excitement if goin' on, and one of the cops walks Dad and the dog down the block to the house. Dad brings the guy right on in, and I happened to be there. The cop kind of noses around a little, and the other one comes into the house, too. They talk to me about the deplorable condition of the house and of Mom and Dad. They said they'd have to take Dad down to St. Mary's Hospital and have him checked out because of the fall and because of the call from the old lady. So, off they go with Dad sitting in the backseat of the cop car. Damn, you know, he was down there in that hospital five days. I guess he had some cracked ribs and I don't know what else. Mom says it was only three days, but I know it was really five."

It's my turn to be shocked, as this is the first I've heard of this hospital trip. I ponder dates and times as Rolf continues.

"I used the time that Dad was in the hospital to do some cleaning around the place. I took two of the old cars off the driveway to avoid police action on an old abatement notice. That's one of the things the cop brought up when he was in the house. Then me and my friend Shortie cleaned out that whole driveway area from the front street to the garage door. Wouldn't you know Mom placed herself right there in the middle of our work area and hollered the whole time, 'Rolf, you've got your dad flat on his back in that hospital and here you go hauling off his stuff. Those cars are valuable, and those tires, too. Dad needs those.' Shortie and me just kept hauling."

I couldn't resist and I broke into his monolog. "Rolf, cleaning up that kind of stuff is necessary, but I'm not sure I can agree with you on doing it like that. I didn't even know about Dad's hospital trip, and I'm not sure you should be doing what you and Shortie did with their property--at least not how you did it. I know it's all junk and needs to be moved, but some of those things really are their treasures. It seems like the job could be done without totally ignoring them and running over them."

"Well, that's where you're wrong, little sister. When me and Shortie finished, we had his truck loaded up pretty good. I had Mom give me the cash to pay for dumping, and I gave the change to Shortie for his help."

I turn in my chair to face Rolf more directly. "Okay, Rolf, I get your point, but I'm going to agree to disagree with your method of cleaning things up *and* with your method of barging into their finances like that, especially with cash."

Mr. Hinson glances at his watch. "Time is moving along on us here. I've made an appointment for the two of you to meet with a possible court-appointed *ad litem* person. He's a necessary element in a guardianship proceeding, and he will explain his role to you. He's an attorney whose office is located in the building just to the north of this one. He's expecting you in a few minutes."

As Rolf and I leave and walk up the street to the second appointment, he growls at me, "Sis, all that shit had to be removed from the front yard and the driveway. I couldn't do it by myself, and I couldn't expect Shortie to work for nothin'. I'm tellin' ya, you just don't know what it's like at the house!"

"I don't know a lot of things, Rolf."

I clinch my teeth until I feel pain in my jaw, squelching any further response to his lame one-sided defense of his actions. My nostrils flare as I suck in each short breath and expel the used air. My eyes squint and I force myself to look straight ahead, concentrating on the nothingness of the pavement. I'm thankful it's a short walk and we are admitted immediately to Mr. Mason's office without even having time to sit down.

Mr. Mason has discussed our situation with Mr. Hinson, and he proceeds immediately to give an explanation of the *ad litem* role in pursuit of a guardianship. "I will not be working for you. I'm a representative of the court. My job will be to oversee the rights and properties of the parties for whom you are seeking the guardianship and to share my perceptions with the court at various times throughout the duration of the guardianship."

He pauses to ask if we have any questions. His quick overview didn't really sink in. I feel entangled in legalese, anger, frustration, and whatever other emotions are still causing a painful tightening of my jaw. But before I can formulate even a semi-intelligent question, Rolf launches another diatribe, relating several episodes he feels justify the pursuit of a guardianship. He gives his rendition of Dad's screw-up of the mail that caused him time in jail a while back; and he runs from that story into a description of Dad's latest mail screw-up and *his* need to write a check on Malfaits' emergency account for his most recent citation in order to prevent his having to spend another night in jail.

Old Parents and Purple Tulips

I can stand it no longer.

Anger wins out and I explode. "For God's sake, Rolf, we're supposed to be here to figure out what's best for Mom and Dad--not what's best for you! I don't care how senile they are nor how deplorable their living conditions are, you don't have any right to be writing checks out of their account for your personal benefit. Your tickets are your business! You shouldn't be paying for such things from their personal funds. I don't think I can *ever* have my name on some guardianship checking account with you. I will share any other guardianship decisions pertaining to our parents--their living conditions, their health, or whatever--but I will not--repeat--*will not ever*--share a checking account intended for their benefit with you!"

"What the hell do you mean by that?"

"I mean just that. I will not share a guardianship checking account with you. You have a history of financial irresponsibility. You don't keep a checking account for yourself. You don't keep a budget book. You don't pay attention to deadlines. You prefer to do everything in cash yourself--and for them, too. No one can tell what's been paid or hasn't been paid. Mother opened a checking account with you, and you sat right here and related how you used those funds to rescue yourself. I could never agree to that. It isn't right. I will share personal decisions in this process but not a check-book!"

The attorney's office feels like a blast furnace. The heated atmosphere dissipates into momentary silence, but unspoken embers pelt against my sweaty skin. I sense Mr. Mason's desire to get us both out of his office. He manages to do so by indicating in a quiet, professional voice that we can work out details of the guardianship as we go along. He'll need to see us again, and he'll call and let us know when.

I still don't know exactly what a guardianship actually entails. I don't feel like knowing any more right now, and I don't think Mr. Mason feels like explaining. I already have the application papers. I know they need to be filled out.

Rolf and I are politely ushered out.

On the sidewalk our argument erupts anew into an enraged verbal battle. Rolf shouts at me, "I don't know why you have to be such a God-damned know-it-all!"

"Rolf, if this thing is a partnership, then each of us has to do the things that we are good at. I can do the bill paying. I can keep a budget book. I can pay things on time and show accounting for everything. I can do yard work. I can do the washing and grocery shopping. I'm willing to do my part to make this thing work."

"Where do you get off saying I never pay my bills? That's a God-damned lie!"

"Rolf, you have a history of poor financial management. You never pay on time. Right now your box of mail in their house is full of unopened bills."

"Well, the point is that I *always* pay. Yeah, it may not be on a specific time schedule, but I always pay!"

"Rolf, that's not how the business world works, and you know it. When you don't pay on the specific schedule, you get bad credit. Then you're stuck when the time comes for you to need credit. That's how you got Mom and Dad into that consolidation mortgage in the first place. You got yourself in way over your head, and you didn't pay. You couldn't get credit from *anyone* in this town."

"That's bullshit! There was a time when my name *was* credit."

"You know what--that may be, but you couldn't even get credit *with* your senile parents now!"

At this moment a friend of Rolf's ambles up. Rolf abruptly turns off his anger and turns on an air of ingratiating congeniality. I am ignored and definitely not introduced. I stand behind him in numb angry silence. When the conversation with his friend is concluded, he and I walk on toward my truck. I have to hurry to keep pace with him. Once inside the truck, he releases another irate outburst, "I don't know what makes you think you know so fuckin' much?"

I lower my voice and try to be calm as I fumble with the keys. "I really mean it, Rolf. I won't have my name on a checking account with you. It just won't work." I turn the key and start the engine, but Rolf isn't through shouting at me.

"Are you so damned paranoid you think I'd steal from it?"

I move the gear into place and turn to check traffic. Rolf's face is scarlet and he looks as if he may explode at any moment. I return the gear to neutral. "Rolf, not wanting to do a checking account with you doesn't make you a thief. It's saying you're careless. You pay things in cash. You don't pay your bills on time. You say you'll pay them when you can. Rolf, that would drive me crazy. I couldn't live that way. I don't live that way. I have *never* bounced a check. That doesn't mean I'm better. It just means I carry on my business differently than you do."

"That may be good, but I do pay my bills--" Rolf leans toward me and barks, "And I ain't no thief like some people!"

I turn off the engine and face him squarely. "Now, wait a minute, Rolf.." My volume rises to match his. "Be specific. Name a time when I have ever cheated you or misused your property, money, or anything else. Say it very specifically. What are you referring to? *Who* are you referring to?"

Rolf thrusts his body against the door frame and window and crosses his arms as if preventing them from pummeling me. His eyes squeeze into narrow slits, and he rages, "Get this thing going,, and take me back to the motel! I have a couple of things I gotta do. Get this truck headed back there--*now!*"

Seething silence engulfs the cab of the truck for the few minutes it takes to reach The Sterling. I pull slowly to the curb. My clinched jaw is throbbing. Rolf throws his shoulder against the truck door, as if the door release is not sufficient. He gets out and slams the door. With his back to me, and already in stride toward the motel, he shouts, "I'll see you at the house in an hour!"

I drive away. I probably will never see him again, and that may be just as well. Now he definitely won't be cooperative toward a guardianship or any other plan that involves working together.

I continue on to Malfaits' house, where I am greeted with the usual ordinary bizarre banter. My jaw relaxes in the comfort of this quieter oblivion.

Rolf arrives about an hour later. He acts as if nothing happened. In fact, he is quite pleasant, and we all sit around the cluttered kitchen table and discuss the tax delinquency problem with the Whidbey Island land. We all agree we will go to the bank tomorrow and have a check drawn to pay at least one year's taxes. I don't ask what happened to the church bond money that was to be used for that purpose. I volunteer to drive to Whidbey and do this task in person. Paying in person seems to appease all of them. For me, it means wasted time, a hundred mile trip, and two ferry rides. Oh well, if that's going to settle some of the furor, then I simply will do it.

Secondly, we agree to get a certified check made out to Neilson Insurance Company for an insurance policy that pays the difference between what Medicaid covers for Dad and what total hospital or other medical charges might be. Rolf has driven to Portland and paid this bill in person previously, an occasion which prevented cancellation of the policy at one time. Mom and Dad both express appreciation for Rolf's vigilance in watching out for this bill, paying it in person, and knowing right where to go. Thus this task is a natural for Rolf to do. I, of course, have some reservations about their trust level with cash, but I say nothing as silence seems a better option allowing us to settle on a financial plan for other bill-paying. Besides, hunger is becoming a priority.

I make a quick trip to a local drive-in and return with burgers and shakes, which we all share in the midst of Taco, the cats, and wafts of fecal residue. Some from the animals. Some from the remains of the day's activities. I join my family members at the cleared-off end of the kitchen table and ravenously chomp off huge hunks of my burger and choke it down much as they do, squeezing the bun tightly and licking the greasy drippings from my fingers. I don't know whether I washed my hands or not. I don't care. I silently tease my own brain about possible genetic relationships of eating habits. I slurp the last of my milkshake in noisy, bubbly intake as I rise from the cluttered table to make my departure.

Mother and Dad are unaware I am staying at a motel. They simply say goodnight.

Rolf follows me out to my truck and asks for a ride to the motel where he makes himself at home in my room until about 10:30 PM before he finally goes to his own room. During this time he visits pleasantly with no mention of the appointments with either of the attorneys earlier in the day. It's as if that part of the day didn't happen. He rattles incessantly but in calm tones, mostly about his long-haul truck work. He gives me a rehash of the ordeal of losing his log truck. He tells a bizarre story of reporting a man from Newcastle as a potential murder suspect to the Green River Task Force. The FBI actually picked the man up and held him for questioning based on Rolf's evidence. Is that possible? He tells me of his special work in Ridgeview and how he makes reports to the County Drug Task Force. All this information is new and strange to me. Is any of this plausible?

CHAPTER 18

———✸———

A Family Financial Plan

THE NEXT MORNING Rolf comes by my motel room at precisely 9:00 AM. We leave together and go directly to Malfaits. They are just getting up and have forgotten we are coming. Our first event of the day is a noisy recall of yesterday's plan for bill-paying followed by an equally noisy search for the recent Social Security and pension checks.

Finally we seem ready, but that is not to be. Mother insists all four of us must go. Neither Rolf nor Dad want to oblige, and I can't take all four of us in my truck. After another round of loud family dialog, Mother wins. We clear out the seats in one of Dad's old cars, and all of us set off to the bank. I drive. Mother sits in front, a combination navigator and driver-trainer instructor. Dad and Rolf sit in the back seat, each staring out his respective window into his own personal oblivion.

At the bank our bizarre familial unit shuffles through the big glass doors, Mother first, then Dad, Rolf, and me. Each of us struggles independently against the weight of the heavy glass door. In past years Dad or Rolf would have held the door for Mother. Or, if it was just Mother and me, I would have held the door for her.

Not today.

Inside the bank we take our place in a crowded customer line. People in front of us turn to look to see what wafted in. People behind step back. People in nearby lines look over and stare. Mother stands beside Dad clutching her black bulging shoulder strap purse tightly against her once light tan London Fog raincoat--a quality lady, a quality raincoat, both now tattered and filthy. Dad looks straight ahead, arms hanging loosely at his sides. He is wearing a nasty deerskin jacket melded to his body by years of hard wear. His attire is completed by his favorite dress-up wide-brimmed hat, the hat-band permeated by a greasy ring from longtime use of Brylcreem, and more recently plain Vaseline, in combing his thinning hair. The front of the hat brim bears smudged fingerprints from years of turning it down and bending it to curve a little lower over the right eye than the left.

Rolf stands behind Dad, a bushy, wild-looking man in logging garb, puffed up to his fullest height, arms crossed over his chest. His glances flick from the counter back to our family with occasional wheezy, impatient sighs.

I stand behind Mother, odd-man-out in my classic teacher attire of casual tan slacks and an unobtrusive matching striped sweater.

I'm in this family.

I'm not in this family.

I love this family.

I hate this family.

What a sad comedy!

Mother keeps us all shuffling up a step at a time toward the teller, as if we are children visiting the bank for the first time. When it's our turn, she asks, "May I see Mr. Tim, please? He's that nice looking, helpful young man who worked with me the other day when I was doing some business here."

The teller departs and returns shortly, directing us to Mr. Tim's desk.

Mother and Dad seat themselves. Rolf and I stand.

Mr. Tim, a pleasant young man in banker pin stripes, takes his place behind the desk. "Good morning, Mrs. Malfait. How are you today?"

"Just fine, thank you. I want you to meet my family. You already know my husband, Roger. These are our kids, Rolf and Betty.

Mr. Tim smiles and nods to Rolf and me with no indication he has met either one of us previously.

Mother continues, "I want to cash some checks today, and I need to get a couple of cashier's checks. I also want to take care of the business you and I talked about the other day."

Rolf pulls a sheaf of papers from his overstuffed shirt pocket and sorts through them, finally drawing out Dad's pension check, "Here, Dad, you better get this one cashed too."

"Oh, Jesus, I've been wondering where that was."

In the next few minutes Mr. Tim cashes their checks and follows Mother's directions, putting some of the money in their account and the remainder in a stack in front of her.

Mother counts the money and looks up, "Now, Mr. Tim, I want you to take Rolf's name off that new account and add Betty's name to it--today."

Beside me I hear Rolf's sudden raspy intake of air. He shifts from one Romeo-clad foot to the other and clenches his arms tighter across his chest, exhaling a noisy sigh of frustration. I am surprised by Mother's request. I stand in frozen silence. Is this really happening? Is she really this lucid? Will tomorrow be total oblivion and she'll have us all down here to change the names back again?

Mother continues, "Yes, that's why we're *all* here today, and that's how Dad and I want it set up. The children are going to be helping us with bill-paying, and Betty's name will be the one on the account."

Mr. Tim shuffles several papers and cards and gets the necessary signatures. Meanwhile Mother counts out a stack of paper money and some change and piles it on top of the envelope containing the land tax statement. She licks her thumb and prepares another stack of money on top of the Neilson Insurance bill. She shoves each preparation across the desk toward Mr. Tim, "I also need a cashier's check for this tax bill on our Whidbey Island land and another cashier's check for this Neilson Insurance bill, which is for Dad's insurance for when Medicare doesn't cover things."

Mr. Tim glances over her statements, counts the money, and completes the requested tasks placing the checks in front of Mother. "Is there anything else today, Mrs. Malfait?"

"Just this." Mother remains seated, scoops up one of the bill statements and its accompanying check and turns toward Rolf. "Here, you take this Neilson check." She turns back to the desk and extracts a single bill from the pile of cash, " And, here--here's $50.00 cash for your expenses to go to Portland." She returns to the pile of cash and extracts a twenty and a ten and turns again to Rolf, "And here's $30.00 to pay the Cablevision bill."

Mr. Tim looks both embarrassed and puzzled but says nothing. Mother squints momentarily at the remaining stacks in front of her, and then picks up the other cashier's check and turns to me, "Here, Betty, here's the check for the Whidbey taxes."

Mother gathers the remaining money, crams it in her bulging purse, and thanks Mr. Tim. She and Dad rise and we all shuffle in odd tandem back through the heavy glass doors, each again struggling against the weight of the doors.

Once in the car Mother directs, "Betty, take us to the Fibex Credit Union. I have some business there, too."

Rolf adds, "Yeah, so do I. I need to find out about those checks they said would be coming."

Mother looks back over the car seat at him, "Those checks came, and I put them right in my nightstand by the bed. You won't be needing them."

In strained silence we travel the remaining few short blocks to the credit union where all four of us disembark and troop into the busy counter area, looking like raggedy ducklings obediently following a raggedy mama duck.

Rolf breaks rank and steps up to a free teller's station. "Yeah, I want to check on those checks for the Malfait account you were gonna mail to the house. Mom and I arranged for them here the other day. I'm worried because the folks closed that account, and Dad, here, might get confused over those checks coming to the house, and he might try to write a check on one of them."

Dad stirs from his obedient blank forward stare beside Mother and glances back over his shoulder to me, "Oh, shit."

The teller's bright red fingernails click on the computer keys. She looks back to Rolf and assures, "There were no checks mailed to Francine nor Roger Malfait--nor to Rolf Malfait. They will not be mailed, if that's what you'd like."

Rolf responds, "Well, that's good, because I've had to go down to their bank a couple of times lately and straighten out their account when Dad wrote checks for which they had no funds."

Dad again turns back toward me and chirps, "Oh, shit."

Rolf seems to be conducting the business. I am a dumb post. Mother and Dad stand in frozen silence. I'm not sure what's going on. A few minutes ago I heard Mother say the checks had come and they were in her nightstand. Now I hear the teller say they haven't been mailed out. I don't know how many accounts Malfaits have, which ones they've closed out, whether they have check-books, balances or whatever.

As we stand in the credit union line, Dad's utterances seem apropos. If he chirps it again, I think I'll join him.

My frustrated musing is shattered as Mother pushes past Rolf, steps up to the counter, and commands, "Mr. Malfait and I want you to take Rolf's name off all accounts here, and we want you to add Betty's name to those same accounts--today."

The clerk's eyelashes flutter their heavy burden of mascara as she scans through our ranks. No one speaks. No one moves. She obediently goes about changing the names on the account. I identify with her rote responses--without the mascara load--she obeys Mother, despite knowing something is wrong. I know many things are wrong, but here I stand also obeying Mother.

My sarcastic musing is interrupted. "Get over here, Betty, and sign these new signature cards."

I step forward as commanded. I can see there is about $1400 in the savings account, and I remind Mother, "You know the mortgage payment here is two months past due. I know that's not your debt, but you and Dad are responsible for it at this time." Behind me I hear another nasal wheeze from Rolf.

"I guess you're right." Mother turns to the teller. "Transfer enough from the savings to take care of that, please."

The clerk's bright red fingernails dance over the keys again, and she announces, "That's $942.80 with late fees, and I've transferred it to make those payments. Your savings balance is now $470.52."

Mother shakes her head lamenting, "I just never seem to get any-where with saving anything. It goes out faster than it comes in."

The clerk turns away to concentrate on comparing the information on the computer screen with the receipt she has printed out.

Mother's lamentation continues to blather toward a large gold loop ear-ring partially exposed from one side of the perfectly coifed clerk. "We all work so hard. Rolf works hard, too, and he's had so much bad luck. That costs us all. Well, Rolf is getting back on his feet. He'll be coming in here to make those payments to you himself soon."

The red fingernails make a dull click as they stab the receipt, push it across the desk, then retreat.

I don't dare question when *soon* will be.

An awkward silence prevails. The mascara-laden lashes remain steadily downward as the clerk rearranges pens, pencils, and paperwork in preparation for the next customer.

Mother turns from the counter and leads our pathetic tandem out of the credit union.

I feel a painful stab of compassion as I sense her eternal hope that Rolf will honor his debt agreement, but I think even in her disoriented thinking she knows it will never happen.

As we settle in the car, Mother again directs, "Betty, take us down to Chuck's Wagon. Dad needs to eat."

Eat is Dad's cue to harmonize with Mother. "Yes sir, we all need to sit down together as a family and have a bite to eat."

For me, eating is a low priority at this moment, nauseatingly low. "You guys--oh, please--I really appreciate the thought, but I need to get on the road headed home."

Dad's concern for hunger takes on new urgency. "I'm starving, and you must be too, kid. You gotta eat. You can't drive all that way on an empty gut. Come on, let's all sit down together as a family just for a few minutes."

Old Parents and Purple Tulips

I would adore sitting down as a family, but at the moment my whole being is racked with a multitude of emotions, none of which signal hunger. I'm a human blender pureeing guilt, shame, humility, humiliation, love, obedience, defiance, anger...

Rolf interrupts my mental list, "I'll tell you what, Sis, take us back to the house. You left your truck there. You could get on your way, and I'll bring Mom and Dad back down to Chuck's Wagon and eat with them. I'll pay for my own, of course, but I'll stay and eat with them."

My gastrointestinal blender gives a gigantic pulse. Someone who just allowed his mother and father to pay his overdue mortgage payments for some $942.00, plus give him generous expense money to *help* them pay *their* bills is now going to pay out $6.50 for his own meal and sit with them at Chuck's Wagon. As far as I'm concerned Rolf has been pulled up to the familial chuck-wagon for years. He is chronically seeking a free lunch. We will never be a family again, not even for just a bite to eat. I want out of here--out of this car, out of this town, out of this *family*!

I follow Rolf's directions back to 516.

CHAPTER 19

⸺⦾⸺

Dear God, What is Your Will?

ON MY TRIP home my mind wanders in and out of recalled happenings and conversations from the weekend. I can't help speaking aloud.

Dear God, who are these family strangers? What about Rolf reporting someone from Newcastle to the Green River Task Force as a possible murder suspect? Did he really do that? Was that reality, fantasy, or some kind of subtle intimidation to me? Sometimes I have been afraid of him. He's big. He's rough and crude. I don't like his philosophy in regard to guns. He has a huge collection, which he himself says is worth forty to fifty thousand dollars. He has been a collector since he was a teenager. He has a permit to carry a concealed weapon. He has a loaded 38 in his jeans pocket. I don't like all those guns in Malfaits' house. Most of the guns are in racks upstairs, and Mom and Dad are not likely to go up there, as the stairwell is pretty well blocked off. But there are guns around the downstairs living room and the bedroom areas. Then there's the loaded gun purchased from Wilma. None of us knows where that is.

I feel very insecure when Rolf speaks of his hatred for the guy who ruined him financially and stole his logging truck piece by piece, which was what brought about his debt crisis and the co-signed loan with Mom and Dad. Rolf said the other night he would like to kill that guy, and it's only the power of the Lord that holds him back from doing the deed. He says some day he'll get his opportunity, and it will be done in such a way there won't be any evidence pointing toward him.

If Rolf hates that person that much, he probably hates me even more. I have confronted Rolf on more basic issues than why he didn't pay for his truck repairs.

He says he has tried often to get Mom and Dad to clean up. But look at him! He looks as bad as they do--or worse! He seems to take pride in his eccentricity. When is it eccentricity, and when is it a mental problem? He works, but he seems to live off of them. What does he do with his money? Is he living in their house? Is he just in and out staying overnight sometimes?

Malfaits have made no major purchases for years. They have a bit over $1800 per month coming in, and even with the $468.90 going out for his mortgage, there's money there for home improvements and self improvements. They can't be eating over $1,000 per month! Rolf himself says, 'Their money just disappears. I can't keep track, but they ain't eatin' out that much!'

My mind races trying to absorb, rehash, assimilate—trying to make anything meaningful of my random thoughts. I have no tears at this moment, but beads of sweat form on my forehead and trickle down my temples making me itch. My armpits feel sticky. I am also aware that my mind is not the only thing racing. I lift my foot from the gas pedal, signal, and move into the slower freeway lane.

Dear God, please protect me in all that I do, including my driving.

Dear God, I am scared, partly because I really don't know what I'm doing. I am so alone. The parents who raised me are gone. The people who vaguely resemble them and bear the appropriate names are impossible to relate to except in bits and pieces. That fragmentation is enhanced by my inability to talk meaningfully with Rolf.

God, Rolf is not my brother of earlier times. He is not the off-the-wall fun companion of my youth. He is not the high school and college buddy of later years. He is not the cherished uncle whom I allowed my children to ride with all over Southwest Washington in his log truck. He is not the brother who has had a house key and an open welcome to any home Don and I have had. He is not my loving, caring friend.

God, he's bizarre, irrational. He's an easily enraged someone I don't even know. He seems to exercise no moral or ethical values, although he proclaims to be a child of God.

What god? You?

Dear God, I don't trust him, but he is my brother, and somehow I feel compelled to work with him in the role of parenting our parents.

Dear God, this is crazy! May I be guided by a higher power than my own! Please help me know what to do. What is Your will?

CHAPTER 20

Mexican Drug Deals, The Green
River Task Force, and Rolf

A COUPLE WEEKS later Rolf calls me collect. He seems calm but tired and frustrated. "I been workin' all week sortin' that stuff in the living room. I no sooner get it out in stacks and they come along and cover it over with newspapers or junk mail. It's damned hard to figure anything out when it keeps gettin' messed up."

I offer no sympathy. "Well, Rolf, I went to Whidbey and paid the taxes. Have you gone to Portland and paid the insurance?"

"No, no, I ain't been able to do that. I talked to a trucker friend out here at a truckstop on the Interstate, and he told me it snowed one of them freak snowstorms north of Portland. I'll go when the snow's over."

"Isn't the bill past due?"

"It's close, but there's a grace period. I still got time. Anyway, I've been pretty busy this week. I been doin' some observations, and I've had some meetings with the County Drug Task Force. You know, this whole neighborhood has gone to hell in a handcart. We got a bunch of Mexicans doing drug deals down here at the corner store. Actually, I can see 'em right now from this phone booth I'm callin' you from."

"How do you know they're doing drug deals?"

"Well, I seen this one guy down at The Sterling the other day. He's suave, sophisticated, drivin' a big Monte Carlo."

"That doesn't mean anything."

"Oh, but it does, 'cause I seen the same car here in the neighborhood. They think they're pretty clever, you know. I was makin' a phone call from this corner booth, and I seen this carload of Mexicans in that same Monte Carlo. Their activity was sorta suspicious when I spotted 'em the first time at The Sterling, so I wrote down the license number. Well, get this, the same guy I seen at The Sterling is drivin' the Monte Carlo, but the license plate number is different than it was when he was at motel."

"So you reported all this?"

"Yeah, the Task Force is investigating. They're real happy to get the info."

"Listen, Rolf, how are things going with Mom and Dad?"

"Actually that's what I called you about. The two of them went for coffee about noon to Ocean Espresso. When they came back, either Dad couldn't or wouldn't talk. He could walk okay, but he messed his underwear. I caught him going out to put it in the dumpster in the alley."

"What are you saying? Was he embarrassed and not talking because of messing himself, or has he had another stroke?"

"Hell, I don't know. Could have been either or both."

"Well, did you have him checked?"

"No, he seems okay now. He ate like he was okay a little bit ago. He ate a hamburger and a milkshake, and he stuffed it in like some starvin' kid."

"Rolf, I don't think that's really enough of a check."

"Well, everything seems pretty calm now. He don't wanta go to the doctor, and Mom don't want him to go to the hospital. He just kind of mumbles. I don't know exactly what he's sayin, but he makes it very clear he ain't goin' to no doctor. Actually he's resting now."

"I don't know, Rolf. To say he's eating fine and he doesn't *want* to see a doctor doesn't seem like enough of a check."

"Well, do you think I should run him down to the hospital?"

"You could call his doctor, but I'm sure he would need to see him—and I know what Dad would say to that. It's difficult enough to get him to cooperate for his regular medical appointments even when he says he feels good. Forcing him to go might make things worse. I guess I have to agree with you. Just let him rest."

Rolf calls back a few hours later to update me, "Mom's bein' about as big a problem as Dad is. I guess they're both okay—enough to be arguin'."

"What about his speech?"

"He's talkin' more. He's very emphatic he ain't goin' to no hospital. There's no mumblin' about that at all."

I agree with Rolf based on his telephone report, but I'm not sure. I know I couldn't do anything more with them if I were there. When they both agree on something, a brick wall forms around them. How can I expect Rolf to be any more successful? I feel guilty for not being there, but it's a three hour drive, and it's practically midnight now. If I were there, it would be a two-to-two standoff. And Rolf and I would lose.

Finally my own tiredness wins out, and I go to bed. I drift off with a fuzzy notion that if death comes stalking tonight, I can't do anything about it. And if their stubbornness measures up to its usual mark, they will defeat the Grim Reaper and survive by their shear orneriness—at least until the weekend and my regular trip time.

The weekend arrives and my drive down is nasty with heavy rain competing with tired, frayed window wiper blades, and the whole vehicle being buffeted steadily by a southerly wind. Hopefully this is not an omen for the rest of the weekend.

When I get to the house, Rolf's old junker car is out front. Malfaits are just getting up. Dad has his pants on backwards and is trying to change his socks which have urine and fecal matter on them. Mother is helping him, and despite her frustration with his attempted independence, she is doing so relatively quietly. Dad is happy to see me. He smiles, makes animated gestures, and mumbles pleasant, babyish sounds. He answers yes and no to my questions and speaks some short phrases very slowly. I am stunned by the scene, and I have a rush of guilt for not having come sooner. That instantly dissipates when I attempt to talk about going to the doctor or to the hospital. Dad shakes everything he can shake and does his nonsensical mumbling at his loudest volume indicating his unwillingness to go. Neither Rolf nor I know what to do.

Dad speaks slowly but decisively, "All I want—and need—is food!"

Mother chimes in, "I want Dad right here where I can take care of him. I can do it better than anyone at that hospital. Dad's right. We just need to eat!"

Rolf and I are both wimps about forcing the issue. The dominant pair continues their chanting dialogue about food and their gnawing hunger. I fear we are about one stanza away from a command to go to Chuck's Wagon, so I interject, "Okay, let me just run out to my truck. I've got some home-made stew and other goodies I brought with me. It won't take but a minute to heat it up."

Everyone's attention instantly refocuses. I hurry and get the stew heating on the stove. Dad is very cooperative and lets me help him get redressed and sort of cleaned up. When the stew is served, both Mother and Dad eat enthusiastically. Dad finishes off two big bowls, finds the coconut chocolate chip cookies, and eats half a dozen of them with his third bowl of stew. He tops this "breakfast" off with a couple of sticks of peppermint candy and two glasses of milk. He then pulls himself up from the table without any help and unsteadily makes his way to the living room grasping, chairs, tables, and the wall along the way. He puts on his filthy, body-fitting deerskin coat and his floppy-brimmed dress hat, adjusting it low over his right eye. He sits down on the couch with an air of authority and complete control over sheer oblivion.

Mother gives Rolf and me instructions for bill-paying, handing us the statements one at a time, each with an appropriate amount of money tucked in its own envelope. She gives us another five dollar bill for purchasing two cans of cat food, eggs, milk and bread. I don't suggest five dollars is probably not enough for the required purchases. I'd like to report about the Whidbey taxes and ask about the Nielson Insurance bill. Again, I hold back.

Once Rolf and I are in the car and off on our mission, I ask, "Have you made that trip to Portland to pay the insurance bill?"

"Nah, I haven't got to that yet."

I grit my teeth and snort out air through my nostrils. "Rolf, first it snowed. Then you were on a couple of truck-driving jobs. Okay, that's excusable, but what else has prevented you from doing what you promised?"

"Well, I made some little trips here and there—to Winlock, Vader, and Ryderwood. I visited some people up that way. I got a lot of good information from 'em, but mostly I just had to get away."

"They still have snow up in those towns, don't they?"

"Well, yeah, they still have too much snow for them guys to be workin' in the woods, but the roads are pretty clear."

"Geez, Rolf, if you could be running off to places like that to visit friends, I would think you could make it to Portland."

"Well, like I said, I had to get away for a little while."

I take his failure in this assignment as an indication that our new shared financial arrangement is not going any better than the previous non-arrangement. I don't feel like fighting with him.

When we return to the house I give Mother her bill-paying change, the latter secured in each appropriate envelope. She reads each receipt, counts her money carefully, and complains, "I'm having a hard time keeping track of my money. It seems like nothing adds up right lately."

"Mother, every penny of your change is there!"

"I don't mean this money," she says as she crams all of the change into her little square black purse and snaps it shut. "This morning I had money missing from my bank envelope. I thought I already had money for the next two weeks and plenty for renting a commercial vacuum and getting our vacuum cleaner from the repair shop. I've counted it several times, and I'm short $120.00." She shakes her little purse in my direction. "And not only that, there's $90.00 missing from this purse, too."

My shoulders sag. I stand helplessly waiting for her accusation. It doesn't come.

Rolf speaks up, "Remember, Mom, you gave me $20.00 for hamburgers one day last week and $6.00 the day we took the vacuum cleaner in for repair. And you did a fifty-dollar grocery shopping. Other than that, I don't know anything about your money."

I feel the blender pulse in my stomach. The amounts of money Rolf recited are not the same as the amounts he told me on the phone this past week. Which one of us will she accuse? I'm nauseated. I muster all my possible restraint and make an exit to the bathroom where I plop onto the toilet and sink my head into my hands, squeeze my eyes shut, and release my bowels.

Dear God, please forgive me for talking to you in this particular place of urgency, but I am beside myself. I feel as if I may explode any moment. You know I didn't take her money, but there's been no one else here but Rolf and me. Please give me strength from my own past hurt resulting from false accusations. I can't help thinking it, but please don't let me do to Rolf what they did to me and my family! Please don't let me accuse anyone of thievery.

I return to the kitchen wishing I could release and flush away the fecal material of my life as quickly as that in my daily bodily functioning. Rolf and Mother are still arguing about what had been spent during the week. I make no accusations. I say nothing. It's crazy here in Ridgeview, and Malfaits are not the only qualifying parties. Rolf is just as nutso. And I wonder what the hell *I'm* doing standing here in the midst of this surreal turmoil.

Nothing is settled, but Mother decides she and I will go to the bank by ourselves. Rolf should stay home with Dad.

All the way to the bank she complains about the missing money and makes innuendos about Rolf's possibly helping himself to it. I maintain silence. I listen. I make no accusations.

Once we're in the bank and it's her turn at the counter, Mother draws out the necessary money for expenses for two weeks, all the while explaining to the kind lady across the counter, "I thought I already did this. I guess not. This money ought to be enough until Betty comes down again in two weeks. May I see Mr. Tim now?"

"I'm sorry, he's not in today, but maybe I could help you."

"I don't think so. I've had missing money this week at home. Mr. Tim is watching our account here, and I want to be sure no one is taking money out without my permission."

"Mr. Tim did speak to me the other day about your situation."

"Well, I need to know if my son, Rolf, has been in to the bank and withdrawn money from Dad's and my account?"

"Oh, no. The day you all had the conference with Mr. Tim, we flagged that account. It's not likely that could happen. Let me check— no, I see no withdrawals since that date."

"Well, thank God for that. Maybe I forgot and didn't take out any more household money. It's awfully hard to remember every time I take money out, and it all disappears so quickly."

"Francine, you have your daughter's name on this account, and you have her with you today. You said you're happy to have her helping you pay the bills. May I make a very valuable suggestion that would help you both?"

"Yes, tell me anything that will help me."

"Francine, why don't you give your daughter **Power of Attorney** in addition to having her name on your account? That would give her the permission she needs to really help you effectively with your banking, as well as other business."

"Mr. Tim already spoke to me about that awhile back. He thought it would be a good idea and be less worry. I probably do need to do that, but for right now I don't want to give anyone any more power, especially with money. For today I'll just leave things as they are."

The lady presses gently, "But, Francine, it's really the only *legal* way to give the person whom you trust to help you with your finances the actual ability to do that. You do trust Betty, don't you?"

"Yes."

"She is the person you want to help you pay bills and write checks?"

"Yes."

"The **Power of Attorney** would allow that to happen so much more easily."

I say nothing. Mother remains firm in her decision. "No, I just don't want to give anyone any more power right now."

As we leave the bank, Mother decides we need a little break. "Come on, Betty, I can't remember when I've had a cup of coffee at Woolworth's counter."

Over the years lots of happy memories and good things came from trips to Woolworth's: the pleasure and diversion of a cheap toy or trinket, rewards for achievements, sometimes a quick lunch or a comfort pause. Are we doing that now? As we wander the aisles, we submerge ourselves in the sales. I choose some soft slippers for Dad and a large roll of duct tape. We make our way to the checkstand.

"Betty, what in the world are you going to tape up with that?"

"Well, Mother, since you won't part with that old bank envelope, I thought I'd tape up the sides with this."

"Oh, that will be nice. It'll be all silvery, and that ought to really make it last."

"My God, Betty, did you see the price tag on those slippers before you picked them up? That's highway robbery. They want $9.00 for those flimsy little things." Mother rummages through her purse. "Here, let me give you this to help pay for them." She presses $3.00 into my hand. People are lining up behind us and she won't take no for an answer. I feel like a *rolf.*

Mother has chosen three chocolate peanut butter eggs for El for a treat and a dishtowel for her hope-chest. She is slow with her money but very precise as she counts out $3.47 exactly and pays for her purchases.

We amble over to the lunch counter. The waitress recognizes Mother and before we can even seat ourselves on the stools, she calls out, "You want coffee—black—right? How're you doin'? Where's your papa today? Is he sick? I haven't seen you guys for a long time."

Mother fills her in as to why they haven't been in. The waitress serves our coffee, commiserates, and scurries back to the kitchen, where we can see her laughing with the two cooks. Their glances in our direction and their facial grimaces give me the distinct impression the joke is not in the kitchen. In her unrehearsed charade, the waitress' twirling fingers beside her ear and her wrinkled nose clearly speak weirdness and repulsion. My inward blender simultaneously pulses anger with empathy.

Other people, including Dad's doctor, have not been so insensitive in their observations as this rude waitress, but I suppose the bottom line is the same. I cannot deny the odor of urine as I sip my coffee, but it disturbs me that this waitress is so ingratiating and yet so cruel. Is she a person who would charge 'pretty high' for a cup of coffee? Is she as fast making change as she has been with the coffee pot, faster than old eyes and trembling hands can follow? Am I seeing everyone as a cheat?

I place a single penny beside my empty coffee cup and rotate my stool away from the counter. I'm glad I didn't accuse Rolf earlier.

Mother and I walk back down the other side of the street to my vehicle and go home. She is refreshed. I am more disturbed. Rolf is reading the paper, and Dad is sitting in the same spot as when we left. They both look grumpy.

Before we can comment, Rolf speaks up. "Yeah, Dad, here, wanted to go down to the little store, but I told him no. He's mad at me because I won't let him go."

Mother affirms Rolf's decision as she chides Dad, "You know you can't just go down to that store any time you want."

Dad says nothing.

Rolf continues, "He's pouting. He won't say nothin' to ya. Well, I take that back. When I told him he couldn't go, he clearly said 'Shit!' and then he sat back down and started his pout. His speech was pretty clear on that!"

Dad looks up and pulls his hat brim lower over his right eye. "Shit!"

A short while later Rolf and I leave to go to the vacuum cleaner shop. Rolf is about as grumpy as Dad, "Oh, man, Sis, the old man is harder than ever to manage. I've had a hell of a week. I can't keep up with either one of them. I really think the nursing home is close at hand, at least for Dad. I was talkin' to some friends the other day, and they tell me there's a law that lets Medicaid pay the whole bill for nursing home care, but the folks can't own anything. You know, in order to qualify it's important to have Mother have the house in her name—or in *someone else's* name."

"Rolf, I'm a little hesitant to have them sign anything changing property ownership now, because we've already started the paperwork for a guardianship based on their mental incompetence."

"Well, I'm just tellin' ya what my friends I was visitin' in Ryderwood told me. They've had experience with senile parents, and they told me this thing called ***Transfer of Ownership*** is somethin' we ought to get the folks to do—and to do it right away."

"Rolf, that may be a good idea, but I think it's too late. Mr. Hinson already told us it was too late to be doing any transfer of property. I guess we could ask him again, but I think by pursuing a guardianship, we've already said we don't think they are capable of caring for themselves, that includes making legal decisions such as changing property ownership.

"Besides, if you're in such an all-fired hurry to do something *right away,* why don't you get to the bill-paying you said you would do? You haven't paid the insurance bill, and the grace period is probably up. You don't even seem concerned. Instead you're asking me to think about helping influence Mom and Dad to make legal decisions about their property in the middle of filing for a guardianship. That just doesn't set right!

"Something else that doesn't set right is all this arguing about money and missing money. Rolf, when Mother was recounting her money after we shopped this morning and you two were arguing, she said she fills your gas tank for you sometimes and maybe that's why she came up short. If that's the case, I'm not sure that's real kosher for you to be running the gas out taking trips to Vader and Ryderwood to visit your logger friends for legal advice about transferring ownership of Mom and

Dad's property. The Portland bill-paying assignment is in the opposite direction. If you were so in need to get away, you should have made the trip to Portland."

"Mom's damned well mistaken. She didn't fill my gas tank at all."

"Rolf, I don't know whether she filled your gas tank or not, but I know she gave you ample money to make the trip to Portland that day we were all in the bank. She gave you fifty bucks."

"She's damned mistaken about filling the gas tank!"

I pull into a parking spot in front of the vacuum repair shop, and Rolf tells me, "I'll just run in here. I'll only be a minute. Wait for me."

I gladly remain in the truck. I need to get away! Through the store window I see Rolf gabbing with the repair man. Fifty-five minutes later he returns to the truck. I guess he needed to get away, too.

We're both hungry. I don't want to go back to Malfaits' and eat warmed up stew, and knowing Rolf doesn't have money to eat out, I try to make an atoning offer, "There's a bunch of fast-food places in this part of town. Can I take you to lunch at one of these nearby drive-ins?"

"Yeah, that'd be great. I am hungry, but I'm not much on drive-ins. I'll tell you what, there's a nice little place just down the street—and not too expensive."

We drive down the street and pull up to the curb in front of the restaurant. It *is* a nice little place and probably not too expensive, especially if you're not paying for it yourself.

Rolf removes his 38 pistol from his pants pocket and lays it down on the seat of the truck pointed in my direction.

"What the hell are you doing? Is that thing loaded?"

"Yeah."

"Well, why is it necessary to carry that in to a vacuum cleaner shop, and to the laundry—and to have lunch?"

"Here, let me just slip it under that cushion you're sitting on there. You forget I have a permit to carry. I carry it all the time."

"Rolf, I can tell you this. I'm tired. I'm hungry. I don't want that damned gun under the cushion I sit on when I'm driving this truck. I don't want to climb back in here and forget it's here and blow my ass off due to forgetfulness. Furthermore, if such a thing happens, I have made enough notes in my journal that you'll spend a long time explaining the circumstances of my missing ass! Now, get that thing back on your side of the seat, and let's go eat!"

Rolf obliges and covers the gun with loose newspapers on the front seat.

Out on the curb Rolf insists we stop for a moment and talk in low voices so people won't hear us. He wants to watch some people at another restaurant down the street. He begins a rambling tale about how busy he has been with the County Drug Task Force this past week, repeating the whole account of the Mexicans, the license plate changes, and The Sterling. "Yeah, the Task Force guys were real glad to get filled in on that, and I've since met with a couple of cops on the Regional Drug Task Force, Elvin Ramose and Curt Viner. That meeting took place about 1:00 AM in the morning here a week or so ago right there at that little restaurant you see down the street where those guys are standin' there smokin.'

"And who should I see when we walk in to have coffee but this guy named Jim Olison. Ol' Olison was sittin' at the counter. You know, he's part of a drug deal that went sour, and the other half of his partnership, a guy named Gramchy, is doin' time in Oregon State Penn."

"Did you carry your loaded 38 that evening?"

"Hell, no."

"Oh, you just do that when you go to lunch with your sister?"

"Well, I figured Ramose and Viner probably had enough steel to cover us. Anyway, I didn't want to be seen with those guys on the Drug Task Force and be sittin' in there near Olison, so I went back outside."

"Well, are we going *inside* here at *this* restaurant?"

As if I had not spoken at all, Rolf rambles on about the drug activities at The Sterling. "Yeah, you know, I'd just gone outside my room there to get me a Coke from one of their machines, and I noticed these suspicious looking Mexicans lurking in the shadows. A little bit later I went out to get myself another Coke, and the same guys were still there. Now that really got my attention. The next mornin' I talked to the maid, and she told me about this black residue left in the bathtub in the room where them guys had been. Yeah, and someone had urinated in the bathtub, too. What I think is them damn Mexicans are part of some kind of black tar heroin importing ring."

"Rolf, I don't get the connection. I don't know any of these people. I haven't seen any of these people in the neighborhood nor at The Sterling. I don't know anything about making black tar heroin in bathtubs. I just know I have had enough of your narration crammed down my throat. I need something more substantial, and probably the Drug Task Force does too. Damn it, can we go in now and eat?"

We enter the restaurant, are seated, and we both order club house sandwiches. We're served quickly, and I am thankful. I devour my sandwich while Rolf prattles on about the drug deal. When I am finished, he is only half way through his meal. He waves the third wedge of his clubhouse in my direction and launches into a monologue describing his theories about the Green River killer. I pull a tablet and pen from my purse and start taking notes, writing under the table as he labors on.

"There's somethin' real bad wrong with the bastard that's doin' that."

For the next half hour I say nothing. It doesn't matter. Without any pause his Green River killer filibuster moves into a repeat dissertation on the loss of his logging truck. "Speaking of bastards, I can tell you one I really hate is the one that stole my logging truck."

"But the truck wasn't stolen, was it?"

"Well, no, not stolen as such, but he out and out robbed me."

"How could he steal the truck if it was locked up? You actually went to court over that, didn't you?"

"Yeah, yeah, it went to trial."

"Did you win or lose the court battle?"

"I lost the battle regardin' the repair costs. I hadn't been able to pay the guy, but the judge awarded me the truck. The ringer was when I went to pick it up, it'd been stripped. The guy took the engine out and put it in one of his rigs and was runnin' it."

"So what were you supposed to do?"

"My only recourse was to sue him. I was strapped financially, and I still am. I can't afford to make any moves at all. Work ain't too steady for me right now. I haven't worked this past week because of being busy with Mom and Dad, and I'll probably not be able to get any work next week. My last check was only $150.00, but I still have 60 bucks of that left.

"I'll tell you what though, that son-of-a-bitch is gonna get his. In fact, I myself have been keepin' an eye on him. I know where he works, and he has to work late pretty often. I go over there and sit in my car in the parkin' lot. I get a kick out of playin' mind games with him, and he better be watchin' his behind at all times, no matter whether he's at work or somewhere else. Sometimes I sit there in the parkin' lot and spy on him through the rifle scope.

"Do you realize what a power surge that is just to place those cross-hairs precisely? You can decide whether you want to shoot him in the right eye-ball or the left eyeball."

"Rolf, that's sick, and if that's what you're really doing, *you're* sick!"

I feel as if I am watching a poorly rated television episode without the TV set.

The waitress whirls by and refills my coffee cup. Rolf speaks up, "Yeah, would you bring me two more glasses of water?

"You know, Sis, that coffee isn't good for you, especially black. I almost never drink the stuff anymore.

"Say, do you remember Bart Strekowsky?"

"Of course, I remember Bart. We went to school together from first grade on."

"Did you know his wife is a Superior Court Judge?"

"Yes, I know that."

"Yeah, well, she's the one who judged me over this last citation involving the missing medical card. That cost me over $150.00."

"I hate to interrupt your story, but may I remind you that you told me before it was $135.00—so now it's $150.00 plus the additional $50.00 you took out of Malfaits' bank account for expenses. Whatever it is, I guess you could say that cost *them*!"

"Yeah, yeah. Well, I explained that previously, and I still think I had a right to those funds in that emergency account because Dad screwed up my mail. Anyway, this judge kind of sat up there on her high bench and stared down over her pompous nose and found me guilty. I felt like lookin' right back up at her and lettin' her know she wasn't much of a judge, and a lot less of a person, for imposin' fines like that on people who could ill-afford them. She'd be a lot better off to spend her time and energy at home on her family. She might have prevented her son from meetin' his fate smashin' head-on into a loggin' truck after a drunken' party with his rich little high school friends down there at the railroad crossing near the river bank. That smash-up squished the whole carload of them rich little bastards, and the truck driver—well, he was pretty shaken up, but he come out of it unscathed."

"Jesus Christ-on-a-rock, Rolf! How can you even think such a thing and imagine that it has any association whatsoever with you or your friggin' truck citation? You really are sick! Maybe you ought to listen to what you're saying."

"Maybe you ought to realize half of what I'm sayin' s just in jest."

"When you're speaking of kids drinking and a horrible accident squishing a car full of kids head on into the front end of a logging truck, I see no jest! That's a nightmare for any family—I don't care whose it is! And as for the truck driver, he has to live with that memory forever, even if it wasn't his fault. I doubt that's being unscathed."

Quietness befalls our table.

Dear God, please, where are You? Please be here. I am afraid. I'm afraid because of Rolf's vindictive nature and his pent up hatred for other people. And, perhaps most of all, I'm afraid of the hatred which he has for himself. Please help us all!

Rolf finishes his meal and gulps down the second glass of water in silence. I pay the check, and we return to the truck and go on to the laundromat. Neither of us speaks during the trip.

Any conversation at the laundromat is minimal and relevant to our work. When the wash is completed, we drive back to 516. I am lost in my own thoughts, still trying to process the lunch-time conversation. Rolf continues to be non-conversant, and I'm glad. I hope he's perceiving that he *is* sick!

Once we're at the house I tug the laundry bag from the front seat of the truck and scoop up the used newspapers for recycling. For the first time since before lunch, I wonder about the whereabouts of the gun Rolf left on the truck seat under these papers before lunch. I don't ask. He is busy unloading boxes of laundry from the truck bed. I guess I should be thankful my ass is in tact.

In the house Mom and Dad don't question where we've been for so long. Rolf and I are both tired from our laundry mission which totaled $15.75. We simply add the piles to the boxes at one end of the couch.

We leave again and head to the grocery store to do the shopping. By the time we finish that chore and return to 516, it's late and the house is dark.

Rolf shouts through the door wicket, "Where the hell is everyone? We need some help here getting these groceries in."

"Rolf, leave them alone. We don't have that many groceries. We can get it done by ourselves."

"Damn it, they're not helpless!" Rolf fumbles with the key. Once inside, he stomps over to their bedroom door and pushes it open, still clutching his bags of groceries. "Get yourselves out here and give us a hand."

Mother mumbles, "I don't want to get up. I'm cold."

"If you want this shit hauled in and put away, you better get out here and help!"

Rolf follows me to the kitchen, and Mother walks stiffly behind us. I begin to put items away, and she tries to help. Her sleepy-eyed attempt to unpack bags quiets Rolf, and he goes back for the remaining groceries. I hurry the rest of the unpacking, tell Mother goodnight, and ask her to please go back to bed.

Rolf comes into the kitchen and drops the last bag non-too-gently on the cleared end of the table. "That's all."

"I'm fine here by myself. Why don't you go on your way and try to get some rest? Thanks for your help today."

"Yeah, sure." He turns and leaves the kitchen.

I hurry through the last bag and give a final wipe-down to the cleared end of the table and the counter. Then I try to escape quietly through the living room where Rolf is hidden behind a newspaper. I say nothing, but he lowers the paper and snaps it shut, rises and follows me out to my truck.

I fumble with the keys in the darkness. I hope the one I have selected is the key that opens the door and not the ignition key. Rolf stands close behind me on the lawn, arms crossed, a massive blackened form silhouetted dimly from the light filtering through the living room drapes and casting a shadow over my truck door. I guess if his arms remain crossed, the gun will remain in his pocket. I will not ask him to move. My hands shake as I feel for the keyhole. I hope I'm not putting too many scratches in proximity to the key slot.

"You know, Sis, there's an awful lot of confusion around here."

The lock releases. I remove my key and turn partially toward him but still clutch the door handle. "I'm really pooped, Rolf. I need to get on my way. I have a long drive."

"Yeah, I'm bushed too. But there's just so much confusion around here all the time, and there's definitely a lack of communication. It's real unfortunate there's been all the painful accusations over missing money and household items over the years."

I re-grip the truck door handle and move my thumb over the release button. What is he going to say? Is this the beginning of his being sorry? Or, is he about to make more accusations?

Rolf stands mutely on the grass. My hand remains frozen to the door handle.

"Yeah, it's a real shame. Sis, we really need to work together on things now."

I'd like to work together. I'd like to trust Rolf. I do know and understand his frustration in trying to deal with Malfaits. I don't like how he vents his anger. Much of this whole day has been him venting his anger, and that episode a few minutes ago with Mother was outrageous. I'd like to hit him one right now, right between the eyes. Maybe that's how he feels too. Somehow I know I can't depend on him, though. The bill-paying I was to do, I did. The bill-paying he was to do is not done. He was supposed to help watch their money, and yet $184 is unaccounted for in the past two weeks. I can't accuse anyone. I *won't* accuse anyone. Most certainly not him.

"Well, Rolf..." I open the truck door and climb in. Close the door and depress the lock button with my elbow. I start the engine and roll down the window part way, focusing on the bulky shadow on the grass, "I agree, there's a lot of work to do, more than one person can do by themselves."

Rolf steps closer to the open truck window and grimaces but maintains crossed arms. "You know, some day we'll get this whole family thing about the missing money straightened out. When I finish digging through the house and sorting stuff, I know I can come up with some answers, probably even find some of the missing items."

"I don't know, Rolf. That house is so packed full no one could find anything."

"We could at least talk some things out, you know, with your kids and all."

I give the window another crank downward. "You know, Rolf, when Nick and El were children, they adored you. Uncle Rolf could do no wrong. They loved staying over with you in the house in Newcastle. And riding to work with you in your logging truck was a venture into another world. You were a hero. However, your loud-mouthed, macho, narrow-minded accusing tactics have alienated them—probably forever. I would say you robbed them of a relationship with their grandparents at a time when it would have been very beneficial to them, and likewise beneficial to Mom and Dad. You've robbed yourself of a relationship with two really wonderful people."

"Well, when I get all the digging and sorting done, we'll find some answers."

"Rolf, I'm not so sure of that, but I appreciate the fact we have been able to talk as much as we have recently, and to work together. We could at least attempt to keep that up."

I release the brake and let the truck move slowly down the driveway, leaving Rolf standing on the lawn, arms still crossed—an unyielding, mute, statuesque advertisement for Old Hickory shirts.

CHAPTER 21

∽∾∽

The Dam Breaks

As I leave Ridgeview I stop at the local Golden Arches and wash off a layer of grit in the restroom. I order my usual cheap hamburger dinner to occupy me as I drive. I am not really hungry, but the mechanics of eating is soothing, and the warmth feels good. As the thumping of the tires on the patch strips on the Interstate vibrates through the truck, my brain surges with thought fragments.

I wish I could understand the big picture. I wish I could trust and depend on Rolf. But, I can't. I don't approve of his tactics with Mom and Dad. His behaviors with them are cruel—sometimes when I'm there, and probably more so when I'm not there.

There's something more wrong here than a dirty sink and dirty bodies. Dad's condition is worse, but on some things he is very clear. Even today he didn't say words but complained with hand gestures and pointed to Rolf. Was he not speaking because he has had another stroke, or is he afraid of Rolf? He was making hitting motions. No, Rolf wouldn't do that. I told Dad I understood, and things will be all right. But I *don't* understand, and things are *not* all right.

I try to refocus on my hamburger. I'm only a few miles out of town. I can't swallow. I feel as if I'm choking. What's wrong with me? I pull off the freeway at a roadside rest area.

The dam breaks. The tears flow. My body heaves and wrenches. My hamburger returns to the bag, both the eaten and uneaten parts.

Dear God, why does my father have to be locked in a body that doesn't function—and now with a mouth that can't talk? I'd rather

see him dead! God, what am I supposed to be understanding here?
Which one of them am I supposed to be helping? It's so impossible.
Dad and Mother are beyond help. They're not coming back, but
there must be a better way to die than this. And what about Rolf?
I'm trying so hard not to be accusing. I try to not make things worse,
but he is filled with such sick, violent anger. What happened to him?
Or, am I the sick one? Is there something I'm not getting? My whole
weekend has been a continual exercise in humiliation and humility,
restraint, and patience. I'm kind of dense, I know. But, God, I'm
trying to understand.

Please, God, please help me. Please help us all.

The tears subside. I blow my nose noisily into the restaurant napkins, wipe my face and hands with damp baby-wipes from the glove
compartment, get rid of my garbage and make my way back onto the
Interstate.

Thank you, God. I know you won't give me more than I can handle.
I don't know what I'm doing, but I'll keep trying.

Over the next two weeks the fury over finances and other frustra-
tions continues in Ridgeview. Rolf's calls become more frequent.

"Oh man, Sis, it's a mess down here. We've had another snow, and
that causes all kinds of havoc. Taco got out again, and I had a hell of a
time catching him. But Dad's worse than the dog—he wandered off twice
yesterday. I'm tellin' ya, if he keeps doin' that, I'm gonna kick his ass."

"Rolf, I'm tellin' *you*, you had better not do that."

"Well, I'm not—not really. But there's no let-up around here. I just
get back to the house from roundin' up Dad, and Mom starts hollerin'
she needs to go to Safeway. Hell, that's clear across town, and that ain't
no treat in this ice and snow. I said I'd take her down here to the corner
market, but she won't have it that way. I feel like kickin' her ass, too."

"My God, Rolf, are you listening to yourself?"

"Yeah, yeah. I ain't gonna do that. What I really need is for both Mom and Dad to be more cooperative with me."

"I won't promise you that will happen, but Mom hasn't called for a while. I'll call her tomorrow."

When Mother answers the phone, she seems happy that I've called, but she is evasive and non-committal about how things are going. I feel something is more amiss than usual. "Mom, are you busy? I could call you later."

"No."

"You seem hesitant. Can you not speak freely with me right now?"

"No."

"Do you have company?"

"No."

"Is it because Rolf is right there?"

"Yes."

"Are you okay?"

"Yes."

"Are you upset because everyone is fighting?"

"Sort of."

"I know he gets angry and loud, but he's not hitting either you or Dad, is he?"

"No."

"He's not touching either of you in any other way that's upsetting you? I mean he's not hitting or smacking you around, is he?"

"No."

I hear her open the door and move out of the kitchen onto the back porch. Maybe she needs privacy and will tell me more. I repeat questions but get only short negative replies and no details.

"Well, Mom, do you think if you were a little more cooperative with Rolf, maybe he would be less angry and argumentative?"

"If Rolf doesn't like the way things are around here, he should get on out of here. He has his own place. He doesn't need to be hanging around here all the time. He keeps things in a continual uproar. He doesn't do any of us any good."

My efforts at persuading her are only half-hearted. I understand how they both feel about Rolf's attitude. I also understand how frustrated Rolf gets trying to cope with their irrationality. There's verbal abuse on all of their parts. There's disorientation in all of them.

I change the subject, "Have you shopped this week, Mom? Do you have groceries like meat, eggs and milk?"

"Yes, I have a roast on now."

"How'd you get to the store to get that in the stormy weather?"

"Rolf took me."

"Well, at least he took you. He must be doing some good around there."

"Rolf never takes us anyplace."

"He says he takes you both around to a lot of places."

"He does no such thing! He doesn't take us anyplace! The other day Dad and I walked to the grocery store. He saw us after we finished shopping, and he never even offered us to ride. We had a cart full of groceries, too. We went across the street to the credit union, and when we came out, he was there in the parking lot. And he still never gave us to ride."

"Maybe he really didn't see you, Mother."

"Oh yes, he did. He drove up by us and we talked to him. Then he drove off and left us standing there with our groceries. We had to push that cart over a mile to get home."

"Do you need me to come down so we can talk about this more freely?"

"No, I don't want you to drive down here in this nasty, cold weather, but we do need to talk."

"Do you have money for groceries and for going out to coffee?"

"Yes, I have eighty dollars."

"Will that be okay until Friday? That's four days away."

"That's more than enough. We'll be fine. Will we see you on the weekend?"

"Yes." The knowledge that I will be coming down has a calming effect.

It's only two days later when Rolf calls to say things are in a royal turmoil and they have *no* money. He still hasn't paid the Neilson Insurance bill because he can't afford to go. I don't ask about the expense money she gave him. It's evidently gone, as is the money for the Cablevision bill—and probably money she gave him to fix a distributor cap—*and* money from whatever purse or bank envelope she may be trying to hide.

Rolf reminds me, "You know, it takes a lot of cash to do their required running around here, much less a trip to Portland."

"Are you really taking them in the car to do the running around as you call it?"

"Well, I gotta chase after the dog whenever Dad lets him out that gate, and it seems like they want to go to the store every couple of days."

"Actually, Rolf, I have to tell you Mother told me of a recent instance in which they had walked to the grocery store and shopped, and you saw them there with a full cart of groceries and did not offer them a ride home."

"Yeah, that's right. They shopped. Then they went across the street to the credit union. I'd already told them their retirement checks wouldn't be there, but you know them, they went anyway. I drove across and watched. When they come back out, they had nothin'. You're damned right I didn't offer them a ride. They didn't ask me for a ride, and I just drove off and left them."

"I guess I don't understand your reasoning, Rolf."

"No, you probably don't, but I've got to have some access to their funds to be able to work with these shortages. They won't give me anything to work with. Something has to be done."

Senile or not, if I were Mother I wouldn't give him any more cash either. But he's right, something has to be done! I don't know what, and

I don't know how. I don't know what Rolf does with the cash he does get his hands on. It's more than enough for groceries for three people. I am not sure what all the *required* running around for them is. They seem to walk or ride the bus everyplace they go.

On my next weekend trip to Ridgeview, I am received at the front door by Mother wearing only a blouse and panties but no slacks or skirt. She has never been shy, but this is a new kind of weirdness.

"Mother, you shouldn't be opening the door like that."

"It's only you. So what?"

Dad joins her at the door in a partially buttoned shirt and unzipped pants. "Come on--kid--let's go get--something to eat."

There is practically no food in the house and neither of them has *any* money. I have juice, coffee and sweet rolls with me, and I break them out immediately. They eat ravenously.

After this bite of breakfast, Mother insists we get to the bank. Once we are parked Dad is happy to stay in the truck and promises he won't wander off. As I help Mother down from the passenger side, I notice the seat is slightly wet. "Mother, that's such a big step down, it looks as if you've strained a bit. Do you need to go to the bathroom?"

"No, I don't need to go."

"Are you sure? There's a public restroom right across the parking lot."

"I don't *need* to go!"

As usual, I give in. We enter the bank and take our place in a line of customers. I notice a small wet spot on the carpet at Mother's feet. I lean over and whisper, "Mother, I think I really need to get you out of here to a restroom. Come on, let's go. We'll come right back and do the banking."

Mother's reply is *not* in a whisper, "I *don't need to go to the bathroom!*"

The spot gets bigger, as does another spot around the crotch of her slacks.

"Mother, please. Let's leave."

"Betty, I have a condition that is brought on by extreme nervousness. I can't help it. That's just the way it is. I do not need to go to the bathroom. And I am not leaving!"

I don't know whether to wish to be invisible or wish I could create my own wet spot on the carpet and not allow her to be alone in her uncontrollable humiliating nervous condition. Once outside the bank and back in the truck, she maintains she doesn't want to find a bathroom. All things considered, I guess she doesn't need one now.

Dad commiserates in our dilemma, "Hell--kid--I don't--need a bathroom."

I start the truck and head for home. Once we arrive at the house, Mother says she is very tired. She and Dad both go into their bedroom and lie down to rest.

I want to ask them to clean up--to at least change clothes. I want to yell at them and make them realize what just happened. My appalled, mute body stands staring at the closed bedroom door.

I turn and go to the kitchen where I attack the disaster zone in the sink. I need the reality of the dirty dishes and the moldy scraps in the pots and pans. I lean close over the sink and scrub furiously. In only a short while I feel droplets of sweat on my forehead. Bleach fumes sting in my nostrils. It's soothing. It's good. It's what needs to be done. It's something I *can do!*

With no forewarning, Rolf appears in the kitchen doorway and booms out to the back of my head, "Let's get the hell out of here and get some grocery shopping done."

"My God, Rolf, where did you come from? I didn't hear you come in."

"Ah, I was around. Let's get going!"

I thought I was stressed and nervous with Mom and Dad on our *soggy* bank trip, but Rolf is really a case! As we drive along, his brow is wrinkled in tight creases. He's sweating, and his fingers drum constantly. Those on the right hand drum against the handle to the wing window of the truck and those on the left hand against his leg.

"Here, take a right and go down by the lake."

Silently I turn onto the street, a street I've traveled thousands of times and for which I don't need directions.

"Watch out for them bastards parking in front of the hospital, They don't know what the hell they're doing--here, turn left at the next corner. Oh, oh, there's some little high school peckerhead in that low-rider. Watch out for him. He ain't gonna stop."

I miss the peckerhead and turn into the grocery store parking lot.

Rolf's directions continue, "It's been the shits to find parking places in this lot lately. Let's go down to the other end of the lot."

"Rolf, are you aware that you have said nothing to me but bark directions and criticisms of other drivers and pedestrians the whole way down here?"

"Well, I may be a little edgy."

"It seems more than a little. You need to listen to yourself and watch the way you speak to other people--that means Mom and Dad--*and me*!

"Here, right here--get this thing parked right here in this one."

I glide slowly past the spot he has been vigorously motioning to and roll into a place two slots down. He gets out, slams the door, stomps into the store, only to realize the shopping carts are outside. He stomps back out, rips a cart out of the line-up and then tries to drive the cart into the store through the exit. By the time I lock my door and run around to the other side and lock his, he gets the cart through the correct entryway and I catch up with him. He growls his way through fruits and vegetables, canned goods, and paper products. He is uncooperative about almost all selections. Near the completion of the usual items on our list, he gathers a few things he favors himself. Choosing these things seems to calm him.

This newly established composure lasts for the trip back to the house. I myself begin to relax--that is, until Rolf can't find his door key while juggling his two grocery bags and searching his pockets on the front door step.

Suddenly he drops both bags of groceries from about waist height as if they are filled with hot coals. He flings his arms skyward. "Goddam, fucking cocksucker--fuck me a blind man!" He jumps off the front porch into the yard and stomps in tight circles, flailing his arms and yelling his initial refrain repeatedly, "Goddamn, fucking cocksucker--fuck me a blind man!" These irrational volleys go on for several minutes as he continues circling, stomping, and kicking at the grass.

I stand midway on the sidewalk which leads to the front steps, clutching my own two bags of groceries, mouth agape. I have never seen anything like this. Is this really happening? Am I dreaming?

Mother opens the door and looks around as if nothing is going on, "Oh, Rolf and Betty are back with the groceries."

Rolf stomps back to the front steps and picks up his grocery bags. Miraculously the heavy-duty bags have not split open. "What the hell took you so long?" He elbows his way around Mother and into the living room, throws the bags of groceries down on the couch, and begins rifling through the pockets of his clothing scattered about on the furniture. He finds his keys in a jacket and mutters something about remembering that's where he left them. He grabs the grocery bags and proceeds to the kitchen, where he begins throwing groceries on the table and the counter.

Thank goodness, the eggs are in my bags.

When we go back out for more groceries, Rosy from next door comes over, seemingly to visit with me. She waits until Rolf has gone back into the house.

"I saw you and Rolf drive in just now. I couldn't help but hear a little bit, too. I wanted to call you when I seen you here last time. In fact, I've thought about calling you up at your home several times this week. I'm real concerned about how Rolf is treating your Mom and Dad."

"What do you mean?"

"He's just not very nice to them."

"Mother has said that, too, Rosy. I don't exactly know what's going on, and I don't know what *not very nice* means."

"Well, a couple of days ago was one example. Rolf and your dad were going someplace, and they got into an argument out on the front street because your Dad wouldn't get in the car fast enough. You know, Betty, he was doing the best he could, but he just wasn't fast enough for Rolf's wishes."

"So what happened?"

"Well, Rolf was hollering and screaming at him about like he was a few minutes ago out here in the yard. Then he pushed him down on the sidewalk. It was awful. He just sort of flung him down. Now, Betty, you know that isn't right."

Rosy and Malfaits have not been friends over the years, and Mom and Dad usually refer to her as Nosy-bill. But they have been neighborly. And even though they say she steals their flowers, whenever they have lots of apples or cherries ripening or they've been making jelly, they always send some over to her. Rolf never has liked her, and I don't think she likes Rolf. But I don't think she would concoct stories about any of them to cause me any trouble. I've always been friendly with her and her family. Her account today of this incident seems to be made in genuine concern. And her nosiness, though it may not be pleasant, may be something I need to heed.

"I'm trying hard to be helpful to my mom and dad, Rosy--and to figure out what's going on. I, too, have concerns about how Rolf treats them--and how they treat each other. I don't know what to tell you, because I don't really know how to handle the situation myself. I do know the problem is way too big for me. Rolf and I do not agree on things, but I certainly can't combat Rolf."

"Oh, my God, I wouldn't want you to even try that, with him and all those guns. But other neighbors have noticed his meanness, too. Pushing your dad down on the sidewalk isn't the only time. He's got to stop doing what he's doing."

"Rosy, I can't speak *for* you, but I suggest you report to the authorities what you've noticed. I don't know what agency acts on things like that, but I can tell you we have begun the process for a guardianship for Malfaits, and I can give you the name of the court-appointed ad litem figure. He is supposed to be a neutral person who is evaluating the living condition for Malfaits."

"My God, I can't see Rolf being a guardian to no one. He can't take care of himself!"

"Rosy, I think you really need to call the ad litem person and tell him your observations--and ask him about to whom you should report any future incidents."

As I leave Ridgeview, my trip to my own home is more depressing than usual. I know there's something to the abuse that Nosy-bill described. After witnessing Rolf's doorstep tantrum, I feel he is definitely capable of hurting them. Even if not intentional, dangerous things could result from his irresponsible, irrational flailing and stomping.

Dear God, where are You? I am so scared. I am so frustrated. I am so furious. I feel sick. I feel guilty. I feel helpless. I feel hopeless.

CHAPTER 22

Beware, The Ides of March

I DON'T HAVE time to wallow in my fear, my frustration, my helplessness, my hopelessness--or anything else. It's the first of March--time for another jaunt to Ridgeview for more cleaning, more grocery shopping, more bill-paying--more, more, more! Who cares how March comes in--or goes out?

Upon arrival at 516 I walk into the routine furor. Mother is missing $150.00. Rolf says she put $125.00 in the bank according to her bank book. No one can find the bank book. Mother is raving about the Neilson Insurance bill still not being paid. Today is the final day of the grace period. Yeah, yeah, Rolf's been meaning to get down to Portland and do that. He says he damn well needs a break and to get the hell out of the house.

He needs a break? *I am about to break, and I've been here less than an hour!*

A short while later Rolf and I are in *my* car driving to Portland. I want to scream at him! Why? Why do *I* have to make this trip today? Can't you do anything you're depended on to do? What have you been doing? What did you do with the cash Mother gave you?

Instead, I weakly chastise, "Rolf, don't you realize how much Dad needs this coverage? It pays beyond Medicare coverage. It has saved them hundreds of dollars just this year in medical expenses for Dad's little 'street fighting' incident."

"Yeah, sure, but I knew you'd be down this weekend, and we could still get to Portland before the insurance office closed."

"Geez, Rolf, what about wrecks or unforeseen things? Something might have prevented me from being here on time--or at all?"

"But it didn't happen, did it? We're gettin' there just fine."

Rolf leans back and changes the subject. "Check that out down there on the river. That's a brand new saw mill. They're takin' a lot of real small trees and runnin' 'em through there. They can load 'em right there on the river on the ships that take 'em straight to Japan. And they're gettin' top dollar for them spindly little things. I wouldn't want to haul for an outfit like that, but a lot of guys are doin' it. It sure is good for employment in the area."

The Portland trip passes in a blur of trivial prattle mixed with relief at finally getting the Neilson bill paid. The chores on the rest of the weekend pass in another blur. My exasperation with Rolf dwindles somewhat as I note improvements in the appearance of the house and yard. I can see where he has spent some of his time.

Rolf and I work together as usual on the washing and grocery shopping. We discuss the purchase of a new bathroom sink and agree Mom and Dad could afford about $150.00.

We patiently listen to Mother's directions for the regular local bill-paying trip. Under her watchful eye we locate each statement and attach the designated amount of money. But because of our earlier Portland trip, we run out of time and are unable to finish this chore. Rolf assures me he will take Mother to town Monday to finish paying them. I have my usual *cash doubts,* but I can't do everything.

When I leave Sunday afternoon all seems calm.

Being in my own home a distance away does not insulate me from the financial furor which continues to usher in the month of March. On March 3rd I pick up the phone and Rolf roars into my ear, "We got a problem down here! I can't get a damn thing straight with either one of them! I been shopping for that bathroom sink you and I talked about. I couldn't find nothin' worthwhile for $150.00, but I found one for $192.00. It has a wooden vanity--real wood, you know--but it's got a small crack near the top. When it's all in place and hooked up that wouldn't show at all."

"That's a little more than we talked about, Rolf, but it sounds okay. What's the problem?"

"Mom gave me money for the thing, but I can't find the rest of her money. I know they both got their retirement checks and their Social Security checks. And I know they cashed them. I want her to tell me how much money she has and to count it out for me. She won't cooperate at all."

"But she did give you enough money for the sink?"

"Yeah, but I need to know she's got enough for food and such. She's right here. See if you can get anything straight out of her."

There's a quiet shuffle as Rolf and Mother exchange the phone. I hear her open the backdoor and step out on the porch.

"Hi, Mom. I thought things were fine when I left Sunday. We were all agreed about the bill-paying and the sink, but it sounds like everyone is angry all over again."

"Yes, I'm angry! Rolf is trying to run everything. He has a shitty, domineering attitude about things! I can keep better track of my money when he stays out of it."

"Well, he needs money to buy the sink. You've needed a new one ever since Mavis was there. You are going to let him get it and put it in, aren't you?"

"Yes, of course, I want that done, but I already gave him the $192.00. He doesn't need to know how much more money I have. I'm mad because he always grabs my money out of my hand, and I feel like I don't get it all back. I don't want him grabbing things away from me. I can count my money myself!"

"Mother, I don't blame you. I wouldn't like him grabbing things out of my hands either, especially my money. Would you mind just taking it out now and counting it yourself, as I am listening on the phone?"

I hear her shuffle back into the kitchen, unsnap her purse, and smooth the bills out on the counter. She licks her fingers. "Twenty, forty, sixty, eighty--one hundred. Twenty, forty, sixty, eighty--two hundred. Twenty, forty, sixty, eighty--three hundred. Ten, fifteen, twenty, twenty-one. I have three hundred twenty-one dollars.

She gathers the money, taps it against the countertop, and counts it all over again via long distance. If I were she and counted that well, I wouldn't let Rolf count it either!

When I left Ridgeview yesterday she had $155.00 left from their pension checks. Both of their Social Security checks equal $915. That's $1070.00 minus Rolf's mortgage payment of $468.10--that's 601.90--minus the $192.00 for the sink is $409.90 that she *should* have. Yes, she's short. That's $88.00 missing in two days. I'd be nervous about money being grabbed out of my hands, too. I make note of the discrepancy. I don't ask about the missing money. I know they have coffee out each day, and they probably *give* Rolf money. That's not my business. I need to be positive and encouraging.

"Mom, maybe you and Dad should take a walk to the bank tomorrow. Your money would be much safer there than either one of you walking around with all that cash. Nobody could grab it away then."

"We might just do that."

"How about if I chat with Rolf a bit more now?"

"He's right here--Well, he *was* right here. Just a minute."

I hear Mother walking through the house yelling his name.

There's a quiet click on the phone line.

I'll be darned! He slipped off and went upstairs and listened in on the extension. I forgot they even had a phone extension. No, he wouldn't do that. I'm being paranoid. I'm as bad as Mom and Dad. But I do remember Rolf talking about slamming the front door and sitting in the darkened living room listening to Mother and Dad exchange their private thoughts. I'm so naive! I will no longer be surprised at anything that goes on down there. All of them are crazy!

After several minutes Mother picks up the phone, "Betty, I can't find him anyplace. He was here just a minute ago. He's always going off somewhere."

"Well, Mother, you counted your money just fine today. Be sure you don't keep it all in the same purse and count your change each time you buy something. And, Mother, please think about putting at least some of your money in the bank."

"Yes, I think that's a good idea. We'll put half of it in the bank tomorrow."

Days go by. Did they go to the bank? Did they lose any more money? Do people at the corner market or the little cafe cheat them? I know they give money to Rolf, but I wonder if Rolf *takes* money from them--like a hundred dollars or more at a time. Does he take their money and then make them think they lose it and that they can't keep track of it themselves?

Rolf calls midweek. "Well, I got the new bathroom sink and new faucets. That cost $192.00, and with a senior citizen discount. It'll be another $95.94 for installation."

"Geez, that's almost three hundred bucks. That seems high for a bathroom sink--and installation? I thought you were going to install it yourself."

"Yeah, these guys are highway robbers with their installation fees. They get about forty bucks an hour. But you know Dad's plumbing work just hasn't held up."

"But I thought *you* were going to put it in."

"Yeah, yeah, I was. But, you know, they've needed to get this done for over a year, and I thought we better get on with it and be sure it was done right. The three hundred bucks will be money well spent--and the bill won't come 'til the end of next month."

To myself, What bill? Mother told me she gave you $192.00 already. *You* said she gave you the money. Betty, keep your mouth shut. You're not going to get into a he-said-she-said argument with the two of them."

"I guess you've got a point, but that's a mighty expensive sink." I scramble for pen and paper and my journal and scratch down $192.00 plus $95.04. "Geez, Rolf, that means Mother's going to have a bill at the end of the month for $287.94."

"Yeah, well the job will be done right."

Silently on my paper I add another $192.00 cash she already gave him. Good God, that's $479.94--maybe more by the time the work is finally done--and that's for a sink with a crack in it. Hmmm, the sink's not the only thing with a crack in it!

Rolf interrupts my thoughts, "At least the job's done, and maybe I can get them to be cleaner now. But, you know, Sis, they probably aren't going to have enough money to last the month. Yesterday Mom only had $360.00."

I page back through my journal notes. When Mother counted her money for me on the phone, she had $321.00. She counted it twice. How can she have *more* today than she had a few days ago? Who's right and who's wrong? I wonder if Mom and Dad took that walk to the bank.

Rolf complains, "I really don't think they can get through the month on that."

I am slow to respond, "I don't know, Rolf. I think we'll have to let them try. I'll be seeing them again before the end of the month. We'll just have to wait and see."

I guess Rolf senses the silent wall between us. He says an abrupt goodbye.

The next day he calls again. "Mom's on the war path."

"What is it this time?"

"They need to have money on hand for staples, you know. They're out of milk, and I want her to give me some money so I can get some. She's raisin' holy hullabaloo and says she's not gonna give me any money."

"Rolf, they had a gallon and a half of milk on Sunday when I left. It's only Thursday. Maybe she figures they don't need to buy another gallon today."

"Hell, I don't know what they had on Sunday. *Today* they're out. They need milk, and they ain't got any money--or at least she ain't gonna give me any money to get some.

"Yesterday they banked fifty or sixty bucks. Today they went to the bank twice. First they banked another forty or fifty bucks, and the second trip they banked $218.00."

I would like to laugh, but I refrain. "That's a lot of banking in two days. Are they walking down town to do all this?"

"I guess so. I ain't takin' 'em."

"How do you know they're doing that?"

"I can read their bank book."

"Rolf, based on what she counted out to me last Sunday, and even if they banked $218.00, they still should have a few bucks left. If you're reading the bank book for the deposits, how come you don't know exactly what the deposits are?"

Rolf explodes into the phone, "I don't know where the hell they walk every time they go out the door. Damn it! I just can't make this thing work. There is no milk! They have no money! I work hard as hell around here. All I get for it is to be shit on!"

"Rolf, calm down. Is there food in the house? It can't be all gone. You and I did a huge shopping last weekend."

"Well, yeah, there's food in the house. There's plenty of food. It's just the day-to-day things. There's no milk, and there's no money to buy that kind of stuff."

"Rolf, these are the kinds of things you need to explain to the court-appointed lawyer. If you're going to be there as a care-giver, how much do you need to get along on? How do you get access to such money correctly and legally--not by grabbing it out of their hands. I know for sure the numbers you tell me and what Mother tells me don't add up. Also, I believe Mom and Dad should use the bank and not be wandering around town carrying large amounts of cash stuffed in Dad's shirt pocket or pinned in Mother's bra. Like you say, the repetitive banking is crazy, and I know the food supply is erratic. But the way you're taking over everything isn't helping. I don't agree with the way you're doing things, and I'm not going to support you in that grab-their-money-out-of-their-hands routine."

"Well, I'm sure as shit gonna have that session with that ad litem guy. I'm goin' down there tomorrow and tell him just how it is around here. And he either better shit or get off the pot! This guardianship thing needs to get moving!

"And the next thing I'm gonna do is toss a couple of cats out the door!"

"Rolf, Rolf--it's time-out. It's no secret they think more of the cats and Taco than either you or me. That's nothing new, so what's the big deal? You need to hang up this phone and go walk around the block--several times. Also, if you're going to talk to Mr. Mason tomorrow, you might want to be careful and not give him cause to write your behavior up in his report. You're as bad as Mom and Dad, and this is not the first time I've told you that!"

"Yeah, yeah, I know. I'll go take that walk."

"I'll call later and try to talk to Mother about some operating expense money until I can come down again, but I already know what she's going say."

"Yeah, what's that?"

"She's going to say, 'Rolf eats like a horse, and he buys nothing. We're not going to feed him so's he can lie around and rest up and abuse us.' She's already said that to you and to me."

"Yeah, she's said it a bunch of times to me, but I gotta' have some way to manage things better around here."

"Okay, I'll talk to her, but I doubt it will do any good."

As I hang up I know I'll probably make the call but not with much conviction. Sometimes I just don't care how miserable and frustrated he gets. I feel as if deep in this demented soap opera there is some degree of justice in the current situation that makes up for all the years he disappeared when I needed him so desperately. Maybe right now he deserves to be right where he is.

I remind myself to 'Do unto others....' And 'Judge not lest ye be judged....'

Dear God, grant me wisdom that whatever I say or do will be according to Your will for all parties concerned! I truly don't understand how these two old people could have eaten over a hundred dollars worth of food since Sunday and consumed almost two gallons of milk; but aside from that information, it's not right for Rolf to grab their money out of their hands. Maybe both Malfaits and Rolf have justification for anger. I know their money will not last through the month of March at this rate, and I cannot identify the drain for sure. I don't want to be mean or unreasonable. I don't want to accuse my brother or anyone else. God, please direct my search, my quest, or whatever it is I'm supposed to be doing in this situation.

On March 9th I talk to Rolf again. He seems calm, almost pleased, as he tells me, "Yeah, they're out of money. She was cryin' on my shoulder this morning about havin' no money to go to coffee. 'Boo hoo. I don't know what we're gonna do. We're flat broke.' I told her I was flat busted, too."

"You seem sort of pleased about all this."

"I just flat out told 'em they'd have to get off their asses and get down to the bank and get some money if they wanted to eat or go to coffee or anything else."

"And?"

"I really don't know. I been busy workin' in the shop out back. I been movin' junk from the living room out there. I haven't had any hauling jobs for over two weeks out at McCray's Logging, or any place else for that matter. Mike from over at Stimson Freight called, but that was probably just a small local hauling job. Hell, I don't even know what it was. Mom screwed it up and didn't give me the message in time for me to call back. I've been so upset I took yesterday off--I mean completely off. I did nothing. I stayed home and tried to rest."

"Do you need me to come down and spell you for a day or two? It isn't my usual weekend, but I could come if you need me."

"No, there ain't much point in that. There's really nothin' you can do. If Mom gets the money today, she gets the money. If she doesn't, she doesn't. I'm just gonna stay out of it. I'll pinch my pennies and make do. I didn't do nothin' yesterday, and I ain't gonna do nothin' today either."

"Well, if you need me this coming weekend, you better say so. I have a wedding I'd like to go to. It's for a former student."

"Naw, go on and go to your wedding. Things will be okay here."

"Rolf, I'll change my plans if you need me to. Or, I'll come for part of the weekend, but I need to know now."

"Things are okay right now. I'm sure they'll be fine. No, don't come down."

I hang up thinking to myself, He doesn't *want* me to come down. He seems pretty sure Mother went to the bank, and he's probably just waiting to get his hands on her money. I know he can't be there day in and day out with no money at all, but it's really strange he would stay there two days and do nothing but rest. Even when he doesn't have hauling jobs he usually doesn't just lie around their house. He sounds more like a waiting vulture.

His work schedule has always been sporadic, even in good times. Is he living at their house all the time? Does he consider himself *the* care-taker? Is he taking care of *them* or *him*? He can't just eat and do nothing day after day. Can he? Is he really looking for work? What is he trying to do?'

I call on March 14th and Rolf answers, "Yeah, well, the latest event is that there's shit in the bed. Actually, that was about four days ago. It got all over that big puffy comforter thing you gave 'em for Christmas." Rolf laughs. "It don't look so new and puffy now."

"Are you just leaving it like that?"

"Well, no, not exactly. They cleaned up after themselves. They wiped it and smeared it around."

"That's it?"

"Yep! That's it unless they do it better themselves. That ain't the only thing that's shitty. I know damn well Mom went to the bank that day we were talkin' on the phone, but I ain't seen any of the money and there ain't no food around here. Me, I'm living on two tacos a day. I guess I'll just have to wait 'em out."

"Are they eating?"

"I don't know. They go out. I guess they're going down to the corner place or maybe out to Ocean Espresso."

"Shall I try to talk to Mom?"

"No, no, I don't think so. Just let things be."

The next day my phone rings again. "Well, Mom finally admitted she'd gone to the bank and taken out some money. She said she got $100.00. She gave me $5.00. Big deal! I bought one gallon of milk, two loaves of bread and a dozen eggs."

"Did they do any other shopping?"

"I really don't know. And as far as any other money, I don't know nothin' about that either. I been busy cleanin' out the shop out behind the garage, and I went downtown and got an estimate on lawnmower repair for the big mower. You know how many gas mowers Dad's got? Six. None of them work good. And you couldn't possibly guess how many push mowers I found in that shop. There was eight of 'em!"

"That's a bunch of mowers for so little mowing that gets done."

"Yeah, when I got all that stuff lined up on the lawn, there was a hell of a lot. But it's all back in the shop now. Dad put up a real howl about my takin' all his stuff out. But you can't tell what needs fixin' unless you know what you got. I got rid of some of it, too. But I kept four of the push mowers."

"How many lawnmowers are there all together?"

"Hell, I don't know. There's just so damn much stuff in there you can't really tell what's what. Shortie, the guy who lives across the street, come over the other day. He said for a hundred bucks he'd help with the yard clean-up. He said he'd trade work for the old mowers. That sounds like a good deal to me. What do you think?"

"Well, for sure the yard work needs to be done. That sounds fair, especially since cash is a problem right now. I have no idea what a fair price is for mowers or tools. I'll have to accept your judgment."

"Yeah, okay. I hoped you'd see it that way. Maybe you could give Mom a call a little later and explain that to her. They're out somewhere right now. We need to get some grocery shopping done, but she won't go. Right now I got a load of tools and mowers in my car. I need to get going."

Later in the afternoon I call and Mom answers. "How are things going?"

"Just fine."

"I'm just calling to be sure you've got plenty of groceries? You know, bread, milk, eggs and stuff like that?"

Her voice is pleasant and reassuring, "I've got plenty of everything. I have money, and we've been to the store. I didn't lose any hundred dollars either. We're having hamburgers for lunch right now. We have bread, milk, peanut butter, eggs. Nobody is starving! What are you asking about that stuff for? We're fine."

I let the comment pass regarding any lost hundred dollars. Rolf had not mentioned any lost money when I spoke with him earlier. I can only wonder if there has been more missing money.

"Mom, remember, I told you about my former student's wedding. It's this weekend, and I just wanted to be sure you didn't need me and that you and Dad are okay--that you have everything you need."

"Of course, we have everything we need. We have lots of food. We're having hamburgers right now. We're fine."

Her words are reassuring, but her voice is flat and unemotional. "Well, Mother, Rolf said there was no food at all in the house, and you wouldn't go to the store with him. I was kind of worried about that."

"Of course, I'll go to the store with Rolf. I never said I wouldn't go to the store with him. I said I will not give *him* money to go shopping. He can think again if that's what he wants, and you don't need to be asking me to give him any money either."

"Mother, I'm not asking you to give anything to anyone. I'm just reminding you I won't be down this weekend. It's Susan and John's wedding. I wanted to be sure you guys were--"

"Betty, you don't need to be worrying about us. We're fine. You need to be getting yourself ready for that wedding. Susan's that little Greek girl, isn't she? And that's that big fancy Greek wedding you were telling me about. You go on and have a good time."

It was a long while back when I told her about the invitation. How come her memory is fine on some details, especially ones that seem to have no relevance to her? I want to believe her about the food and that everything is fine.

"Is Rolf right there where you can see him while we're talking?"

"Yes."

"You're sure you have plenty of food?"

"Yes."

"Are you angry with Rolf?"

"Yes."

"Do you want to say why?"

"No."

"Do you want me to call back later, so we could talk?"

"No, you don't need to be worrying about things down here. And don't be coming down this weekend. Things are fine."

"Okay. If Rolf's still there, may I speak with him?"

I hear them shuffle about as they exchange places. "Hi, Rolf. Are you really having hamburgers now?"

"Yeah, charred at that."

"You guys must have gotten some shopping done since we talked this morning. What about the other food she named? Is that there, too?"

"Yeah, yeah. We have peanut butter, bread, milk and potatoes, hamburger and a roast. And you know who bought it, too. Right?"

"No. I'm not really sure who bought what! Rolf, she said she *would* go shopping with you. Maybe if you ask her instead of ordering her, it would help."

"Fine. Then maybe I'll get my $70.00 back. Then again, there's always the check book I'm carryin' in my pocket. That's still got about $80.00 in it."

I don't know if it's their checkbook or Rolf's. I feel the undertow of pressure toward me, as if I can loosen up the bucks if I want to--or, it's my fault her money is in the bank and they're having to do without.

I guess it *is* my fault since I was the one who suggested they walk to the bank, but I don't know if they did. As usual, I sense right and wrong on both sides, but I can do nothing from a distance. In fact, my suggestions may have already made the problem worse.

Four days later, March 18th, is my next call from Rolf. "I don't know what the hell's going on. They got no money again. Neither one of them has any. I went to the store a little bit ago and bought a gallon of milk with my own money. Mom wants to feed some of it to the cats. I told her, 'No way, you're not touchin' that for them damned cats!' She been hasslin' me ever since.

"That ain't all. Yesterday I worked from about seven in the evening until five o'clock in the morning cleanin' up the shop area. Then I went in the house and crashed, and just when I was gettin' to sleep good, Dad went out on the front sidewalk and wandered off. I had to go find him. While I was gone, Shortie come over to start on the yard work he and I had talked about. Mom told him to go home, because there wasn't any work at their place for him. I barely got home in time to get that straightened out."

I make no comment about Rolf's strange working hours, but I think that's more weird than Dad going out at 7:00 AM and wandering off or Mother sending Shortie home.

"Well, Rolf, Mother probably just got confused about Shortie. She doesn't like him anyway, does she?"

"Naw, she don't like him, but he's okay. He's having it kind of rough right now, but he's a good worker. Today we worked all day cleaning up that area by the shop entrance and out there by the garage and the back door to the house. We got rid of all kinds of old flower pots, stacks of lumber, and piles of brush from old pruning jobs. Dad tried to help. But wouldn't you know it, he screwed that up, too."

"What happened?"

"He poked a hole in Nosy-bill's garage window while he was stackin' brush."

"Oh, no, what did she say?"

"Well, actually nothing since they're gone. I just nailed a board over the hole 'til they get back and I can tell her what happened. I also paid

Shortie $20.00 apiece to prune two fruit trees, and that took the very last of my money to do that."

I do not respond to *my money,* though I've never known Rolf to pay for anything for Mom and Dad with his money, much less a pruning job. The amount of yard work Rolf describes sounds like a lot, far more than could have been accomplished in one day. As for pruning the fruit trees, if they really did that, $20.00 apiece is a pittance. Something about this financial accounting doesn't ring true, but before I can question specifically about hours, tasks, or pay, Rolf rambles on.

"You know, it's just doggone hard to get all the work done and keep track of the old man, too. He wandered off while Shortie and me were busy, and he went into the shop and found my glasses and pocketed them. Later I saw 'em in his shirt pocket. Now let me tell ya before anyone else has a chance to tattle. I grabbed 'em right out of his shirt pocket, and I slapped his hands three or four times and told him to stay out of the shop. If he is going to act like a child, I am going to treat him like a child."

"Rolf, where the hell do you get off acting like that? The man is *not* a child. He's your father, and he's old and sick! What makes you think that kind of pissed-off anger and slapping would be appropriate for a child or an old person?"

"Well, I didn't hurt him much. In fact, I didn't hurt him at all, but Dad acted as if he was hurt. Really, he was *mad!*"

"Rolf, you have no idea how mad I am right now. There is something dreadfully wrong with what you're doing. You are not an authority on how to treat senile elderly people, and you're certainly not an expert on treatment of children. It's a damned good thing you never had any!"

"Well, I suggest you come down this next weekend and stay over and really understand the situation. You gotta be down here and see the shit that goes on."

"You know, Rolf, I've had that experience, and some of it for more years than you have. I do understand, and I don't think your treatment of them is in any way justifiable."

"Sis, you just don't know how bad things are. A few months ago I could at least talk to Mom. I could manage her, but Dad's problem is dragging her down. They're both paranoid and filthy, and this stinginess is really bad! I bought three loaves of bread on Friday, and they just sit and eat until it's all gone. They eat bread, butter and jelly sandwiches--with sugar on them. Today is Sunday, and there's nothing left. I only have nine bucks to my name. You get it? There's no food here--*nothing*!"

I remain a calm but unsympathetic listener to Rolf's venting. "Well, there's not much I can do from here. I'll be down next weekend."

"Yeah. Okay." Rolf slams the phone down.

I rub my ear and replace my receiver.

The distance away and my familiarity with Rolf's embellishments allow me to put aside my emotional reactions and growing mistrust of his behavior. I almost don't care what happens to any of them. There's wrong from each of them, and I don't want to hear any more from any of them until I have to.

I let days pass without calling. I don't know how--or if--they'll survive on *nothing*.

On March 21st, Rolf calls to tell me, "The pruning's all done. That took us damn near three days. The front yard is mowed and edged. I want you to know I had to dip into my own money again and fork out $24.00 to the mower repairman for the edger. And, I had to give him two other edgers besides to meet the debt. I picked up two power mowers he worked on, and that was $90.00 for getting them in shape."

"That sounds okay to me if the repairman will take the extra mowers as partial payment. Dad doesn't need them anyway. If everyone's short of cash, I guess that's a good way to pay for service." My mind is flooded with previous *facts* Rolf has given me. The numbers aren't jiving. He also said he only had nine bucks to his name. How does he 'dip into his own'? I also wonder how they did all that work on bread and butter and jelly sandwiches--even with sugar on top?

Later in the evening I call Mother, and she gives me her variation of the work. "Oh, my, we're so tired, both Dad and me. We've all worked hard, but everything looks so nice. It's costing plenty though. I went down to the bank and took out $250.00 and paid out $165.00 of it for the mowing and pruning. Shortie works for $7.00 an hour, and I gave Rolf $80.00 for his work."

As usual the numbers don't jive, but I guess that's what Rolf meant by his *own money.* "Mom, do you have enough money for food until your next checks come?"

"Oh, yeah. I've got $40.00 left for food, and we have everything we need."

I can hear Rolf fussing in the background. "Rolf must be with you now. May I speak to him?" I hear her call out to him and hand him the phone.

"Hey, Rolf, you said there was no food in the house, but Mom tells me they have all the food they need. Is she right?"

"I don't know whether they eat or not. I suppose they do. The whole house smells like burned toast. They must have had something to eat."

"How about all this yard work? Mother says *she* paid for it, but you said you dipped into *your* money to pay for it. Which is it? I thought you only had nine bucks to your name."

Rolf doesn't miss a beat. "Well, I hauled a couple of small jobs a little while back, and that's how I had a few bucks."

His answer is quick and smooth. He mentioned no word at all that Mother had given him $80.00. Maybe she pays him, and she's the *someone* he did a couple small hauling jobs for--like to the dump or the recycling station.

"You know, Sis, I'll be damned if Taco isn't giving me a bad time too. He stole a head of cabbage from the grocery shopping bag. He took that and an open can of dog food and drag 'em under the dining table. I was tryin' to wrestle those things away from him, and I was down on my knees under the table when about then here comes the old man and he had to get his nose into it."

"What does that mean? He didn't get under the table too, did he?"

"Naw, but you know how Dad feeds them cats. He uses one big can and a table knife, and he spoons out for each one of the three into separate dishes. Well, he'd done that, and he was comin' back through the house. He couldn't get through the dining room with me down half way under the table and blockin' his way. Now you know how he just can't wait for nothin' anymore. Well, he started hittin' me on the back with that knife and tellin' me to get out of his way. I want you to know I came flyin' up from under that table and grabbed him and slammed him up against the wall. He just ain't gonna do that to me. I told him, 'Don't you ever do that to me again, or I'll beat your head in'."

"Rolf, your geriatric technique sucks shit! How could you do that? You are an abuser by your very own description of the episode."

"Yeah, yeah, maybe. But he ain't gonna go around hittin' me with a knife!"

"For God's sake, Rolf, the man was using the handle of a table knife. How could that hurt you? I think you're more zingy than they are!"

"I wish you would speak to your friend Gary. He's the one whose wife works in a nursing home, Right? You won't listen to me, but I know without even being there personally she will tell you what you're doing is wrong. She may be able to give you some effective techniques for getting along better. Rolf, what you're doing is so terribly wrong. It's making everything worse!"

"Well, maybe I do have a few things to learn, but I can't let Dad get by with stuff like that. The next time it could just as well be a butcher knife."

"Now who's being paranoid? Rolf, please talk to Gary and his wife right away. You definitely should not be doing what you're doing. And please make that call tomorrow. I can't come down until next weekend."

"Yeah, yeah. I'll call Gary and Peggy Sue. And I'll call that Mason guy, too, and see if he can't move this guardianship thing faster.

"By the way, you can expect a bill from the garden shop, too. Me and Shortie bought about $180.00 worth of seed, fertilizer, and stuff like that."

"Huh? Rolf, I can't even keep the amounts straight for the work you and Shortie did. And Mother's figures don't match yours. Now, we're going to have another big bill at the end of this month?"

"Well, Sis, all I can tell you is things add up pretty quick when everything is gettin' done at once."

My mind rages silently. Bullshit, Rolf, my classroom students used $95.00 worth of seeds and grew over 8,500 plants. They could seed all of Ridgeview! What did you spend $180.00 on? I want to scream--*Liar!* But accusations are of no benefit to anyone at this moment, and surely not via long distance. All of the money amounts are mumble-jumble and there are no receipts. It doesn't matter. There's more than one reason *now* that I do not want my name on any kind of guardianship deal with Rolf, and it's not just money management.

A call from Rolf on March 27th rings repetitiously. "Yeah, there's cat litter all over the bedroom. Dad's job is to clean it up. You know him--he rubs it in until he says it's clean. That's pretty much how it goes. We're still workin' on the yard."

"I thought that project was done. How much more could there possibly be?"

"Well, I'll tell you, we carried off another eleven hundred pounds. Totally, that's over three tons. That was another $16.00 for the dump fee, and $28.00 more to Shortie."

I don't ask if that's the same job as before or new work. At least the money amounts are getting smaller. But I wish I could figure out mathematically if it's possible to remove over three tons of limbs from two small pie cherry trees, a crab apple, a Bing cherry and a white cherry tree.

Rolf rattles on, "My biggest problem now is I can't get Mom to understand the bedroom is dirty and they're both filthy. She's so defensive, and she says, 'We don't smell'. You know damn well they stink big time!"

"Part of it is how you say it, you know."

"Yeah, yeah. Dad is still eating butter and sugar sandwiches, and he's had several occasions of uncontrollable runs all over the toilet."

"Who cleans that up?"

"Well, if it gets cleaned up, they do it."

"Did you call Mr. Mason about the guardianship?"

"No, no. I haven't gotten to that."

"Are you ever going to?"

"Yeah, yeah. I'm gonna get to it."

"What about cash flow?"

"Well, they should be getting their pension checks soon--hers in a couple days and his the first of the month. Social Security checks come on the 3rd of the month."

"Are you all going to make it until the checks come in?"

"Yeah, yeah, we'll be fine."

On March 29th, Rolf calls again, "Dad's pension check came, and he cashed it. I just relieved him of the cash. I figure he shouldn't be handling that kind of money. He's pissed, but there ain't much he can do about it."

"I don't think you should be doing that."

"Mom got her retirement check and cashed it. She's got $200.00 left from her $407-dollar check."

"Where's the other $207.00?"

"I really don't know. I guess she paid a few things."

"Rolf, I don't think you have any legal right to take their cash from their checks, even if you do think you can make it go further.

"What about the guardianship procedure? Did you call Mr. Mason?"

"Well, you know, to tell you the truth, I think Mr. Mason is one of those little sleaze-balls who worked with Sam Wilderman to defend the crook who stole my truck from me. I'm not so sure I want anything to do with him."

"Rolf, you met the man personally. It shouldn't take you this long to decide if he was a lawyer in a case against you. Your procrastination is not helping. I can't make sense of anything you're doing."

"Well, little sister, you're not here to see the day-to-day needs. You're just a little know-it-all who thinks you can manage their money better than they can--or better than I can. You always think you're 100% right. I know God-damned well I can carry that $190.00 from Dad's pension check and get more out of it than Dad can."

"Rolf, we're back to square one. I have been trying to get you to co-operate and get this guardianship process moving. It's three weeks later, and you've done nothing. You are not that busy. You just want to continue doing everything on a cash basis with you managing the cash. That means with a lot of grabbing and hollering."

"Well, maybe in the next three weeks I'll be able to get the fuck out of here and on the road again. I got a couple of opportunities comin' up."

"Good luck. That may help everyone!"

"You don't understand a damned thing! I can manage their money fine."

"I think you're wrong to do what you're doing--to take over everything, command them to do things, and grab all their cash. You don't have any legal authority in regard to their business. And you don't have any right to manage them like you do--physically nor emotionally! You're being abusive! As far as your cash management technique, it's in the same category as your geriatric technique!"

March came in like a lion, and it's going out like a lion! BEWARE!

CHAPTER 23

An Ad Litem Home Visit

FROM DEEP WITHIN myself comes the message, Betty, no more waiting for big brother to take the lead. Stop your own procrastination. You cannot deny uncontrolled anger. Verbal abuse and danger in your family are daily happenings. It's not just Dad--or Dad and Mom. It's Rolf, too. Betty, do something!

I pick up the phone and call Mr. Mason, the court-appointed ad litem figure. I'm not going to tell him to relieve himself or get off the pot, but I am going to update him on recent Malfait happenings and make an appointment to see him *by myself.*

In our conversation, Mr. Mason informs me, "Betty, I have almost all the paperwork completed and a judge has been assigned to the case. However, I am required to visit Malfaits in their home. That's an absolute necessity in the guardianship process. As yet I've not been able to catch them at the house, and I've stopped by there several times."

"They do go out to coffee almost every day, and they walk quite a bit."

"Well, the earliest available date I can see you will be April 14th. That's two weeks away. I'll try very hard to complete my visit during that time frame."

As I hang up the phone, I'm thinking I didn't cause him to get off the pot any sooner than Rolf would have. It seems waiting is a routine part of the guardianship procedure. Nothing happens on my timeline--and perhaps it shouldn't.

I go on a spring break vacation with my family and return to Ridgeview April 14th. On my way through town I pick up a bag of culinary fare from the Golden Arches. Malfaits are happy to see me and delighted to join me for a picnic down by the lake near their home.

Mom reaches for the food bag and rolls her eyes in my direction, "My goodness, Betty, you're so tan and it's only April. Where have you been?"

"I've been to Mexico for spring vacation."

Both Mom and Dad laugh incredulously, and Mother comments, "You *didn't* do that! Rolf has gone to California, and that's a vacation for

Dad and me!" Mother opens the food bag and begins dealing out the hamburgers. I do not clarify that my family really did go to Mexico for spring break.

Later in the afternoon I keep the appointment with Mr. Mason--without Rolf. He tells me, "I still haven't been able to visit Malfaits in their home. I've made three trips down there since we last spoke, but I've not been able to be admitted to the house. On one occasion, I saw them in the front yard when I pulled up, but by the time I got out of my car they had disappeared."

Author's mother and father enjoy spring blooms on WA State Capital grounds

"You might have scared them, or they may have thought you were a salesman. I have talked to them about the guardianship. They seem to understand someone is supposed to come and discuss with them about bill-paying, light and water turn-offs, and such--and it's a person who is to be helpful. I've told them it's a necessary legal step to allow me to help them, but I don't know what they *really* might be thinking."

Mr. Mason continues, "The third time I was there I know for sure they saw me, and they heard me. I was already parked on the street, and I could see them coming down the sidewalk from the little corner store. As they went in their front door I was walking up the walkway. But as I stepped up on the steps, I heard the deadbolt click. I rang the bell several times. It's a beautiful four-tone chime. No one answered. I called out to them by name, but not a sound came from inside."

"Mr. Mason, I may have to be present in order for you to be admitted to the house. I'll be there tomorrow to do the usual chores, but you don't work on Saturdays. Usually I'm only there on weekends."

"I have a family gathering myself near that neighborhood tomorrow. Could you be at their house at 11:00 AM?"

The next day I make sure to arrive at 516 well before 11:00 AM. No one answers the door bell. I may be in the same category as Mr. Mason. I search all around, check with neighbors, the little corner store, and the Ocean Espresso. I drive back to their house and search the yard, shop and the garage again. Finally, I return to my truck parked on their driveway. I pull out my pillow and quilt from behind the truck seat, flop down against my suitcase, and fall asleep.

A slamming car door awakens me a short while later. Mr. Mason is right on time for the designated 11:00 AM visit. We go to the front door together and ring the bell. There is no answer. We search all around the property.

As we return to the front sidewalk, a green junker car rounds the corner and comes slowly up the street. "Oh, God, that looks like their car coming now. They haven't driven in years." As the car gets nearer, "Oh, thank God, that's not them. It's my brother, Rolf. Mother said he was in California, but he must have gotten back." The car slowly passes by us.

"Well, what was that about? I know it was Rolf. I saw him. He had to see us standing here and me waving at him. I guess I've been ignored. I'm getting kind of used to being ignored by some people in my family."

"Well, Betty, it seems like neither one of us is going to see Malfaits right now." Mr. Mason takes a business card out and writes a phone number on the back.

The green junker rounds the corner a second time and pulls slowly over to the curb as Mr. Mason tells me, "Listen, if they come back anytime soon, I'm at my family function just a few blocks from here. Give me a call. I'll come right over. I can be here in five minutes."

I turn as Rolf saunters up. "Well, I guess you saw us after all. You remember Mr. Mason?"

"Yeah, yeah, I know Mr. Mason. What's up?"

Mr. Mason tells him, "The general appearance of your folks' place is vastly improved since I was here the other day. I do need to see them in person though, and I'll have to try another time." He hands me the business card.

After Mr. Mason departs, Rolf asks nothing about him nor the guardianship. He tells me, "I seen Mom and Dad over near Ocean Espresso. They won't be home for quite a while."

I grab some cold drinks from my ice chest in the truck, and the two of us head for the lawn chairs in the back yard, admiring all the work that's been done as we go. The flowers and trees are blooming profusely. It's a pleasant reminder of years past, as everything Malfaits ever planted flourished.

"So, how was your trip to California with Mike?"

"It was good for me. I feel a lot better."

"When did you get back?"

"A couple of days ago."

"The yard looks great."

"It should--I busted my ass on it. There's still some more stuff I'd like to get done around here. But let me warn you--the inside of the place is a disaster zone. Urine smell, cat litter, soiled newspapers, shit. You name it.

"*And,* before they tell you, let me tell you we had a big flap about cleanliness. Dad got a little upset. I just told them they stink, and I'm not gonna take 'em any place lookin' and smellin' like they do. They even got a note from the city bus driver. I found it all crumpled up in Mom's pocket. *You and your husband smell, please bathe.* I guess you know something's gotta be done to make that situation better. I flat out told 'em they're gonna have a bath, if I have to throw them in the tub myself."

I let the reason for Rolf's being in Mother's pocket and his physical threats about bathing pass, but the note is not the only indication of how much more their personal cleanliness has deteriorated as I learn a short time later when Ruthie, one of my favorite people who lives down the block from Malfaits, walks by and invites me to walk home with her and have a cup of coffee. "Oh, Betty, I just hate how much your folks have failed. They've been such wonderful people to everyone hereabouts for so many years. It isn't right for them to be like they are now. I feel so bad about them, but I don't think Rolf helps the situation. He's so loud and mean, and I see him pushing your Dad around. That ought not to be going on. I'm kind of scared to say anything to Rolf though. Maybe you can get him to not do that."

I know she's being kind. I know she feels I could, or should, do something about it. But she isn't aware of the total tempest raging in our family teapot. "Ruthie, Rolf and I began the steps toward a legal guardianship, but Rolf isn't easy to work with. He has balked repeatedly for months. I've decided I'm going to proceed on my own. I know what you're trying to say, and I can't let things go on as they are."

Any further explanation to Ruthie is interrupted as we both notice Mother and Dad coming down the street. Ruthie opens her front door and calls, "Hey, you all, get on in here and have a cup of coffee with us."

Mother comes slowly to the door. Dad continues on down the street staring straight ahead as if he didn't hear Ruthie. From the hall entryway Mother's odor precedes her into the living room, a repulsive announcement of her arrival. I can't tell if it's cat urine or her own. She seems more frail and acts as if she can't see very well. She enters the living room and stands momentarily beside my chair. She turns around, returns to the front entryway and seats herself on a wooden bench. "I'm too filthy to come into your living room, Ruthie. Dad and I have been working in the yard. I'd ruin your nice furniture. I'll just rest a spell before I catch up to Dad. We've been out for a walk, and we've already had our morning coffee."

Mother's friend and neighbor of almost fifty years doesn't press her further to come into the living room. I'm sure she smells the same odors I do. Though we are having our coffee in mugs, Ruthie takes a china cup and saucer from the china hutch and goes to the kitchen. She returns to the entryway shortly. "Here, Francine. There's always room for a half cup."

Mother notices me for the first time. "Why, Betty, what are you doing here? How long have you been here?"

"Not too long. I just stopped in for a visit with Ruthie." I rise and take my mug to the kitchen sink. I don't feel like any more coffee nor visiting. The pathetic slow motion tragedy of a friendship dying in the front hallway screams silently at me as Mother swills the entire half-cup in one slurp and returns the cup and saucer to Ruthie. I take Mother's hand and help her up.

She clings hard on my arm. As we make our exit she tells me, "These old legs just aren't what they used to be. I'm so tired."

Once out on the sidewalk, Mother continues to hold my hand as we move down the block. It's a childlike gesture. She is the child. I am the parent.

When we're almost to her driveway, I pull my fingers gently from her grip, "Oh darn, I've left my truck keys at Ruthie's. I'll have to run back. You go on. Dad is standing there on the steps waiting for you to unlock the front door."

I feel a nasty twinge of guilt, as I have not told my mother a lie since about age ten when I wore my Easter suit she had made for me, spilled my pop-sickle juice on it, and then lied about having worn it. I feel bad all over again, about the Easter suit and a lot more, as I run back to Ruthie's.

I call the number Mr. Mason jotted on the back of the business card. He says he'll be over in a few minutes. I race out the door and catch up with Mother who is just unlocking the front door.

"Dad, quit standing there like a wooden post and get yourself in this house!"

I start up the front steps and pretend not to notice Mother is less than gentle as she shoves Dad into the darkened entryway. I block out the pain of my churning stomach with the jangling of my string of found keys hoping to distract Mother from further aggression.

"I found my keys. Boy, that's a relief."

At that moment Rolf emerges from the back yard, and Mother comes back out onto the steps where we all again admire the restored beauty of the gardens. Shortly Mother laments, "That old sun is getting downright hot. Let's get into the house where it's nice and cool."

The savoring of beauty on the exterior is crushed instantly with the first step into the living room. Cool, maybe--but definitely not nice. It's a scene of deplorable, odorous chaos. After a brief flurry of moving piles of unknown debris, Dad, Mom, Rolf and I each find a place to sit among the torn-up newspapers, wads of Taco's dog hair, boxes, guns, dirty clothes, "clean" clothes, and God knows what else.

I lean over and peek into their bedroom. Deplorable is a relative term. It's worse in there. There is kitty litter all over. Mounds of cat feces in the litter pan and out. The bedding is piled up and reeks of urine and human feces. I try to imagine where I'm going to even begin with chores. I assure Mother, "Mom, Rolf and I will get right to that washing. It looks as if you have it all ready to go."

"Oh, no, I don't want my quilts or that comforter washed at the laundromat. I cleaned those myself. They're not dirty. They're just rolled up there and ready to put back on the bed."

Before I can figure how to change her mind about washing them, the doorbell chimes. Mr. Mason has arrived. He is friendly and gracious. Mother invites him in as if she knows him. He comes into the living room, into our family filth, and sits down in a spot Mother clears off for him.

I speak up, "Mother, this is Mr. Mason, the court-appointed person I've told you about." She smiles and stacks the papers and mail on top of another nearby stack. "This is my father, Roger, and you've met my brother, Rolf."

Mr. Mason directs his comments to Mother and Dad. "Your yard is so beautiful. I've tried before to see you both, but I kept missing you. I can tell you've been working very hard."

Mother appreciates his remarks. "Thank you. It's a lot of hard work, and it's getting to be a little bit too hard for Dad and me to do all that needs to be done."

Mr. Mason smiles. "As the years come upon us, we all need a bit more help."

Mother is quick to reply, "We do the best we can, but we don't need any help."

Mr. Mason asks, "Did you get the letter I sent you back on February 12th?"

"No, we didn't get any letter from you. Dad and I keep track of all the mail that comes in around here."

Mr. Mason continues, "Rolf, here, confirmed that it *did* arrive. I was able to chat with him a little bit one day when you weren't here."

"That's news to me. Rolf, you didn't say anything about that visit."

Mother trains a suspicious eye on Rolf. "Why did you bring him here? Dad and I are managing just fine on our own."

Rolf is unresponsiveness, expressionless.

"No, no," Mr. Mason interjects, "Rolf didn't bring me here. The letter that I mentioned states that your daughter, Betty, has asked the Superior Court of this county to allow her to assist you in your legal and financial matters."

Mother glares at me. "Why did you do that? Dad and I are managing fine."

"Mother, I know in some things you are doing fine, but if you truly want me to help with your bill-paying, taxes, and such, I have to have legal authority to do it. Mr. Mason is not my lawyer. I didn't hire him. He has been appointed by the court to come here and talk with you and Dad to see if you really do need my help."

Dad expresses his opinion in conversational chirping directed at no one in particular, "Well, see here now, I have plenty of money in the Fibex Credit Union. I don't need anybody's help."

Mr. Mason looks toward Mother. "Betty feels there are some bills that need to be brought up to date, particularly property taxes."

Before Mother can respond, Dad pipes in, "Well, say now, I'll go right down to that credit union and see Dennis, and I'll get your tax money. Mama, what's his name who has all my money?"

Mr. Mason answers for him, "Dennis Cushion."

"Yes, that's it." Dad questions Mr. Mason, "Do you know Dennis?"

"Oh, yes. I know Dennis. Now, Mrs. Malfait, the problem with the property taxes is that here on your two lots and the house they are three years in arrears."

Mother looks shocked. "Well, I don't see how that could be."

Dad leans over toward Mr. Mason, "Do you have any money in the credit union?"

"Yes, yes, I do." Mr. Mason struggles with his billfold and shows Dad an American Express credit card.

At the same time Mother says, "I don't know where you get your figures. We pay our taxes."

Dad stares at the credit card and moves it in and out trying to focus as he asks, "How much money do you have with Dennis in the credit union?"

"Well, Mrs. Malfait, the county records show the taxes on your property here have *not* been paid in three years. That's the official record, and that's what I checked."

"We'll go right down tomorrow and pay them then."

Rolf and I remain quiet. My last trip to the credit union with her when she paid Rolf's late mortgage payments reduced their savings to a few hundred dollars and the same was true at their bank. Their savings accounts at one time may have been ample to do what she is proposing, but I know they can't do that now.

Mother repeats her lack of belief at the situation but expresses her willingness to pay the taxes. All the while Dad chatters about how much money he has in the credit union. As Mr. Mason retrieves his American Express card, Dad shakes a finger at him, "You know, Dennis *admonishes* his customers about lawyers."

Dad's verbiage catches everyone's attention, and he takes advantage of the moment, "Dennis told me I have enough in the credit union to live on for five years."

Mother snaps, "Shut up, you old fool. Dennis never told you any such thing. We always pay our bills. We've never had any problems, and we have excellent credit."

Dad uncrosses his legs and leans forward as if to get up. "Mama, I told you, we'll go down and see Dennis *right now* and get the money for the taxes."

I turn to Dad to try to occupy his attention and quiet him before he does get up from the couch and tries to go see Dennis *right now*. "Dad, Dad, hush and let the man talk to Mother. You can go to the credit union later and do your business."

Dad leans back on the couch. "Well, we'll just do that."

"I know you will, but for right now, let's try to be quiet and share the conversation time." I smile at him and reach over and gently pat his scrawny bushy bearded face. "Yuck! What the hell is that?" The room stands still as I run my fingers over two scabby lumps about two inches long behind each of Dad's ears. "My God, what *is* that? Mother, what has he done to his ears? These are bloody scabs. He's been hurt!"

Dad speaks haltingly, "Rolf--pulled my ears. It--hurt."

Mother is annoyed at my interruption, "Yes, Rolf pulled his ears, but he's okay!"

I crawl over the piles of stuff on the couch between Dad and me and bend his head toward the light. I can see the smears of dried blood and the lumpy hard scabs of evidence that his ears have been pulled until they tore from his face. In stunned silence all eyes turn to Rolf, who sits like a granite torso, arms folded over his chest.

Without unfolding his arms, Rolf shrugs, "I didn't do that much to his ears. I just pulled them a little bit."

With eyes downcast and picking make-believe lint from his trouser legs, Dad adds, "The garbage can lid--fell on my head."

Rolf glares at me, "You know how Dad is. He's just so unmanageable. And, yeah, I did pull his ears, but it wasn't that hard."

Dad falters, "That damned--can lid--was heavy."

Mr. Mason speaks up, "We're about finished here, I think. Rolf and Betty, may I speak to both of you outside."

As we all stand Mother assures Mr. Mason, "We'll get right down to the credit union on Monday and get those taxes caught up."

Rolf is already outside on the front doorstep. Mother leads Mr. Mason through the living room clutter toward the door.

Dad pulls up his pant leg. "That wasn't all, Betty. Rolf--threw a--lawnmower at me. Look-it here."

I call out, "Mother, wait a minute. Is there anything else you should tell Mr. Mason about the thing with Dad's ears? Or about these?" I lean over and point to the scabs on Dad's legs. There is one on each upper shin, and they're about the size of fifty-cent pieces. "What are these? Dad says Rolf threw a lawnmower at him. Is that true? I don't believe this! Tell me, Mother, is it true?"

My head is pulsating. My stomach is doing the same. I should have known back when Dad couldn't speak clearly and was making the punching motions pleadingly. I should have known Dad wouldn't have--couldn't have--made that up. My moments of self-chastisement crash against a brick wall as Mother speaks.

"Dad and Rolf had a little disagreement, but Dad's okay now. His legs are fine. You don't be worrying about his legs."

Mr. Mason looks at Dad's legs but says nothing.

I make my way to the front door and follow Mr. Mason into the yard where Rolf stands motionless, arms crossed over his chest. Mother closes the heavy door behind us. She and Dad stay inside. I walk up close to Rolf. Clinching my fists to the sides of my quivering body, I glare up into his eyes--really up his nostrils--and scream, "What the hell did you think you were doing?"

Rolf shifts his feet slightly away from me. His arms remain crossed. He thrusts his chin out and locks eye-contact with me. "Yeah, yeah, I did pull his ears a little, but it was just a little." Rolf jerks his head toward the front step. "The rest of that was probably just like he said, from one of those big garbage dumpster lids out in the alley."

I back away from Rolf and cross my own arms close to my body and shove my clinched fists in my armpits clamping them down with my elbows. "Oh, sure, and it even hit him down on his shins. Rolf, you are such a despicable piece of shit! How can you stand there and make such flimsy excuses!"

Mr. Mason steps up close to us and speaks quietly, "I think I saw as much as I needed to see with your folks today."

I want to hit Rolf. I want to smash his defiant chin clear back between his ears. I force myself to focus on Mr. Mason. I release my arms, unclench my fists and let my arms fall to my sides. I suck in a deep, shaky breath and wait for Mr. Mason to make any critical remarks and admonishments to Rolf. I tell myself that's why the court appointed him and that's why he wanted to see the two of us outside.

Mr. Mason looks at Rolf and continues in the same quiet voice, "Those garbage dumpster lids can really be hard on the head. I have the same kind of dumpsters at my house."

I remain immobile, in a silent rage. I would like to shut Rolf in a garbage dumpster--forever!

Mr. Mason's voice seems far away. "The next thing I have to do is get a doctor's report for your dad. That will conclude my part of the guardianship process. The judge will do the evaluating." He pauses, unfurls his pages of notes, and replaces his pen in his shirt pocket. "I'll be on my way now." He turns and walks to his car.

Neither Rolf nor I speak--not to Mr. Mason nor to each other. I stare at Rolf. I can't speak. I have never before felt the emotional turmoil that is surging in me at this moment. A mental image of the wounds and the scabs flashes like a red neon light in my brain. I have a nauseous churning in my gut. In this seething stillness, Rolf and I both turn and go back into the house.

Mom and Dad are discussing their paranoid thoughts about Mr. Mason and why he had been in their home. Rolf plops down in the big arm chair, stone-faced, and recrosses his arms. Mother moves over behind Rolf's chair out of his vision and makes frantic arm motions for me to come and go with her.

"Betty, I need to go to the store."

I break from my frozen position in the entryway, "All right. I'll go with you."

As Mother and I walk along toward the corner grocery, she takes my arm. I can feel her hand trembling. "Rolf and Dad *were* fighting--something about the dog under the table. Dad wanted Rolf to move out of the way. Rolf got awful mad, and he pushed Dad. Dad grabbed him by the beard and pulled. Rolf, in turn, grabbed onto Dad's ears and banged his head against the wall several times."

"What did *you* do?"

"I was going to call you."

"Why didn't you?"

"Rolf wouldn't let me."

"Did he pull your ears too?"

"No. He held his hands on either side of my face and shook my face. I said I was going to call anyway, and he put his hands over mine on the telephone and held them. He wouldn't let me dial."

"Mother, I'm trying so hard to help, but I can't make good decisions when I don't know things. Rolf tells me one thing. You tell me another. Dad never knows what the hell anything is. I should have really listened to him a while back. He was trying to tell me. He was trying to ask for help. I should have believed him then."

As we approach the corner store, I wrestle with my own truth. I saw the scabs. I *felt* them! Neither she nor Dad is making that up.

Mother and I get our coffee and go outside to sit at a picnic table in the sunshine. "Mother, Mr. Mason really is the person to whom you should have told all this. I have taken the steps that I have taken so far pretty much based on suspicions. Mr. Mason is not my lawyer. He is court-appointed. He's neutral. He's the one looking for truth in this matter. Mother, nobody can make anything better without all the information. I know Dad didn't know what was going on with Mr. Mason, but why didn't *you* tell?"

"Because Rolf was sitting right there. I couldn't!"

"Mother, Rolf is part of the reason that today even happened. I can't do this all by myself. I can't help either one of you, if you won't *let* me help."

"Well, I thought Mr. Mason was someone Rolf hired. He's always trying to get his hands on what's not his and to get his name on legal things."

Get his name on legal things is disturbing, but I don't want to cause more confusion and upset. "Mother, I just want to be able to help, to see the taxes and other bills get paid, to know that you're not going to lose your home in foreclosure, which is what it says in those letters from the credit union. Then there's all the other things like health and cleaning and caring. Rolf is lousy about doing those things for himself. How can I, or you, really expect him to do them for you and Dad? He's so angry and spiteful. He's not helpful to you nor himself. I don't know what he's trying to prove."

"Yes, he's awfully mean to us both, especially to Dad. He's always hollering and shouting, and pushing and shoving. He tried to pick Dad up and shove him into the bathtub. That scared us both, but I screamed enough that he gave up."

"Mother, Mr. Mason needed to know that, to know how you felt, and that you are afraid. He needed to know how Rolf really treats you; and he needed to know *that* more than whether you paid your taxes or have money in the Fibex Credit Union."

"Look up there, Betty. I can't even go have a cup of coffee with you without Rolf spying on me. Here he comes up the street. He never goes to coffee with me. He never takes Dad and me to coffee or anyplace else.

He doesn't even drink coffee. He just doesn't want us out of his sight for a minute."

"Mother, he probably doesn't want the two of us here by ourselves discussing what Mr. Mason said. I guess I'd be anxious, too, if I had done what he did."

Mother and I gulp down the last of our coffee as Rolf walks up, "Hey, I wondered what was keeping you two so long. I got that laundry bagged up and ready to go, Sis."

"Mom and I are having a cup of coffee and unwinding a little bit. The session with Mr. Mason was very upsetting to everyone...Yeah, I'm ready to go to the laundromat."

Mother takes my arm and we start back toward the house with Rolf ambling along behind us. We are a trio in angry silence.

The trip to do the washing gives Rolf opportunity to fill me in on his version of what happened. "You know how filthy it is around the place. Dad and Mom are worse than the house, and they won't do anything about it."

"That's what you all got into a fight over?"

"Yeah, you might say that--about not taking baths and not cleaning up after themselves. You know, my cleanliness standards ain't too high. I just want them to bathe and *try* to control the odors."

"I know, Rolf, but you can't *throw* people into the bathtub."

"Funny you should say it like that. I know I can't throw them in, but it was to the point where they both were going to *have* to take a bath."

I don't know if he actually did it or not. The odors of both of them make me think he was not successful. "You know, Rolf, if everyone who ever wanted *you* to take a bath got into a physical match with you, you'd have more than your ears pulled. You can't force behaviors like that, especially things as personal as bathing and bathroom duties."

"Yeah, I know, but they had to have a bath."

"So did you physically force them?"

"Well, you might say that. They weren't going to go otherwise."

"Rolf, you're being abusive. Right now, while we're here in a public place--in this laundromat--how would you feel or react if you saw some big, burly, not-so-squeaky-clean brute pulling the ears of an 80-year-old frail, senile man and banging his head against the wall, screaming at him that he needed a bath?"

Rolf crosses his arms over his chest, juts his chin out and growls, "Well, I guess I'd figure he needed a bath." Then he grins and drops his arms, "It's almost funny when you put it like that."

"No, Rolf, it isn't funny. How would you *really* see that scene here in this public place in front of other people--right here, and not behind the filthy walls of 516?"

"Well, yeah, yeah--I guess that would look pretty bad."

"Can you also see that *public* doesn't matter? Your behavior toward them in private can never be questioned if it's just as acceptable in public. And, Rolf, that's the way it *has* to be!"

Rolf's reaction to my demand is as casual as his description of the episode had been in front of Mr. Mason. He seems to understand his errors, but he isn't about to acknowledge any wrongdoing. I have no confidence he won't do it again.

Rolf interrupts my mental free-flow. "You know, it coulda been just like Dad said--the dumpster lid could of fallen on his head."

"Damn it, Rolf, did it fall on your head, too? Did it fall on both sides of his head at the same time? Did he line his head up in the groove like a penny on a railroad track and get those matching scabby twin wounds on both of his ears? Quit bullshitting me!"

"All right. All right. I'm just sayin' the lid might have fallen on his head, and they bled again where I pulled 'em because they were already hurt."

I turn my attention to the wash, actually turning from one nauseating experience to another, but at least the shit on the comforter can be washed away.

Thank God for bleach! I wish I could use it on me, too!

A short while later I leave Rolf to stay with the dryers, and I run to the nearby store to get some more soap and use a pay phone.

"Hello, Mr. Mason, did you get all the information you needed for your report?"

"Yes, I did. I can certainly understand your urgency. You have several problems with both parents--*and* your brother."

"What is your advice? I don't know what to do next."

"I'm really not in a position to advise you. Rolf is for sure not a good choice for the primary care person. You need to consult your own attorney for further advice. I'll have my report to him on Monday."

CHAPTER 24

Easter Sunrise Service

I THROW MYSELF into the never-ending work at 516, and it's late Sunday evening before I start my three-hour trip to my own home. Exhaustion overtakes me as I near a little town called Allwyn. My eyes are open, but I know my brain has been asleep for a number of miles. It's almost 4:00 AM. It's a good thing there are few cars on the road at this hour, as I know I've been over the center highway line numerous times. I pull over and ease the truck into a parking lot in front of a small restaurant which is closed at this hour of the morning. In one continuous motion I turn off the key, reach for the quilt behind the truck seat, and let my head fall against my suitcase.

Dear God, please, just thirty minutes of sleep. Then, please, will You awaken me? If You don't, I'll be here in this restaurant parking lot when the breakfast crowd arrives. Please help.

A short while later my eyes suddenly pop open. I struggle to an upright position, rub the grit from my eyes and tip my arm so as to see my watch using the light from the neon light of the restaurant. Mickey Mouse's long hand is pointing between his feet, and the shorter hand is on the four. It's 4:30 AM on the dot.

I gaze across the highway toward a little saltwater bay. Slivers of orange and yellow sunlight shimmer across the tidal ripples introducing a gorgeous sunrise. "Oh, my God, Mickey, it's Easter Sunday morning." I grip the steering wheel and lean forward closing my eyes.

271

Dear God, I mean no disrespect here. In my heart of hearts, I know Jesus died on the cross for each of us. I know that's what this day is all about, honoring our Lord for carrying that cross. I know there are people all over the world who are rejoicing in this day. And God, I know each of us has a cross to bear just to live on this earth, but I'm feeling mine is too heavy. Way inside myself I feel there's justice and goodness that will win out from all this painful chaos. And, God, I know You say You won't ask me to bear a heavier cross than I am able to. God, please strengthen me.

And, God, please don't let Malfaits suffer beyond their ability either—especially because I seem not to be able to do the things that need to be done or that I am not strong enough to face up to Rolf or to protect them. Oh, God, please keep them in Your will even in their senility and protect them in all things. God, please be with me. Help me get out of this horror chamber. Help me find an escape door. I will be more compassionate, a stronger human being as a result of these experiences.

Dear God, despite all my muttering and complaints, thank you for this special day, for the resurrection of Jesus Christ, so that we humans in our frailty and ignorance might have hope of a better way and ultimately hope of a joyful eternity!

And, God, right now please just help me to get home safely and to continue working in all things according to Your will.

CHAPTER 25

─ⲟⲝⲟ ─

Procrastination is Over, But the

Ship of Fools Sails On

I START THE truck engine and ease out onto the empty highway. About forty minutes later, I make my way into the comfort of my home, my family, and my bed. As the rest of my family goes to early Easter sunrise service, I fall into an instant, deep sleep. I've already had my church service.

Mom calls about 10:15 AM. "You know those bill-paying envelopes you left where we marked each of the things that needed to be paid?"

"Yeah. I left them right on your nightstand beside your bed."

"I know you did, but I put them under my pillow when I went to bed. I counted the money again just before I put it there. It was fine then, but it's not fine now. The one that had $500.00 cash in it when you left only has $400.00 in it now."

My sleepy blur erases. "Do you have the envelopes in your hands right now?"

"Yes, I do."

"One of them has the bills with the amounts of money you need to pay clipped on each one. Can you tell which one that is?"

"Yes, those are all just like they were. Everything's there."

"The other one had $500.00 cash in it."

"Yes, I know it did."

"Count it for me, please."

The envelope crinkles. I hear the familiar finger-licking sound.

"Fifty and fifty is one hundred—one hundred fifty—two hundred—two hundred fifty---three hundred—and a hundred dollar bill makes four hundred."

There is a painful, silent long-distance pause.

"Betty, when you left yesterday there were *two* one hundred dollar bills. They were there when I counted just before I put the envelope under my pillow. Betty, do you think Rolf took one of them? The envelopes weren't just under the pillow. I had them inside my pillow case. He must have taken it out of the pillow case during the night."

"Mother I don't know. I can't be accusing anyone. You're in Ridgeview and I'm up here. We're trying to count money long-distance. I *know* yesterday when I left I counted each one of those envelopes several times. And I am *very* sure that's what was in them last night!"

"I know that, too, Betty. I'm positive."

"Have you asked Rolf?"

"No, he would just blow up. There's no use asking."

"Mother, I can't really do anything from up here. This is another reason you should be putting those checks in the bank or let them be banked automatically. Is Rolf there with you now?"

"No."

"Where is he?"

"He's sleeping in the back yard. Oh, no, here he comes into the house right now. I'll just step out onto the back porch, and we can continue talking."

"No, Mother, I don't think that will do any good. If he wants to listen, he'll go upstairs and listen on the extension. I'll say goodbye now, and you can do as you like about telling Rolf you have $100.00 missing from the bill-paying envelope. Okay?"

"Okay. Goodbye."

I throw the bed covers back and sit momentarily in the streaming morning sunlight. *This* is why I must trust God Himself to take care of Malfaits, because I can't! I scrub at my sleepy face and recall the paradoxical elation of my personal 4:30 AM Easter sunrise service and at the same time try to focus on the present reality lesson that my brother is a prodigal son and a common thief. There were no other players this time. There are no other possibilities. I lower my head and close my eyes.

Dear God, I'm so sorry, but I must accept that my brother abuses his parents, and he steals from them! What do you want me to do?

A little later in the morning Rolf calls. "Yeah, how are things up there?"

I mumble some trivial comment about not having been up long enough to know how things are, but to myself I am thinking, 'What good is it to tell you how things are anyhow? You're playing games with all of us.'

"It's the usual shit down here. Dad cut the plug off the garage freezer. All the stuff thawed. I discovered it today, because I was trying to use the table saw in the garage, and the thing wouldn't run. I went to flip a circuit breaker, and when that didn't work, I started tracing plugs. I used that saw a few days ago, so I knew it worked. Well, when I got to looking, there was the freezer cord, the wires all cut apart and twisted back together and loosely taped. Whoever plugged it back in blew the circuit breaker. It had to be Dad. It's a wonder someone didn't get killed."

"I don't know what to tell you about how to fix that."

"It can't be fixed. I can tell you for sure the food can't be used. I guess I'll just get up about daybreak tomorrow and throw it out since tomorrow is garbage day. The meat is already rotten and smellin' up the garage."

In *my* mind that's not the only thing that's rotten. I'm not very responsive nor sympathetic to Rolf's problem, and I'm glad when he says good-bye shortly.

Rolf is again on the phone four days later. "Yeah, about that freezer, I taped the old cord together and just plugged her back in and refroze the rotten mess. By the way, how do I go about getting my name on the petition for this guardianship?"

"At this point you need to call Mr. Mason or Mr. Hinson yourself and ask them that question. I don't know where the process is right now, and I don't know what to tell you. You wouldn't budge for so long that I went ahead by myself. If you suddenly feel different now, *you* follow up and see how it's supposed to be done. Do it on your own. I've given up on you."

"Okay, I'll do that. I'll call 'em myself and find out about it. If something doesn't happen here soon, I'm gonna just head out of here and never look back."

"Well, Rolf, I could care less. That may be healthier for all parties concerned. I certainly didn't appreciate all the new knowledge revealed last weekend about your particular brand of care-taking. I told you before your geriatric techniques suck shit, and this past weekend validated my thoughts."

Another long distance call is short and unsweet.

I wish he *would* leave! Whatever guardianship means, at this point there is more than a checking account that I don't want to share with Rolf Malfait. I wish we didn't even share the same last name. He's worse than Mom and Dad put together.

My mind wanders back to his story about watching the logging truck culprit through the sites of his rifle. Would he do that to me? I wish I could watch *him* through a rifle scope. *I wish I could squeeze the trigger!*

Please, dear God, forgive me. May the only rotten Malfait stuff be the meat in the freezer. God, please don't let me sink to their level. There must be a better way! Please help me.

On Monday I get my next Rolf-call. "They're really crazy now. Mom took all the cash and went to pay the taxes."

"By herself?"

"Well, no, Dad went along, too."

"Rolf, they'd have to go clear to Riverton to the courthouse to pay the taxes. That's over six miles. Are you sure that's what they're doing?"

"I don't know. She just said she was going out, and she and Dad left."

"Well, maybe they're just going to coffee."

"Mom's all bent out of shape about Mr. Mason and last Saturday. She said the taxes have to be paid, and they weren't going to let that sneaky little shit sell their property right out from under them. They're going to go pay the taxes while they still have enough money left to pay them with."

"Rolf, she knows I'll be down to help her take care of that when we pay bills next time. I really don't think they will walk clear to Riverton."

"Well, I don't know either, but here's another thing you ought to know—I visited Wilma and Ruthie today. They're both real aware of how much deterioration there's been in the folks."

"We're all going to get there someday, Rolf."

"Yeah, you're right there."

I want to scream at him, And who's going to take care of you the way you've taken care of them, Rolf?

On April 22nd, Mr. Hinson, the guardianship attorney, calls, "We're on the court docket in three weeks. Civil cases are always on Fridays. You need to plan to attend, and to have your parents there also."

"What about Rolf?"

"Yes, he seems to have shown some concern lately. As far as his participation in the guardianship, his name cannot be automatically added. If he wants that to happen, he should come to the scheduled hearing and speak as a concerned party then. Personally, I don't feel Rolf's name would be likely to be added based on the ad litem report, even if he did file his own petition. His behaviors and time spent with both Mr. Mason and me do not convince either one of us that he would be a good caretaker."

By the end of April Rolf's negative phone calls are almost daily. "There's no let-up around here. Things are worse than ever. Dad and Mom have both been at each other lately. One night here recently they got into a scuffle and Dad hit her. Now you know that's not standard.

The whole fuss was over Dad's craving for sweets. He eats all those sugar sandwiches and then he can't control his bowels. She knows that, and she wants him not to eat all that shit.

"Then, of course, their friend Norma has been real sick. That weighs on 'em pretty heavy, too. Norma's had five strokes, and she's in a nursing home now.

"Actually part of that was kind of funny. Mom wanted to go visit her in the nursing home, but Dad, he got all bent out of shape and didn't want to go. He raised a terrible fuss. And as it turned out he was afraid I'd take 'em to visit and leave him there in the nursing home. It was pretty funny, but I guess you had to be there."

Days with repeated similar phone calls pass in a blur until I arrive at 516 May 5th for a working weekend. There's no one around. Malfaits must have forgotten I was coming, despite the usual phone call. I start my routine search.

Sally, their friend and proprietor of the little corner café, tells me, "They weren't in today, but they were in yesterday. You know, Betty, actually I've been kind of worried about them. I almost called you."

"What about?"

"They were fighting about something. Mama got really mad at Papa. She all but ran out of here and just left him at the counter by himself."

"What did Dad do?"

"He said he was going to stay right here as long as he liked, and he did stay. When he finally got up to leave he seemed confused, and I asked him if he wanted me to walk with him. He said no, that he was going right straight home. I was kind of concerned about the fighting, because in all the time they've been coming in here, they've never acted like that. Mama is usually very helpful with Papa, and she is very protective of him. For them to fight in here, and for her to leave him alone like that was pretty upsetting."

I thank Sally and continue my search to Ocean Espresso, by the hospital, around the lake, up and down the main streets of town, then back to 516. No luck.

Nosy-bill, the next-door neighbor drives in. "Hi, Betty, are you looking for your folks? They were working in the yard earlier, and I think they headed out for coffee."

"Thanks. I'll check again."

"Oh, say, I was kind of concerned because your mom had blood on her face. I asked what happened, and she said she was unaware of any blood on her. You know, I could see it right there, and I asked her again. Well, then she got really short with me and she wouldn't give no details other than to say she and Dad had been working in the yard and she musta got scratched by the briars."

"Thanks. I'll check it out."

As I am worrying about the blood on her face and whether to check the hospitals, Rolf drives up. He pops out of nowhere so often I wonder if he hangs out somewhere close by and spies on the house.

"Hey, you been looking for Mom and Dad? I just seen 'em. They went out for coffee. I told 'em you were here and waitin' for 'em."

"How far away are they, Rolf?"

"They just turned onto Oak Street. They're ten or twelve blocks away."

"As usual you didn't offer them a ride?"

"Walkin' is good for 'em. This has been kind of a hard week for them. Norma died. Mom and Dad, you know, they wanted to go to the funeral, but I didn't take 'em. They're pretty mad at me about that. But hell, I ain't gonna take them places lookin' like they do."

I glare at Rolf's bushy-bearded face and unkempt figure. He is garbed in his dirty hacked-off logging jeans and black, gray and white hickory shirt, set off by wide, red suspenders stretched over a gastric bulk that has prevented him from seeing his belt buckle for years. "And did *you* go to Norma's funeral?"

"I went to the house, you know, and visited with the family. They were expecting all these people, so I grabbed a lawn mower out of the barn, and I managed to get all that cow-manure-enriched front yard cut down so's the visitors could at least see their house. That was one hell of a job!.."

"Well, did you go to the funeral?"

"Yeah, yeah. I stayed for the funeral, though I hadn't intended to stay when I went to the house."

"And what did you wear to the funeral?"

"I went just like I am now."

"You're kidding. You went to a funeral dressed like that and after doing the hell of a lawn-mowing job? Yet you wouldn't take your parents to that same funeral—the funeral of one of their oldest and dearest friends—because they wouldn't be dressed right?"

"Well, they won't get cleaned up."

"And you did?"

"Well, I guess I wasn't any too clean myself, but I didn't have much choice. That's how I am, and people who know me, know that. I paid my respects."

Before we can continue our verbal fracas, Mom and Dad shuffle up. "My God, Dad, what the hell happened to you?"

I stare at a huge black eye, bluish coloration stretching from his forehead down over his right cheek bone.

Rolf is immediate in his response, "I didn't touch him."

Dad says simply, "Oh, don't worry about a little scratch, kid. I slipped and fell."

Mother takes over the narrative. "The old fool was collecting rocks out by the bridge. He says we need them for putting around the bottoms of our fruit tree trunks. He slipped and rolled down the bank into the blackberry briars."

As Mother is speaking, my mouth falls open. "And you? What's that on you?"

"What about me? I sure wasn't collecting rocks."

"Mother, your left eye is black and blue and you have a big scrape on your forehead above your eyebrow. There's a scratch from the top of your nose going the other way down your cheek under your right eye."

"Oh shit! I don't have all that wrong with me."

Rolf is standing in his usual pose with arms crossed. "Well, I want you to know right now I don't know nothin' about any of this!"

There is a shred of believability in his denial. "Mother, did you try to help Dad when he fell? Is that how you got all bruised and scratched?"

"No, I didn't help him. He rolled all the way down the hill. I didn't go down there with these old legs. He got out by himself."

I believe *going down there with these old legs* is exactly what she did, but the story will never be told. "Well, Mother, you certainly got a shiner some how."

"I don't think I have a black eye. I don't hurt any place."

I wonder if she is afraid again because Rolf is standing right here. In a quieter voice I ask, "Rolf, are you sure you don't know anything about all this?"

Mother speaks immediately. "No, Rolf wasn't anyplace near us. Dad was determined he was going to get those rocks for our trees, and he went after them. I couldn't stop him." She laughs almost lovingly. "He's such an old fool. He just goes off any old place, and he's always getting way ahead of me. He picks up rocks everywhere we go.

"I can't keep him from going right into people's yards. The old man in the next block buys those special white rocks for the garden in his front yard. He's probably had to buy some more lately." She laughs again. "When I scold Dad about taking other people's rocks, he says he's getting them for El; she likes rocks. Look right here by the front door step. Rolf makes him empty his pockets before he goes in the house."

Piled on either side of the front door step is at least five gallons of rocks of various sizes and shapes, predominately white ones.

"Betty, he's got rocks all over our house. Look in there at my lamp table."

Peering through the screen door, I can see her beautiful maple lamp table, adorned by a hand-painted china lamp with a ring of crystal baubles hanging around the base. In haphazard array all around it are probably fifty rocks, mostly white, scattered among old flashlights and a mass of other unidentifiable debris.

"Betty, I honestly don't know how I got a black eye. I guess it is a shiner, but it doesn't hurt. Maybe Dad bumped me in his sleep because he always sleeps with his arms up above his head and he rolls about a lot. He can't ever seem to relax, whether he's awake or asleep."

I don't press further. I think Rolf is as surprised as I am at their appearance, and this time he's probably not the culprit. Dad doesn't object or add to the story. He simply stands staring at passing cars.

Mother continues, "Just about every night Dad rolls and tosses all night long until we neither one can get any sleep. The other night he rolled over on me, and he wouldn't get off. Rolf was out on the living room couch, and I finally had to yell for him to come and get him off of me."

"Was he fighting you or beating on you?"

"It wasn't exactly like that. He just doesn't know what he's doing half the time. He was asleep, and he wouldn't move. Then when he did move, he jabbed me with his old elbow. That really hurt, and he may have blacked my eye then. Who knows?"

Rolf joins in, "Yeah, Mom, she was yellin' her head off that Dad was beatin' up on her. I had to get in there in their bedroom and get him back on his side of the bed. Hell, I told you, I can't watch 'em every minute day and night."

Mother picks up the challenge, "Dad and I don't need to be watched every minute. We don't need to be watched at all. You'd do well to watch out for you!"

Nosy-bill, Malfaits' next-door neighbor, steps out onto her front porch to shake a rug and just in time to catch the increase in volume as Rolf admonishes Mother, "You better get going to get your bill-paying done. You gotta be watched for that, too, and it ain't done!"

Mother raises her volume above Rolf's, "You don't know what you're saying. It is so. All the bills are paid."

Rolf faces her squarely and moves closer, "They're not paid! They're not paid at all! You haven't done it, and you've had plenty of time!"

"I've had no time for anything. We've been very busy around here."

Rolf thrusts his face up inches away from her nose and bellows, "Well, very busy around here doesn't cut it. Nothing's cleaned up. You're both filthy, and I'm getting to where I don't care if you and Dad both drop dead with your cocksucking cats and up to your ears in shit!"

Mother holds her ground and shouts back but at a somewhat lesser volume, "You don't know what you're talking about!"

Rolf continues the volley of shouted expletives, "What's to know? I don't have to be no God-damned genius to know it's just damned fucking dirty around here, and you're both filthy! What's to know?" His hands are held stiff-armed down at his sides and pushed back behind him, his fingers rotating furiously in tight circular patterns.

God, please. Be here now

I feel as if I am rotating in my own tight circles. I want to tear into him with my bare hands. I want to knock him flat to the ground. My whole body is trembling. I take a step toward him, but I feel as if I am laboring in slow motion and my arms are locked to my sides. I hear my own breathing, long noisy shaking inhalations and trembling exhalations playing in tandem with jerking motions in my stomach and chest. Each intake of air lessons the quaking. Finally a calmness engulfs me, embraces me, soothes me. I am unable to move any closer to him.

I force myself to speak, and I am incredulous at my low, steady, almost whispered voice. At least, I think it's my voice, "Rolf, Rolf, you're being a jerk. You're making a fool of yourself. You're saying all kinds of things I'm sure you don't mean, and if you will notice, you're providing this show for all the neighbors. You need to back off. Go! Just get the hell away from here. Now!"

Rolf turns and stomps off down the street without another word. We all stand watching his bulky shadow move in an angry lurching gait until he finally disappears around the corner.

Mother turns toward the front door, "I'll get my bills and my purse."

Dad asks, "Betty, where'd Rolf go in such a hurry?"

Without answering him, I go into the house and follow the kitty litter walkway through the living room. A peek into their bedroom reveals Dad has broken a ball point pen and smeared it all over the comforter. It doesn't matter though, because there's human waste smeared over the ink.

Mom and I look through the bed, in drawers, in pillow cases, and all the other illogical places for their bills. I begin collecting them in a paper bag. The bills are definitely not paid. The telephone bill is $124, a $100 over the usual amount. And there's a red tag from the utility company on the nightstand. Mother doesn't know anything about it.

Rolf, who is supposedly cooled off, comes back into the house as I am figuring out that the red tag is announcing the intent of the water district to turn off the water supply for failure to pay the bill.

He states calmly, "Yeah, Mike saw that thing stapled on the front door, but I didn't see it because Mom took it down and hid it."

Mother pipes in, "We always pay our bills, and your friend Mike was running his nose in where it didn't belong."

I try to avoid another flare-up. "Rolf, we've sacked all this wash. Please lug it out to the truck for me."

I guess he wants to avoid further conflict, as well. He turns immediately and leaves with the washing. Once he's out the door I focus on Mother and in the same quiet demeanor I felt in the front yard I try to get her to share my sense of urgency. "Mother, we've got to keep on task here. Some of these businesses will close at noon. Tomorrow the water will be turned off. Then we'll all be standing around screaming at one another." I gently touch her arm and lower my voice, "Mother, *please, help me. I need* you right now. I can't do this without *you!*"

She locks eye contact with me and whispers, "What do you want me to do?"

"We've got to get the bills and get downtown immediately. Put every envelope you can find that even looks like a bill in this paper bag. We'll sort them later."

The two of us scurry around the living room and drop anything that looks semi-official into my paper bag. Mother continues to complain but in a whisper, "If Rolf would quit taking our stuff out of the mailbox, we could keep better track of it."

"Mother, he says he puts it all right here on the top of the TV."

"Maybe he does, and maybe he doesn't."

"Well, I think we've found what we need for today. I guess our scheme with the marked envelopes and cash paper-clipped to each bill wasn't much help this last time around. Mother, would you please make a trip to the bathroom before we go?"

"I don't need to go."

"Sure you do. If you remember last time we rode in my truck, you told me you didn't need to go, and I ended up with a wet truck seat."

"Well, I don't need to go, and I'm *not* going."

I clutch the paper sack of bills extra hard and grit my teeth. Despite my better judgment, I give in. I help her down the steps and out to the truck. I place the little single step stool in the appropriate spot. Mother pulls herself up onto the seat. A warmth spreads over my hands as I reach to fasten her seat belt.

I remove my hand. "Mom, I can't let you go like this. You're wet. I am, too."

"I'm okay; it won't show."

"Now, Mother, I'm really sorry, but I just *can't* let you sit in my truck like that and let the pee soak through on the seat. I'm sorry it's such a high step up and you have to strain to get in. But I only have this one truck, and I worked hard to get it. Mother, please, I just can't let you pee in it. *Please* understand." I say nothing more. I stand quietly gripping the truck door handle and wait.

Mother finally turns and slides back down to the ground from the truck-seat. I take the wet quilt down. She can see it's sopping.

"Lord God-A-Mighty, who would have thought I had that much pee in me!"

"Don't worry about it. It's laundry day." I quietly pitch the wet quilt in the back with the rest of the laundry and rearrange the large plastic bag that had been underneath the quilt. I try to make the plastic bag look as if I just that moment pulled it from under the seat.

"Betty, I don't know what I can do. I don't have any other pants. They're all in the laundry."

"From the size of the load of clothes in the truck bed, I'm pretty sure I do have all of your pairs of slacks.

" Well, Mom, we'll just have to have our Mother's Day celebration early right here in my truck." I reach behind the seat and pull out the bags of unwrapped gifts I have purchased for her and place them on the black plastic bag covering the front truck seat.

"What a wonderful surprise!" She reaches back into the truck and tears at the paper store bags with every bit as much excitement as if the gifts had been exquisitely wrapped. "Oh, these are beautiful." She lays out the pants, shirt, and sweater on the truck seat. "What's this little bag? Oh what beautiful panties! I sure do need those. My God, people out here on the street will see me waving my drawers around. I'll just go into the house and put these things on."

I follow her back into the house and pick up her soiled clothing as she changes in the middle of the living room. I am not going to worry about her not bathing. She loves the gifts. It didn't matter about no wrappings nor the truck cab celebration. She is a happy child at this moment. I am a blubbering idiot!

We return to the truck and she pulls herself up onto the black plastic with no complaints.

The bill-paying venture proceeds smoothly, and we are both much relieved as we reach the last place on the list just before closing time. Mother asks me to go in with her to the Fibex Credit Union. We step up to a teller, and I ask Mother for her bank envelope. She cooperates quietly, and I count the necessary cash out onto the counter. The teller nods in my direction. "Who are you?"

My jaw drops momentarily as I look up and squint at the teller. This is the same woman who was unimpressed when I previously identified myself. I lick my dry lips and swallow. "I'm Francine's daughter. I'm helping her pay her bills today."

The teller counts the bills without looking at me. "This loan is Rolf Malfait's mortgage. Is that your brother?" She doesn't wait for my reply before she asks, "Why does Francine pay Rolf's mortgage all the time?"

"Because he *doesn't*. Mother says she co-signed the note. If Rolf doesn't pay, she has to. Is that correct?"

"Well, I'm not supposed to share the details of this file with *you*, but since Francine is with you today, maybe it's okay."

She turns the computer screen around toward me. The figures that blur into my bi-focal view show the original loan was taken out 12/6/80 for the amount of $35,700.00 at 12%, which would accumulate finance charges of $31,821.00 over a twelve year payment plan at $468.90 per month. The final payment will be 12/6/92, over three years into the future for a grand total pay-out of $67,521.60.

Yes, the credit union holds a lien on the Malfait house as collateral. Mother and Dad both signed it. From what Mother says and what the teller says, I'm sure Rolf does nothing about it. I've been helping her with bill-paying since Dad had the stroke in July of 1987, and each payment has been in cash and from their monthly income. I'm confident they have paid in cash the years before, as well.

A flood of anger surges within me! I can't afford anger right now. Besides, whom shall I direct the anger to? Mother and Dad? Why? Because they love Rolf and want him to make something of his life, and they are willing to sacrifice to help that happen? At Rolf? Yes, but what good will that do? Right now, Betty, you don't have any business even knowing their business!

Rolf is at the house when we get back. Mother is tired and goes to lie down. Rolf offers to accompany me to the laundromat. Neither of us has much to say as we fill eight regular washers plus two of the big ones. There's a lot more wash than usual and it's nastier, but so is everything else in this family situation. Rolf is helpful throughout the washing, but when all the dryers are loaded up, he says, "I'm gonna go across the street for a Coke."

About an hour later, I see him coming back through the parking lot munching away. I've finished folding the laundry and have it all in boxes and bags to take home. I'm waiting. I'm thirsty. I'm hungry. I haven't eaten all day!

Rolf comes up licking his fingers. "Yeah, I was kinda hungry. I got myself a couple of egg rolls at the Chinese restaurant over there." He shoves the remaining bite of a candy bar into his mouth. "Let me give you a hand with them clean clothes and get 'em to the truck."

I refuse to react. What good would it do? A jerk of Rolf's quality who has such a long-term record of *jerkdom* would have no concern for how tired or hungry I might be. Once we are underway in the truck, without any explanation, I drive through a fast food place and order some chicken sandwiches and then go on to 516.

Mother greets us at the door, "Let's get all of us down to Chuck's Wagon."

"Mother, I already got chicken sandwiches for us."

"I don't want that. I want to go to Chuck's Wagon."

"But, Mother, I spent twelve bucks and it's hot. Let's just eat. I don't feel like going to Chuck's Wagon."

"Well, I don't want that shit. You can give it to Dad."

I pitch the bags of food down on top of other stacks in the living room and go to the kitchen without any further word. I haven't been in the kitchen yet today, but I am confident work awaits me there. When I approach the sink, I literally gag. There's rotten food in pans and peelings from fruit, and God knows what some of the stuff *was!* I spray everything directly with "409" and gag some more. Throwing up is one of my least favorite things to do, and it's a good thing I don't have anything in me to throw up!

I clean what I can clean. I soak what I can soak. As I leave to go do their grocery shopping, Mom and Dad are in the living room eating chicken sandwiches. They don't ask where I'm going. I don't know where Rolf is.

An hour or so later when I return with the groceries, I pick up their sandwich garbage which is strewn about the living room and re-attack the soaking items in the kitchen. By 9:30 PM the sink is clean, the table is clean on the half they eat on, the groceries are well stocked and put away. The beds are clean and Mother and Dad are both wearing new night clothes. As I leave the house, I know it's probably only momentary. By tomorrow night it will all be back to *normal chaos*.

I move my truck slowly off the driveway and down the dark, tree-lined streets to my weekend home, The Sterling. I am beyond tired. I am beyond crying. I am numb! It hurts so much I can't even feel it. I barely feel the sting of the hot shower water and the rough nubs of the cheap towel. I drink a warm Diet Coke from my no longer cool cooler and eat some Peanut Butter finger cookies.

Dear God, I am so inadequate. I'm not getting anywhere. Every time I think I have gotten a bit of a handle on some aspect of these Malfait family problems, the whole thing goes to hell. We all have to die. Is this the only way? God, I do think it would be better to be dead than to live like this.

CHAPTER 26

⊸⊶⊷

A Day in Court

IT's MID-JUNE, 1990. Almost time for another trip to Ridgeview. Another trip into oblivion. I wish I were immune to oblivion. I wish I were immune to Rolf's phone calls. He knows I'll be down in a couple of days, but he has a chronic need to vent.

"Yeah, you know that back bedroom—Dad's bedroom—well, I like to go in there and open the window and rest. It's the only way I can get any fresh air in this damn place. Well, get this, there's a big wet circle on the quilt back there. I mean *big*—like two feet across. I got on 'em about it right away, and they both denied doing it. Mom said neither one of them would do anything like that, and probably I had done it myself. Now that's about all I could stand! I know it's them damned cats. I took that one they call Butchie and threw him out. Mom's howling could be heard clear out to the alley—regular sobbing and wailing. But, before you yell at me, too, I finally found the damned cat out in the shop and let him back in the house. And, I only did that to shut her up!"

"You should have known better than to throw one of their cats out. You know they think more of their cats than you or me, or anybody else."

"Yeah, I know, but they're around them damn cats so much, they don't even smell 'em. I was out to Ocean Espresso having coffee the other day, and the folks, you know, they come in. I could smell 'em from the next booth. They didn't even know I was there. I just got up and left."

"Rolf, compared to some of your other reactions, that may have been the best thing you could have done."

"Yeah, well, hey, we got that notice about the court hearing comin' up here in a couple of days. I explained it to 'em, but I doubt they really understand it."

"I hope they understand enough to go—and that you'll be going, too."

"Oh, yeah, I'll be going. I already been over to the courthouse. I know the right rooms, and I already read the docket. It's a Judge Fox presiding. He's a good man—very fair. He's the one who heard my logging truck case."

That's not the name I remember him telling me, but I let that thought pass. "You seem upbeat at least about the schedule."

"Yeah, we need to get this guardian thing over with. I think justice will be done, and we'll be treated fairly by him."

Rolf seems so confident. I wonder if he talked to the judge. As far as I'm concerned, the approaching date is going to be a nasty day. We're not dealing with some argument over a logging truck and indebtedness. June 15, 1990, is the scheduled day for the competency hearing for our parents. The Superior Court will record documentation that shows our parents are mentally incompetent. I hate this. I feel sick. Fairness? Justice? There isn't any such thing!

I arrive at The Sterling the evening of June 14th. Rolf stops by, saying he just happened to see my vehicle. He immediately starts talking about expectations for the next day. "Yeah, I've re-explained that court letter to 'em a dozen times. I'm not sure they get it. I don't know if they'll go to the courthouse or not."

"I guess we'll just have to ask them at the moment when it's near time and hope they'll be cooperative."

"Well, I don't know about cooperative. So far, the reaction to the letter has been a lot of ranting about how one or both of us are tryin' to get what they have."

"And, Rolf, I wonder how much of that reaction is due to how you present the information to them."

"Yeah, yeah, but we need to get on with this guardianship thing. We need to get things set up so that lumber bill of theirs can get taken care of right away."

"What lumber bill is that?"

"Oh, you don't know about that? Well, it's a biggie. Mom and me have been arguing about that one all week."

"How big of a biggie?"

"Actually, it's $540.00."

"Oh, geez! You're right, that's a biggie! What the hell did they buy?"

"It's for some boards and sheets of plywood—and, well, about $250.00 of it is for a couple of saws. One is a jig saw, and one is a skill saw."

"Rolf, they didn't buy that stuff. Dad can't even use a garden shovel anymore. How could he use a jig saw or a skill saw? They couldn't carry all that stuff out of the store, and they couldn't use it if they got it home. What the hell is this all about? What have you done?"

"Well, yeah, *I* actually bought the stuff. I needed some things to work with for doin' repairs around the house. I fixed up some more lawn chairs and their picnic table. Then, of course, I had to shore up that garden shed I bought for them that's out there by the clothesline."

"Rolf, I haven't seen five hundred dollars worth of lumber anywhere on their property. Fixing two lawn chairs and a table didn't take that. That old shed you bought second-hand for less than fifty bucks at a garage sale. You surely didn't put any five hundred dollar foundation under it."

"Well, I did do those repairs I mentioned, but I also used *some* of it to fix some gun racks upstairs."

"Yeah, and that gives *them* a huge bill, and I'm not sure whether that's for your benefit or theirs. If most of the guns were Dad's, and if he was the one who was able to use a jig saw and a skill saw, that would be one thing—or if I could see some other improvements you had done around their house, maybe I could see the need."

"Sis, you just don't get it. Things ain't easy around there. I have my own financial stresses. Hell, I'm gonna have to go down and file for unemployment."

293

"You've been saying you're going to do that since January."

"Well, I've picked up enough work I haven't had to do it, but now I've gotta file. I don't have any money at all. Hell, I used four tanks of gas just last week running around after Taco."

"Yeah, and Taco is *your* dog. If he wasn't at their house, they wouldn't have to feed him and you wouldn't have to run around after him. He's more of a danger to them than a comfort."

"Oh, I don't know about that. I have to run around checkin' on Mom and Dad, too, and takin' 'em places."

I open the motel desk drawer, pick up a pen and paper, and begin scribbling. "I don't know, Rolf. You must get lousy gas mileage. You have about a twenty gallon tank. You said four tanks, right? If you only got *ten* miles per gallon—hmmm, that would be 800 miles last week. That's over a hundred miles per day. Either Mom and Dad or your dog Taco are getting a hell of a run *daily*."

Rolf scowls at my scribbles then grins. "Yeah, yeah, it's pretty funny when you put it that way. Well, once in a while I can con her out of a tank of gas, and that helps me a little."

"Yes, and *con* is a pretty good word. I don't know how much help that is to either of you."

Rolf stands abruptly, "Well, I better call it a night and get back to my place; tomorrow will be an early day. I'm down here in my usual room. We better try to pick the folks up about nine o'clock or so. Can you give me a ride to their place?"

"That's fine. I'll see you a little before nine."

As I fasten the deadbolt on the motel room door, I shake my head and mutter aloud, "I'm glad he's gone. I couldn't stand to listen to him much more. I'm dreadfully tired, but I don't think I can sleep right now."

I dig out my schoolwork and set about grading papers. It's 2:00 AM before exhaustion forces me to fall into bed.

I'm jolted awake by two harsh telephone buzzes. It's my 7:00 AM wake-up call. I force my body out of bed and into the shower. I throw on whatever clothes I can rummage from my suitcase and rush out the door to meet Rolf at the agreed hour. We go together to pick up our parents for the dreaded court hearing.

As usual, they're not home. We drive around to all the places they frequent. No luck. Their usual twelve-block route to Ocean Espresso is blocked off due to sewer construction, but I cruise slowly through an alley and see them about six blocks over moving slowly along. I can't get my truck down to where they are, so I pull up close to the curb where they'll have to walk to cross the street. Rolf decides to walk back to their house to take care of Taco before we have to leave.

Finally Mom and Dad shuffle up near my truck. When they almost bump into the passenger door, they look up directly into the open truck window.

Mother smiles. "Oh, Glory, Roger, look who's here."

Dad leans forward and squints in the passenger window. "Well, hi there, kid. Come on, Francine, we're going to ride the rest of the way."

I hurry around to their side of the truck to make sure they get safely in from the curbside and to roll up the window. "Did you forget I was coming at nine this morning, and we're all supposed to go to court for the hearing?"

"Dad and I have had our breakfast. We're ready to go."

"I think I'll have to take you just like you are. We don't have time to go home and change clothes or anything."

Mother responds with vague defensiveness, "That's fine. We don't need to dress up to go there."

Dad chimes in, "We're just fine. Let's get going, kid."

I run back around and climb in on the driver's side. Both of them are congenial and jabber about the weather, the yard, and their breakfast. I have a difficult time chatting. I'm nervous over the impending court proceedings, and they are filthy and smell of urine, and worse. I can see brown fecal material clinging to Dad's socks and pant cuffs. I can't chat and gag at the same time.

Mother breaks my nauseous trance, "Dad and I didn't forget you were coming. We were hurrying to get back to the house."

Dad joins in, "Yeah, kid, you just tell us what you need us to testify to, and we'll get her done."

"Dad, I don't know what will happen in court today."

"Well, whoever's there, we're going to talk to them." Dad pulls up his pants leg and shows me his shins. "Rolf did this to me."

I glance at the bright redness of freshly formed scabs. "Oh, man, I don't want to know about this. Are those old wounds or are they new? Geez, people, you're the ones who have to decide if it's bad enough you want to tell it to a judge. I can't help you if you won't tell. What do you expect? Do you want me to get into some kind of fist-o-cuffs with Rolf and knock the shit out of him for you?"

Friendly demeanor is gone. They both wail away at each other and at the same time at no one in particular. They give bits and pieces of abusive details, and they lambaste Rolf anew. I don't know what to believe. Dad is indefinite about the new scabs. They could have been from another tumble down the riverbank or a sidewalk fall—or he could have picked the old scabs off and the wounds bled again. I can't tell. All Mother will say is that Rolf is really mean all the time now, but she doesn't tell *how* he is mean. Maybe some of this new information will be revealed in court today. As I pull up to the curb in front of 516, Rolf climbs into the bed of the pickup.

Dad blurts, "Jesus Christ, Mama, what the hell is Rolf doing back there?"

Mother matches the volume, "How can he be so cruel as to take us to court?"

"Mother, Rolf isn't taking you to court. He left his car downtown last night, and I am dropping him off at his car. Then we're going to follow him to the courthouse. He checked out the specific rooms and times, and he knows right where we should report. This court thing is something we all have to do to try to get a better plan of action going about keeping you and Dad healthy and safe."

We arrive at the courthouse and make our way into the empty courtroom. It's a large room with seating for more than a hundred. The judge's bench and other official desks dominate the front under dimmed lights and dark mahogany silence. The four of us choose seats in a far corner at the back. Presently the room begins to fill, and though several people wander over near us, no one stays long. Some of them even sit down, but they don't remain in *our* corner.

Mr. Hinson, the guardianship attorney, arrives. He's a small man dressed appropriately in his court-room, dark-gray, pin-stripe power suit and carrying a huge brief case, all factors enhancing his legalistic persona. I introduce him to Malfaits.

Dad stands and shakes his hand vigorously. In a loud voice he tells him, "If Betty chose you, you are an honorable man—for a lawyer!"

There are some nearby appreciative sniggers.

Mr. Hinson is both embarrassed and amused as he returns the handshake and nods to Mother. "I am pleased to meet you both."

There is no exchange of greeting between Rolf and Mr. Hinson, though Rolf leans over in his direction and bends his ear anyway, "You see that guy over there in the checkered shirt. I'd like to know what he's here for today. He's the son-of-a-bitch who owes me about $2,000.00 in unpaid wages."

Without looking up, Mr. Hinson shuffles papers in his briefcase and extracts a fresh legal pad.

A door opens near the front of the courtroom. The audience rises as directed. The judge is seated and immediately calls Mr. Hinson to the bench. They carry on an inaudible conference for several minutes.

Mr. Hinson returns to where we are seated and speaks to me, "The judge wants an additional ad litem figure for this case. He also wants a recent medical report on both Malfaits—and, he wants a psychological report on each family member. Mr. Jim Keys is a counselor located here in the courthouse and serving the Offender Service Program. He's a well-qualified professional counselor and someone with whom Judge Fox often works in his cases. He's had considerable experience in counseling the elderly and doing guardianship work. The judge is adamant in these demands, and his main reason is the likely contesting of the guardianship proceeding by your brother."

I turn to Rolf. "How did you spend your day at the courthouse on Thursday? Did you in any way formally or informally contest this proceeding?"

"No. I definitely did not."

I press again, "Rolf, *do you contest it now?*"

"No, No, I don't contest nothin'. I feel we should *both* be involved in decisions here. But in regard to the paperwork—no, I didn't contest it."

My own thought is, Rolf, I don't believe you, even now in front of Mr. Hinson. I'm disappointed at the delay, but in this whole process I am continually re-educated on the *un*importance of my time-lines.

Dear God, I am where I am at this very moment on blind faith, trying to seek justice for an unjust family situation. If I have perceived things incorrectly, may You correct me. And may You, through the courts, provide what is right and just. This whole thing seems like an exercise in futility. It would have been so much easier to manage for all concerned if Rolf and I were able to cooperate and trust one another. I can't have that relationship with Rolf, but I know I can have that with You. But, God, I'm so sorry—I feel like I've failed You. I have tried with Rolf, but I don't think trust is ever going to be there again. Where is my brother? Where are my parents? Who are these people? Oh, God, help us all now.

Our pathetic party leaves the courtroom and follows Mr. Hinson to a small conference room nearby. Mom and Dad are confused but cooperative as we're seated. Still standing in the doorway, Rolf, announces, "I'd like to see what's gonna happen to that guy I saw earlier there in the courtroom. He's really a slick operator. He buys trucks, hires drivers, runs the wheels off the trucks, claims to lose them and then never makes final payments to owner-companies or drivers. I'm gonna drop back in and check it out." Rolf backs out into the hallway and shuts the door.

Mr. Hinson and I look at each other and shrug. He turns his attention to Mother and Dad and explains what the appointment with the counselor will be about. "Each of you should talk to him just like you would to the judge. Tell him all the things you want him to know about your living situation. You'll need to fill out this paperwork from Judge Fox, and Betty can help you with that if you need. Mr. Keys may want to talk about some of your answers to these questions." Mr. Hinson hands some of the papers to Mother but continues to make eye contact and concentrate on both Mother and Dad. "We all know sometimes this paper stuff is a little confusing—the real important thing today is to talk openly to Mr. Keys. He's a good listener. Just tell him in your own words. He'll make notes about what you say, and he'll share all this information with Judge Fox."

Mr. Hinson turns and hands me the remaining papers. "Mr. Keys' office is on the third floor, the same floor as the county jail. That's where he does most of his counseling work. Don't be concerned about the signs on that floor about the jail. There is no activity in that area right now, and Mr. Keys is expecting you." Mr. Hinson rises and hefts his big briefcase from the table, "Now, if you'll excuse me, I need to hurry to go to another appointment. The elevator to the third floor is just outside this room and to the right."

Mom and Dad and I find our way as we were instructed and seat ourselves on benches outside Mr. Keys' office. Dad shifts about awkwardly and remarks, "Well, I'll say one thing—this here counselor fella doesn't have much for a waiting room. These little metal benches are uncomfortable and damned cold!"

Mother squelches any further complaints. "You better sit still and hush, Roger. That sign right above your head says 'Jail Entry'. You go wandering off here, and they'll keep you for sure."

Dad squints upward at the sign, folds his hands in his lap and stares straight ahead. Mother and I begin filling out the judge's paperwork.

After a few minutes Rolf finds us and seats himself on the metal bench. He leans over to read the paperwork I've been working on. "What's that you're havin' to fill out for this guy?"

I fold my completed papers away from his eyes and select out blank copies. "Here, Mr. Hinson gave me copies for you to fill out, too. It's a request for bonding. You have to be bonded to be able to be a guardian for someone else."

"Yeah, how much is that for?"

"I don't really know what the requirements are."

"Well, how are *you* filling the thing out? You know, just 'cause you got a few bucks and I don't, don't mean you'd make any better guardian."

"Look, Rolf, I can work and co-operate with you on many things, but finances and financial responsibility are *not* going to be among them. If you're still pissed off about my attitude on that, that's fine. I'll drop the whole proceeding and you can do the guardianship or caretaking or whatever this becomes by yourself. I *cannot* manage finances with you!"

"There you go, starting in on my integrity again."

"No, Rolf, the issue here is *not* integrity. It's financial responsibility. I believe in checking accounts and receipts and meeting deadlines. I *will not* have any kind of financial management arrangement shared with you! Now fill out your *own* forms."

Author, Jr. High School, and Rolf, High School

Our argument is interrupted as Mr. Keys comes out of his office. He is congenial in greeting all of us and invites Malfaits to come in and confer with him first. Rolf and I sit in our respective places on the metal bench in metallic silence.

About half an hour later, Mom and Dad exit the office guided by Mr. Keys. The atmosphere around them seems amicable and business-like. Mr. Keys walks them down the hall around the corner and asks them to wait there and not talk to anyone else for a few minutes. Rolf remains seated on the metal bench bent over his paperwork.

I am the next one invited into Mr. Keys' office. He is very direct, making quick notes as to my age, marital status, children, drug habits, alcohol use, occupation, and general outlook on life. He pauses to reread the judge's note.

"One of the most important parts the judge has asked for today is your folks' medical history. Can you provide that?"

"I doubt Mother has been to the doctor in twenty years or more. Actually she's been a very healthy person, and so was Dad until he had the stroke. I don't think Mother even has any medical records."

"What about your Dad's records since his stroke?"

"Sure, Dr. Kettle has seen him several times. Then, of course, he has records at St. Mary's Hospital."

"Great. Those are vital to this hearing process. If we had those records for Mr. Malfait, the court could probably make a final ruling on the guardianship fairly quickly, and it wouldn't require your driving back down here for another day in court. Could you get the health records either from the doctor or the hospital and hand-deliver them back to me here at the courthouse before 5:00 PM?"

A door off to the right of Mr. Keys' desk opens and Mr. Hinson pokes his head into the office. "Mr. Keys, you may not know but Dr. Kettle is on vacation. He'll be gone at least ten days. My people have been unable to get anyone in his office to release those records."

Is Mr. Hinson eavesdropping from the adjoining room? Is the judge in there, too? Was that his other appointment? I remain silent.

Mr. Keys looks at me expectantly. "Maybe it will make a difference if Betty tries to pick up the records herself. Can you do that?"

"I'll try."

Mr. Hinson closes the door, and Mr. Keys continues, "Now, I need to find out about this big mortgage that has Malfaits' house as the collateral."

I draw in a deep breath in anticipation of giving my perceptions on this subject, but Mr. Keys is around to my side of the desk and very smoothly ushers me out the door before I have a chance to say word one. I am escorted down the hall to join Mom and Dad who are sitting like mute wax images in the anteroom.

"I thank you all for coming up to my offices. I know this is not the most pleasant part of the court house, but I appreciate your cooperation and we got the job done. I think we have everything we need except those medical records. I'm hopeful you'll still have enough time to get those to me today."

Mr. Keys makes his departure, and I hear him down the hall invite Rolf into his office.

I interrupt Malfaits' dazed calm. "We're finished with interviews. Let's find a bathroom."

Mother is quick to reply, "We went to the bathroom before we came. I don't need to go."

"Yeah, but Mom, you and Dad had been to coffee and were walking home when I picked you up. That was hours ago. Besides, *I* need to go."

Dad bounces up in anticipation. "Well, I sure do need to go, kid. I wondered if they even had any toilets in this place!"

Once in the lady's room, Mother and I both make very good use. "Let's wash our hands, too."

This is a signal for Mother. "Thank God, maybe then we can go find some lunch. I know Dad must be starved."

"You're both hungry, I'm sure."

"Not too bad for me, but poor old Dad really needs to eat."

As we come back out and meet Dad, he senses the subject of conversation and announces, "I'm about starved to death."

Mother's concern for 'poor old Dad' must have been left in the restroom. "Why, you old fool, you ate a big breakfast. You had a chicken breast and jo-joes. I only had a wing and a leg. If anyone should be hungry, I should be."

"Well, Jesus Christ, Honey, a man can't live all day on that."

I know they are both starving literally and figuratively, but my watch dictates that I have a race against time to accommodate Mr. Keys' five o'clock deadline. I ignore their hunger and their bickering as I help them into my truck and point it in the direction of Dr. Kettle's office across town.

For about the first time ever I make every green light in my crosstown route, and only a short time passes before I enter the doctor's office where I am greeted by an office attendant who understands my problem immediately. "Oh, yes, I know exactly what you want. Yes, that's a very standard request in guardianship hearings. I'd like to help you, but I really can't help you today. Dr. Kettle is on vacation, you know. He's the only one who has the authority to grant permission for such requests."

I listen to her prattle as long as I can stand it, and suddenly I erupt vocally in a manner that surprises both me and the office attendant. "Holy Jesus Christ on a rock! *HELP!* You people are supposed to be in a helping position, and you're claiming to understand my predicament. Understanding I have! Where is your *HELP?*"

The girl stammers, "I, I—I just don't know..."

From somewhere in the illustrious medically elite office sanctum, a calmer feminine voice sings out, "You know, there may be a way we could help." A nurse-type emerges and approaches the waiting room desk. "We really *can't* give you his records. But if your dad is with you, you could go over to St. Mary's to the Records Department. Your dad can request his own records."

I shake my head in despair as the tears well up. "That's unreal. He's the *subject* of the competency hearing. The court needs his medical records in order to complete the judgment that will declare him incompetent—you're suggesting he pick up the records which would do this to himself!"

The knowledgeable nurse-type shakes her head and sighs, "I know that sounds a bit unreal, but he can do that. Then, if the hospital does need to call back here, I'll get a doctor here to approve the record release to him. You have to hurry though—it's 4:20 now."

My thank-yous are curt, even to Holy Jesus on His rock, to whom I quietly apologize and thank as I run to my truck—and to whom I further implore to help Dad and me be quick. Jerking open the truck door, I find Dad and Mom both dozing. Dad's head rests against his chest and Mother is leaned against the window glass of the passenger door, mouth hanging open snoring loudly. "Dad, they won't give me your records here."

Mother's mouth snaps shut, and she's instantly wide awake. "That little Dr. K has been a bastard about everything else. What did you expect?"

I ignore her attack. "Dad, the lady said if we go to the hospital and *you* go in with me and give *your* permission, we might get your records that way. Will you do that?"

"Sure, let's get the hell out of here. Get this truck moving, kid."

Hurrying in slow motion is a recurring paradox in all of our family scenes in senility. We make the short trip from the doctor's office to St. Mary's. Dad and I get out of the truck, and he steadies himself looping his arm through mine. We begin a slow race toward the door. Just inside I stop. "Wait, Dad, we're at the Emergency Entrance. Records surely won't be any place close to this area. For the past fifty years this was the front door of the hospital. I'm more turned around than you."

Dad stares up at the arched doors and the Emergency Entrance sign. "E-M-E-R-G-E-N-C-Y. Oh, yeah, they rebuilt the front of the hospital about five years ago. It looks like they did a pretty good job. I haven't been here in ten years or more."

"But look, Dad. Look down the hall there on the right." I tug on his arm and begin to move us both toward the sign.

Dad comes to a sudden standstill and squints. "Where? Where are you looking? What sign?"

"Come on, Dad, this way. It says 'Records'."

I step forward, but Dad is still standing and squinting. I am jerked to a halt.

Dad raises his free hand to shield his eyes. "R-E-C-O-R-D-S. Records. Good. I'll just tell them to give my records right out to us. We're in a big hurry."

We begin anew our fast shuffle toward the sign. Bingo! A wonderful lady helps us immediately and with few questions. We thank her, and I clutch the thick brown envelope close. Dad loops his arm through mine again, and we retrace our steps to the exit through the Emergency Door. All is going well until I turn left toward the parking area, but Dad turns right. Our looped arms separate, and before I can catch him, Dad plunges head first into a large trash bin and begins retrieving aluminum cans and stuffing them in his pockets.

"Dad, Dad, we can't do that now. Remember we have to hurry."

"I *am* hurrying."

"Dad, we only have fifteen minutes to get back to the courthouse."

"This won't take long."

Dad keeps rummaging. I move up close and gently take hold of his arm speaking quietly very near his ear, "Please, Dad, go with me—*now*. I'll come back and get a big plastic bag and go with you to hunt for aluminum cans all day if you like. But *please,* just come with me—*now*."

Dad comes up with two more cans and stuffs them in his already full pockets. "Oh, shit! We could take a minute or two here."

I feel his arm slip gently back through mine. "Okay, Dad, let's get into fast shuffle overdrive, and you keep step with me."

We maintain a steady pace to the truck. I help him in on the passenger side and run around to my side. I hastily move out into the traffic and head for the truck route hoping to save valuable minutes but fearing I will never be so lucky again with the green lights. As I drive, and despite the danger, I take the records out and read en route. Upon arrival at the courthouse, I jam the truck into a parking spot, gather the papers, and hurry across the lot into the building. I manage to read a few more lines while I'm in the elevator. The records of January are there, including the conflict of chasing the dog and being taken to the hospital by the police. In the summary it very specifically says Dad has Alzheimer's and should be in a nursing home. A note at the bottom says the family has been informed Dad needs to be in a care facility, but they were unreceptive to that choice. I don't know who *they* refers to. Who has been informed? Who is unreceptive? I am further confused because I thought Alzheimer's could not be absolutely determined until after death and a brain autopsy. The report is definite, "Mr. Malfait has Alzheimer's." At no time did Dr. Kettle use that diagnostic term in talking with me. It looks as if every possible condition is ruled out, and when there is nothing else to test for, then the diagnosis is Alzheimer's. I guess that's the way doctors do it. How should I know? I don't even know what Alzheimer's is, and these reports don't sound as if doctors know either.

When I arrive at Mr. Keys' office, I tell the girl at a reception desk, "I didn't get the whole report read in my rush to get here, and I don't understand very well the parts I did read. Could you please run off a copy for me?"

"Oh, I couldn't possibly do that. That isn't kosher."

"But there's too much material to read in a few minutes, and I had to rush to get these over here to you people before five o'clock."

"Oh, it's not the time. *You're* not supposed to read them at all. These are intended to be placed as part of the confidential court record, and for right now they are only for the eyes of Mr. Keys and Judge Fox."

When I get back to the truck Malfaits are having their second nap, but only a slight suggestion of food arouses Dad. "Oh, Jesus, kid, I'm about starved to death."

Mother takes up the cause, "I'm hungry, too. We've got to get Dad to Chuck's Wagon right now and get some food in him."

"Mother, that's clear across town. Couldn't' we pick up something quick right here close by?"

Mother is adamant. "No, we're not going to run into some little cheap drive-in and pick something up. We're starving, and we need to sit down to a nice meal."

"But, Mom, it's the dinner hour at Chuck's Wagon. It will be really crowded."

"I don't care. We're hungry, and we need something warm. We're dressed just fine, and Dad needs to eat. I do, too, for that matter."

"I know we're all hungry, Mother. I'm hungry too, but we're really not dressed very well. Remember I picked you and Dad up right off the street, and you people had been out in the yard—or something."

Mother is relentless. "Chuck's Wagon is no kind of fancy place. We go there all the time looking like this. And it's right on the way home."

Dad chimes in with his usual support of Mother's decisions—at least ones related to food. "Now, kid, Chuck's Wagon is nothing fancy. We all need a good warm meal. We're almost there right now. Oh, sweet Jesus, kid, I'm soooo hungry."

They are still in their nasty "court dress" and the stench is unchanged. No matter how many times I try, I am unable to change their minds. They wear me down.

CHAPTER 27

Chuck's Wagon with Mom &
Dad—Denny's with Rolf

MOVING THROUGH THE line at Chuck's Wagon, Dad assumes *fast shuffle overdrive* as in our earlier hospital walk, and Mother has to hurry to keep up with him on the way to a table. Without taking the plates off the trays, they both lean over their trays and attack. Dad consumes two huge meaty ribs, two pieces of fried chicken, eight deep-fried shrimp, a healthy helping of macaroni and cheese, a mound of stewed carrots, a mountain of mashed potatoes and gravy, eight or ten jo-joes, a monstrous green salad, and a cinnamon roll the size of a luncheon plate and covered with thick frosting. Mother doesn't eat quite that much, but she's a close second.

It's not just the quantity of food that is amazing. Dad, particularly, eats savagely! He tears and stabs and shovels his food. He works at the tray as if he is clearing weeds for planting a garden. This is a man who for as long as I can remember has eaten large amounts of food, but who always considered eating one of life's great pleasures to be planned for, savored, and surely not rushed. This same man now uses both hands to rip the chicken from the bones and before that is even chewed, to shovel in great mounds of whatever is next in front of his spoon or fork. His hands and face become a greasy bearded blur of gnashing and gnawing. At brief pauses the coffee cup becomes his central focus. No matter whether old coffee or a freshened cup, Dad holds a sugar packet in proximity to the cup and rips the bag apart, causing most of the sugar to hit the coffee and the rest to fly wherever. Their behaviors today in Chuck's Wagon may be accentuated due to their extreme hunger, but I have noticed in both of them this gross, vicious attack on food becoming commonplace, along with insatiable appetites.

When we leave the restaurant, my throat feels like I have a rib bone stuck in it. My little green salad, a piece of chicken and some coffee push in a pulsating glob under my ribs. I would like to rename the restaurant "Upchuck Wagon."

Out on the street Dad loops his arm through mine and pats my hand with his free hand. He moves more spryly than he has all day, and I have to hold him back to wait for Mother. At the corner crosswalk he cautions, "Look out here, kid. You gotta be watching for these pedestrian lights. You can't be crossing when it flashes 'Do Not Walk'. Betty, I'm so happy we had dinner together."

I get Malfaits back to their house. After discerning Rolf is not there, I leave and drive out to Ocean Espresso and locate his car parked near his friend Mike's double-trailer rig. He's sitting in the cab with Mike, who is getting ready to make another run to California. I know they see. No one acknowledges me, but silent invisible rays of anger sear down from the big rig into my truck—into me!

I sit for a moment. Finally I roll down my window and look up to the truck window on the side where Rolf is sitting. "I took Mom and Dad home, and you weren't there. I wondered if you were still with Mr. Keys."

"Yeah, well I spent an hour and a half with him. I just told him everything. I really laid it on the line."

"That's what those sessions are for. I'm sure he wanted to hear exactly how each person felt."

I wonder what Rolf means by *really laid it on the line.* I doubt he told Mr. Keys of any of his conning or abusive care-taking. He had to have told him about the mortgage though, because that was the subject Mr. Keys brought up right at the end of my session. I don't know what the law says exactly, but I *do* know that Malfaits' house and property are theirs. If it takes it all for care for them, that's the way it has to be. Their house is not Rolf's. Their money is not Rolf's. Rolf should get the hell out of their house and quit wallowing in his ten year old *poor-me-the-mountain-erupted-I-lost-my-truck-my-dad-caused-me-to-go-to-jail-I-need-help-attitude.* I am so sick of his lamentations. Malfaits owe him nothing. And he owes them more than he'll *ever* be able to repay!

From up in the cab of the rig Mike leans across Rolf and shouts down, "You know, there's a law in Washington regarding senile parents—one of them can put everything in the other one's name. Then the impoverished one can get care and it's paid for by the State."

I respond, "I'm sure that's something Rolf and I should know more about."

That is the extent of Mike's profound legal counsel. Rolf says nothing more. Is Mike looking out for Rolf? Do either of them really care how Malfaits look and live and are cared for?

"Look, Rolf, I'm tired. I'm going back to The Sterling."

Rolf leans out his window as I begin to turn my truck away from the big rig and shouts, "Give me five minutes and pick me up at the house."

I want to yell back, 'Screw you!' but my thoughts dissipate into the wind as I pull onto the street and take the long route around the lake to Malfaits' house. It's no more than ten minutes, but Rolf beats me to the house, and he runs out to the car as soon as I drive up. He tells me Mom and Dad are sleeping, so I do not go in. I take him to Denny's for a bite to eat since he missed the big feed at Chuck's Wagon and I know he doesn't have any money. I also know my stomach won't tolerate this repast any better than the earlier episode, but I order ice cream anyway—a pacifying notion from happier childhood days.

Rolf eats practically like Dad, except that Dad devotes his full attention to the savagery. Rolf talks while eating, especially with his mouth full. He gesticulates vigorously with greasy hands, as I get a replay of the infamous D.B. Cooper bank robbery-parachuting crime and how Rolf himself may have been a suspect because of his serving on a United States Army Sky Diving Team and later teaching sky-diving lessons. I also get a recap of Green River Task Force activities, a recalling of Rolf's fraternity days at WSU, and an account of a conference in the courthouse men's room just this morning with the lawyer of the opposing side for the man Rolf had spied across the courtroom during the Malfait hearing that didn't happen. In conclusion, Rolf swipes a large chunk of bread in circular motions across his plate sopping up the last droplets of gravy from his meal. He shoves the soggy glob in his mouth with other unchewed food and wipes his mouth with the back of his hand.

I pay the check. There's no thank-you from Rolf. I guess Mom and Dad owe him a lot, and I must at least owe him some meals. Somehow the world owes Rolf everything!

"How about running me back to The Sterling? We can talk a little bit."

Once we're settled in my room, he talks nonstop until after midnight. He is not too revealing about his time with the counselor nor about any other part of the day. Neither does he talk about the angry, awkward scene at Mike's rig. It's as if none of it happened, and we're just catching up on old times. In fact, most of his vocal marathon is a rerun of his dinnertime monologue.

"You know that Green River Task Force thing is something I've followed pretty close. As a matter of fact, I felt real close to one particular girl who got done in. Her name was Linda."

"Did you know her?"

"Well, no, but I followed that case real close. I know the restaurant from where she disappeared. It's a little place I been to myself a number of times. In fact, after she disappeared from there, I've made it a point to go back there several times for coffee and hamburgers.

"That's an eerie thing to do."

"Well, maybe. I just felt real close to her. I prayed fervently that her body would be found. You know, ultimately it was found a few blocks away in a playground landfill. The body was just a few inches one way or the other from a drilling bit. The cops was pretty damned lucky to find it when they did."

"I still think that's kind of a spooky thing to do. It doesn't make sense to me."

Rolf shifts into another story almost without taking a breath. "You know me—I'm a person of pretty strong religious faith. I felt compelled to be there close by and to pray for them to find her.

"And, say, you know that thing with Dean Stearns up there at Centralia at the trucking company—now that's a deal that doesn't make sense."

"You used to work there, right? Did you quit or were you fired?"

"Naw, I wasn't fired. I worked there about four years. You might say I was "put on vacation". Old Dean, he was a guy who just made too quick a rise. He accumulated way too much too fast. He made a mass purchase of trucks and trailer rigs. Man, he bought all kinds of equipment—way more than he should have been buying. Then he kind of got caught with his pants down, so to speak. That kind of financial pressure may have caused him to get involved in some possible drug transport."

"What makes you think there was any kind of drug transport?"

"Well, Dean sure wasn't makin' the kind of money he needed to make all them payments."

"How do you know stuff like that about the owner of a company whom you only worked for?"

"Well, you know, the bookkeeper gal, she was always pretty friendly. I'd take time to visit with her every time I come in from a run. You know, one of his trucks got stopped once and searched. The cops evidently gave it a real goin' over."

"Was it one you were driving?"

"Naw, I wasn't drivin' that one. I had shared earlier with Dean about my private interests in contributing to the Green River Task Force and to the local county drug task force. I figure Dean was gettin' nervous and couldn't afford to have me haulin' anymore and him knowin' I was kinda sniffin' around. I may have been gettin' a little too close."

"A little too close to what?"

"Ah, hell, there wasn't any other reason for me being put on vacation. I was probably gettin' real close."

I'm not too interested in Rolf's sniffing around. To myself I'm thinking, 'Yeah, Rolf, you drove truck for that company for four steady years of big rig driving, and not once did you pay your $468.90 per month. Your parents rescued you financially because you *accumulated way too much too fast*. As I recall, there was a brand new GTO car, the house in Newcastle, a pick-up truck, two gill-netter boats, nets for the boats, and Alaska fishing licenses. I wonder if someone who would do what you've done to your parents may have some other habits that might be less than desirable. I don't know if you're describing yourself or Dean in your ramblings.'

Rolf's saga continues on in a repeated diatribe about the use of the rooms here at The Sterling. "You know, the prostitutes like that corner room down here. That's where they had their big drug party just the other day."

"And did you attend? Were you patronizing the prostitutes or were you checking on the drugs?"

"Well, you know I wasn't really part of the party. I can learn a lot from the maids the next day."

"Rolf, it's almost midnight. If you keep jabbering, I'm not going to need the maids in my room tomorrow because I won't have slept in my bed. You need to get out of here."

"Yeah, yeah. We need to get the wash done tomorrow. I'll meet you at nine at the house. For right now, can you run me over to where I left my car near Mike's rig?"

Despite the late hour, I do that. We don't talk much on the way over, and we part—estranged but without argument. I don't know where Rolf is spending the night, and I don't really care.

As I return to my room at The Sterling, other women are coming into the motel at the same hour. I wonder if Rolf knows them. I wonder if he's ever partied with them—or patronized them. I chuckle and hope I don't get mugged or beaten up because someone might think I'm moving in on their business territory. One thing for sure, we can't all be in this town doing what I'm doing. On the other hand, what the hell *am* I doing here? What am I *really* doing?

CHAPTER 28

———

God, Please Be Here

THE NEXT MORNING I arrive at Malfaits about nine thirty. There is no Rolf. I should have been here at nine, as that's when Rolf said to meet him so we could go do the wash. He stayed in my motel room awfully late last night. Maybe he slept in. I would have slept in, but Don called early to tell me Mother had called a couple of times last night and asked for me. She seemed confused and wouldn't tell him what she wanted. He was a little bit worried since I had not called him last night.

I tap lightly on the front door and listen at the wicket. Malfaits are just getting up. They admit me to the confusion of their morning dressing routine.

"Say, Mother, I talked to Don this morning, and he said you called last night a couple of times. Is there something you wanted?"

"Why, I didn't call Don last night. I never talked to him."

"You *didn't*? Don said he got the first call at 8:50 and the next one at 11:50."

"Well, I never talked to Don."

Before we can pursue this difference, I hear Rolf's old car pull up on the driveway. I guess a hole in the muffler is as good as a door bell. He comes through the door with no hello, boo, or kiss my fan to anyone. He stomps through the living room snarling, "Jesus, the air is so God-damn thick in here this morning, how can any of you stand it? It's like breathin' fuckin' cat hair."

"Man, Rolf, are you stressed because I'm half an hour late?"

"No." He continues on toward the kitchen.

Mother interjects, "He's always like that. He has a filthy mouth."

Rolf whirls around and storms back into the living room, "I can't even find a fuckin' place to sit." He swats his own boxes of junk out of the way and flops down on the couch. He grabs a newspaper, opens it to a middle page, and raises it in front of his face with snapping motions to force it upright. The snapping motions fail. The paper falls against his face making him angrier.

Mother helps things to an even higher pitch as she sits down on the arm of the couch and slowly brushes her long, straggly white hair. "You don't need to have such a filthy mouth about things."

Rolf snaps the paper again and it defiantly crinkles back over his face. He jerks the paper down and yells at her, "You're the one with the God-damned fuckin' dirty mouth!"

Oh, God, please...

I try for some degree of calmness. "Rolf, I thought things were okay last night when I dropped you off. What's wrong now? Are you having a bad morning?"

"No, I ain't havin' no bad mornin'!"

"Well, did yesterday get to you that much?"

"No. I just didn't sleep very well. In fact, I didn't sleep at all. Who the hell could sleep in this God-damned, cocksucking hell-hole?" He raises the paper back up over his face and continues muttering volleys of expletives at the inert black ink.

With each stroke of her brush Mother delivers a new barb. "You're mean to Dad—You have a foul mouth—You need to get a job."

I interrupt the fracas. "Mom, you and Dad need to hurry up and get on your way for your morning coffee. You're really not helping here. Please."

Dad paces through the living room babbling, "Rolf, you leave Betty alone. You hear me? Don't you touch her."

I sense Mom and Dad don't want to leave, and they are afraid Rolf will harm me. I am incredulous of the current rage and vileness Rolf has shown. In fact, I *am* afraid—terrified! Maybe he'll snap me like the newspaper.

God, please be here—now! God, if he's going to kill me, it better be now, because I'm not leaving, and I'm not going to let go.

Almost immediately I feel totally enclosed in an invisible, comfortable, protective balm. It's a strange sensation. It's surreal. I'm here, but I'm removed from the situation. I feel Rolf can't hurt me.

Rolf looks out from behind his crumpled shield and breaks the angry, frozen quiet. "I ain't gonna hurt no one. Go on to your coffee."

Dad seeks affirmation, "Now, Rolf, I'm telling you, you better not hurt anyone."

I open the front door for Mom and Dad. "You guys go on to breakfast. Rolf and I are fine."

They both move toward the door. Dad pauses, squints a warning glare toward Rolf, jerks his chin to one side and thrusts a silent pointed finger at him.

As the door closes I turn toward Rolf. "I don't understand your rage. You were fine when we parted last night. What's the problem now? What's bothering you? Why don't you lay all the cards out on the table?"

He snaps at the uncooperative paper and when the pages again defy his command and fall into his face, he hurls it across the coffee table in my direction. The pages flutter apart and nestle onto various piles of clutter. Rolf lurches himself to the edge of his seat on the couch and shouts, "Well, you know that Whidbey Island property may be worth a lot of money some day, and I'd hate to see that strangely end up with a deed with only your name on it—or find that you had purchased it for under the actual value."

"Listen, Rolf, all that Malfaits own is the 516 property and the Whidbey Island land, and none of it is mine nor is it yours. Both of those properties are theirs and should be used for their benefit as long as they live, and that means for whatever kind of care they require. Is a dumb piece of land what you're so angry about?"

"Well, I hate to think you'd become the owner of twenty acres of cheap land in this guardianship thing."

"Rolf, I have no intentions in this guardianship of becoming the owner of twenty acres of cheap land. That's not what this is about. By the same token, what's theirs is not automatically yours—not the 516 house, the land, nor their money!"

"I just don't want to get screwed over."

"Rolf, this process is about providing care for our parents with their assets. It's not a legal way to screw *you*. The assets are not yours, nor are they mine. I think a large part of the problem that makes our relationship unworkable is because you have this paranoia about being screwed by other people, and you feel you have to beat people to the draw and do it to them first. In regard to Malfaits, you have accepted far too much already—they offering in the guise of helping, and you taking as if what's theirs you have entitlement to, whether it's food, storage space in their house, or money. It's ridiculous that you have a place in Newcastle and yet keep a mailing address at their house, and then when mail gets lost you hold them financially responsible for rectification of situations such as your night in jail in Oregon, your traffic ticket, your overdue tire bills, your overdue repair bills. You've been doing this shit for years. You take and take and blame and blame. It has to stop. It's *going* to stop!"

"That's not true. I never *ever* borrowed anything from them I didn't pay back."

"My God, Rolf, how can you say that? You have never made any of the $468.90 payments to Fibex, and don't say you have because I've been helping Mother with the bill-paying since Dad had the stroke, and I know firsthand you haven't paid that payment for years. Way before that Mother griped about you never doing what you promised to do in regard to the repayment of that loan."

Rolf looks thoughtful. "You know, I just don't know what Mom and Dad have done with all their money they've had over the years. They have about $1800.00 a month coming in."

"Actually, Rolf, the amount is $1705 per month, but even if you rounded it off and said $20,000 per year. Over the past five years that would have been $100,000. I can tell you that $468.90 per month is about $5600 per year, and that's $28,000 total. In other words, Rolf, more than one-fourth of their total income has been spent on *your* debt consolidation."

"Yeah, yeah, and I fully intend to pay them back."

"You won't live long enough to pay them back! They'll end up paying another $20,000 or more before the debt is totally cleared, and for what, Rolf? What will they have at the end of that debt? They have many hard feelings toward you about the debt now, because they wanted to *help* you, and they had enough confidence in you that they co-signed and used their most precious asset, their home, as collateral. But, *you*, Rolf—you were supposed to take over the payments when you got on your feet. And you have never made any of the payments—not even when you did work, did you?"

"Well, I'm gonna pay it back."

"Rolf, neither one of us is doing well with the events of yesterday, but perish the thought, what if they died next week? What would you do to manage their affairs?"

"Well, I'd pay everything off and straighten things out, but I'd still pay off my debt to them, even if they were dead. Then I'd get the hell out of here and get a decent job."

"See, Rolf, in my mind I don't believe you'd do that. You have done nothing so far that gives me any confidence you would carry through and do it. You'd probably get the job and get the hell out, but I really doubt you'd pay anything off. There is no paperwork that would insist that you do, and I doubt you would. I can tell you, you'll never be an honorable person in my mind until you've got sixty-seven thousand, five hundred bucks to lay on the table for them and say thank you!"

"Well, I can administer things as well as you."

"No, Rolf, the difference is if I were administering, I would pay off all debts, including your past debts. It would gall me to the bone, but

I would act in their behalf. Then I would use all their remaining assets for their benefit only. And upon their deaths, if there was anything left, I would split it 50/50. As for your paying them back—whether they're dead or alive—I think that's just a $67,500 chuckle and a lost cause."

"That ain't no chuckle! I tell you, I'm gonna pay it back—every red cent. I always pay back."

"Rolf, where would you like to be five years from now?"

I'd like to be out of debt and able to look the bastards in the eye who fucked me over with my truck and be in a position to do the same to them!"

"Rolf, those are the kinds of comments that scare hell out of me. You seem to be listening, and you travel right down the moral pathway—then, BOOM! Your intent is suddenly manipulation, vengeance and vindictiveness. Those comments make people who would like to trust you very uneasy. You make *me* very uneasy."

"Yeah, yeah. Well, maybe I say a lot of stuff I don't mean. You really make me angry just coming in here and taking over. You never even asked me to be part of this guardianship deal. It doesn't have my name on it. You just did it on your own. It ain't fair because one child in the family has fallen on hard times and can't be bonded and all that legal shit—it just ain't fair for that person not to have any say in what happens to the senile parents. Contrary to what you might think, I really do care."

I want to contradict the error about never asking him, but instead I choose to react only to his last comment. "I know you care, but your physical behavior and abuse have not been actions that suggest you care in a healthy, safe manner—at least they do not suggest you would be a very good care-taker."

"Well, I do care."

"Rolf, if you made a list of all the good, positive things you've done to show you care, how long would the list be? What would be on the list?"

"Well, I've put up with a lot of shit over the last two years and all during the time I was working for Dean Stearns."

"What does that have to do with what we're talking about? You didn't live with Mom and Dad during that time. In fact, it appears you have only actually lived *in* the house since January of this year. Prior to that, you cruised in and out of their lives giving them directions about things to do, but not actually doing anything *for* them or *with* them. In January of this year you dumped your junk all over their house, until it was impossible to even get through their living room. That's not living with them or caring for them."

"Now, wait a minute, most of that clutter is *their* shit from years of saving and from spending splurges at Salvation Army and Goodwill. All that shit is not mine."

"I disagree! I've cleaned and moved and packed and stacked many times. I *know* whose shit most of it is. I will agree to disagree though!

Rolf slumps back on the couch and folds his arms. Icy silence prevails as he stares into nothingness.

I begin picking up the pieces of the failed newspaper shield. Moments pass. "Rolf, do you ever think maybe this whole thing is bigger than just us? I mean, does it ever occur to you this ordeal with our parents is a masterful orchestration of events by a higher power—by Almighty God—and you and I are supposed to be learning from all this?"

"Yeah, yeah. That thought has occurred to me."

"Rolf, I've thought about it more than once. Maybe the whole thing—the progress, sequence, and timing of these events is out of our control for the most part, and it has been for a long time—maybe even for years, clear back to the big family hoopla over theft. You know, all along the way, we each have had choices to make—choices of right and wrong."

"Yeah, yeah. I know there's bigger things than my control, but I just don't want to get screwed here."

"Rolf, that's not going to happen. I don't think I'm ever going to be able to agree with you on a lot of things. I know I can't be totally correct in my perceptions, especially after the family rift and my five-year hiatus. All these family episodes have been like a very bad movie we've both been watching, but we're not arriving at the same observations and conclusions. In fact, I'm not even sure I'm watching the same movie as you."

Rolf chuckles, "Yeah, definitely a low budget film."

"Rolf, I hear your words. I'm really sorry you've had such bad luck in your work and finances, but my bigger concern is with Mom and Dad. I feel they deserve to live at a more humane level than like street bag people with the whole town looking on—some laughing, some repulsed and aghast, some taking financial advantage."

"I agree with you there, but I don't want to get fucked over."

"Rolf, I wouldn't do that, but I don't know how to make you believe that. We can communicate and mutually decide on many things, but we cannot share financial matters. We just don't operate the same way. You can't do it my way, and I can't do it your way. I will *not* share a savings nor a checking account with you."

"I don't understand that. I have never done anything to warrant your attitude. Furthermore, up until I lost my truck, I had outstanding financial standing in this community."

"Only you know about that, Rolf. All I know is that you have dogged me just about every step of the way from the beginning of this guardianship process, as well as anything either Mother or I depended on you to do relevant to paying bills—especially with cash. You have repeatedly treated their money as if it's yours."

"Well, how'd you get that idea?"

I clamp my teeth and draw in a long, slow breath and expel the air slowly. I squelch words like liar, thief, and bilk. Instead I answer, "Number one was the money for the trip to pay the Neilson Insurance. Number two was the money for the sink. Number three was the window repair money. Number four was the Cablevision money. Number five is the recent five hundred-plus dollar lumber bill. Rolf, the list goes on and on."

"Well, all those examples are things that I had to do differently from your directions in order to help them."

"Rolf, I say no! Discussion never took place. There are no receipts to show when or if things got paid. I can't work cooperatively with you in regard to money matters without records, a check book, and receipts."

There is a rattling of the mailbox on the front porch. Rolf goes to see who's there and comes back into the living room ripping open a letter. "Ah, here's a new Sears Credit Card for Mom and Dad. I may need it to buy a new plastic mattress cover." He tucks the credit card in his over-stuffed shirt pocket.

I make no objection. Maybe he will buy a new plastic mattress cover. I just hope there are no more saws or building materials on the next Sears bill.

Another metallic scraping of the screen door being opened announces Mom and Dad's return.

I resume my task of gathering laundry. Mother and Dad enter the living room pleasantly enough and make no mention of the tension and fear which preceded their leaving to go to coffee. "Oh my, Betty, you should have waited and let me help you with all that laundry." She rummages through her big black purse and extracts her little square purse. "Let me get you some money for the laundromat." She counts her money meticulously, then recounts. "My God, I'm $100.00 short again."

Rolf declares immediately, "Well, I don't know nothin' about any of this."

"Mother, I don't know how that could happen. I counted it with you last night."

"Betty, I know you counted it with me last night. I had it all in the envelope when I went to bed—in that bank envelope you put all that silver duct tape on."

"I know, Mom. Where's the envelope? You just took all your money out of that little black change purse. Maybe most of the money is still in the silver envelope."

She shrugs, "I don't know where it is."

I begin a search for the envelope and find it in their bedroom all crumpled up and hidden under the cushion of the chair beside the bed.

Hurried thoughts surge through my brain about where Rolf was last evening before he ran out to catch a ride with me to The Sterling. I hadn't gone into the house at all. Most likely at that hour no one else had gone into their house—surely not into their bedroom—surely not into her 'pillow-case-duct-tape-encased-purse-envelope'. However, this morning their money is not in the envelope. Rolf was not here when I arrived. They've been out to breakfast. Who waited on them at the corner café? Who else had access to the envelope? I make no accusations. I drop the duct-taped envelope into the trash basket with no comment. I cram the remainder of the dirty clothes in the big black plastic bag, heft it over my shoulder, and head for the door.

Rolf does not offer to accompany me to do the wash.

About two blocks away from the house my tears gush—tears of frustration, tears of restraint from not allowing myself to accuse Rolf, and tears for both of my parents' decline and the untrusting atmosphere in which they must live. I grab a crumpled napkin from the truck seat and scrub across my face as I continue to drive. By the time I arrive at the laundromat the tears have dried up. Soggy bits from the napkin cling to the front of my black sweatshirt. I wish I could brush the debris of my life away as easily as the tear-soaked paper crumbs. Instead I refocus on the task at hand and attack the laundry.

On the way back to 516 I stop and do a grocery shopping.

At the house I haul in the groceries and the clean wash. Mom and Dad are both hungry, and I cut a cantaloupe for them and put each half on a plate with spoons and get them both seated at the kitchen table. My next trip through the house, laden with four more grocery bags, I find Rolf sitting in the living room with one of the cantaloupe halves. In the kitchen Mother is spooning her way through the other half. Dad is sitting at his place at the kitchen table watching Mother eat.

I would like to kick Rolf wherever it would hurt the most, but it's quicker to just fix another cantaloupe. I heat water for cups of soup, get out the milk and two clean glasses. I pour the milk and drop some bread in the toaster. Rolf comes into the kitchen, picks up one of the milk glasses, gulps it down, refills the glass and drains it a second time. He sets the empty glass down near Dad and leaves the kitchen. Now I would like to do more than kick him, but I simply get another clean glass for Dad.

I barely get this one on the table when Rolf bursts back into the kitchen yelling at top volume, "Here, here, Betty—you may as well see what we're having to live with from these fuckin' cats!"

"Rolf, look at yourself waving your cantaloupe in one hand and that big gob of cat shit in the other. You're acting like they act toward each other, and what you're doing serves no purpose. You're gross! You're liable to get so excited and hyperventilate so much you'll forget which hand the cat shit is in and eat it, and I really don't care! In fact, I might get a great deal of satisfaction out of seeing that event. Now get the hell out of the kitchen and away from the table!"

Surprisingly, he turns and leaves the kitchen without argument. Shortly I make my way through the house to depart for my drive home, Malfaits call out a thank you for all my work, but they don't get up from the table. They are engrossed in polishing off a package of doughnuts and drinking more milk.

On the way out of town I swing into a drive-through window and order a hamburger meal. I force myself to eat my first meal of the day, other than the day-old apple fritter I gobbled while the wash was in the dryer. I choke down the bites of warm burger and greasy fries with slurps of a diet cola, and as I pull onto the Interstate I feel the lumps wallowing in my gurgling, belching gut. Geez, I'm as gross as any other Malfait!

Food provides no comfort. I am filled with a smorgasbord of emotions: love, hate, anger, frustration, desperation, fear.

I turn on the radio and find a music station, hoping for some relaxation. The only station that will come in clearly on the truck radio is blaring some foot-stomping gospel lyrics—*finding something to be thankful for can make all the bad things go away.* Each resounding verse brings another deluge of tears, as my brain dredges through the events of the weekend. I clench the steering wheel and shout back at the twangy, nasal voice, "What's to be thankful for? I want to smash something—maybe you—preferably Rolf!"

Suddenly the same invisible, eerie wrap from earlier in the day enfolds me. My anger is quelled. My tears stop. I feel warm. I am quiet. My brain recalls the calmness in the confrontation with Rolf when he was enraged. I'm not overly brave, and I'm not a fool. I know the loaded 38 was his pocket. It was a dangerous confrontation. But at this moment I feel calm—protected—strange—almost pleasant.

Is that you, God?
Dear God, I do have doubts and fear, but I do thank You for Your presence and personal protection today. I don't pretend to understand this, but I know You're with me. I feel Your presence. I know You care for me personally. Thank you.

The gospel music continues to blare as another part of my brain chides, 'You're acting as nutso as your relatives. What are these ill-formed prayers of yours? You're no saint in action here. You know very well there's millions of people who have done far greater deeds at far greater personal cost than whatever it is that you're trying to do with your parents.

God, I'm not Mother Theresa. I'm no place close to that kind of contribution and loving devotion. I have so much more to learn from You. God, please help me to go the distance to do whatever you want me to do—in the name of Jesus.

I glance at the speedometer. I'm at 70 mph. I've already passed Pleasanton and the mall. I'm nearing Allwyn. I have no recollection of the past hour and a half of interstate driving. Reality tells me to slow down. I'm a danger to other drivers and to myself. I don't want to have to take a nap again in the Allwyn restaurant parking lot. I cut my speed back to the legal 60 mph and open my truck window to help me stay in reality mode until I get home.

The next morning Rolf calls about ten o'clock. "Hell's a poppin' here! Did you leave any money in the Father's Day card you left on the freezer?"

"No."

"Well, Dad said you had left him money for Father's Day, and it was gone. Of course, he felt I had taken it."

"Geez, I'm sorry. It was so confusing this weekend, and I was awfully tired. I wanted to be home for Fathers' Day. If I had said that yesterday, Dad would have gotten all maudlin about it and would have said, 'You stay here. I'm your father, and this is home. This may be the last one, kid!' I just couldn't bear that, so I thought I'd leave a little surprise in the kitchen instead. Right now it seems food is a big deal, so I left him that pie with the card on top."

"Well, food may be a big deal, but Dad says he ain't eatin' that God-damned pie. He's going to huck it off the back porch."

"I don't see how he could get so mad about a pie. It's blueberry, too. That's a favorite of his."

"Well, to tell you the truth, I think it had more to do with the card. You signed the card 'Love from Betty and Rolf'. Dad seemed to have some suspicions about what might be in the pie—poisons or such."

"*You've got to be kidding!* Is Mother there?"

"Yeah, yeah."

"Let me talk to her, and I'll try to explain the pie."

Rolf and Mother exchange places at the phone. "Mother, listen, I forgot to mention the pie. I just plain forgot. When I finished the shopping yesterday the lady was putting the pies out fresh from the bakery. I thought it would be a nice surprise for Fathers' Day morning, so I left it out by your breadbox on the freezer. I'm sorry about the misunderstanding about money. I usually do put money in his Father's Day card, but this time I didn't have any cash. I'm sorry if that caused a problem."

"Oh, Dad gets upset too easily lately. He thought it was like your other cards, and that you would have left money in the card."

"Well, it would have been that way, but I ran out of time—and frankly, I was also out of cash. Do you want me to talk to him and try to explain?"

"No, I'll explain it to him."

"Well, you tell him I will get him a present and I'll bring it down next time. I'm really sorry for the hubbub. It's confusing around there anyway, and things get misunderstood easily."

"Oh, don't worry about it. Dad just got all worked up over nothing. And the money doesn't matter at all. I get a little short myself sometimes. You worked so hard this weekend. I just hope I don't owe you anything."

"No, Mother, you don't owe me anything. I didn't have any cash, and I didn't have my checkbook along.

"You people will eat the pie, won't you? It was freshly baked yesterday."

"It looks wonderful. Of course, we'll eat it."

I hear Rolf take the phone back, "I've thought a lot about these last two days, and I think I'd like to find one of those Alzheimer's support groups."

"Good. I think that would be helpful for all of us."

"Mr. Keys gave me a couple of numbers. I'll contact one of them real soon."

As the month of June concludes, the guardianship is complete except for Judge Fox signing the papers. My attorney advises me to go ahead and plan for Malfaits' care and finances. In planning those details I have to visit the courthouse, and I run into Mr. Keys in the entryway. He tells me Rolf will *not* be a part of the guardianship. Rolf had come back in to see him the next day and spent about an hour with him. And he called him again later in the week to ask some more questions.

During that second visit Mr. Keys told Rolf of the final court decision. Rolf was disappointed as he had thought there would be a formal time in front of the judge, and he had a few things he wanted to say.

"I'm sure he would have a lot to say. May I ask you now that you have spent more time with Rolf, do you feel he is dangerous with all his threats, guns, and intimidation, as well as having a file with Adult Protective Service verifying his abuse to our parents? Do you feel he is dangerous to either Malfaits or me?"

"Well, probably not, but you never can tell about these people who are gun bunnies."

CHAPTER 29

────⚮────

Fourth of July Fireworks

I PULL INTO Malfait's driveway July 4, 1990. It's almost noon. Dad is standing on the front steps holding the door open behind him.

I call out across the yard, "Hi, Dad."

Dad squints in my direction then turns his view back up the street toward Ruthie's house. I grab a couple of packages off the front seat, slide out of the truck, and cut across the lawn. When I am a few feet away, I try again. "Hi, Dad."

"I don't see—her—anywhere," he mumbles.

I step up close to his face. "Dad, I'm here. Helloooo."

"Oh, it's you, Betty. Well, you can come in."

"Dad, why don't you give me a hand carrying some things in? Here, you can take these presents. They're birthday presents for Mother, and there's a belated Father's Day gift for you." I shove the packages toward him.

Dad glances once more up and down the street, takes the presents, and disappears into the house. I return to the truck for a second load, but when I get back to the front door, I find I am locked out. After several repeated melodious four-tone doorbell repetitions, I hear Dad coming back through the house. Taco is barking loudly.

"Just—hold your horses—there. I'm coming. Taco, get out of the way! Taco, hush! I'm coming. You hold up there a minute—until I get this damned dog—out of the way!"

It's quiet for a moment. I hear the deadbolt clank and finally the door opens. "Oh, it's you. I don't know what's happened to Francine. She's been gone and gone."

331

"I'm sure she's around somewhere, Dad. What did you do with the presents?"

"What presents?"

Without a response to Dad, I begin a search for the presents and find them on top of the garbage cans on the back porch. Further out in the backyard under the cherry tree sits Mother in an old wooden lawn chair half hidden in the tall grass.

"Hi, Mom. What are you doing out there?"

She pulls herself up in the chair and concentrates in my direction, raising a hand clutching several pieces of silverware to shade her eyes. "Dad took our lunch dishes in, and he was going to get me some birthday cake. The old fool is probably lost. He's been gone so long, I'm about to fall asleep."

I follow a pathway through the overgrown grass to where she is sitting. "Geez, what's with the hayfield? You told me on the phone Rolf had mowed the lawn again and you paid him thirty bucks to do the job. Didn't that include the backyard?"

"I wanted him to do the backyard, too. I don't know why he didn't do it. He knows this is our favorite place to sit. It's always cool out here under the cherry tree and the grape arbor. It's been awful hot this week."

I peek over my shoulder into the tool shed. "The front yard looks great. The mower's here in the shed. That's weird he didn't mow this part, too." I turn back to Mother who is slumped in the chair still clutching the silverware staring sleepily straight ahead. "Oh well, maybe he ran out of gas."

"I don't think so. He mowed two days ago, and there's more gas in the shed. I don't think he intends to mow this part."

Dad shuffles through the grass to the picnic table. "Jesus Christ, Francine, where have you been? I've been looking all over for you."

Mother snaps to alertness, "Why, you old fool, I've been sitting right here waiting for you to bring me my birthday cake."

"Oh, Jesus, I forgot your cake! I don't know what's the matter with me lately. I left it in the kitchen."

Before Dad can turn around, I head back to the house calling over my shoulder, "You both sit here in the shade. I'll run in and get the cake."

On the kitchen counter I find two dinner plates with huge hunks of cake on them. They're so big I doubt Dad could have carried them anyway. I quickly lop off portions from each of the pieces and prepare a third dinner plate. Grabbing another fork and balancing the three plates, I return to the backyard.

It's two days before her actual birthday, but the three of us share Mother's birthday treat as she opens her presents in the cool of the backyard deep in the weed jungle. Dad happily rips open his belated Fathers' Day present, and no one mentions the blueberry pie incident. They don't care whose birthday it is or when Father's Day was, and the weeds don't matter. They are engrossed in celebration with childlike pleasure.

"Yoo-hoo, Betty." A neighbor calls me over to the fence. "Hi, kid. I don't want to interrupt your party, but I want to tell you real quick your Mom fell down and bruised her left arm and left knee. She's been limping pretty bad for a couple of days now. It supposedly happened tripping over a chair in the house. I don't know—you know, the way Rolf acts and all—I just thought you ought to know it happened."

"Thanks for telling me. I'll ask her about it, but if it's anything other than falling, she probably won't tell me."

Dear God, please let it be a fall and not some 'rolf' thing!

A little later on the way back into the house, I ask, "Hey, Mom, what happened to your leg? You're limping."

"Oh, I fell over the kitchen chair. Dad, the old fool, left it right out in the middle of the floor."

As we open the back door and move into the kitchen I wonder where the middle of the floor is. The table and chairs are stacked high with pots and pans, canned goods, and piles of dirty dishes. The stacks are *everywhere* on top of the 'permanent stacks' of past clutter, and in the floor, as well. How can they do this in the short amount of time since I was last here? No wonder they ate lunch in the back yard. They would have had to stand up in order to eat in the kitchen.

I waste no time launching my dish-soap-bleach attack on whatever is in the sink. Three hours later the dishes are done and the 'eating end' of the table is useable. The permanent stacks are restacked and stabilized. I consolidate three large grocery sacks chocked full of empty cans, reused paper plates, moldy jars of partially eaten jelly, and bits and pieces of unknowns into one big black heavy duty garbage bag. As I pass through the living room with the bag on my shoulder, I am thankful Mom and Dad are engrossed in the newspaper and ask no questions about what they don't see within the black plastic. I huck the bag out the front door under the camellia bush and relish a small degree of success at avoiding an argument over 'salvageable' food items and 'good jelly jars'. I'll take the bag around to the garbage dumpster in the alley after dark.

Later, we all sit at the 'eating end' of the kitchen table and have supper. Mother and Dad appreciate the improved surroundings but lament that they haven't been much help. After our meal, I invite them to dry dishes. They fuss about which one gets to do it, but we settle the argument by having them both help. It's messier and slower passing the dishes from the sink to the table where they are seated, but they like their assigned jobs and scrub happily at each dish.

"How are your legs now, Mother, after such a hot day?"

"These old legs have just been killing me lately."

Dad offers helpfully, "I tell your mama I'll help her get all this work caught up."

"Did you really fall here in the kitchen, or did you hurt yourself some other way?"

"I've not hurt myself at all. Sometimes I just can't stand very well. Someday when you get as old as Dad and me, you'll see your legs don't work so well either."

"Maybe I could find someone to come in and assist with some of this housework. Maybe even some of the yard work."

There is an immediate simultaneous 'No!' from both of them.

Mother continues, "Dad and I don't want any strangers in the house. Those people who come into your home to work generally rob you blind."

Dad adds, "Now, Betty, if *you* wanted to come in here that would be different. Why, you could just come on with Don and the kids and move right in here with Mama and me. We have plenty of room, and we sure do need to hold together as a family right now. Your mom *needs* some help."

"Dad, that's really nice of you, but you know I have my own family and a job."

"You bring Nick and El and Don right with you. We have plenty of room."

I work on the pots and pans with a harsh metal scrub pad as Mother defends my unspoken position, "Dad, you know Betty can't quit her teaching job and come down here and clean up after us."

I offer another option, "Maybe the two of you would like to live closer to me and my family. Then I wouldn't have these long trips to make, and we could see you more often. Would you and Dad like to have a little apartment or something up near where I live? Does that sound at all interesting?"

Dad speaks up, "Well now, I for one don't want to live in no apartment, but your mama and me have always liked Whidbey Island, and I'd like to build another house and live on our property up there. That's nearer to you, isn't it? I don't see why we couldn't build our own house on our own land there."

Mother adds, "Yes, we both like Whidbey. I'd love to live there. But, Dad, you and I are too old to be thinking about building another house. I'm not going to go through that with you again."

Mother's words express a fifty year old unpleasant memory of the building experience of 516. Dad laughs good naturedly and shrugs, "Why, Francine, I built this house just fine, and I could do it again."

Before Mother can recall the true agony of house-building, Rolf materializes in their kitchen. Mother demands, "Where have you been?"

"Oh, I've been around. I been to Oregon to talk to a couple of people, and I worked a couple of days this past week."

The vague answer seem to satisfy Mother. She asks for no additional detail.

Dad speaks up, "Jesus, people, it's getting dark and time for the fireworks down by the lake."

"Now, Dad, my old legs are not going take me down by that lake for any fireworks this year."

"Oh, dearie, that's okay. We can watch the sky off the front steps. I'll keep you company, and we'll see the whole show from right here." Dad scrapes his chair back from the table. "Rolf, help me move these chairs out to the front yard."

Author and brother Rolf

The evening passes pleasantly in the cool front yard, including feasting on a juicy ripe watermelon. Shortly after 10:00 PM Rolf turns to me, "I'm pretty beat. How about I drive up to The Sterling behind you and run up to your room and grab a shower?"

"That's fine by me. Any Malfait who *asks* to take a shower will not be refused, no matter how tired *I* am."

Rolf chuckles, "Yeah, I gotta report at 6:00 AM tomorrow on a log hauling job. Old man Whitfield who lives down near my place in New Castle has over a couple of hundred acres up north a little ways. Should be good haulin' for a while."

Rolf helps me get Mom and Dad and the chairs moved back inside. He goes out to his car, and I run in the house to remind Mother about bill-paying tomorrow. I grab up all the bills I can find, while she counts her money. I count her money again with her and then run to my truck.

At The Sterling Rolf showers, puts on a change of work clothes, and plops down and stays until 1:00 AM. We rehash Mom and Dad's continued decline, how much care they need, and what Rolf should do with his stuff all over their house, especially if someone has to come in to help with the cleaning.

"Well, Rolf, I don't think we're arriving at any answers, but we're certainly agreeing on a bunch of areas where help is needed."

"Yeah, and maybe one of the first things to do might be to get 'em both in for medical check-ups."

"I can try to get them to do that, but I don't have much confidence either one of them will go."

"I been readin' lately about oxygen starvation to the brain. I'm sure they both got symptoms of that. I guess a doctor would have to say for sure."

"Rolf, all this house cleaning is more than they can ever do. It's getting to be more than I can get half-way done on weekends down here. It's become too big a job for me by myself. We really need to consider what kind of institutional care, or at least personal care, they need on a permanent basis."

"Betty, I don't know about that. They both want to stay there in the house as long as possible, and it would be pretty expensive to get someone in to help."

"I don't think we could get anyone to come into their home as it is now. I know very well I couldn't live there with all the cats and my allergies. I haven't slept in their house for years, although Dad said today he wants me to come and move in with them. He told me to come on down and bring Don and the kids and move right in. They have plenty of room."

Rolf laughs incredulously, "Yeah, like that would really work. Sis, nobody should quit their job to do this, but Mom and Dad do need help."

"Well, my family isn't going to be making that move. You don't need to worry about that. I'll have to see what community services are available and if they qualify. I've got to have some help whether they want anyone in the house or not."

I spend most of the rest of July getting acquainted with Senior Citizen Services in their community. Malfaits do not qualify for any of the available services, because they have too many assets. Their need is urgent, but their Whidbey Island property is a stone around their necks. Also paying the $468.90 per month for Rolf's mortgage is not considered their debt, but paying it prevents them from having funds to hire help or to use any kind of senior assistance program.

In recent weeks as Mother and I have tried to manage financially, continued disappearances of cash have occurred regularly, and that's another entanglement. It's harder each time for me to refrain from accusation. I know Rolf runs their car ragged and gas money has to come from somewhere, 'con' job or not. Along with their bills this month, I also find two bills on the coffee table for Alaskan fishing licenses due in the amount of over $300.00 apiece. Rolf hasn't worked much recently. He won't want to lose those licenses, and he probably doesn't have money to renew them. I know June's household cash is gone, and July's Social Security checks have been cashed.

The next day I try to confront financial issues with Rolf without being accusing, "Rolf, have you taken them shopping since I was down last?"

Rolf is immediately defensive. "No, I ain't havin' anything to do with their shopping, and I don't eat at their place. I don't know nothin' about their money. Mom gave me $30.00 here the other day to mow the lawn, and another day she give me $30.00 for groceries. She's given me no more than sixty bucks—max! That's it! I don't know nothin' more than that!"

Rolf is so sure when he wants to be sure. Malfaits themselves cannot help me account for the cash. The hearing date in court is over, but I don't have any formal guardianship paperwork yet, and I am frustrated by the slowness of court action. Without the paperwork businesses will not divulge information, and I feel as if I am still in the dark on many issues.

Being under a guardianship doesn't mean Malfaits are no longer responsible for Rolf's debt at Fibex. When Mother and I go in to make the loan payment, I explain to the clerk the court hearing is over and I am now Malfaits' legal guardian, although the formal papers have not yet arrived.

The clerk's response is, "Well then, as guardian, what do you want to do about your Dad's *other* loan?"

"What other loan?"

The clerk's fingers click across the computer keyboard and she rotates the screen toward me. "You can see there's another mortgage for Malfaits. Mr. Malfait has $98.50 in his savings, but he borrowed $55.00 on May 14th of this year. On the application it says it was for 'living expenses.' On an added note it says they didn't know Francine's Social Security Number, but Roger had *his* card."

"Why did you people loan him any more money? Why would anyone give Dad a loan for $55.00?"

Mother speaks up, "I most certainly do know my Social Security number, but I don't know anything about Dad doing that little bit of business."

The clerk looks at me helplessly, "Actually, Betty, until you have your papers with you, I shouldn't be describing the details of any of these loans to you, even if Francine is with you."

Mother turns her anger toward the woman. "Guardianship or not, why would you people give a loan to the old fool? You don't have any more sense than he does."

"Mother, you and I will straighten this out later." To the clerk I assure, "This will be taken care of." To myself I say, 'Hang on tight, Betty. Mother, in your less-than-full-strength mental capacity, you are so right. This credit union, which is so obligated to rules and regulations that they can tell me nothing about my parents' finances, can make loans to my only partially recognizable father, a senile shell of his former self. That's as bizarre as my trip to St. Mary's Hospital Records Department where the senile person may pick up his records to be used in a court hearing against himself. Who is really incompetent? On which side of the desks do the incompetent ones sit?'

Mother and I go back by the house to check on Dad. She is still irritated about the credit union episode and becomes further agitated as she looks for her money. She shakes her little black square purse at me, "Look at this, Betty. I don't have any money at all! I don't have a thing in my purse!" She carefully counts out nine pennies from the purse into her hand.

I laugh, "Well, let's be positive—you've got nine cents."

"That's not funny. I don't have a damned thing! I had $199.00 in it last night."

"Mother, we were the only ones here last night. And we were the only ones here this morning. We counted again just before we went to the grocery store and to the credit union. Your money is only misplaced. Let's look." We search the living room, the bedroom, and several purses before I ask, "Mother, have you looked in your bra? You have been known to carry money there."

"Well, I most certainly don't carry money there!"

"Mother, you're the one who just this morning raised the whole front of your shirt at the checkstand in the grocery store."

"That's a stupid place for anyone to carry money!"

"Mother, please look. You really did have money tucked in there this morning."

"Why, I never have put my purse or money there! Someone just came in while I was sleeping last night and stole it! That's all there is to it! You *knew* I had the money in the little black purse. *Someone* stole it."

I bristle. "Mother, don't do this. Don't go there. I doubt anyone stole your money—not last night—not this morning. And you know *I* wouldn't do that."

"Well, you scooped everything up off the coffee table last night—checks and all."

I concentrate on my slow breathing routine. "I know, but those were the bills we paid today. *You* kept the money. We counted it together last night. We counted it again this morning before we left. Mother, *please* look in your bra."

She raises her shirt reluctantly and bulging in her cleavage is another little square black purse. My response is instant, "I didn't know you had *two* of them!"

"Two what's?" She look up and giggles.

"Mother! Two of those black purses!" Then we both laugh at the almost-joke.

She counts her money twice. It's all there. "I think Dad and I will just go off someplace where we won't have to pay bills!"

"Mother, I would like to do the same. I know bill-paying is confusing, but the right purse is found now, and it's all right."

"I think Dad and I are able now to handle our own affairs and pay our own bills."

I struggle for calmness. "Mother, you and I can pay them together. That's part of what the guardianship is about—only the two of us will be involved in the bill-paying now. That will help you and me both to know the paying is done right. I think we could keep track of it that way, don't you?"

"But I want to do it by myself."

I have no response. I understand how she feels. I know she *knows* she can't, but she wants to! I take her hand and stroke it. The two of us sit quietly in the cluttered kitchen for several minutes. I can hear the ticking of the clock above the chest freezer.

"Betty, you can come down any time you want to visit, but Dad and I want to take care of our own business."

"I know you do. Couldn't I just help see that all the things get paid?"

"No, we want to do it ourselves. You and Rolf just want to get Dad and me out of the house and into a rest home."

"Mother, that's not the case, but you and Dad do need help, and there's so much to do around here. Even when we all pitch in, it's hard to keep up."

"Well, you don't need to come down and work. You don't need to do the wash either. I can go right down here to the corner laundromat and do it myself."

"I know you can, Mom, but it's a lot harder now when you have so much soiled bedding and heavy laundry loads. You *need* help."

"No. I want to do it myself."

The two of us sit—dejected, spent, motionless. Things are relatively clean right now, and she's sort of clean, too. However, some of yesterday's laundry is already soiled. I can see the darkened spot and smell the urine on her slacks as we sit holding hands in the gray afternoon stillness of the kitchen. She is totally unaware. The Depends we purchased are unopened in the bathroom.

"Mother, I love you and Dad so much, and I want for life to be better for both of you. I want for you to be able to do for yourself and to take care of Dad, but I fear it's never going to be quite how you want it again! Dad's illness has taken a toll on you. Rolf has added to the stress, and I guess I have, too. Mother, I've tried hard to be accurate and to save receipts and return change. I don't ever want you to think I take things from you and Dad. We spent so many wasted years over that foolishness, and we all missed a lot."

"I do trust you, but I don't trust everyone."

"Mother, it's okay about forgetting where the purse was. It's easy to confuse those two purses, and I didn't know you had two just alike. We all have to be careful about accusing people though. Thank you for not accusing anyone this time. You know it would have been a terrible error, and everyone would have been hurt by that. Rolf was out in his car when we counted the money last night. He didn't stay here last night. He wasn't here this morning when we came in the house and couldn't find the purse. It couldn't have been he who took your money. And it would have hurt me all over again if you had accused me—and I felt you were going to. Thank you for not doing that."

Mother's tears spill over, but she doesn't say anything. She wipes her face and blows her nose on a paper towel. I know she knows she was wrong this time. She may even know she was wrong about her accusations of Don and the children years ago, though she has never said so.

"Mom, just try hard to hang on to your purses and your money."

"I *am* trying hard to do that."

"I know you are, and I know when you put them in your bra you are trying hard to keep them from being rifled. And when you put things in your pillow case at night, you are trying to be careful. I *do* understand, and you *are* trying hard." To myself I say, 'Damn, no one should have to try that hard, especially in their own home.'

I get up from the table and prepare to leave for my trip to my home. "Mom, we spent $110.00 for groceries. You have $90.00 in your little purse for coffee money for about twelve days. Is that enough?"

Mother nods, blows her nose, and wipes her eyes again.

Dad enters the kitchen and sees I'm about ready to leave and that Mother has been crying. "Betty, you need to stay a while longer."

"Dad, I can't. I'm already over an hour late from when I wanted to get started."

"Oh, one hour won't make any difference. We need to be together a while."

"I know, Dad. I can't stay though, but I love you. I love you, too, Mom."

My own tears burn my cheeks as I turn my back and walk away from them through the living room. Rolf is standing at the front door. I don't know if he's coming in or going out—or if he's been listening the whole time. He follows me outside and down the sidewalk. "I see you're highly frustrated. I guess now you know what I go through day in and day out tryin' to take care of them the last two or three years!"

I whirl around in the darkness causing the burly, lumbering blur to almost crash into me. "Don't dump your God-damned bullshit all over me the way you do them! You haven't *been* here the last two or three years, and what you do to take care of them sure as hell isn't care-taking! You're part of the problem! Don't talk down to me as if I don't understand the situation or know what's going on! I've known for a long time.

I've pleaded for your help and cooperation. You dogged me at every turn, and you do it every chance you get—even now! Nothing adds up around here!"

Rolf stammers, "I didn't take their money. I don't take their checks. If you want to know what all the lumber is used for, get back in the house and look at the invoices."

"I don't want to look at invoices. I didn't say anything about lumber. I didn't say you stole their money. I said nothing adds up around here. I can't find anything! I can't find the receipts or the envelopes I leave cash in. Yes, I'm highly frustrated. And you go dump your bullshit elsewhere. Leave them alone—and leave me alone! I'll see you in two weeks at the end of July!"

Once I'm in the privacy of my truck and on the way down the street, my tears extinguish all memory of Fourth of July fireworks. By the time I pull onto the freeway it's raining hard outside, too. I blurt out to the empty truck cab, "Damn, today was her birthday. Happy Birthday, Mom! In all the chaos, I didn't even remember to tell you on the right day. So what the hell were seventy-six years for?"

CHAPTER 30

What is a Guardianship?

As JULY PHASES into August I investigate every possible senior service available in Ridgeview. I learn the difference between CAP and CHORE. I become familiar with the Kiwanis Van Program. I distinguish Medicare from Medicaid. I visit several different in-home caretakers, foster homes, and nursing homes.

I arrange for a CHORE interviewer to talk with Mom. Mom agrees to have the service, but when the workers show up, they are told their services are not needed and have not been asked for. I try for Meals on Wheels. Dad rebels, 'There's no way I'm going to eat those damned TV dinners for old people!' Mother is supportive of Dad's opinion, 'I can do the cooking around here. And besides, we're not that old!'

As idealistic as the goal of Senior Service is to help elderly people stay in their homes as long as possible before a nursing home or other assisted care is required, it isn't going to work for Malfaits. My guardianship papers have changed nothing.

A few days before my first August care-taking trip I call to check on Mom and Dad and be sure their money is lasting. Mother is confident. "Oh, yes, we've got plenty of money for this week and probably longer."

"That's good, but I have been looking over your bills, and you're going to have to be more careful about some of them—particularly your phone bill."

"How bad is that one?"

"It's $186.15."

"Why that can't be right!"

345

"I'm afraid it is right. Mother, you said you wanted to cut back on your expenses. That would be a good place to begin."

"I couldn't have talked to that many people. I don't know how I could have such a huge phone bill. I haven't been calling anyone."

"Mother, the billing lags behind when the actual calls are made, and you may forget you've made them. Maybe you could cut down a little bit on your calls to your sister Mavis. There's an awful lot of those."

"I only made one call to Mavis in West Virginia and one to Maurine in Texas."

"Mother, it's true you only made one to Maurine in Texas. But the bill is very specific, and it says you called West Virginia on the 12th, 13th, 19th, 20th, 27th, and 30th. Most of them are twenty to thirty minutes. It's your money, and you can do as you like, but I thought if you were going to try to cut down on monthly expenses, that might be a good place to start."

"I guess I didn't realize I made that many calls to Mavis. I don't need to be doing that much calling."

Loud male voices erupt in the background. "What's all the noise? Is Rolf there?"

"Yes, he just came in. Do you want to talk to him?"

Without waiting for my reply, I hear them changing places at the telephone. Rolf barks his usual greeting, "Yeah, what's up?"

"Mom and I were discussing the latest phone bill for down there. It's $186.15."

"Yeah?"

"Yes, and it appears that you put $52.27 of long distance calls on their bill."

"Yeah, yeah, well, those are mostly calls related to jobs."

"Well, you've got six of them on there to your friends Gary and Mike, and they're long distance calls. Those may be in regard to jobs, but with your other nineteen calls, that's a lot. Your calls to your friends are about thirty minutes apiece. That's more time than I've spent in some job interviews. The usual phone bill for Mom and Dad is $24.00, and they can't afford ones of this size. You need to cut that down."

"Well, maybe there are a few extra calls there."

"Rolf, there's three to Weed, California. What's that for?"

"I don't know who they'd call there?"

"These calls are very short—about a minute each."

"Oh, yeah, I guess I made those. They were to check on some lottery tickets I bought when I drove down with Mike in his rig."

"Rolf, you need to make those kinds of calls from a phone booth."

"Well, Betty, you better get ready for a couple more long distance calls to those lawyers who were looking for the 'missing trucks.' You remember back that day when we were in the courthouse and I went back in to that other trial?"

"Yes, I remember."

"Well, I thought I had some information for them that was worth sharing, and the cost of the calls was money well spent."

"Whose money well spent? Malfaits would not have spent *their* money doing that, and *you* don't have the right to spend their money doing that either. They don't even know those people!"

"Yeah, maybe not, but those calls will be coming on the next phone bill anyway. Good-bye."

I think I just struck out in my new guardianship status.

A few days later my trip down to care-take doesn't do much to improve my score. Since it's almost noon, I stop outside of town and call to see if Malfaits have had lunch.

Dad answers the phone. "Hell, no, I haven't had lunch. I haven't eaten for twenty days, kid. I am soooo hungry!"

"You be waiting, Dad. I'll bring us all a picnic lunch."

I stop at a deli and pick up sandwiches, melons, a bucket of fried chicken, and cold drinks. When I arrive at 516, both Mom and Dad are sitting on the front doorstep waiting. Dad is up and across the lawn before I can get out of the truck.

"Kid, I'm soooo hungry. I haven't eaten in twenty days."

Mother is right behind him. "Why, you old fool, you had bacon and eggs and toast at Sally's Café this morning."

"Well, I know, honey, but that doesn't last a man all day."

"Well, you're not starving by any means. It's only noon. You help Betty get this stuff unloaded and out to the picnic table in the back yard."

As we settle around the table in the cool shade of the cherry tree and sate our appetites, I bring up the subject of the guardianship. "You know, for the most part this guardianship thing means I will help you with decisions that normally would stress you, like the taxes and bill-paying and getting some help with house cleaning. It doesn't mean I'll be taking over your lives. In order to do what I'm supposed to do though, I need to know what *you* really want to do. What do you want from me?"

Mother immediately answers, "We want to live right here in the house that Dad built for us. And we *don't* want to live with Rolf. Rolf is mean—especially to Dad. This week he's been awful to both of us."

"Is Rolf living here?"

Mother is very direct, "No, but he's in and out all the time."

Dad's adds, "He *acts* like he lives here. He acts like he *owns* the place!"

"Last time I was here we talked about Whidbey Island. Would you guys ever like to live there?"

Mother speaks up quickly, "That would be nice. We both like Whidbey, but this is the house that Dad built for us. We don't want to sell it."

"Mother, there are other options. Maybe we could sell the timber off your land up there—or sell part of the land. That would free up some money to pay off the debt on this place and also make some much needed repairs on the house—and we might still be able to afford to build on Whidbey."

Mother re-emphasizes, "We'd like to live closer to you and Don, but we don't want to sell this place."

"I hear what you're saying, Mother. Don and I have always wanted to live on Whidbey, and that's our intent when we retire. We want to build on the land we own up there. Would you like to live on Whidbey near us?"

Dad opens his mouth as if he's going to say something, but Mother beats him to a response. "Yes, but Don probably wouldn't want us up there under his feet."

"Mom, there are lots of things we could all enjoy on Whidbey, and you wouldn't have to be under anyone's feet."

"Well, Betty, I know one thing, we can't all live together. You and I each need our separate space."

Mother and I pause, look directly at each other, and chuckle at the profoundness of her comment. "I agree, Mom."

Dad rummages through the remaining chicken pieces and finding no more breast portions comes up with a drum stick which he points rhythmically in Mother's direction. "Now, Mama, I don't know about that." The chicken baton jerks toward me. "Kid, I've told you before, you and Don and Nick and El can all come right in here to 516 with Mama and me. We have plenty of separate space."

"Dad, that's very generous of you, but no thanks."

Mother continues, "Maybe Dad and I could have an apartment or rent a little house on Whidbey. I know Dad would be fine if he could just go fishing again. There's a lot of fishing around Whidbey Island. You know that friend you have up there, Doris Musieleski—I wonder if she would know anybody that Dad and I could live with or rent from until you and Don retire. There must be some little place on that whole big island."

"Mother, you amaze me. How did you remember *her* name? I taught with Doris twenty years ago, and I haven't seen her for years. You've never even met her. I'm not sure she still lives there. How did you think of her?"

"Well, like I said, I know Dad would be fine if he could just go salmon fishing again—and if we could have a little garden."

I know Mom and Dad are grasping at unreal dreams. I try to bring us back to reality. "Do you both realize if the day comes that we could all live on Whidbey Island, we may *have* to sell this house in order to make it financially possible for you to have a house there?"

Mother is quick. "No, Betty, Dad and I don't want to ever sell this house."

"But, Mom, you don't have the kind of money it takes to have a place up there and this house, too. I don't think you could afford to have both."

"Well, Dad and I may go to West Virginia. Mavis has a room all ready for us."

"Mother, you and Dad can't just move in on Mavis."

"Now, Betty, she said she has a bedroom all ready and waiting for us."

"I'm sure she meant she has a bedroom ready for you to come *visit* her."

"Well, we could surely live with her a year or so until we got on our feet and got our own place. She lived with us more than that one time until she got settled."

Our conversation is interrupted by an explosive boom from the street in front of the house. Rolf's old car pulls up to the curb. The vehicle belches a cloud of blue smoke and sputters a few more defiant rattles before the engine quits. Mother leans toward me and lowers her voice, "He's been real mean-natured all week. He's mad because his name isn't on that court paper, and he's jealous because Dad and I want you to manage our affairs. He's been really nasty to both of us."

Rolf crosses the lawn to the backyard picnic table where we've been eating. "What's going on here?"

I answer, "We're having lunch. Want to join us? We've been talking about how Mom and Dad feel about things—what they would like to do around here and in the future. You're welcome to join us."

Rolf whirls away from the table and stomps off shouting over his shoulder, "Don't let me interrupt your little intimate private chat!"

I yell back. "Geez, Rolf, this isn't an intimate private chat!" He doesn't stop. I turn to Mom and Dad, "He's welcome to join in on this kind of talk if he wants. It's on bill-paying and money matters that I won't work with him."

Old Parents and Purple Tulips

Mother shakes her head and searches for a wing piece of chicken. "Don't worry about it. All week long he's answered every question either of us asked with, 'Betty will have to answer that for you. She's managing all your affairs now'."

"Guys, I'm sorry you have to put up with all this. It's so destructive, and it isn't what this guardianship thing is about." I get up from my 'weedy picnic chair' feeling as if the weeds have overgrown all three of us in the last few minutes. I don't feel like dreaming anymore. I make my way to the tool shed.

It's been two weeks and Rolf still hasn't mowed the backyard. I only thought the grass was high before. I take out the smaller of the two power mowers. It has gas in it, so I pull the starter cord. The mower is mute, but it's as if the pull cord starts Rolf from somewhere within the house. He jumps out on the back porch glaring angrily as I struggle several more times with the cord.

"That one ain't workin' very well," he growls.

With a renewed surge I yank the cord again, and the engine splutters to life. I turn it away from Rolf and immediately run it into a row of bricks that forms an edge around the flower gardens but is hidden in the tall grass.

He yells at me, "That's my only God-damned decent mower!"

I shout back, "I thought you said it didn't work very well. Now all of a sudden it's decent—and it's *yours*! It's *THEIRS*! If I break it or ruin the blade, I'll buy them a new blade. Or, if necessary, I'll buy them a whole new lawnmower!"

His volume booms over the lawnmower. "You're such a God-damned arrogant son-of-a-bitchin' know-it-all little fuckhead!"

I guess I am. It's a scorching day and a stupid time to be mowing lawn. My anger is surpassed by my tenacity—and my own irrationality. Rolf follows me on the mowed path around the corner of the house screaming a constant volley of verbal abuses. I purposely aim for the gate to the front yard. I open the mower to full throttle and run it in a wide circle through the part of the lawn which he mowed two weeks ago. I then turn back

351

toward the backyard making jerking motions against the tall grass along the path. I fight my way through the growth around the shed and under the cherry tree and grape arbor, where Mom and Dad are still sitting. I pause the mower near them. I am amazed by my own strength as I lift the wooden picnic table and each of the two unoccupied chairs out of the way. Mom and Dad get up and struggle with their two chairs. I mow the grass in their favorite spot and replace the lawn furniture.

When I glance toward the front street, Rolf is still standing near the gate observing every green swath I make and muttering occasional obscenities in my direction. I wheel the lawnmower around and attack the open area of grass away from the cherry tree and grape arbor. A few minutes later the mower gives out gasping and sputtering near where Rolf is standing by the gate. I can almost feel a slight breeze as he stomps past me heading toward his car. His old car roars to life. He revs the engine a couple of times and drives off leaving a cloud of blue smoke hanging over the asphalt.

With sweat streaming down my face and back, grass stuck to my knees, and my arms and shoulders vibrating from the past half hour of bucking the Toro at full throttle, I grab a gas can from the shed and pass by the cherry tree near Mom and Dad. "I'm going for more fuel." If they made a reply, I didn't hear it.

As I move my truck down the street under the shaded coolness of old maple trees, my legs feel itchy and uncomfortable against the rough seat covers. I feel sticky sweat in my arm pits and my hands tingle in Toro rhythm. I itch all over, but I resist an urge to scratch. I wonder what this past week at 516 has really been like.

As I near the gas station I signal to change lanes and veer away from my destination, continuing down the avenue to Mr. Hinson's office. I guess he's *my* attorney now. I don't have an appointment, but I need to see him.

I don't know if it's the grass stuck to my sweaty body or the fire flashing in my eyes, but when I push open the office door to Hinson-Harkness,

Attorneys at Law, two secretaries look up with startled owl eyes. The one nearest the counter rises quickly and ushers me into a private room then flutters off to get me a drink of water.

Mr. Hinson comes in soon afterward. He tells me he's glad I stopped by. He just finished compiling a list of things for me to do within the guardianship.

I glance over the list and feel some sense of accomplishment as I've already done the first two items. (1) Cancel all credit cards; (2) Transfer utility, telephone and other billings to my name and address; (3) Establish an estate checking and savings account which only I can access; (4) Take Letters of Guardianship to Social Security and apply to have Malfaits' checks automatically banked; (5) Follow the same process with pension checks; (6) Pay the $270.00 bond fee as a guardian; (7) Get a new home owners insurance policy. (8) In regard to Rolf I have three choices: a) Talk to him again and ask for his co-operation; b) Ask him to leave the house and take all his things; or c) Evict him.

Mr. Hinson favors the latter choice, and the sooner the better.

I leave the attorney's office thinking, I like Mr. Hinson—but I wish I had more confidence in him. He was so organized and straight forward today, but I wonder if he is learning along with me as to what a guardianship is. Maybe I should have searched for an attorney whose specialty is senior citizen law. What *really* bothers me is for him to be so emphatic about favoring eviction for Rolf. And the sooner the better? Rolf has been a pain in my posterior, but I have a hard time visualizing myself evicting him. I get scared just hearing the word.

I should at least seek a second legal opinion.

On the way home I stop for the lawn mower fuel. Arriving at 516 I gas the mower, start it, and mow for the next three hours. I lean the mower back on two wheels taking off the top of the tall grass with jerking motions, run over it a second time at high cut, and a third time at low cut. I zip across the entire front yard again to erase the fresh cuts of the angry circle I mowed earlier. With three rows left by the front sidewalk the mower conks out. No amount of pride or anger is enough against the red hot fuming Toro and my own exhaustion to get either of us going again.

Mother, who has been sitting on the front steps, hollers back into the house, "Dad! Dad! Get out here and help Betty get this thing started."

Dad comes out and does a fast shuffle across the lawn. I steady the mower, and he tries several times, but he can't pull the cord all the way out. I close my eyes and see flashes of my younger, muscular father pulling a lawn mower cord as simply as I might flick on a light switch. I see a finished lush green lawn and colorful edged flower beds—the prettiest yard on the block.

Mother leaves her front steps viewing perch and crosses the lawn shouting, "Pull harder, Dad! There's only three rows left. We need to finish before dark."

I wipe the sweat from my brow and rub my aching hands. "Mother, please, let's go rest on the front steps. I'm pooped. I'm sure I can start it after it cools down."

She turns back toward the steps commanding over her shoulder, "Dad, you work on that thing. We've got to get it started."

Mother and I both plop down on the cool cement. "Mother, please don't fuss at him. He's tried as hard as he can. Neither one of us is strong enough this time."

Dad continues to stare at the defiant mower and wiggle one part and then another. The fragrance of beautiful blue and pink phlox wafts in soothingly on my right side. The aroma of urine rasps at my exhaustion from the left and from where Mother yells out her futile cheerleading, "Dad, hurry up, hurry up! Get it started!"

If the mower cranked as well as Mother, it would start by itself. My hands are bruised. My knuckles are cracked and bleeding. Tears come easily. "Mother, I'm just not strong enough, and Dad has even less strength than I do. Please leave him alone. The mower will cool. We'll get it started and finish the lawn in a little bit."

"Well, do you want me to go out there and try?"

"Heavens no!" I laugh through the tears. In her whole life she couldn't start any mower they ever had. And she wasn't too adept even with the little push mower the few times she tried that. Besides, whenever she mowed the yard, Dad always mowed over her work because he deemed her rows to be 'crooked as a dog's hind leg.'

Mother looks up. "Oh glory, here's Rolf driving up. Now we'll get it started. Surely he's cooled off by now. He won't leave us with just those three little strips."

As Rolf comes up the walkway to the front doorstep, she asks, "Rolf, we've all worked awful hard, and we've got it all done but that little bit by the sidewalk. Would you *please* go help Dad pull the cord and get the mower started?"

Rolf steps between Mother and me and reaches over our heads for the screen door handle. "I really don't know what you're going to do about that. You'll have to ask Betty. I've got some phone calls to make."

His words string. I'm too tired to be confrontational, but I do feel some remorse about the angry circle I mowed through his front yard mowing job and my abuse to the lawnmower which he had just gotten repaired. I go to the kitchen to get a drink of water and try to talk to him.

The kitchen is empty. As I replace the water pitcher in the refrigerator, I am startled by a booming voice coming from outside on the back porch. 'Yeah, things are worse than ever around here. I'm just gonna have to get the fuck back out on the road.'

I take my glass with me and leave the kitchen. Unlike Rolf, even when I want to, I'm not an eavesdropper. He's probably on long distance to Gary or Mike. Malfaits will have another huge phone bill, and I have no idea how a guardian is supposed to stop abusive phone usage short of disconnecting the phone. My new guardianship seems to exacerbate abuse of all kinds.

By the time I get to the front steps, any remorse I had has dissipated. The tired Toro is the recipient of my frustration and repressed anger. I practically dislocate my shoulder, but I get the mower going on the first pull. I finish the last three rows of uncut lawn at high speed. I return the mower to the shed, sweep it off and put away the tools. Everything is in better shape than I found it, except the mower blade. I go back to rest a few more minutes on the front porch where Mother is still sitting. We both admire the results of *our* labor.

"Well, Mom, neither of us wants to cook tonight. How about if Dad and I run down to the Colonel's and get some chicken?"

The idea is appealing to both of them. I am relieved. I guess they've forgotten our earlier lunch menu.

By the time we get back Dad has told me at least ten times he hasn't eaten for twenty days. He is definitely ready! Though I didn't see Rolf again before we left, I bought for four people just in case. That was a good decision, as Dad immediately settles into two big breast portions and a half a pint of cold slaw. He adds two cups of mashed potatoes with more than ample gravy and two biscuits. He washes it down with a 32-ounce Dr. Pepper. When Mother only drinks half of her Dr. Pepper, he drinks the rest of hers, too. How can he do that and remain so scrawny in physique?

As we are finishing, Rolf walks up the sidewalk toward the front door. He sees us at the picnic table. I invite him to join us.

His tone is civil. "No thanks." He turns away.

I reach in my pocket and pull out a letter and call to him, "Rolf, I have to talk to you, at least about this." I run toward the front yard. "It was in with their bills. It looks like a tax statement or something."

Rolf takes a few steps toward me and grabs the envelope out of my hand. "Let me see that. It's a license tax bill on a boat. They'll get their money when they get it."

"Rolf, do you not want to talk to me at all? If you don't, that's fine. Just tell me so, and I won't try. I don't want to pester you."

"I don't know. I just don't know."

"Rolf, this guardianship thing has caused all of us a lot of stress, and I can't change the court decision. But I *do* want to work with you on the things we are able to work on together."

"Well, I don't know about that."

"Rolf, I'm sorry about the mower. I'll get the blade sharpened or get another one. I just wanted to get that tall grass mowed down, and I was angry with you because you hadn't done it. That's their favorite place to sit under the cherry tree."

"Yeah, well I don't know if I want to provide any input into a situation where I bust my butt working and I have no authority at all."

"It's not a matter of authority. It's important what *they* want. I think they're confused and do goofy things, but some of the things they want and care about are the same as they were in their coherent days."

"Yeah, but what you think is a more suitable or dignified way to live just may not be better."

"Rolf, you've made up your mind that I want to put them in a nursing home right away. That's not a correct assumption. The object is to keep them in their own home as long as possible. But as things progress, a nursing home—or some kind of more concentrated care—is a very real issue. You and I have to talk about that. I do want us to make those decisions together. In the meantime, it's not very constructive for you to take every possible opportunity to tell them, 'Now that Betty's your guardian, she's going to put you both right in the nursing home.' Rolf, you know that's not true."

"Yeah, yeah, I did tell them that a few times. I told 'em when they're up there near you sitting on the porch of some nursing home holding hands, they'd be wishing they were back here and they'd be too late. So maybe I did tell them that, but at the same time, I didn't appreciate you telling Mom in your secretive little whispers and hand motions in the kitchen that the lumber bill was too much."

"We didn't have any secret whispers. It's no secret. The lumber bill *is* too much."

"Betty, you're a God-damned two-faced liar! I heard you and *saw* you motioning with your hands that you guys were being overheard, and at the same time you told her the bill was too much."

"Rolf, the only way you could see and hear us, as you say you did, was for you to be hiding in the dining room, as we used to do as children, and be watching in the corner cabinet glass to spy on the people in the kitchen. I don't think that's very nice, and the view is certainly distorted. You have to remember Mom was very upset because she had nearly accused one or both of us of taking her $199.00. And I think she knew she was wrong, because we had both been to the laundromat away from the house at the time. She understands what falsely accusing has done to us as a family. I really think she didn't want to do that again. Yes, I did want her to hush about it, but I was trying to hush her so she wouldn't make a mistake and accuse anyone. If you saw that differently, you should have come out from your hiding place and participated in the conversation.

"As for the lumber bill, I *do* think $250.00 for saws and $300.00 or more for lumber and materials is too much right now with all the other bills and delinquent taxes on both the house and the Whidbey property. Dad can't even use that stuff."

Rolf leans up close to my face and jabs his finger toward me in emphatic accord with his words. "You're a God-damned liar, and if you want to know where the wood is, look at the invoices!"

I step back and strive for calm, "I did look at the invoices. That doesn't tell me *where* the stuff is. Where are the sheets of plywood? Where are the saws?"

"I have the saws locked up so some cock-sucking son-of-a-bitch doesn't steal them. If you want to know about the wood, look!" He thrusts his arms in wild circular motions over the yard.

I keep my focus locked on Rolf. "I did look, and I'm telling you I think three hundred-plus dollars is a bit much to put under that cheap little rusty metal tool shed you bought at a garage sale. That's the only improvement I can see you've built for them. I don't see $300.00 in the frame it's sitting on, nor in the shoring up you did to the inside."

Rolf stomps off across the yard, gesticulating wildly, "Look! Look around you!" He rips off the twisto-wire which holds the gate to the back yard closed. "Get your ass back here! Pull your head out of your ass and look! He wildly jabs his arms in stabbing motions toward the ground. "Here! Here, get over here!"

I freeze in my tracks.

God, Help me! Please, God.

My body relaxes. A low, calm voice which I'm not sure is even mine speaks, "Rolf, if you want to call Taco that way, that's one thing, but I'm not your dog, and I'm not going to respond to your uncivilized orders and your name-calling."

Rolf bellows a fusillade of curses and begins stomping in his goose-step march in little circles in the gateway area in the front yard. Nosy-bill next door opens her front door and steps out on her porch. Rolf continues his bizarre circular march and his cursing. Nosy-bill is getting her eyes and ears full. It's okay with me. If he does me harm, I'll at least have a witness. Keeping one eye on Rolf's irrational routine, I edge my way slowly to the gate and close it, pick up the wires and secure the gate to keep Taco, who is tied to the cherry tree and now barking wildly, in the backyard. I feel as if I'm in slow motion. When I look up Rolf is still stomping in circles and muttering vile comments but at a somewhat lower volume. He suddenly throws both arms up in the air, turns, and goes in the house.

I glance behind me to the picnic area under the cherry tree. Mother and Dad are sitting there quietly eating chicken. Nosy-bill turns her head away from me and makes a quick retreat into her house.

Mother calls out, "Did Rolf talk mean to you?"

My lips are still frozen. My teeth are clenched so hard my jaw hurts. My whole body shivers in the darkness. My guts feel as if I've swallowed the Toro. A swarming mass moves about me in its own frenzied rampage. Lumps begin to swell on my arms, legs and neck. At least mosquitoes are real—and they like me!

Continuing in slow motion I force my gelatinous, quivering body to the picnic area and begin picking up garbage and left-overs. Mother and Dad attempt to help, and soon our three laden forms move awkwardly through the darkness toward the back door. Once in the kitchen I am greeted by the usual stacks of dirty dishes and pots and pans. It's late now, and I realize I have not done any work in the house all day. My attention turns to a large pot of what *may* have been a very healthy, hearty soup with all kinds of veggies. It sits in the sink, nestled under a blue blanket of mold. The whole kitchen smells like compost. Mother and Dad begin arguing about the rotten soup and who should take it to the garden and dump it. I'm just glad they don't want to eat it.

"Dad, you get this rotten mess out of the sink and take it out to the garden and dump it so Betty can get something done."

"Why, honey, I don't have my glasses on. I can't see a thing out there in that garden in the dark."

"Why, you old fool, you don't need glasses to see out there. Your glasses are reading glasses."

"Well, it's dark out there, and I can't see a damned thing."

Mother swats at the light switch by the back door. "There, I've turned on the shop floodlights. You can see all over Ridgeview."

"Honey, I'm not going out there tonight."

"Well, shit! Give me that pot!"

I am not in the mood for their childish verbal games. No wonder Rolf turned into a crazy, dancing fool in the front yard. I hand her the pot. After the past hour, I am convinced it's a genetic trait just waiting to be expressed in me! In fact, it's already manifesting itself or I wouldn't be standing here in this kitchen anyway. I turn to Dad and throw a dishtowel in his direction, "Here. If Mother has to do your garbage detail, then you're going to have to do her work. Let's get started."

"That's fine, kid. I'll do that." He sits down at the table. I stack things to drain on a towel in front of him, and as he begins to dry he tells me, "You know, kid, I've just been up to Olympia for a job interview this week."

"Huh? I didn't know that."

"Oh yeah. I had a fine interview. And I'm going to have to get out of here and get on with this thing. It's really big. It pays $232.00 a year! I can't afford to pass it up."

"That's fine, Dad. I'm glad the interview went well for you."

I'm glad for the dirty dishes and I scrub harder.

"Now, that fellow that interviewed me, why he said to me, 'Mr. Malfait, you are one of the most pleasant, well-mannered gentlemen I have *ever* interviewed'."

"Dad, you *are* a fine, pleasant gentleman; but sometimes you get a bit stubborn, especially with Mother."

"Where *is* Mama?"

"She went to the garden to get rid of that rotten soup."

"Well, Lord God-a-Mighty, she shouldn't be out in the dark doing that. Why didn't she call me? Why, she's had time to go to Portland and back."

"Yeah, she has been gone a while. I'll go check on her in a minute. We're about finished with the dishes. How about if I trim your beard and mustache next?"

"Okay, but Mama ought to be here to help with that for sure."

I hand him the last pot to dry and I go get out the towels and hair-cutting tools. When I return to the kitchen, Dad says no more about Mom being present for the trimming and I forge ahead with the task. By the time we finish, Mother comes back in with the empty pot. I don't really want to know what she did with the contents. She left by going out the back door, but she re-entered the house by the *front* door. I hope that doesn't mean there's a new problem in Nosy-bill's yard.

"My God, who is this new man in my kitchen? I haven't seen your face in so long I almost forgot what you look like. Betty, you did a wonderful job! That's even better than his last trip to the barber."

I take my leave from their house while they have something pleasant to admire. Rolf's car isn't on the street, and I'm glad not to see him. I have a long late-night drive back to my home.

Dear God, this is crazy! God, I'm so angry and frustrated! I can't solve this satisfactorily for everyone. In fact, God, I can't solve it at all! I truly believe whatever I've done up to now, or said up to this point, has been morally right. I don't like where I am and what I'm doing, but God, I'm striving to do what's right according to Your will. God, I hate this!

I arrive home and go directly to bed. Don and the children are on an overnight outing with his family. I am glad to be alone. I fall into an exhausted sleep almost before my head hits the pillow. The next morning I feel nauseous. I have a headache and a stuffy nose. My face hurts. I try to go back to sleep. It doesn't happen. I try to stretch and relax. I fail. I pick up a book from the nightstand and head out into the warm summer sun, fumbling with the pages to find exactly where I left off in <u>One Flew Over the Cuckoo's Nest</u>. My poor reading selection, my own sweat, bugs and bites drive me back indoors.

In the coolness and comfort of my bedroom, I get to the scene where the cuckoos are going on their fishing trip. I reach for a tissue to attend to my compassionate sniffles, but the tears come faster than the tissue can handle. I make myself get up, but after only a couple of steps my legs give way and my body crumples to the floor dragging the comforter with me, heaving deep, mournful, wrenching sobs.

Finally I pull myself up. I replace the comforter. I make myself walk—a trip to the bathroom, then to the kitchen. I wash dishes. I wash the floor. I wash the cupboards. I clean the oven. Aloud to myself I claim and reclaim God's promise.

God, I know You don't give us more than we can bear. You've promised that. God, I know You don't make mistakes. I know there will be a satisfactory end to all of this. God, please don't give me more than I can handle.

My prayerful muttering continues as I keep busy from the kitchen to the bathroom. By the time I finish scrubbing down the bathroom, I have a temporary plan in mind for the next step in being a guardian to Malfaits. It's time for me to locate a nursing home or some other group care facility. I *have* to do it.

CHAPTER 31

‐⊸⊛⊶‐

Guardianship Research

IN THE NEXT few days I go to Anacortes, Oak Harbor, Mr. Vernon, Coupeville, Port Townsend and several places in between. I ease my own personal fears and misconceptions about nursing homes. For the most part I find the personnel very knowledgeable and helpful, and they try to provide information related to my particular situation. I visit residents. I talk to other 'parents of parents.' I learn prices. I learn certification and licensing standards. I learn recent legislation. I learn about foster care and other care options. I learn more often than not when the person needing care is moved to a facility, there is a window period for a month or two. Then, in most cases, the person finds they are happier in their new surrounding than they were living independently.

After all these visits, I decide Mom and Dad are *not ready* for nursing home care at this time. Even if the condition in both of them is Alzheimer's, they are far above the veggie-type and chronic moaners I have observed on my trips. By my crude standard they are still fairly alert and physically in good shape. They walk regularly two or more miles a day, and they seem strong. Verbally, some of their information is very accurate, probably more accurate than *I* might be, especially in older memories. And when they are in error, they are creatively and enthusiastically in error. It must take a still active brain to devise those scenes.

Oh the other hand, it may be that *I* am not ready for them to be in nursing home care.

On my research trips I share my personal story so many times I grow weary hearing myself. I find what I thought was my unique and tragic family story is common in the current senior population in the United States. Bilking and other schemes of financial mismanagement, abuse, neglect, confusion and mental disorientation—all these factors plague our older population in their fears of aging and often in their daily existence. But my interviews affirm my own perception that abusive behavior is totally unacceptable. Despite the fact the abuse results from understandable anger and frustration on the part of the family member or the care-giver trying to help older persons whose degenerative conditions cause them to be hurtful and disruptive to themselves or others, such behavior is inexcusable and cannot be ignored.

Repeatedly nursing home personnel emphasized to me: (1) Rolf's geriatric techniques are not acceptable anywhere. (2) Rolf must be removed from the care-taking scene, whether by selling Malfaits' property and getting them into nursing home care, or getting Rolf out of their home and some kind of home services in. Malfaits should be kept in their own home as long as possible, and they seem to still have enough awareness and ingenuity to be there. (4) Interview carefully whatever level of care I choose for them. Ask questions such as, 'If Mom and Dad mess themselves, how will you handle that? If they refuse to bathe, what will you do? What are your references? What is your previous experience with cases similar to mine?'

While on Whidbey Island, I look up my friend Doris Musieleski and renew a friendship, telling her it was my mother who remembered her living on Whidbey. After hearing some of my family situation, Doris takes me for a drop-in visit with Janice, a friend of hers who operates a foster care facility in a lovely wooded setting nearby.

Janice is committed to working with the elderly. She has three residents, though she's licensed for five. She has a mom-and-pop apartment in the basement which is vacant. The house is clean and has lovely furnishings. Lunch smells wonderful: ham, scalloped potatoes, carrots and fresh home-baked apple pie. The kitchen is spotless and obviously equipped by someone who loves to cook. Janice is a single divorced woman who feels God has been good to her. She is positive and caring and feels God is directing her talents in a useful manner to provide a valuable service as well as a good income for her. My mind is abuzz with excitement. This is manna from heaven. This is perfect for my family situation.

Oh, God, why did I ever doubt? Your guidance is awe-some. It was incredulous that Mother even remembered Doris' name--and more incred-ulous that Doris has this par-ticular friend. Oh, God, I'm so ashamed to have doubted! This is so perfect--the woods, the deer, the kitchen, the mom-and-pop apartment.

Before my adulation can soar higher, Janice tells me, "I've had some folks with me for four or five years. I screen them myself. I don't take clients who are always trying to run away, I can't keep up with that--and, I don't take clients who are incontinent, I can't deal with that either."

Author's mom and dad in Author's home

"Un--You don't take persons who are incontinent?"

"Oh, no. That's too hard for me. The amount of extra work, you know. There's so much more washing--clothes and bedding. And the extra precautions here in my home and when I take my people out places. No, that's just too much. I can't deal with that. Are your mom and dad incontinent?"

"Dad isn't, but Mother is. I haven't been too successful in getting her to wear protection."

Janice is kind in her reply, "Well, my place is probably not for them, but I can give you a list of places nearby who deal with that level of care. Of course, you know incontinence may be stress-related or a dietary problem. Sometimes peace and quiet, medication, and proper diet alleviate the problem. A doctor has to make that evaluation. I don't ever take a new client until after they have had a thorough physical examination by a doctor anyway, so maybe there's still a possibility for your folks here."

I'm disappointed, but I understand. I haven't been able to get Mother to deal with her incontinence. Besides, Malfaits don't *want* to leave their home in Ridgeview, and I doubt I could get the two of them to a doctor for a thorough physical. I was only able to satisfy the court requirement for medical documentation because of Dad's medical records and doctors' observations of Mother's behaviors as related to Dad's situation.

My hopes are dashed, but meeting Janice was a special experience. I might say Providential, but I'm not sure. I was quick with my awe and appreciation of God's guidance, and I am equally quick falling back in doubtful despair. I guess I have to keep plugging along in the day to day nitty-gritty decisions and not try to rely so heavily on Divine Providence, which may rank right up there with Justice and Fairness--nonexistent.

God, I'm sorry for my doubtfulness, and I guess it was presumptuous of me to think You would be right here with me providing the immediate perfect solution to all my problems. I shouldn't be so quick to assess and so lofty in my assumptions. Maybe Rolf's right--I am sort of a know-it-all--and whatever the rest of his phrase was.

CHAPTER 32

※※

Is God Really Involved in
Guardianship Research?

On my next trip to Ridgeview a few days later I contemplate my huge
Things-To-Do-List on the way into town. One of the items is to get a
second opinion from Mr. Oats, an attorney who has been highly recommended by several of the senior services personnel with whom I have
been discussing Malfaits' needs, and who was lauded in a recent local
newspaper article for his expertise and contributions to senior citizens
in this community. His office is on the main thoroughfare and easily
accessible, and I'm right on time for our appointment. As we become
acquainted, he covers pretty much the same procedures and options as
Mr. Hinson, including his personal feeling that eviction of Rolf is a necessary step at this time. He is much quicker with his responses and legal
references pertaining to seniors. And because senior law is his area of
expertise, I feel a growing sense of confidence in him. By the end of the
appointment, I make a decision to transfer my guardianship business to
Mr. Oats. I tell him I will contact him further after I've talked with Mr.
Hinson.

Leaving Mr. Oats' office I find myself in the far right-hand lane at a
major intersection in heavy late afternoon traffic. How can I be so stupid
as to get caught over here in this lane? I've been through here thousands
of times. Well, I can't fight my way over two lanes. I guess I'll have to
turn right with the flow of traffic. Oh well, I can still get to 516 by this

street. Wow, there Malfaits' old church. They haven't attended for years, but it used to be a huge part of their lives.

Without a signal I make an abrupt right turn at the next street corner and enter a back entrance to the church parking lot. I pull the truck into a space near a side door of the church. A voice in my head chides, 'Wait a minute. What are you doing here? You've never been to church here. This isn't on your Things-To-Do-List. What do you expect to find here--God? You're whole family is nutso, including you, Betty. This is one of your desperate whims! Who's in charge here? Are you crazy?'

The side door is unlocked, and I enter the church. A short hallway leads to the church office, where I find an older secretary who tells me Malfaits' favorite pastor has been gone from this church for a couple of years. However, she remembers Francine and Roger well. In fact, she occasionally calls them and offers them a ride to church. They always politely decline.

The secretary is sad to hear a partial update on Malfaits. She had no idea of the severity of their current condition, as their telephone de-meanor is always very friendly. She refers me to John Chaliss, an assistant pastor during the years Malfaits attended regularly. He is now the direc-tor of a local church-sponsored retirement facility. She assures me he will want to know the current family situation.

The retirement center is only a few blocks away, and I drive from the church directly there. I find John's office and he welcomes me to come in and visit. He remembers Malfaits as wonderful participants in the congregation. They especially loved to help beautify the church grounds, and they were always caring for their pastors by gifting them with gar-den produce and jams and jellies. John did recall some problems about the time Dad had his stroke. He had asked Malfaits to allow some men in the church to come to the house and help finish a roofing job which he thought was too dangerous for Dad. Their help was emphatically re-fused, and so were all visits from church friends and pastors thereafter.

John is knowledgeable, compassionate, and very perceptive. He un-derstands so much without my even having to say it. He affirms that death can be sudden or death can be slow, and either way we grieve. During our conversation he helps me to accept that any time sequence is out of my power. I need to proceed one move at a time, one day at a time, seeking God's guidance constantly and making decisions based on my understanding of that guidance. John cannot help me in a practical sense regarding a living space for Malfaits in the church-sponsored retirement home of which he is the director, because they have too many assets. They live a wretched existence, but their ownership of twenty acres on Whidbey Island is again a stone around their necks.

I'm glad I came here and personally counseled with John. I felt an epiphany in those moments with him. 'Betty, you're not God, and you can't *do* everything. Tune into His real true power, power of the entire universe. It's at your disposal just for the asking. Your actions so far are supported by scripture and you are trying to honor your father and mother. You are not responsible, nor should you feel guilty, for Rolf's actions. Keep your attention focused on care of your parents.'

As I turn my truck back into the busy traffic, I savor the feeling that God truly has given me some wonderful individual attention in these moments, and He has been with me all the time over these past years--whether I thought so or not--even in the right-hand traffic lane.

I go to the downtown area and proceed with items on my Things-To-Do-List before going to Malfaits' house. My errands go well, and my list shrinks fast. I arrive at 516 about 5:45 PM, tired but feeling successful and renewed.

Reality, or lack of it, bangs me square between the eyes. Malfaits are pathetically huddled over their kitchen table eating boiled potatoes and bread. Dad has an open can of pork and beans beside his plate, and he's eating them out of the can. Mother fusses at him about this. He responds with his own cranky comments.

I have brought cantaloupe, cheeses, and fresh home-made apple pie. Without getting into their fracas, I quietly unpack my picnic box, slice generous wedges of apple pie, top them with thick cheddar slices, and heat them in the microwave. Without any objection from either of them,

I remove their dinner plates and the bean can and offer the more appetizing fare. They dive in eagerly.

"Gosh, Mother, how come your dinner was so Spartan?"

"Well, that's all we've got."

"Didn't you buy any groceries?"

"We didn't have any money."

"But, Mom, when we talked on Tuesday, you said your pension checks had come and you and Dad were going to shop then."

"Oh my God, what day is this?"

"It's Friday, Mom."

"Friday? That can't be right."

"Yes, I'm afraid it is."

Mother drops her fork and starts to rise from her chair, "Let me get that check and let's get downtown and get it cashed right away."

"We can't do that now, Mother. It's too late. You'll have to wait until tomorrow morning."

I could take them and go find a Friday night check-cashing place, but I'm tired myself. I say nothing more, and she sits back down and resumes eating.

I ask, "Did you guys go to coffee this morning?"

Mother responds immediately. "No, we didn't go to coffee this morning. I told you, we didn't have enough money."

"Oh that's right. Well, you and Dad work on that pie. I'll run out to the truck and unload a few things. I leave them for a few minutes to relish the apple pie, and I drive down to the corner store for a quart of milk. I notice the cafe next door is closed, but Sally is doing her books at one of the booths. I rap lightly on the window. She recognizes me and comes to the door.

"I'm sorry to bother you. I just wanted to know if Mom and Dad have been coming in this week for their usual coffee or breakfast?"

"Oh, yes, they've been in every morning. They were here today. Is anything wrong?"

"No, I was just checking."

"They were fine this morning. They had their usual--bacon, eggs-over-easy and toast. Papa had two pancakes, too. He said he was awfully hungry."

"Did they have enough money to pay?"

"Oh, yes, Mama paid with a ten dollar bill. She had it in her little square purse. They were fine today and ate a good breakfast. Are they okay now?"

"Yeah, pretty much. I'm just checking. If they ever didn't have enough money, would you feed them anyway and keep a tab?"

"Oh, yes, for sure I'd do that. You don't even need to ask."

I arrive back at 516 in time to fill glasses of milk for them to go with second helpings of pie. I open my thermos bottle and pour coffee all around for us, and I join them at the cluttered end of the table. "Things seem more piled up in your living room. Has Rolf been around lately?"

Mother answers, "No, he's worked all this last week. That's good. It keeps him away and out of our hair."

"How's his crankiness when he is around?"

Mother replies, "Well, he's not so bad when he works."

"The last time I was here you both said you didn't want him living in this house, and you didn't want to live with him. Is that really how you feel? Do you want him to be living in this house?"

There is an emphatic duet, 'No!'

"Is he living here all the time now?"

Mother takes over, "He's in and out of here, but he doesn't live here. He's gone for days at a time--sometimes weeks."

I take a few more sips of cold coffee and think, Yeah, and you people didn't eat breakfast at Sally's this morning either. What *is* real?

Dad puts his coffee cup down and pushes back from the table. "Rolf comes by here now and again, and he sleeps here sometimes. I don't reckon I'd say he lives here--and I don't want him to either."

"For someone who doesn't live here he's got an awful lot of stuff piled all over your house. What do you want me to do about that?"

Dad tells me, "Well, I want him to get the hell out of here."

Mother takes over, "I don't know. He's so mean sometimes. He orders everyone around to suit himself. He pushes and shoves both of us, and he eats everything in sight, but he's better off when he's working. Dad and I do just fine when he's not here."

"Do you want me to have him evicted?"

Mother gasps. "Oh, my God, no, I couldn't just turn him out on the street! I wouldn't do that to *you*!"

That declaration ends our conversation. I clean up their kitchen and head for The Sterling.

God, what do I do now? After today, somehow I know eviction is in the future, no matter who the guardianship attorney is. How can you evict someone who doesn't even live here for sure? Oh, God, please guide me.

I return to 516 in the morning to do the laundry. Mother wants to go with me to help. Dad stays home to rest and 'do a little work Mama has ordered up.'

At the laundromat Mother pushes through the door and goes directly to a seat by the window as if she's about to watch a movie. I am caught in the double doorway maneuvering two grocery carts of dirty laundry. In the next three and a half hours I use nine of the regular washing machines plus a big washer for the comforter. The total expended is $7.00 for soap and bleach and $17.00 in quarters. When the last load is in a dryer, I flop down next to her in the comfort of one of those cold plastic butt-molded chairs.

"Mother, can you see now what Rolf and I do when we come here? See how long it takes and how much we spend?. We always ask you for a twenty dollar bill, and you always try to tell us that $5.00 ought to do for a wash. It normally would, I guess, but Dad creates more wash than he used to--and maybe you do, too."

"Oh, I can see you did a big job today."

"Mother, you have an awful lot more wash than you used to. Can you understand why we need to get some help coming into the house?"

"Well, I think I could do it."

"I know you could, Mother, but it's too much for you. It's too heavy. There were bags of laundry today that you couldn't--and *shouldn't*--lift. *I* couldn't carry them. I had to roll them off the truck bed onto the shopping carts and wheel them in."

"Well, I'm tired from helping you today, too, but I think I could get it done a little each week."

I can't ask, What help were you to me today? I know she wants to work, and she evidently thinks she has today as she sat the whole time in her plastic chair watching the soap suds whirl about. When school starts and I am back in the classroom, I won't have this kind of time nor energy. I have renewed anger for Rolf, too. It's not just a matter of today, because I'm glad he is working, and I hope that work will become steady for him. However, he is totally unwilling any longer to help with their laundry or any of the household tasks. He now has an even angrier, more abusive, domineering attitude, and he won't cooperate with them nor me. Personally he's a filthy mess. Any time I come back after a week or two, not only do I find Mom and Dad dressed in the same clothing I left them in from the underwear out, but I find Rolf wearing the same clothing; and he doesn't even wear underwear, as I learned from past laundry experience with him. I guess I should be thankful he doesn't throw his laundry in with theirs now.

When Mom and I get back to the house, Dad meets us at the front door. "I just got done changing the kitty litter pans in our bedroom, Mama, just like you wanted."

"Well, it's about time." Mother heads directly for the bathroom.

I lug in the bags of clean laundry. A dusty grayish haze hangs heavy in the living room. Mother emerges from the bathroom and explodes, "My God, Roger, what have you done? Did you let those damned cats into something?" She shuffles toward their bedroom and crashes into the door. "What in the world have you done to the door? I can't get it open."

The plastic runners from the bathroom to the bedroom form a gravelly pathway scattered with kitty litter. Mother pushes and jerks on the bedroom door. I help her, and when we finally get it wedged open we discover a large pile of used kitty litter behind the door.

At top volume Mother bellows, "Roger, get the broom and dust pan in here."

Dad pushes through the narrow space of the jammed door, "Well, Jesus Christ, I don't know what happened here. You must have spilled that, Francine. I had that all in a nice pile."

"You get that shit swept up right now."

Dad tries to sweep the litter from the pile into the dust pan, but he isn't coordinated enough to get the sweepings in the pan and with each brush of the broom kitty litter flies off every which way.

Mother continues her fury. "My God, Dad, you're ruining our good wool carpet. We'll never be able to get that shit cleaned out of it."

In my own silent ineptness I'm thinking, 'There is so much sticky waste residue from the dog, cats, and people ground into this good wool carpet I doubt anyone could ever get the shit cleaned out of it.'

Mother goes to the kitchen, and I watch Dad continue the clumsy strokes with the broom against the plastic runner. When he gets a recognizable pile of kitty litter, he pushes it onto the dustpan and carries it to the bedroom where he reaches in and dumps it behind the door. Out of sight is clean. That makes sense--to him. And to me as to why we couldn't get the bedroom door opened.

"Hey, Dad, let me give you a hand. I'll sweep and you hold the dust pan."

Dad obediently takes the pan. We fill it several times and dump it into a paper sack. It's no place close to clean, but the vacuum cleaner is out of the question, as it is so full of dog hair it won't suck anything. Another repair job having to wait.

Dad surveys the room, "Now, what does your mama mean that's not good enough? It's cleaner than it's ever been."

"It sure is, Dad, and you're a wonderful helper."

"Hell, kid, hardly any of it was spilled anyway. That little bit couldn't ruin a carpet."

CHAPTER 33

⸺ ❧ ⸺

Mrs. Vink, The Social Security

Perspective of Guardianship

THE LAUNDRY AND the kitty litter clean-up are not the only fecalistic experiences of my new guardianship care-taking weekend, as I learn on Monday when I keep an appointment at the Social Security office. My goal is to have Malfaits' checks automatically banked. This change can only be done after a personal interview. When it's my turn at the counter, Mrs. Vink, my assigned interviewer, immediately establishes her power in my life as she glances through my paperwork, clicks her fingers over her computer keyboard, and without looking up at me inquires, "Oh my, what kind of manager for your parents' affairs *are* you?"

I'm not sure what she means and I look at the side of her head as I explain, "I'm their legal guardian."

She continues staring at her keyboard. "You have the wrong Social Security number for your father. The number you gave me belongs to a person living in a foreign country. Don't you *know* your father's correct number?"

"I'm sorry, I must have copied it incorrectly. Can you look it up from other information I've given you?"

Mrs. Vink tucks her chin close, twists her head slightly toward me, and looks over the top rim of her glasses. "Yes, I've located his number here on my computer screen, but by law I can't give it to you. You'll have to bring in his Social Security card. You know a lot of family members just want to get the old folks' checks in the bank so they can have access to the money. You need to bring me some acceptable documentation with his number on it. And as to these Letters of Guardianship, these are practically meaningless."

"But those are the documents that were issued by the Superior Court of this county. They have Judge Fox's signature on them and the official county seal."

"Really? Well, *I'm* saying they're worthless."

"But those *are* the official Letters of Guardianship from ..."

Mrs. Vink cuts me off, "You're going to need a recent doctor's report for each of your parents, indicating they are incompetent to manage their financial affairs." She increases her volume and leans toward me, "It will have to be a report that uses the word *incompetent!* Do you understand?"

"But these papers were issued after a long, detailed court process in which--"

Mrs. Vink's foghorn voice slices through my words, "I can't help what the process was. I have to read the word *incompetent* on the document!"

I glance away from the counter. A dozen pairs of eyes in the waiting area refuse my eye contact, and lowered heads pretend they don't hear. I strive to breathe deeply as I focus on an ink stain on the counter. My face burns. I have no defense to Mrs. Vink's public derision of my family. I already feel inadequate to deal with my parents--or Rolf. And I am more inadequate--perhaps even incompetent--to deal with this omnipotent Social Security Officer. The ink stain on the counter disappears. I can taste my salty tears.

Mrs. Vink's sharp voice cuts into me again, "I also would like you to understand that you can't have both of their checks automatically placed in the same checking account. You must keep their accounts separate."

I retrieve from my pocket a partially used deli napkin from yesterday's picnic lunch and dab at my eyes. "As their guardian, I have to submit a report to the Superior Court of what I do with all their money. Do I have to do it for the Social Security Office, too?"

"You have to keep their money separate. Also you'll have to get doctors' reports on both of them. If you can't get doctors' reports, you cannot bank their checks automatically."

"But doctors' reports have been done for the court action. Don't those count?"

Mrs. Vink looks up at me and shrugs. "I don't have copies of them here in these papers. I guess you could get other letters of verification of their incompetence such as from the water department, the credit union, or their bank. You know, your dad may be incompetent, but your mother may be perfectly able. After all, 'becoming senile' is *not* the same as being *incompetent*! I can't do anything for you until I have the required evidence of your parents' incompetence."

Good God, who is this lady? I escape the Social Security Office masked in my own incompetence.

I am able to get an early afternoon appointment with Mr. Hinson. A search of the material he has in the files shows I had the correct Social Security number for Dad all along. Mrs. Vink was in error. He advises me that doctors' reports are redundant to the court's procedures and requirements. Medical reports and counselor reports have already been carried out. He also says the estate checking account is fine as it has been set up. He feels as I do that Mrs. Vink momentarily landed from a broomstick, but he scratches a short note personally addressed to her and includes further court documentation.

I'm thinking this doesn't seem like an appropriate time to discuss changing attorneys, so I hurry back to the Social Security Office later in the afternoon. Before I can seat myself Mrs. Vink looks up, "Oh my, you do work fast! You may come up to the desk next." She extracts my file from an overburdened stack on her desk, picks out the Letters of Guardianship and proceeds to reread key phrases aloud. "Oh, yes, this is the case that failed to say your parents were *incompetent*."

People in the waiting room look up. I slide the attorney's note and the additional court papers across the counter. "These papers are more explicit."

Mrs. Vink scans the papers and reads aloud. "Let's see, here in the judge's words it says *by reason of incapacity--ah,* and here in the ad litem report it finally says both your parents are *incompetent*. Yes, that's what I need to see."

I offer a feeble explanation, "I've not read those reports myself. The guardian is not privileged to that information nor to the medical reports received by the court."

"I guess not." Mrs. Vink smacks her stapler fastening all the papers in the Malfait file and turns back to her computer screen. She repeatedly messes up the information regarding Dad's marital status. "This new computer program has some mistakes in it. It doesn't always work right." She leans forward and squints as her long fingernails re-attack the keyboard. "Machine, you cannot outsmart me!"

Personally I'm rooting for the machine. By her fifth try, Mrs. Vink is quite exasperated. She continues to face the computer, but her words are for me, "I feel rushed right now because it's actually past my working hours, and I have out-of-town company from Texas coming in tonight. My husband and I recently moved his mother up here, and that's the only reason the company is coming to visit. It's worth moving his mom though to get the rest of the folks to come and visit us."

I want to ask, Is your husband a Legal Guardian for his mother? Is his mother competent? Has she been to the doctor in the last ten years? I bite my tongue. "You completed Mother's verification, and I'm staying overnight here in Ridgeview. Would you like me to come back tomorrow for you to finish Dad's application? That would give you a chance to get home in time to greet your company."

Mrs. Vink's fingers freeze midair and she turns her head a full ninety degrees to face me squarely. "Oh, could you possibly do that?" Without waiting for my reply her fingers return to the keyboard and tap out a short ditty. "Oh, well look here--you won't have to bring in your father's card. Here's his number right here. You were just one digit off. I'm sure the error was on the pension check I was reading from. It won't take very long to do his application tomorrow morning. We open at 9:00 AM, but I come in at 7:30 AM. I'd be happy to have you come at that time. Here, these are Representative Payment forms. You'll have to have your parents sign these. Then tomorrow morning, you just come around here and tap on the window. I'll let you in the side door."

I am gracious in agreeing to the suggested meeting time, but to myself I say, 'I hope I don't trip over your broomstick coming in that side door early in the morning.'

I return to Malfaits' house and find them working in the yard trimming flowers and shrubs. They readily sign the forms with no questions. An invitation to supper out encourages them to change into clean clothes with no arguments. They smell better and look presentable. I don't even broach the subject of washing other than their hands. Actually they both have a healthy, robust appearance with faces browned from summer sun. We enjoy a quick meal at a restaurant close by, and on the way home Mother says she is tired. I drop them off at their house, and I go 'home' to The Sterling. Considering the beginning of the day, I appreciate the quietness and lack of turmoil that ends this day.

The next morning I tap on Mrs. Vink's window shortly before 8:00 A.M.

"Oh, good morning. I was just rereading your mother's file, and I've run a hard copy for you. I had a little computer mess-up on it, too. For the phone number it prints symbols and no numbers. This is just one of the errors in our new program. When it does that, we have to ask people to fill in the number by hand and initial it. These computers aren't quite as smart as people think they are." Within a few minutes Mrs. Vink completes Dad's report, and the whole thing prints out perfectly, including the phone number.

I remain quiet and recall how discombobulated she was with her computer last night and now again this morning. I am secretly happy for her computer anxiety, but I only laugh to myself. 'Computers are wonderful--and you, Mrs. Vink, with all your pink ruffles and frills, your plastic perfect hairdo, your haughtiness, and your moralistic preaching--you, lady, are a deceptive bag of bullshit!'

CHAPTER 34

—⁓—

Mr. Manilow, Adult Protective
Service Defines Guardianship

WHEN I RETURN to the Sterling to gather my things and prepare for my departure to my real home, I note the flashing light on the telephone. A message from Adult Protective Service requests me to keep an 11:00 AM appointment with a Mr. Terry Manilow. Who's that? I don't know anyone by that name. I didn't make any appointment with him. It's not on my Things-To-Do-List. But the name of the agency carries a sense of urgency, and I hurry to keep the appointment.

Mr. Manilow is cordial and gets right to the point. He scans my guardianship documents and pulls a file from his desk drawer. "Let me say first off that you seem awfully slow in progress to gain this guardianship--and I see you haven't transferred ownership of any assets."

"Sir, as for slowness of progress, I'm moving as fast as I can. I'm trying to take care of the most urgent things first and consider what's best for Malfaits each time. Legal procedures such as transfer of ownership of any property is at a standstill because I can't find the deeds to either of their properties. I can't very well transfer an asset which I can't prove they even own. Besides, Malfaits were not at all cooperative about transferring anything by their own volition. By the time my brother and I became knowledgeable about transferring assets as a legal procedure, we were already petitioning for the guardianship based on their incompetence. By that action we were saying our parents were incompetent to manage their affairs and take care of themselves. How could we then ask them to transfer any property ownership?"

"Aside from that, Betty, as a guardian you have certain very specific things which the law has charged you to do, and you must get at them. Right now you have two main problems as Malfaits' guardian. Number one, there is definite lack of supervision of two people whom the courts have declared incompetent. And Number two, you as the guardian must guarantee the abuse, as previously reported, will not occur further.

"Now that you're their Legal Guardian, you must make decisions in their best interest in these areas. And if you don't do it adequately, a year from now at hearing time, I will have to say to the judge, 'That lady you appointed to be Malfaits' guardian did not look out for them very well.' In that case, the judge will take the guardianship away from you and give it to someone who will make better decisions."

"Mr. Manilow, I get the general idea of guardianship, but there's no prescribed method. I haven't been given very much direction. There's no book on it. Things can't happen all at once."

"With the formality of your appointment, I cannot emphasize strongly enough that *you* are henceforth *responsible* for Malfaits! That means *now*!"

My brain is about to explode as I chide myself silently, 'How am I going to address those two main problems while living three hours away and trying to have another life in the sane world?'

Mr. Manilow continues, "In regard to the lack of supervision I had a new complaint about them just this week. It was called in by one of their neighbors. The gist of it was that these senile, smelly people wander freely without any supervision. They are a nuisance and an embarrassment to neighbors with their bickering and disorientation. Aid cars and police have had to be called several times, and that's also an annoyance. They have been outside when not properly dressed--pants open, etc. and they smell awful. This is just one example of the kinds of entries that are in their file. I have other complaints, as well."

"Mr. Manilow, I understand the complaints. They need a lot of help. *I* need help with them!" The tears stream down my face. "These are my parents whom I love, and who were not always a neighborhood embarrassment.

These are people who have given to others their whole lives, and I'm rather sure in some cases very generously to neighbors who now register these complaints. I *know* they need supervision. I am willing and I am trying, but I can't do this by myself. And I can't do it all at once."

"You definitely need help with them, but Malfaits have too many assets to qualify for any DSHS benefits. I suggest you sell their Whidbey Island land or the timber on it, and use the money for their benefit. Not having the cash is not the problem, but the land is too great an asset to qualify for assistance help."

"I know that. I've tried more than once to get COPS services lined up for them. Mother agrees to the help, then when the workers show up she won't let them in. The COPS interviewer told me this was not an unusual circumstance. Just because they need help, they don't have to accept it."

Mr. Manilow concurs. "That's right. They can refuse the help or they can fire the people you hire. Often the older folks will fire people repeatedly, and for no reason, or for very simple things. Your mother is very good at the 'no-admittance technique.' I myself was unable to gain entry when I went out to check on the abuse situation with Rolf. There are several complaints on him from neighbors. How is that behavior at this time? Has his abusive behavior toward them stopped?"

"I think those behaviors have ceased."

"One of the reports says that a neighbor saw Rolf push Mr. Malfait to the ground because he became angry with him when he wouldn't get in the car fast enough. What you have to understand, Betty, is that henceforth *you* are responsible to see that Malfaits are not abused like that by him or anyone else."

"Well, I haven't ever seen him physically abuse them, but I definitely have observed the verbal abuse. I myself have been the recipient of his uncontrolled ranting and raving. And I've seen the scabs on my father which Rolf caused."

"Betty, the answer to the Rolf situation is for *you* to ask Rolf to leave. If he is uncooperative, he should be evicted. Rolf, it seems, has milked them far too long. And a *prudent* person would proceed with eviction."

"But, sir, when I talk to Malfaits, they both do not want Rolf living in their home, but when I use the word eviction, Mother will say, 'No, Betty, if you were out of work and broke, I wouldn't kick you out.' Dad will say, 'Rolf needs to get the hell out of here and get a regular job and quit screwing around.' But, for me, this is especially frustrating because Rolf is my brother; and despite all the mean, nasty things he has said and done, I do care about him, too."

"Betty, you are not a Legal Guardian for *Rolf! You* are the guardian for Malfaits! The Legal Guardian has to make these kinds of decisions *for* Malfaits because they *can't!* If *you* can't--or *don't*--make these decisions appropriately, then I don't think you really have *their* best interests foremost."

"But I feel caught. There isn't a straightforward single right choice."

Mr. Manilow pauses, and then asks, "Are you afraid of Rolf?"

"To be honest, yes. I have been afraid on several occasions. He has over two hundred guns in their house, and he carries a loaded 38 in his pocket. He does have a permit for it, but, yes, I've been afraid--for myself and for Mom and Dad. I feel like he's especially mean and nasty when I'm not there."

"Then you need to make decisions that are rational and prudent for your folks--*and* for you."

"My Aunt Mavis, mother's younger sister, is coming to visit the first part of September. I would feel more comfortable making decisions regarding Rolf after that visit is over. She may be able to be influential in getting Rolf to cooperate."

"Whatever influence your aunt may have is all well and good, but *you* are going to have to feel that *you* are in charge of Malfaits in the same way as if they were toddlers. They have lost all of their rights through guardianship. They can't handle their banking. They can't vote. They can't sign legal documents. However, you can't hire people to work in their home if they don't want them there; and you can't put them in a nursing home if they don't want to go to one. Or you can't keep them in a nursing home against their will."

"That doesn't make much sense if nursing care is what they need."

"I know it doesn't make sense, but if they don't want to be in a nursing home, you as their guardian, cannot force them to be there. That's the law."

Oh, God, deep inside my head and my heart, I know right now what the right decision is. They are slipping away. Each time period between my visits, I note further decline, especially in Dad. They cannot live in the squalid conditions of their house with Rolf's care, because it's not care! They cannot live by themselves! Adult foster homes will not take them because of incontinence--at least not at Janice's. They don't qualify for any of the assistance programs to help keep them in their own home, and they don't have the cash to hire available chore service, at least not as much as they need. They will not now--or ever--go to a nursing home willingly! God, I don't think I can do all the things that have to be done in this guardianship. It's such a 'Catch 22.' I am damned if I proceed with any kind of action to help them or remove Rolf's influence, and I'm damned if I continue as I have been. And this is a Legal Guardianship! God, what do I do now?

CHAPTER 35

God, Do You Really Work On Guardianships And Real Estate Deals?

ON MY NEXT trip to Ridgeview, I consult with Mr. Hinson about changing to an attorney whose emphasis is senior citizen issues.

"Betty, if you feel you'd like to do that I have no objection. Most of my work is in contract law, but I do have experience with guardianships. However, Mr. Oats is a very fine attorney and has established good rapport with the senior population in our community. If you wish to change, I'd be happy to send all the files to his office."

"I appreciate your representation so far, but I do think I would like to make the change. I feel as if I may have several more years of work with Malfaits, and the initiation of the guardianship is a good time to make the change to Mr. Oats' services."

"I agree. If you're going to change, this would be a good time to do it."

Mr. Hinson and I part amicably. I leave his office telling myself he's probably relieved. But however lacking in guardianship knowledge and experience he is, I know even less. I hope choosing Mr. Oats' service is the right move for all of us.

At my next appointment with Mr. Oats, we discuss the potential of Malfaits' Whidbey Island property and how it might be used for their care. "Betty, I think you should sell that property. Use the money for your folks' most pressing house repairs. Pay their delinquent taxes. Get some home help services into their home."

"Mr. Oats, I agree with all those things. But in regard to your first suggestion, I have not been able to find the deed to their Whidbey property. How can I sell land for which I have no deed?"

"That's not a deterrent. Number one, you get a copy of Malfaits' deed at the Auditor's office in Coupeville, the county seat. Secondly, you get a current land valuation on a recent tax statement from the Assessor. Thirdly, get a record of tax payments and overdue amounts from the County Treasurer. Then you get two appraisals of Fair Market Value from certified appraisers, or realtors who are well established and familiar with the area. It's that simple. And you can do all this at the courthouse right there in Coupeville."

I leave Mr. Oats' office feeling confident in his quick grasp of my situation and in his directions for the next steps in the guardianship. Learning which tasks belong to the Assessor, the Auditor, and the Treasurer, however, makes me feel as if I am going through my junior high Washington State History lessons again--and those chapters were near the end of the book. I should have studied them better.

A few days later I make a special trip to Whidbey Island to the courthouse. Hours of searching records in the Auditor's Office with the help of several nice people show there is no deed recorded for Malfaits' property. There are copies of the real estate contract but no copy of a registered deed. A trip to Oak Harbor to the title company that handled the closure of the sale confirms no deed was recorded.

Personnel in both offices tell me their only possible suggestion is a thorough property search. I shudder at that idea. The Malfait home is stacked floor to ceiling, covered in layers of dog hair and kitty debris, and an accumulation of years of filth plus all of Rolf's junk. A deed could be in a shoe box in the garage, under the grape jelly in the can cupboard, or on the third shelf above the sewing machine with quilt scraps--or, it could have been thrown out. Aside from all these possibilities, Malfaits are not likely to allow me to search their home.

I return to Coupeville to the Treasurer's Office. The news there is equally sad. Two years of back taxes amounts to $1,518.83, and next month another year's delinquent taxes will be added to that total. As I leave the courthouse, I pause on the steps, lift my face to the warm summer sun, and suck in several breaths of fresh marine air. How can it smell so good when a person is in a bottomless pit?

I decide to go back to Oak Harbor to the title company. Title companies must have to give some direction to people in my situation. What about fires or other natural disasters? What if someone paid for their property and died before they could record a deed? What would the heirs do? There *has* to be an answer.

The people in the title company aren't too happy so see me again, but after some further conversation with other office personnel, they give me the name of a Seattle investment company which bought the contract during Malfaits' time payment period.

Back out on the street, I stop at the first phone booth I see and place a call to that company. I make connections with a woman named Leah. By the time I labor through an outline of my problems of the day, my rote demeanor dissipates, my voice quivers, and the tears spill over. I sob into the cold, smelly telephone mouthpiece, "I don't know whether to come to Seattle, go to Oak Harbor, or go to Ridgeview and tackle an impossible house search. I have to have a deed, but Malfaits have no money for searches or attorneys. I'm it!"

Leah's compassion transcends the desperation in my voice, "Betty, take a big breath."

No words come into my mind, so I follow Leah's direction and suck in a big breath. Dropping my shoulders and arms in exasperation, I force a gust of air back out, temporarily repelling the tobacco stench of the plastic receiver.

"Now, Betty, first off let me tell you that I do understand your frustration. I don't know the answer to your dilemma, but I am going to try to help you. I want you to find a public fax service in Oak

Harbor. I will find out as much as I can about that contract. I'll call you back at the public phone booth where you are right now. It will probably take me an hour to an hour and a half to get the information. That's past business working hours and closing times--ours here, too--but I can see your circumstances are dire, and I want to help you. I'll stay over and complete the search. You just be sure the fax material can be received at whatever place you find at the time my search is complete. When I call you back, you can give me the fax numbers from the phone booth where you are now. Then you can go back to the fax place and pick up the copy of the search. It will probably be there before you get there."

I hang up the phone and bow my head.

God, thank You for the Leahs of the world, because at this time of the day and after all the discouraging information I've received, I am incapable of devising any plan of action or knowing what the next step is. Leah has done that for me. God, please guide us both.

I turn and struggle with the ill-fitting old glass door of the phone booth and mutter aloud, "Where will I find a fax service in a town I'm unfamiliar with, and one that will be open longer than usual business hours?" I step into the refreshing, cool, late-afternoon air, lift my head, and stare straight into the front doors of the Oak Harbor Public Library. I go in and make my arrangements for receiving a fax. Then I find a cozy spot and try to rest and collect my thoughts for the next hour. Newspapers and magazines do not hold my attention. I wander back outside by the phone booth twenty minutes before the hour and pace nervously nearby. I step into the booth whenever someone comes down the street, so I can be sure to be occupying it at the time I might receive the call. And when the passerby goes into the library instead of seeking *my* phone booth, I breathe a quick *Thank you, God.*

Old Parents and Purple Tulips

At twenty minutes after the hour the ringing from the booth startles me. I grapple with the bulky door and nearly drop the phone as I scramble to answer, "Hello? Hello?"

An excited voice answers back, "Hi, Betty, this is Leah from the investment company. I am so excited. I have such happy news for you!"

"Oh, please, I need to hear some kind of happy news."

"I found the people who purchased your parents' contract. They are both alive and well. In fact, they are investors in our company. I've already talked to them by phone. They are well aware of that particular contract with Malfaits and remembered talking to your folks a couple of times on the phone after they bought the contract. They said they both shared a mutual love for Whidbey Island and fishing. Anyway, they verified the contract was paid in full."

"That's wonderful! Now what do I do?"

"These folks live on south Hood Canal—a little place called Seabeck."

"Good heavens—that's only five or six miles from my home. I probably shop in the same stores and have seen them around town."

"You're probably right. They say they will help in whatever way necessary for you to attain a Warranty Fulfillment Deed. I'm sure your attorney can help you with the paperwork. I am happy this has worked out like this. The Seabeck folks are so cooperative and remember absolutely the contract was paid in full, and they are willing to state that in writing if you need them to do that. It's a very happy find."

"And how do I pay you for the service you have done today?"

"No payment is necessary. You just hang in there and take things one step at a time. Good luck."

Leah is almost as near tears as I am as I thank her and say goodbye. I escape the stench of the phone booth and scramble to the library and my fax copy.

My energy is renewed and on my way to the ferry I stop at the first realty company I spot. It's past business hours, but the lights are on, and

393

the girl behind the desk who is wrapping up for the night is able to give me a business card for a local certified appraiser. "We use him quite often out of this office. I know he's been working the island for over twenty years, because my parents used his services when they bought their place. I was only five years old at that time."

A short while later I spot a second realty office and make a sharp turn into the parking lot spewing gravel across the shoes of a gentleman who is locking up for the day. After a brief introduction, he reopens the office door and invites me back in and listens to my story.

"Betty, I don't think your problem is too difficult. I'm the owner-broker of this office and have been in business for twenty-eight years at this same location. I've sold three parcels of land in proximity to your folks' property during the past couple of years, and two of my sales people have sold parcels recently which I think adjoin the piece you have described. I'd be happy to do an appraisal of Fair Market Value of Malfaits' twenty acre parcel. I'd like to list that property, but I wouldn't do that without a registered deed. That just isn't something a reliable realtor would do, and it could never sell that way."

I accept his offer to do the appraisal. A few minutes later I pull out of the parking lot at a more relaxed pace and with no flying gravel.

The realty agency is near Janice's foster home. It's early evening and getting dark, but she said to stop by any time—so I do. Janice is happy to see me.

"I tried to call you a couple of times last week. I've really been praying about your situation. I know you need help, and I don't like to take clients who are incontinent, but I've been thinking maybe I need to learn to deal with that if I'm going to grow in this business. I know your folks don't have enough money right now to pay my monthly fees, but I'm doing pretty well and I could probably afford to have your mom and dad come up for a while, and I'll wait for payment. You're eventually going to have to sell their house or their Whidbey land, and you could pay me then. Or, maybe they could come up for a temporary time so they could relax and get to feeling better. That might be all they need for right now. Then again, they might decide they would like to live here and that living in a foster home isn't as bad as living in a nursing home—and maybe even better than living on their own."

"Janice, Malfaits want to stay right where they are right now, and I can't imagine how much work it would take to prepare their house for selling it. Also, selling their Whidbey land is a moot issue. I can't find the deed to their property. Today I learned for sure that Malfaits never recorded a deed. I'm working on solving that problem, but no reputable realty office would list it as is without a deed. *And* it has no legal access. That's another little problem I discovered today. The property owner below Malfaits' land has completely fenced his fifty-five acres and developed a dirt bike trail over the old logging road which Malfaits used to drive in on. The old logging road simply isn't there anymore."

"Oh dear, that's too bad. That's just one more problem, isn't it? I do wish I could help you. I wish there was something I could do."

"Thank you for your thoughts, Janice, but the reality is Malfaits' combined monthly incomes wouldn't cover your required monthly fees. I wouldn't feel right about asking you to wait for payment, because I can see from what I have learned today it could take years to unravel their problems and sell either of their properties. There's piles of legal work and more lawsuits waiting to happen. On top of that, Mom and Dad don't want to leave their home, and legally I can't force them to."

"Betty, God will provide an answer. We both need to keep praying, and then we need to listen carefully for the messages God puts before us. He will work it out. Just listen and trust!"

"You know, Janice, some place way inside myself most of the time I think I am trying to earnestly trust God, but right now my communication lines are all on overload, even to God. I'm sure He's as sick of hearing me as I am of hearing myself."

"Now, Betty, that's not possible. You have to trust God will work this whole thing out. It *will* work out for all of you. You'll see."

I doze briefly on the twenty-minute ferry ride to the mainland, and that refreshes me for an hour's drive on the other side. I arrive home and crash in exhaustion.

I am awakened by the phone ringing at 11:30 PM. Mother barks, "Betty, where is my antique wooden bowl? Dad says you took it."

"Oh, Mother, *please...*"

"Now, Betty, Dad says he saw it in your truck."

From my sleepy fog I mumble, "Mother, I don't steal. I never did steal anything from you. I don't like being falsely accused. Dad is wrong. You people need to go to bed and not be making phone calls at this hour of the night to anyone, and especially not to me about such lies!"

"Well, it's gone, and no one else has been here!"

I sit up in bed, and yell into the phone, "Mother, how many times do I have to say it--I am not a thief!"

"Well, here, you better talk to Dad."

I don't know why it even hurts. It's like rolling the clock back eight years and starting the 'great family rift' all over again. At least this time I know I'm *sort* of okay, and they are the whacko ones!

When Dad gets on the phone, he is so upset he can't say anything meaningful. He whimpers, "Jesus, kid, I know--you don't--steal. I just saw--well, I *thought* I saw--that damned bowl in your truck. I thought it was under the seat."

"Dad, there's no reason for a bowl to be under my truck seat. That wooden bread bowl is two feet long. It wouldn't even fit under there."

"Well, I'm sorry, kid. It must have been under Rolf's car seat then."

"Dad, Dad--don't do that. It's not under any car seat."

Dad sobs into the phone, "I'm sorry. I'm sorry, kid."

"Listen, Dad, you don't need to apologize. The next time I'm down, we can both go out to the truck and search thoroughly. If it's there, everyone will be happy. If it's not, you can apologize then. Okay?"

"Yeah, yeah, that'll be fine."

"Goodnight, Dad. I love you."

"Goodnight, Betty. Mom and me love you, too."

God, are You really working this stuff out? What am I supposed to be learning from this? I already know pain. I know compassion. I know forgiveness--and I know I need to work harder on that last part. I'm trying desperately to help and to do what's right for all of us. There are so many tangles to this, I can't seem to comprehend them all nor to act logically on any of them. Help!

CHAPTER 36

Purple Tulips

A FEW DAYS later I make my next trip to Ridgeview. I get there about 11:00 AM. Mother is sitting cross-legged in the front yard weeding the clover out of the lawn. Dad is sitting nearby in one of the old wooden lawn chairs staring off into space. My arrival interrupts his 'space trip' only when he sees me walking across the lawn toward them.

"Mama, Mama, look who's here!"

Though I called her this morning before leaving, Mother shows her usual surprise, "Well, for God's sake! What are you doing here?"

Dad launches into his favorite topic, "Oh, Betty, I'm so glad you're here. I'm soooo hungry! I haven't eaten in twenty days!"

Mother snaps at him, "Why, you old fool, you ate this morning."

"No, I didn't."

"Why, you did so."

"No, sir, Mama, you've been sitting out here in this yard all day. We haven't even gone to coffee yet."

"We don't have any money for coffee today."

I ignore their argument. It could be like last time and they *have* been to coffee and eaten breakfast, or it could be that Dad is right. I heave a silent shrug and go back to my truck and return with cookies, juice and Sprite from my ice chest.

They relish the cold drinks and eat the cookies by handfuls, lawn dirt and all. Dad opens a second can of Sprite and scoops another handful of cookies, "Oh, Jesus, kid, I need this." He shakes a cookie at me and winks."

"Mother, Dad does seem awfully hungry."

Mother returns to her weeding, "Oh, he's always hungry. He'd eat all day long if I'd let him."

Dad drinks the rest of his second can of Sprite and follows it with a can of juice. When he shakes all the remaining cookie crumbs from the container into his hand and tosses them into his mouth.

I bring up the subject of the "stolen" antique wooden bowl. "Did you guys find your bowl yet?"

Dad answers, no. Mother answers, yes.

I kneel beside Dad's lawn chair, look into his eyes, and speak quietly, "Dad, I was very hurt and angry that you accused me of stealing that."

Dad looks back into my eyes and shakes his head, "Now, kid, I didn't accuse you of stealing. I didn't say you stole it. I didn't do that."

"But, Dad, you told Mother you saw it in my truck."

"I did see it in your truck. I saw you take it out of your ice chest."

Conversation with Dad was impossible on the phone. This also seems futile, but I persist in my quiet voice with eye to eye contact, "No, Dad, you didn't see that. You're confused about it. I don't have the bowl. I didn't take the bowl. And I never had it in my truck nor in my ice chest."

Dad breaks our close eye contact and jerks his head away from me and toward the opposite side of the big wooden lawn chair. "Well, I don't know nothing then! I don't know a damned thing!" He folds his hands in his lap and looks down.

"Dad, sometimes people get confused and think they see things. I'm sure that's what happened. I'm sorry the bowl is gone, but I didn't take it. I really want you to understand that I didn't do that." I remain silent in my kneeling position leaning on the opposite chair arm.

Dad looks back into my eyes, his voice relaxed, "Well, I didn't say you took it. In fact, Rolf found the bowl. He ran out to his truck last night, and he came back in with the bowl. That I did see!"

"Dad, Dad, Rolf may have done some other misdeeds, but he just couldn't have had that bowl in his truck. Dad, he doesn't *have* a truck!"

Dad hangs his head, "I just don't know. I don't know a damned thing."

Mother, who has been sitting motionless during this conversation, speaks up nonchalantly, "Rolf found the bowl. It was under the coffee table in the living room."

I turn my attention to her and continue quietly, "Mother, you can't accept everything Dad says and side with him. He doesn't see and remember like he used to. Neither do you. You're really going to have to try harder not to accuse people. It's so hurtful to us all, and it keeps us from working well together."

Mother is a little bit defensive but calm, "That bowl is one of my favorites, and it was gone. I couldn't find it, and I was worried."

"Mother, it wasn't gone. You just couldn't find it. I know that's scary. Part of the problem is you're tired and you're trying so hard to be helpful and supportive of Dad. You have to understand he doesn't see things as clearly as he used to. Remember his vision is severely reduced since his stroke. You both have to *not* accuse people. I understand how scared you were, but I have to tell you I'm *never* going to let you *ever* accuse me unjustly again. I don't steal your bowls or anything else. I never have, and I don't want you saying those bad things to me, to other people, or even to each other. I feel deeply hurt and angry when you both do that."

With no further word, Mother and I get up to leave the yard and go into the house. Dad follows us muttering to himself some sort of blame toward Rolf. Mother punctuates each of his comments by turning and quietly telling him what an old fool he is. The three of us move across the yard in this bizarre, irrational kind of calm. I want desperately to believe there has been some degree of understanding, at least on Mother's part, but I truly doubt it.

In the house we find Mother's two square black purses, and one of them has plenty of coffee money. With that settled, I address their odor and clothing. Dad is wearing the same clothes since my last trip down ten days ago. Ignoring that fact and that he was just sitting in the lawn chair 'spacing' when I drove up, I tell them, "Listen, I know you've *both* been out there working hard in the hot sun and you're all dirty and sweaty." With no mention of the words filthy nor bath, I say, "Let's get you *both* into some fresh clothes, and I'll take you out for lunch."

In looking for clean clothes for Dad, I find the wash from my last trip still packed in bags and boxes on the couch, including all Mother's panties and all of Dad's shorts. Mother rummages through the box, "My God, I've been wondering what happened to all my underwear." She immediately strips naked and dons clean clothes in the middle of the living room. I try not to look, but I don't think she was wearing underclothing.

I busy myself with Dad, who is none too steady, but who is also shedding his clothes in the living room. As I assist him, I discover he for sure has not been wearing underwear. He modestly clutches himself and makes sure every important part is covered as he pulls on a pair of shorts.

In clean underwear with pants zipped up and shirt tucked in, Dad smoothes himself down and says, "Well, I feel a damn sight better now, I'll tell you that."

"And you look a damn sight better, Dad."

Dad smiles as I hold the door for them. We are finally ready and off--*truly off.*

"Where would you two like to go?"

In simultaneous chorus, 'Ocean Espresso.'

"But you go there almost every day for coffee. That's not exactly what I had in mind when I said I'd take you out to lunch."

Mother reaffirms the choice, "Well, that's where we want to go."

Dad echoes, "Yeah, kid, that's where we want to go."

After several repetitions, each of us in the trio speaking our line with increasing volume, I give in. We load into the car and head for Ocean Espresso. At each stop sign and cross street, Dad leans forward, checks both ways and chants in my direction, "You'll like this place, kid. The food's not half bad."

We arrive at Ocean Espresso, park in front, get out of the car to the accompaniment of Dad's monotonous incantation, and move in an awkward triad to the doorway of the restaurant. I hold the door for Mother as Dad booms out his lines once again, "You'll like this place, kid. The food's not half--"

Mother hisses over her shoulder, "Shut up, you old fool! We're out in public."

I smile at Dad, thinking it may be *more than half--*.

We seat ourselves in a small wooden booth by the window. No one else is in the restaurant. The waitress scurries over from behind the counter, swipes one wide wet streak through the middle of the table, picks up a stray catsup bottle, wipes it with the same rag and drops it noisily into its little wire basket container with the mustard, vinegar, and an array of smudged, evil-looking hot sauce bottles. She motions toward Mom and Dad with the clutched rag, "You folks want the usual?"

Dad smiles up at her. "Yes, ma'am. We'll have one chicken breast, one wing, one leg, an order of jo-joes, three burritos and two 32 oz. coffees. Plus, our daughter's with us today, so we'll need whatever she wants."

The waitress points the rag toward to me, "What can I get ya?"

"I'll try the burrito and a Dr. Pepper."

When the food arrives, I do *try* but not too successfully. The middle part is chewable, and hopefully the beans won't be too damaging. I am squishing the over-cooked burrito shell into my napkin as the waitress cruises by again.

Mom and Dad smile at her and order a couple of chocolate cream-filled pastries to top off their lunch. I opt for nursing my 18-oz. plastic bottle of Dr. Pepper.

On the way out of the restaurant, Dad pokes me in the ribs and winks. "Now, that wasn't so bad, was it, kid? Their food's not half bad, is it?"

"No, Dad, it isn't *half*--it's all--fine."

Back at the house as we enter the front door, I peruse the cluttered stacks in the living room and muse silently about the missing property deed. I know now I can get a replacement, but I wonder where in all these haystacks the needle might be?

"You know, guys, when I took care of your Whidbey taxes last week, I learned that you never recorded the deed to the property."

Dad shuffles a stack of old newspapers on the coffee table and selects an outdated, colorful Home Depot insert ad. "Oh, shit, kid, we did that the day we bought it." He shakes the paper out, allowing the remaining pages to fall about his feet.

Mother is half-way to the kitchen and fussing at Taco who is noisy and excited because he knows she has some Ocean Espresso scraps for him. She tosses the food pieces in the general direction of his food bowl and retraces her steps, "My God, Betty, that means we don't own it. We've got to find that deed right now."

"Mother, you *do* own it. I'm sure you do, but if we could find the actual document it would save a lot of time, letter writing, and maybe even legal fees. I already know you can get a replacement deed, but we might be able to find the original one. Would you mind if we started a search here in the front bedroom where you guys sleep? Maybe it just got tucked away."

Mother reaches down and scoops up Elizabeth, one of their scrawny Siamese cats who probably is also hoping for a restaurant treat, "Well, I don't think you'll find anything like that in the bedroom, but you can go ahead and look."

I don't wait for further permission to enter their cluttered bedroom and begin a search. Dad follows me and flops down on the bed clutching his outdated Home Depot ad. He snaps the paper out in a reading position a couple of times, then tosses it aside and launches into a friendly, irrational up-dating on his recent job search in Olympia.

Mother comes in and sits on the edge of the unchanged, stained bed sheets and begins picking fleas off Elizabeth and crushing them between her thumb nails. I shudder and take as much of a breath as the environment of the room will allow and open the top dresser drawer.

Two hours later I have nothing to show for my effort. I've searched Dad's dresser drawers, the built-in closet and storage shelves which go all the way across one side of the twelve foot room, and the two upper drawers of Mother's vanity, which is a heavy mirrored piece wedged in at the foot of their bed. I have only the bottom drawer left to search. It's hard to open this one because of the narrow space at the foot of the bed--and because it's stuffed way past capacity. I finally yank it free, and it belches out a bundle of recipe cards with faded yellow newsprint copies of various delicacies glued to each card. Un-regurgitated stacks underneath contain old birthday cards, letters, news clippings, a broken china cup, and a plastic sac full of unfinished quilting squares. Pressed on the very bottom are several bundles of old Christmas cards, banded and labeled by year. I work my way through each item. Finally I toss the last bundle on the bed. The rubber band breaks with a limp, rotten little snap scattering the cards across the bed. I feel like that rubber band.

I heave a sigh of disappointment and pick up some of the Christmas letters from the scattered bundle and begin reading the news Malfaits' friends and relatives wrote in their cards more than two decades ago. Neatly folded and tucked in the second card I find a heavier, official looking creased paper. I blink to force the bold-faced print into focus--**Warranty Fulfillment Deed**. I allow the black print to snake past my tired eyes a second time. "Whoa, maybe--just maybe--"

Mother is now concentrating on picking and crushing fleas on Susie, the other equally emaciated Siamese kitty. She glances up at me, "Betty, you've worked really hard in here. Don't be worrying about that deed. I'll help you later and we'll search the whole upstairs. I know we can find it."

Dad jerks to wakefulness, tosses Elizabeth off his chest, and strikes up his usual melodic refrain about how hungry he is.

I cram most of the clutter back into the open drawer, holding out the paper with the slithering black letters. I pull myself up off the floor and carry the paper outside to my truck where in the afternoon sunlight I can be sure I have *indeed* found the *deed*. I tuck the precious paper in my journal behind the truck seat.

When I re-enter the house, neither Mom nor Dad has missed me. The only difference in their conversation is that Dad's repetitions have taken on a louder tone conveying the increased urgency of his hunger.

I avoid confirming the finding of the needle in the haystack.

"Dad, you can't be hungry. You ate over $10.00 worth of chicken and jo-joes a little while ago. You can't possibly be hungry."

"Kid, I tell you I'm starving."

"Dad, if you feel the same way in another half hour, then you and I will go out for a milkshake. How's that?"

He smiles silently.

Abruptly, and punctuating her words with the successful crushing of another flea, Mother asks, "Well, Mavis is coming in tomorrow. Who's going to go with you to Portland to the airport to pick her up?"

I had not spoken of Aunt Mavis' arrival, hoping this date like doctors' appointments, my trips to Ridgeview, items on a grocery list, or even the property deed would go unnoticed or be forgotten. I leave their bedroom and seat myself in the living room wrestling silently with my thoughts, 'God Almighty, Mother, your memory loss is incredibly selective! Okay, Betty, how *are* you going to handle this?'

Mother calls out, "Well, who's going to go to Portland with you?"

I assume the same quiet tone as in our earlier front yard discussions of theft accusation and hope logic will prevail as I answer from the living room. "Mother, I think it will be best if I go to Portland by myself because...."

Mother instantly emerges from the bedroom, tosses Susie to the floor, and cuts in, "Well, that's no good. Mavis is my sister, and I haven't seen her for years. She's coming all the way from West Virginia to visit, and she'll be expecting Dad and me to be there to greet her. We always go to Portland to pick her up."

"I know, Mother, but I'm in my truck. It only has one seat, and it's supposed to rain. Mavis will have some baggage, and we'll need to put that in the cab of the truck. There won't be any place for two other people to ride. There will barely be enough room for Mavis and me and her suitcases."

"Why that's ridiculous. Four people can sit on that seat in your truck."

"I know, Mom, but that's not legal and we don't have enough seat belts. And, I'm trying to tell you Mavis will have luggage that has to go in the cab."

Mother booms back, "Well, Dad can sit in the bed of that pickup!"

My own volume rises, "Mother, it's fifty miles to the Portland airport. I'm not going down the freeway with my eighty-year-old frail father bouncing around in the back of the pickup."

"Dad wouldn't mind riding back there at all."

Dad shuffles into the living room in time to chime in, "Hell, no, kid, I'd be fine. I've ridden in the bed of many a pick-up."

I bark at them both, "Well, that isn't going to happen this time! Dad's not riding back there, and that's final!"

Mother offers another option, "Well, we can leave Dad at home then."

"Mother, that may be fine for a trip to the grocery store or the laundromat, but a trip to the Portland airport is too long. It will be over three hours. The plane may be late, and then it would be even longer. All kinds of delays can happen at airports."

Mother is adamant. "Dad would sit right here in this chair while we're gone."

"He won't sit in that chair for one hour, much less three hours. He'd be out on the street looking for you, or he'd walk down town--or he might even try to go to Oregon looking for you. I can't allow that."

Mother blasts back, "Then we all *have* to go! We *will* fit in that truck!"

I suck in air through flared nostrils and release slowly through my mouth. I repeat the aerobic exercise avoiding eye contact with her. "Mother, even after we get to the airport, it's a long a walk from the parking area to where the passengers disembark. Your feet and legs would be killing you, and there aren't very many bathrooms."

Top volume finds a new level as Mother fires back. "I don't know what that has to do with it! I've never pissed in your truck, and Dad hasn't either!"

I draw another big breath and brush imaginary cobwebs from my face as I tell myself, *Keep laughing, Betty. You only have two choices: you either laugh or you cry! To hell with logic. That went out the window years ago. I can't think of any other reasons anyway. Mother has defeated me verbally again. I have a sinking feeling this will not be the last of this battle.*

I glance at my watch. I have an evening appointment with a senior services counselor. I ignore any thoughts about their hunger or what they will eat for dinner. I ignore my promise about Dad's milkshake. I rise from the couch and move toward the front door, "Listen, both of you, I'll be here tomorrow promptly at 9:00 AM. I'll bring your breakfast. If you're both up and dressed, we'll decide about your going then. I can't deal with this any more right now."

It wasn't a yes, but it wasn't a no. I leave with no further argument or explanation. I don't even say goodnight as I quietly shut the heavy front door.

I climb into my truck and proceed to my appointment with Mrs. Zane, a court- recommended counselor who often advises guardianship cases in this county. She has years of experience with senior citizens and problems inherent in helping them, their family members, and their care-takers.

Mrs. Zane is very friendly but at the same time business-like. She reads several pages from my records and affirms my work thus far with the bank account, bill-paying, and budget book. Though she is not nearly as abrupt as Mr. Manilow from Adult Protective Services, she emphasizes three main points that she perceives I must follow in this guardianship: (1) I must be responsible for Malfaits; I must provide supervision for them. (2) Rolf must be out of their house; his deviant and abusive behavior will not cease otherwise. (3) Malfaits must have help in their personal care and daily chores; for right now that appears to be needed in their home, and at some time in the near future that will probably mean in a care facility.

Mrs. Zane compliments me for accomplishing an amazing amount in the short time since the finalization of the guardianship. She shares brief experiences of other adult children who have had to work through guardianships in order to care for loved ones, and she leaves me with renewed hope rather than fear of failure.

It's 10:00 PM by the time I drive through the take-out window of a local drive-in and begin a moonlit dinner by myself in the front seat of my truck. I wolf down some kind of bacon-barbecue-onion thing, as I contemplate my conference with Mrs. Zane and mull over my successes as a guardian. It's not a very long-lasting pep-talk though, as my thoughts turn to how much is yet to do. With the genetics in my family, it is no wonder I'm having this kind of weird Friday night out on the town. No normal person would do this. As I choke down my last bite, I again doubt my guardianship abilities and even my own sanity.

Back at The Sterling, I crash in exhaustion. My dinner disturbance and frustrated insecurities about the guardianship was mild compared to my rolling and tossing in the night as I stress over the Portland airport trip the next day. The daughter wants to please. The prudent novice guardian knows she can't take these two unkempt, senile people to the airport, despite the fact the arriving guest is Mother's much loved sister. After a couple of hours, I give up on sleep, turn on the light and prop myself up in bed. I reread the local newspaper--even the want ads. I poke around in my suitcase and find an old magazine to read.

Still sleep does not come.

My travel clock shows it's 1:30 AM. I turn out the light.

More rolling and tossing. I sweat. I'm cold. Another hour passes.

I get up and take another shower. I rummage through my travel bag for something dry to sleep in. Tucked in pajamas is a love note from my husband and attached to it is an inspirational devotional from Genesis 16:1-13 and 21:14 -17 with a thought for the day: 'God hears and re-sponds to my faintest cry for help.'

I dig out the Gideon Bible from the motel nightstand and read the verses indicated in the devotional, then pray,

Oh, God, I don't know what's happening in my family! Everyone and everything I care about is all screwed up. Oh, God, all Your ministers, Your counselors--they all say, trust God, He will see you through this. Just be faithful! God, I'm not sure I know what this faith stuff is all about. Maybe I've never known. I don't know what's right. I don't know what You want me to do. God, I'll do whatever You want me to do, just help me to know what that is. Please direct my every thought, word and deed through this night and tomorrow morning. If I just could know what it is that I'm supposed to do. I feel so dumb.

God, I'm a visual person. If You want me to go a certain way, give me some kind of sign--send up a purple tulip in the cracks of the side-walk in the snows of December! Then I'll know that's the way You want me to choose, and I'll follow that way. Oh, God, I know that's ridiculous, but sometimes I feel as if I have it all figured out, and then when I'm with Mom and Dad, I lose sight of the goal, especially in regard to Mother. She always outtalks me. What she says doesn't even make sense, and I leave feeling defeated and outmaneuvered.

Dear God, I just give it all to You! I know You can't really do some outrageous thing like send up a purple tulip in the cracks of the sidewalk in the snows of December to point out the way just to me, but, Almighty God, I'll do whatever You direct me to do! In Jesus' name, Amen.

I sleep fitfully.

The next morning I am comforted briefly by the morning sun as I pick up take-out breakfasts, although what usually produces a pleasant aromatic sensation for me, this morning gives me a queasy, nauseous feeling. As I drive to 516, I talk aloud to myself and practice the words of the decision I *think* I have made. "Mother, if you're up and ready, I'll take you. We'll just have to leave Dad and hope the fascination of guarding that big overstuffed chair will keep him in the house. But, Mother, if you're not dressed, you can hate me as much as you like, but you and Dad will have to stay in Ridgeview and wait."

As I stand on the doorstep, I listen to the doorbell chime melodically. Mother opens the door promptly, but she is wearing only a bra and holding her hair brush. She steps back and resumes brushing her long, straggly gray hair which reaches almost to her waist. "Well, my God, look who's here. Come in."

"Jesus Christ on a Rock, Mother, do you always answer the door like that? You did that the other day, too, but at least then you had on a shirt and panties."

"Well, it's only you."

"Yes, but you didn't know that when you opened the door. You didn't even look through the wicket to see who it was."

In my whole life I have never seen my mother clad so briefly. As I step into the entryway, she turns and strolls across the living room, her flabby, sagging, white buttocks flesh stark against the dull drabness of the dim room and all of its clutter.

"Oh well, I guess anyone else would have looked and run away." She sits her bare bottom down on a stack of clean laundry on the couch arm and continues the long sweeping brush strokes.

Dad is in the bathroom. Cutting through the normal cat-dog stench is a penetrating fecal odor. Several flushes in a row let me know he has been successful and probably is using enough paper to plug the toilet. He seems pleased by my breakfast call, and I hope the gurgling sounds of water are from hand washing as I hear him hurrying from the bathroom. Mother makes no move to stop her hair brushing nor to get dressed. Dad passes through the living room, takes the food bags from me, and goes on to the kitchen, holding the bags high and yelling at Taco who keeps jumping up on him. Mother continues her preening in silence.

I remain standing in the entryway screwing up my courage to stick to my decision. "Mother, I told you I'd be by this morning promptly at nine, and if you were ready, we'd decide about your going with me. Well, you're not ready. It's late, and I have to hurry. Good-bye."

I turn and exit through the front door. The pale, nude form continues the silent rhythmic brushing of her hair from her perch atop the laundry on the couch arm.

Ten minutes later I am on the freeway headed south to Portland. Any semblance of comforting morning sunshine has disappeared. Purplish gray clouds well up to the south. Daylight becomes darkness. Light-pelting rain turns to vicious thrashing sheets of water crashing against the windshield. With the window wipers on high power I am barely able to clear the glass enough to see to drive. Repeated wind gusts buffet the truck. I grip the steering wheel tighter and lean forward to follow the watery blur of the tail-lights on the vehicle in front of me and a wiggly white line to my right which I presume to be the edge of the highway. Should I pull over? The speed limit is 70mph, but traffic has slowed to about 35mph. No one is stopping.

A weird sense of jubilation penetrates my intense concentration as I recall the image of my mother answering the door. Did she really do that? What's with all that hair brushing? She usually brushes her hair as a last ritual after she's totally dressed and before going out the door. If they are not going to coffee, she just pulls it back and heads for the kitchen to find something to nibble on until they do go out. She has never been so disinterested in food as she was this morning. Does she hate drive-in food that much? Did she really sit down on the couch arm like that--bare bottom? Maybe she knew I wasn't going to take them and that was her way of giving up the argument. No, she wouldn't have given up. And she's never been that quiet. She behaved as if she was moving in a slow motion--in a trance--as if she wasn't really there.

Dear God, thank you. I think I just got a purple tulip, even if it wasn't sprouting in the cracks of the sidewalk in the snows of December!

Old Parents and Purple Tulips

Suddenly lightning stabs across the sky in huge jagged flashes. A deluge of rain dumps over the truck for several minutes then ceases as quickly as it began.

CHAPTER 37

⸺⬥⸺

Aunt Mavis Lays the Law Down to Rolf

ONCE IN THE airport I feel guilty coming to pick up Aunt Mavis by myself. It seems as if Mother and Dad should be here. After two long delays in flight arrivals due to harsh, stormy weather, I think differently. I did make the right choice.

Mavis finally arrives, and it's a happy reunion for both of us. We return to Ridgeview, where she rents a car; and since it is late afternoon, we pick up a chicken dinner from a deli and go to Malfaits' house. No one is home. Mavis and I go around to their usual hang-outs. Alas, we stop at the little corner cafe where Malfaits usually have breakfast. I run in to check, and there they sit at the counter. I announce to them I have Mavis with me waiting out in the car.

Mother looks up and smiles, "Oh, that's wonderful!" She calls to Sally, the cafe owner, "Did you hear that? My sister Mavis has come all the way from West Virginia to visit us." Sally and several other regular patrons seated at nearby booths cajole about the happy event. Mother rotates her stool back toward the counter and resumes eating her hamburger. Dad has not once looked away from his food.

Did they not understand me? I lean over between them and say, "You guys, she's out in the car in front of the cafe--right now--waiting for you."

Mother calmly replies, "We'll be finished here in a minute."

Dad stabs a fork full of French fries and shakes them in my direction. "We'll be right along, kid."

Both of them stare straight ahead and chew methodically. I stand-- silent, irrelevant--like the dust-catching Christmas cactus Sally has let sleep for years in the corner window of the cafe. A few minutes later

415

without a word, they simultaneously empty their coffee cups, turn their stools toward me, slip down to the floor, and shuffle toward the cafe exit. I hurry to open the door.

When they get up next to the rental car, there is a burst of excitement and joy as Mavis steps out onto the sidewalk. There are repeated hugs and expressions of happiness from all three of them.

Without questioning whose vehicle, Dad climbs into the back seat of the rental car, "Come on, baby sister, get in here with an old man."

Mavis laughs and snuggles up near him in the backseat.

Mother clutches the top of the open door with one hand and the front seat head rest with the other hand as she calls into the open car, "Move over, you two." She sort of falls into the back seat, crushing both Mavis and Dad tighter together.

I stand on the sidewalk somewhat baffled and still in my Christmas cactus persona. Mavis wrenches her arm from under Mother and leans toward the open door. "I'm trapped, Betty. I guess you'll have to drive us."

Thank goodness it's only a couple of blocks back to the house.

On the drive-way we unload and Mom, Dad, and Mavis wander out toward the back yard, admiring the cherry trees and flowers as they go. I guess the deli chicken dinner was a waste, but that doesn't matter if everyone is happy for a change. I grab the food boxes and head for the front door. As usual, it's locked. I find all of them seated at the picnic table in the back yard. Mother immediately opens the boxes and picks out a wing, a roll, some cole slaw and a Dr. Pepper for herself. She lays out a breast portion, a roll, mashed potatoes and gravy, slaw, and a Dr. Pepper for Dad. "Mavis, you better get in here with us or you'll get left out."

Mavis chooses a chicken leg and begins to nibble. I am unnoticed. Despite the hamburgers and fries at the cafe, Mom and Dad eat ravenously at the picnic table. Dad takes two more pieces of chicken in addition to what Mother laid out for him. Noticing a huge candy bar protruding from a side-pocket of Mavis' purse, he helps himself without a word to anyone. What had been Mavis' emergency food supply for her airplane trip became Malfaits' picnic dessert. No mention is made of airplane arrivals or my going to Portland by myself. Hours pass pleasantly.

As darkness approaches Aunt Mavis announces, "Francine and Roger, there really is such a thing as jet lag, and I've got a bad case of it right now. Betty and I need to get out of here and get to bed."

Mother tells her, "Now, Mavis, you can stay overnight here with us."

Dad echoes the hospitality. "Mavis, we have plenty of room right here at 516. We've got four bedrooms, you know."

"Thank you. That's really nice of you, but I don't want to be a burden to anyone while I'm here. I've already arranged for a place. I'll say good-night for now, and I'll see you people tomorrow."

No one raises a fuss or tries to be persuasive. I am not mentioned in the invitation. There are no further questions as to where we're going as Mavis and I leave for The Sterling.

We are barely settled in our room when there is a rap on our door. Aunt Mavis opens the door to the extent of the chain guard. A husky voice bellows, "Yeah, yeah, what's up? Aunt Mavis, you look great!"

Aunt Mavis releases the chain, and she and Rolf hug affectionately. "I'll hug any man at any hour of the day or night who tells me that."

"Yeah, well I saw you two come in and I noticed your light was still on. I wanted to say hello. How was your trip?"

"It was tiring, and I'm suffering jet lag. But I'm more tired from spending the whole afternoon and evening with Roger and Francine. Come on in for a few minutes anyway. I am glad to see you." Aunt Mavis reaches out and embraces Rolf again.

I feel like a piece of motel furniture in the background, but I've become accustomed to not getting much of a greeting from Rolf. Besides, it's nice to see Rolf express genuine affection for someone in his life.

For the next three hours neither Mavis nor I say much, as Rolf dominates the conversation. He gives a detailed description of all the rooms of

Malfaits' house, the dirt and filth, the cats and the general unhealthiness of the conditions. "I guess you know by now it's really bad in their house."

"No, I don't know," Mavis interjects. "We spent the whole afternoon in the backyard. It was sort of one long picnic."

Rolf continues, "Things could be a whole lot better if Mother didn't have to worry about Dad. She can't keep up with the house and the yard and all that goes with it anymore--and then try to keep up with him, too."

Mavis asks, "What do you think ought be done about that, Rolf?"

"I don't know. I just don't know."

Mavis continues, "What are you doing about a job?"

"Oh, I've been working now and again."

"But what are you doing about a real job?"

"Well, you know there's not much around here in Ridgeview anymore."

"You told me a little while back you thought you'd like to go to Alaska again. If you go, what will you do with your stuff?"

"What do you mean my stuff? I ain't got much of anything."

Aunt Mavis persists, "I mean what will you do about your dog, Taco? What will you do with that gun collection? What about anything else you have in Francine and Roger's house?"

Rolf shakes his head. "I don't know. I just don't know."

I can't be still any longer. "Rolf, that's the kind of information I need to know, too. I *have* to know what you're thinking and what you want to do in regards to Mom and Dad--and what you want to do with all your things you have in their house. You've talked about going back to Alaska more than once. If you're going to do that, I need to know about a lot of stuff around their place before you go."

Rolf ignores me and continues facing Aunt Mavis, "Well, I'm about ready to just bag it all. It's damned hard. I have no authority. I have nothing. I'm flat busted. Here recently I went twenty days without eating just to see if I could. I've been surviving lately on a hamburger or two tacos a day--about $1.50 per day."

I don't know if Rolf wants Mavis and me to feel sorry for him or to give him money. I wonder who thought of the phrase *I haven't eaten for twenty days*, him or Dad? No one says anything for several minutes.

Rolf breaks the silence. "You know Betty, here, she just came down and took over. She went out and got a lawyer and proceeded with this guardianship thing. I was never asked to join in the process at all."

I can't help interrupting, "Rolf, that's not true. I asked you several times for over a year. You dogged me time after time on the phone and with appointments regarding the guardianship process."

Rolf glares at me and stabs his finger in my direction. "I never dogged no one on phone calls or anything else. I knew absolutely nothing about this guardianship thing until it had already got going."

"Rolf, how can you say that? You said you wanted the two of us to see the attorney, and when I made the initial appointment, you didn't show. You yourself made the follow-up appointment. We both attended together, and then we walked over to the appointment with the ad litem attorney, Mr. Mason. You *were* involved."

Rolf growls back, "I wasn't notified about any court hearings or decisions. You just got some judge to make the decision without an open hearing. All this shit has been unfair to me."

"Rolf, Rolf, you were there at the hearing. You're the one who directed us all to the right courtroom. You're the one who said that particular judge would be very fair to all of us. He was the one who heard your logging truck case. I don't know any of those people. I didn't arrange the hearing, and I didn't *get* a judge to do anything!"

Rolf's volume increases with each denial, "This whole process has been unfair to me. You're a liar about asking me to participate. You're a liar about me not meeting you for the lawyer's appointment. You're a liar about any phone calls. I never ever promised to call you at any time." Rolf's fingers repeatedly squeeze the arms of the chair as his body jerks forward almost as if he is keeping himself from being launched into the air. "You're a liar about all those phone calls and appointments, and you're a liar about talking to Mom about the lumber bills--and you said I was eavesdropping from the dining room and I wasn't. You're just a liar!"

I release a bit of a nervous laugh. "I guess calling one another a liar is part of dementia, whether the demented, the dementee, or the dementor does the lying. For right now, I see no purpose in this tirade. I agree to disagree."

Mavis has been a mute participant for several minutes. Her presence may have limited Rolf's name-calling to simply calling me a liar without all the other usual accompanying obscenities--and maybe it served to keep him in his chair.

Author and Rolf sit on new family automobile, 1948 Buick

I try to get away from our sibling bickering. "Rolf, we need to get back to the things we can solve. I'm supposed to help make Mom and Dad and their place safer and more livable. I have to know about all that stored stuff. All your boxes of personal stuff and those guns have no business in their house. I have been told in no uncertain terms by Mr. Manilow of Adult Protective Services that providing safety and supervision for Malfaits is my main job. And those guns should not be accessible to senile, incompetent persons. There is no insurance coverage on anything in the house right now either. Mr. Manilow says if lack of supervision continues to be an annotated problem with APS, I won't be a guardian next year at this time. The State will become the guardian, and their people for sure wouldn't know Rolf's stuff from Dad's. The State would just move it or sell it. You really have to decide what to do with your possessions. You can't keep saying, *I just don't know.*"

Rolf grips the chair-arms and leans in my direction, "The State or no one else better come in there tampering with my gun collection, or I might just have to use one of them on someone. That collection is very valuable, at least $40,000, and probably more. I damn well can't afford to leave it at my house in Newcastle. That house is old and kind of falling down. It's too run down to keep my gun collection there safely." He leans back in the chair. "You know, Mom and Dad aren't the only ones with tax problems either. I got unpaid back taxes on my place, too."

Mavis asks, "How much are your taxes there?"

"Oh, the total taxes are about $300 to $350 per year. The house ain't much, but the assessed value of the property is about $50,000. There's really two pieces with about 350 feet on the river."

I can't help but comment, "You sound like Mom and Dad--you've got too many assets, and they become stones around your neck. Couldn't you sell something to allow improvement of your own existence? Boats or guns or something? Selling something would help you, and at the same time Mom and Dad could live better and not have to be giving one-fourth of their monthly income for a mortgage lien against their house that really is your responsibility."

Rolf begins to ramble off on a tangent about his bad luck and his poor financial plight and how the debt consolidation became a necessity.

I become progressively more angry as he talks about the debt with no sense of obligation to pay it, no guilt for having made it, and no understanding of preventing his mother and father from having a more comfortable level of living.

Dear God, on this issue, I need another purple tulip.

My teeth hurt from clamping my jaws shut, but I hold my anger in check for the remainder of Rolf's visit. The evening ends in a blur of words exchanged between Mavis and Rolf about how late it is and jet lag. I am still clamping my jaws when Mavis closes the door after him. She hooks the security chain and turns back toward me, "My God, I'm glad he finally left!"

The next morning I depart from Ridgeview, and Aunt Mavis begins a whirlwind venture that is to be one of the longest weeks of her life. Both Mom and Dad mess in the rental car on more than one occasion, despite the plastic sacks and quilts which I had provided from my truck at the last minute. She and Mother 'lost' Dad when he was supposed to stay in the house while they went shopping. Another time Dad let the dog run off, and he went chasing after it in his fast shuffle with Mother screaming after him. In fact, Mother threw such a tantrum on the lost dog occasion that Mavis feared she was going to hit Dad with the dog's choker chain.

When I rejoin Mavis at the end of the week, she tells me, "Betty, if I stay here much longer, I think *I* may have a stroke!"

"Aunt Mavis, you have to know I love these people who are my parents, but they become less and less recognizable to me, except in occasional fragmented examples. Much of the time I feel I don't know them at all, and other times I don't want to know them. If a severe enough stroke occurred to both of them, I probably would sink to my knees and thank God! I don't mean to be evil in my thoughts, but I don't think I'm capable of doing all that needs to be done with them. I can't be all things to all people. There's not enough of *me!* I have this other life in which I've been very happy and I want to continue it. I feel as if this whole nasty situation is oozing over my entire life and devouring me. I know what I'm saying to you sounds unkind, but the poignancy, the guilt, the ambivalences are crushing!"

"Betty, I've been with them enough this week to know what you mean. And, if that double stroke situation occurs, we will probably both be on our knees giving thanks!"

Way inside myself I know we neither one really want that to happen, but this week Aunt Mavis has walked in my shoes. She does understand!

Mavis and I spend her last evening in Ridgeview in a local laundromat. She doesn't want to leave Malfaits with any extra work. Mother is again reluctant to provide $20.00 to do the wash. As usual, she only wants to give us $5.00. She finally gives in because Mavis is going to accompany me to the laundromat, and she trusts her to keep an eye on the money.

The wash is filthier than usual. Dad left thick fecal streaks in his shorts and the cats have added their deposits to the bedding. Probably with everyone gone so much during the week the cats had to develop new kitty litter repositories. Mavis and I both gag over our task, and we end up with $.50 change from the twenty dollar bill. We scrub ourselves with the remaining bleach and head out to one of the local all night cafes down near the mills to meet Rolf, so Mavis can say good-bye.

Rolf is sitting in a booth with a log truck driver friend when we arrive. He stands, but Aunt Mavis makes no attempt to be affectionate. She moves into the empty side of the booth, and I slide in next to her. Rolf sits opposite us next to his logger friend who makes no attempt to leave and who is not introduced. Rolf is tired and dirty, as he has worked steadily all week driving log truck. He seems happy to be driving again, but he quickly switches the conversation to bend Aunt Mavis' ear with his usual sad, hard luck story. "You know, it's damned hard for a man to make a living--just to make enough to scrape by."

Aunt Mavis waves her hand like an automobile window-wiper in front of her face. "Rolf, I don't have time to listen to that all over again. You need a job that will allow you to work steadily. You need to get a job where you know you will work year-round and have steady income."

"Yeah, yeah."

"Rolf, I've been with your mom and dad the whole week. I'm going to tell you some things, and I want you to listen because I don't have time to tell them over and over again. You need to move on with your life. You need to move those guns out of their house. And Taco is too much for your mom and dad to be chasing after. One of them is going to get hurt sooner or later trying to keep up with that big old dog--and it's not fair to the dog either. You need to take yourself *and* your dog somewhere else. You need to get both of you out of their house! Do I make myself clear?"

"I don't know. I just don't know."

I say nothing. The logger friend at the table says nothing.

Mavis continues, "I left messages a couple of times with the motel lady at The Sterling while I was out with Francine and Roger. I wanted you to come down and talk with your mom and dad *and* me. Did you get the messages?"

"Naw, I didn't get no messages. The managers, you know, they got their kid there now to help them run the place, but he never delivers anything. He's supposed to be helping them, but he ain't good for much."

I refrain from a comment about the likeness between their kid and Malfaits' kid. The motel lady had told me earlier when I checked in, 'I gave your note to Rolf--and I gave him the one from your aunt. I also told him, 'Rolf, brothers and sisters need to talk when dealing with family situations like what you folks have. You've got your aunt here now. That's your mother's sister, and you all need to talk and try to get all this mess straightened out.'

I don't bother to dispute Rolf about the delivery of the messages. He would lie again. It is peculiar though that other people such as truck drivers, loggers, and motel personnel know so much about Malfait family problems.

Rolf leans over in front of his silent logger friend toward my end of the table and asks abruptly, "Who's this Mr. Manilow from Adult Protective Services? I want to set him straight about a couple of things. One of them is that I did push Dad to hurry him to the car, but Dad tripped and fell."

Oh, God, please help me to say the right things here.

"Rolf, I just met Mr. Manilow two weeks ago myself, because he called and left an urgent message at the motel for me to come in to his office and see him. I had never talked to him before that. The purpose of his meeting with me was to inform me of the problems I have as a guardian. He stated them succinctly. Number one is supervision and number two is abuse. And, you, Rolf, are considered one of the abusers by filed reports. Don't ask me whose reports. I don't know. I didn't file them, and I didn't read them. Mr. Manilow didn't share those reports with me. I only know what I was told by him. If you want to know more than that, I'm sure you have a right to confer in greater detail and perhaps you should do that."

Rolf is quiet. His friend still says nothing.

After an awkward lull, Aunt Mavis brings our coffee date to a close. "Well, I hate to end this affair, but I have an early flight tomorrow, and I need to turn in."

Mavis begins to scoot out from our side of the booth, and I move and stand in the aisle. Rolf does not budge. His silent friend does not move. Mavis extends her hand across the table, and Rolf shakes her hand without looking up--a major contrast to their initial greeting.

The next morning Mavis and I are both up, showered and off early to pick up a drive-in breakfast for Malfaits, as she had promised to have coffee with them before her trip to Portland. Once at 516, Mavis and Mom eat and visit in the kitchen. I feed Taco and try to keep him away from Dad's food in the living room. Above the ruckus I can hear parts of the conversation.

"Now, Mavis, I want to go with you and Betty to the airport to say good-bye."

"Francine, I told you yesterday that's why I would come by and have coffee with you and Roger this morning. We can say our good-byes right here, and I'll go on to the airport by myself."

Mother comes into the living room and turns her attack on me, "Betty, you and Mavis could wait just a minute for me to get a coat on and go with you."

"Mother, I'm not going to discuss this with you. It just isn't going to work."

I open the front door and walk out to my truck, leaving Mother and Mavis to continue a heated exchange of words as they both follow me out the door.

"I don't know why you and Betty won't let me go. I wouldn't be in the way."

Mavis and I climb into our respective places in the truck cab. The baggage is piled high between us. Mavis points that out, but it's no deterrent to Mother.

Dad stands helplessly on the front step shading his eyes against the morning sunlight and staring off into space. Mother leans toward my open truck window and shouts, "I should be the one taking her to Portland! It's *my* sister!"

Mavis stifles a chuckle. "But, Francine, you can't drive this truck. I need Betty to drive me down there."

"I don't know why the two of you act like this. Why do you treat us this way?"

"Francine, you can see how much luggage I have. It's starting to rain, and these things have to be inside. There's barely room for me in here."

"We could all fit in there just fine. I don't know why you won't let me go."

I fold the mirror inward on my side to avoid hitting Mother, who has been leaning in toward us each time she shouts her retorts to Aunt Mavis. I slip the gear into reverse. In response to the slight jolt, Mother pulls back. I ease the truck down the driveway onto the street.

Mother stands on the sidewalk babbling as she swipes the over-used breakfast napkin across her eyes, "I don't understand why Dad and I can't go. I just don't know why you all shit on us so!"

I drive slowly away.

———— ❦ ————

CHAPTER 38

The Lull Before the Storm

GENERAL CONFUSION CONTINUES in Malfaits' household throughout my fall visits, guardianship or not. Conflict flares particularly whenever Rolf is in the house. At those times there is a drain on their food budget, and cash disappearances occur coincidentally with his visits. If these instances don't keep Mom and Dad stirred up, his angry verbalizations do, especially in regard to the regular reminders from Fibex Credit Union about past due payments.

A new twist in the overdue mortgage occurs when Mother and Dad receive notices addressed to them about unpaid taxes on Rolf's Newcastle property. They don't understand why they should be responsible for taxes on property they don't own and which is in another county. When I inquire at the credit union about this, the clerk verifies the assessed value of Rolf's property and indicates the current taxes are past due. She says the credit union also holds this property as collateral for the debt that Malfaits co-signed. Last year when Rolf did not pay these taxes, the credit union paid them and added the amount to the mortgage. She says it's their right to protect their collateral in this manner. That makes Rolf responsible, and Malfaits as co-signers, also share the responsibility.

I tend to side with my senile parents on this issue. Shortly after learning of the situation and when Rolf and I are in the Malfait kitchen by ourselves, I bring up the subject of the taxes on his property in Newcastle and tell him what I have learned.

"Yeah, yeah, that don't make any sense at all. I paid my taxes last year."

"But, Rolf, the credit union says you didn't. They say they paid them *for* you."

"That ain't exactly right. The credit union just got ahead of themselves. Yeah, they did pay them, but then I went in and paid them myself at the Grays Harbor County Courthouse. Then the Grays Harbor County Treasurer refunded that money to Fibex. I'm telling you, that's all been taken care of."

"Rolf, Mother and Dad are *not* going to pay your property taxes for you. That's never going to happen again, regardless of who paid them last year. I can't worry about their taxes *and* yours."

"Well, I can't pay taxes if I ain't got anything to pay them with! I don't know what I'm gonna do. I just don't know."

"Well, you better get to knowing! Malfaits have their own problems, and it seems like they get more of them every day. Now the neighbors are complaining about the old cars out front again. This week an abatement notice came addressed to *me*. Am I now guardian for their old cars?"

"So what's the big bitch from the neighbors? It ain't like those cars were just now dumped there."

"I imagine they are concerned with their property values. That old Buick on the driveway hasn't been moved for years. And the old Chev pulled up on the grass in the front yard won't run at all. It's rusty inside and out. I don't know why the neighbors are just now noticing these things, but their complaints are warranted. I imagine they don't like living next door to a junk yard."

Rolf laughs. "Yeah, my car probably gives them fits, too."

"It probably does. It's a regular Cheech and Chong number with the hole in the muffler, the crumpled fenders, and the polka-dot rust spots."

"You know, Betty, my dream is to get some bucks from the lottery and then get all of these old cars running and licensed and leave them parked out on the street and in the driveway. In fact, I'd like to add to the collection. Then as each one of them son-of-a-bitch'n neighbors comes round, I'd tell 'em just what I think. If they get angry and do me in, I'd like to be put face down in my casket, so they could kiss my ass!"

I want to tell Rolf it wouldn't matter which way he faces in his casket; both sides of him look about the same. I opt for a quieter approach, "You might feel differently if you owned one of these houses on either side or across the street from Mom and Dad."

"Yeah, yeah."

The squeaking of the screen door on the back porch brings our exchange to a halt as Mother comes into the kitchen from working in the garden. I remind her, "Mom, you need to get ready to go with me to pay the bills."

"Oh, I know. But, Betty, I can pay those bills on my own."

I ignore her response. "I left a new case of Depends in your bedroom behind the door. You go get ready, and we'll both go. Okay?"

"Oh, all right." She passes through the kitchen to the living room, picks up the latest issue of Sunset, and sits down on the couch and begins to browse.

Despite Mother's griping, the new automatic banking procedure has dramatically improved financial accountability. Mom and Dad still routinely spend about $8.00 per day for their 'coffee' trips. That expense comes out of Mother's retirement check of $407 per month, which I have continued to let come directly to her. Managing that amount of money gives them both some sense of independence and responsibility. It's a major self-esteem thing. Even if they "lose" small amounts, I think it's important for them to handle some money. Mother understands she can spend $100.00 per week on eating out, groceries, gifts or whatever; but she cannot give money to Rolf or anyone else. If she does, she won't have coffee money. I take care of the rest of the bills from the automatic banking account. I have told Rolf in no uncertain terms if he takes money from them, he'll be taking it from their food money. He assures me that will not happen. He is working more hours now. I still don't trust him.

Teaching Mother to wear Depends has been a major accomplishment this fall, and probably one of the greatest challenges of my life. She definitely needs to be in some kind of protection all the time now. She is fairly cooperative but forgetful--and she often discards the used pads in the bathtub for me to "wash" on my next trip down. Each time I simply start over and re-teach, but if I needed a reminder of Rolf's poor geriatric skills, it is brought out dramatically relative to this problem.

Rolf has followed Mother to the living room, and I hear him nagging at her, "Betty told you to get one of them Depends on. You don't need to be sitting there reading <u>Sunset</u>. You need to get to those Depends."

I call out from the kitchen, "Mom, I left that new case behind your bedroom door. I've opened the box for you. Please hurry and get one on, so we can get to town before the stores close."

Mother continues perusing <u>Sunset</u> as she answers, "I don't need one, and I don't need you *and* Rolf telling me I do."

I call back, "I'll be done here in a minute, and you said you wanted to go to town with me. You can't go if you're not ready."

Mother calls back, "I don't need to wear one of those things."

Rolf gets up from the couch where he has been sprawled out watching the news and goes into their bedroom. He drags the whole huge cardboard economy warehouse box of seventy-two pads back into the middle of the living room and jerks the flaps open in front of where Mother is sitting. "Oh yes you do need one of these things!" Rolf waves the Depend in front of her. "Here, go put this thing on!"

Mother lowers the magazine and squints up at him, "No."

Rolf hurls the Depend into her lap and shouts, "Yes!"

"I'm not going to wear that thing!"

Rolf leans in close to her face, "Oh, yes, you are!"

I rush to the living room. "Stop this, both of you!" I step between Rolf and Mother and pick up the Depend, hiding it under my arm. I lean close and whisper, "Shhh, Mother. Please, this is really a very private issue--a *very* private bathroom task. Will you *please* come with me?"

She puts the magazine down, pulls herself up from the couch, and follows me to the bathroom. Behind the closed door I tell her, "Mother, you know women just sometimes have to do this because we strain or sneeze or even laugh and the urine leaks out. It happens to all of us sometimes. You don't want to do that in my car or truck or at a restaurant or anyplace else. Rolf doesn't think of things like that. Men just don't understand this stuff. It's really a very private woman thing. Okay?"

From her seated position on the toilet, she takes the Depend from me and begins to fumble with the tabs. "Well, I wish I'd get over this old flow soon. I don't know what makes it last so long."

I step back a bit to give her some privacy and chant softly, "Irregular! Irregular! Irregular!" Mother pays no attention to my whispers."

Usually at times like this there is a barrage of expletives that flash through my mind--and sometimes my mouth--because I really think Rolf is crazier than Mom and Dad. My friend Doris Musieleski recently sent me a book by Joyce Lansdorf entitled Irregular People, and reading it has been very helpful. I have come to think of Rolf as the epitome of *irregular*, and he is never going to change. He is incapable of truth, and he is never going to be dependable for anything! I'm going to have to work as best I can on my own with guardianship duties--right here in the bathroom and everywhere else! I can at least avoid my own angry blow-ups and the recitation of derogatory expletives that churn through my mind following events such this one.

"Irregular--irregular--irregular."

Actually, I think when Rolf is on the scene, I feel worse about him than I do about Malfaits. When he is away driving a log truck or traveling in the big rig with his friend Mike, everything goes smoother with them. The accounting of money in Mother's little square purse will balance within a dollar. Both she and Dad are happier. They think more clearly and look better--not clean, but better. I see no way to stop Rolf's parasitic behavior until I can move Mom and Dad out of this house and out of his grasp--or move *him* and his stuff out of *their* house. Maybe then I could deal with more mundane aspects of the bizarre nature of their existence.

Mother concludes her bathroom duties and flushes the toilet. She even rinses her hands in a trickle of cold water. "Well, that does feel better. Thank you, Betty."

I follow her back to the living room where she jerks to a sudden stop. "Good God Almighty, Betty, what's this? We can't have this big box of

Depends right here in the middle of the living room. What if someone should stop by?"

"You're right, Mom. Give me a hand and we'll drag it back into your bedroom."

Rolf remains cemented to the couch glaring at the two of us as we labor to move the big cardboard carton back to the bedroom.

Mother and I make our departure to do errands. Throughout the afternoon as we perform our bill-paying and shopping I contemplate a number of things between moments of irrelevant banter. Could I manage Mom and Dad whether Rolf was present or not? I'm not sure. There are so many lost items. Yes, I found the deed to the Whidbey property, but that's only one paper. I've searched the back bedroom and the rest of the downstairs for other legal papers but to no avail. Where are their insurance policies? Where are their wills? I know they updated wills a few years back. I remember discussing that issue with them, but they didn't give me copies of the new wills. They did ask me to be their executor, as I had been named to that task in their previous will. Like the property deed, they probably never recorded their wills.

Mother emerges from a local store front, having paid her electric bill and her garbage bill. As I rush to the other side of the truck and place the single step stool for her to use to get in more easily, she tells me, "Oh Betty, the girls are so nice in there. They were all glad to see me doing my bills all on my own again."

I help her with the seat belt, close the door, and toss the little stool in the truck bed. I mumble aloud as I race around the back of the truck, "Yeah, so I suppose you could have driven yourself down here, too. And you could probably find all the lost things: purses, keys, mail, bills, wills, insurance--then there's Taco's messes on the floor, and his running away. Hell's bells, you guys mess yourselves, but you don't run away. *I'd* like to run away. Shut up, Betty. You sound like they do."

I climb back in the truck and as we head for Fibex Credit Union I silently think, I hate this bill most of all. I would like to be able to get rid of it. I can't refinance it, because it isn't theirs--it's Rolf's. I can't get a loan anyplace else without putting up my own money. And because Washington is a community property state, I can't do anything like that without my husband's signature. Being a guardian for my parents should not require me to encumber Don's and my family finances. I wouldn't mind doing that, and Don probably wouldn't care, but I certainly would not do that for Rolf's benefit. Besides, even though I'm sure Don would co-sign for a loan, I cannot in good conscience let him do that because of old wounds stemming from Malfaits' slander of him. I could never ask him to financially risk for them now.

In the credit union Mother chooses to wait in a line for the clerk who usually helps us.

"Oh, hello, Mrs. Malfait. How are you today?"

She continues to chat about other trivia as she watches Mother count out the required cash for the mortgage payment.

I stand like a dead tree stump. My mind is racing and my jaws are clamped. *Yeah, we're fine. Dad's fine. Everything's fine! The moss is heavy on the roof at 516. The last windstorm blew more shingles off. The roof now leaks, and for the moment I can only put buckets under the leaky places and hope for a dryer spell and maybe enough money in their next paycheck to buy a large tarp. That's how I'm protecting the collateral on this loan. What are you people doing to help?*

I am in deep fecal material in other ways, as well. Urinary incontinence is routine, and bowel incontinence is an occasional problem for both Mom and Dad. I can't tell if they have 'a touch of something' or if it's improper diet. This last wash I had to haul the bed comforter outside and hose it off on the driveway, scrub it with PineSol with a garage broom, and hose it down again. Then I rolled it into a plastic bag and walked all over the plastic covering to squeeze the excess water out. At the laundromat I washed it twice. It still has a fecalistic odor. I am in such deep shit you people couldn't help if you wanted to.

Yeah, everything's fine!

Mother turns and takes my arm and we exit the credit union. I feel her tiredness in the tremble of her hand pulling on my sleeve. "Betty, it feels so good to be doing this all by myself."

I return Mother to 516. I make a number of feeble excuses for myself and depart as quickly as I can.

CHAPTER 39

—✸✸✸—

What Happened to the Last Seven Years?

BACK IN MY "sterling motel home" my mental thrashing continues into the wee hours of the late November, 1990, night. When did this mess start? I don't really know. The first real indicator was the family blow-up with the lies about our children and about Don in the summer of 1983. Next was the four-year separation of our families, then Dad's stroke the summer my family and I were in Florida, and Mother's call for help in August of that summer. I've been flailing away with two trips per month since then and watching continued deterioration. Dad has been totally in "la-la land" for over a year, and Mother is progressively slipping deeper into the "la-la-quicksand." He's taking her down with him, and he doesn't even know it--neither does she!

I continue to be incredulous watching this story unfold before my eyes. I've worked hard, but for the most part I've been ineffective and my accomplishments have been minimal. I may have won in the Depend conflict this afternoon, but Mother still outdoes me in almost every verbal confrontation, whether it has to do with going to coffee at Ocean Espresso or moving Dad to a nursing home. She out-maneuvered all the business people today as she expounded on how improved Dad is and how much better she feels.

She and Dad are bonded in years of loving devotion--and now they are bonded in their senility.

Rolf? Rolf is bonded to himself.

So far losses and dead ends outnumber positive pathways in this guardianship thing. Why did I bother to get into this mess? Why *am* I here? What have I accomplished? Am I such a fool I cannot see what is happening to them may happen to me? After all, I do have the same genes. What does *honor* one's father and mother really mean? How has guardianship helped in that aspect?

I am so damned tired!

Despite all the nastiness of the last few years, I love my parents and care what happens to them. I'm not so sure Mother believes that or trusts my judgment as to what is best for them. But even in his senility, I think Dad does. He knows I want to help, and that I am trying to somehow make their lives better. No matter how much hatred Mother may eventually feel for me, at this point in my best judgment both of them need more concentrated care than I can provide through a work visit every two weeks. They won't allow anyone else in their home, but I just can't do this any longer! They are both slipping away. I can't stop that. I can't help them. And if I don't protect myself better, I may catch up to them!

The verbal fighting between them is almost constant now. They harp away at one another incessantly--what an old fool Dad is--how little Mother does around the house--how she won't help Dad at all. I've noticed Mother sometimes pushes or shoves him. I actually thought she pushed him off the steps the other day when he fell, although he said, 'Oh no, Mama wouldn't do that. I fell.' No matter who pushed whom, the bottom line is they need more attention than my visits.

I *have* to make the arrangements to move them from 516, house that Daddy built or not.

Sometime in the early morning hours, exhausted sleep finally crushes my mental flailing.

When I return to 516 the next morning, it is Mother who brings me back to current issues seeming almost positive and logical in her words and thoughts as she and I share a morning cup of coffee. "You know, Betty, Dad and I had a 23-pound turkey for Thanksgiving last year. It was wonderful, and we enjoyed it so much. When you and I shopped yesterday I saw turkey sales almost everywhere we went--really nice big birds--and cheap. We didn't get to do much for Thanksgiving this year.

It just sort of passed by. It was last week, right? The kids are both away in college and you and Don only had that Thursday and Friday off. We all really missed out. You know, Christmas is coming soon, and they've got all those left-over Thanksgiving birds. Dad and I just need to get us one of those nice big birds to have for Christmas."

"Mom, I'll see that you get all the necessary things to do that. I'm coming back in two weeks, and there will be plenty of turkeys in pre-Christmas grocery sales."

"Oh, that would be wonderful! Then, you and Don and the children can all come down and help us enjoy it at Christmas. We can all be together for Christmas."

"Uhhh..."

Oh, God, how did we get from buying a cheap left-over Thanksgiving turkey to this? I feel the verbal dance revving up.

Mother persists, "You *will* be coming down here for Christmas, won't you?"

"Don and I will see you people for sure during the holidays. I don't know about Nick and El. They're both working now. They may not have enough time off to make a trip down here."

"Well, everyone could make it just for Christmas Day, couldn't they? Dad and I have been talking, and we want us to all be together this holiday."

Dear God, now what do I say? She has no comprehension that we can't all get in her kitchen to cook and eat, and none of us would want to. The dining room is so piled up I haven't seen the table for years and Taco is using it for a doghouse. No one in their right mind could relax and enjoy Christmas in this wretched house, and there is no way to explain that lovingly. Oh, God, I know I have to be strong and tactful. I do need Your guidance. I do need a purple tulip!

CHAPTER 40

⸺ ✸ ⸺

Purple Tulips are not Always in the Cracks

of the Sidewalk in the Snows of December

ON DECEMBER 13TH I return to Ridgeview to shop with Mother for the promised Christmas turkey. Earlier this morning Dad had a non-responsive siege--unable to talk or answer questions, just staring blankly. Suspecting he was having another stroke, Mother and Rolf took him to the hospital.

I arrive in early afternoon and am able to see Dr. Kettle, who gives me an update on Dad's condition. "Actually Mr. Malfait has *not* had another stroke. His deteriorating symptoms are relevant to Alzheimer's. This collapse is just a more dramatic step of decline than what you have been observing over the time period since I last talked to you."

"So how long will he need to recuperate to a level of release? That's about all Mother—"

"Betty, Mr. Malfait will *not* be going home. There are no exceptions. He will be in need of full-time nursing care from now on."

This news does not translate as a purple tulip.

The remainder of December is full of paper work, transferring properties to Mother's name, trying to qualify Dad for Medicaid help--and the eventual move to a nursing home. Interspersed with all this are several depressing visits to the hospital. Dad is weak. He can't speak. He mumbles unintelligibly. He isn't always aware of who is in the room. He can't use his arms nor hands. His heart beat is stable, but he has some kidney and liver problems.

Alas, I have joined ranks with Rolf--*I just don't know*!

While Dad is in the hospital and Mother is with him most of the time, Rolf and I work together cleaning the house. We move everything out of their bedroom and scald and disinfect as much as possible. We use commercial rug shampoo equipment throughout the house. We do a back-breaking laundromat wash that hits an all-time high of $36.75. It seems as if Mother has as many sheets as the hospital, and in the days prior to taking Dad to the hospital, she used them all.

I buy new night clothes for her, and on one of those evenings after she has spent the day with Dad at the hospital, I get her to at least do a wash basin spit-bath. It's been years since a real bath. She snuggles into her newly cleaned bed and bedroom, smiles happily, and begins reading the newspaper. I pick up a part of the paper and sit down in the chair beside her bed.

She lowers the paper and looks at me, "I'm awful tired tonight, Betty. I miss Dad so much, and I'll miss him again tonight, especially his old hot feet. He makes the whole bed warm."

I smile. "Yeah, I know, Mom. Rolf and I are both tired, too. And from the size of the wash we did today, it must have been *very* warm in your bed recently."

Mother tips her chin down and grins mischievously at me over her reading glasses. "It sure was! You know, the other night Dad just rolled right over up close to my back and pissed all over me. It was a huge flood. But, you know, he didn't know he did that. He didn't mean to do it. But you're right, it sure was warm!" She chuckles. "You know, when he gets better and comes home, he won't even remember he did that. He wouldn't believe it if I told him he did it."

"Mother, he may not be home for a while. The doctor says he has to go to a nursing home."

"Well, I think I could care for him here. I could bring him the bed-pan, and I could bring him food."

"No, Mother, this time you can't. It's taking several nurses around the clock to work with him. He can't feed himself. He can't use his arms and legs. He can't talk. He can't go to the bathroom. He's hooked up to all kinds of machinery. You can't do that here. You *have* tried really hard, and you've done a good job trying to care for him since his stroke, but, Mom, this time it's out of our hands. If he ever regains use of hands and legs and can feed himself and go to the bathroom, we can talk about his coming home then."

"How long will that be?"

"Well, Mom, it could be a few weeks--or it could be never. You don't want him to collapse and die here in this house in his own urine and feces, do you?"

"No, but I could bring him a bedpan."

"But, Mom, when he collapsed on the way to the bathroom this time, could you get him up and to the hospital by yourself?"

"No, I couldn't move him at all, but I called Rolf and got him to help. The two of us got him to the hospital."

"See, Mother, right now, Dad's care is way too much for you."

"Which one of those doctors said Dad had to go to a nursing home?"

"Both Dr. Putnam and Dr. Kettle. All the hospital reports consistently recommend that."

Mother still hates Dr. K., but at this point I am thankful for doctors whose sons pursue the medical profession, because she is somewhat accepting of Dr. Putnam's opinion. Young Putnam is the son of the eye-ear-nose-and-throat doctor who helped Dad in years past and from whom Dad got the infamous prescription for Valium.

"Well, that Dr. K. doesn't know shit, but if Dr. Putnam thinks it's time for a nursing home, he must know a thing or two. He fixed Dad's nose pretty good. We used to take them jelly and elk steaks over to their house. Boy, Doc sure loved that."

Mother is quiet for a moment.

I am not about to distinguish between the two Dr. Putnams.

"Here, Betty, take my glasses and paper. I have to get my rest if I'm going to get to the hospital early and be with Dad."

I take the glasses and paper, rise from the chair and kiss her on the cheek. She rolls over with her back to me and mumbles, "Thanks for all your help and hard work today. Goodnight."

The next several days involve many trips to the hospital. Dad is more alert, seems to be trying hard to sit up, to eat, and to be cooperative. Rolf and I continue cleaning other parts of the house, although I'm wondering if he isn't un-stacking and re-stacking a lot of the stuff in the back bedroom. He wants me to go shopping for a bar or handle to put near the front door step for Mother, and he wants to look at a shower that might be installed for her. I'm wondering if Rolf is looking out for Rolf at their expense, and yet I'd like to think better of him. Mother does need the handle on the doorstep--and, oh my God, yes, to a shower!

By the end of the week Dad is more alert, but he still can't talk understandably nor use his hands or arms. Mostly when we visit we just sit and Mother asks him a thousand times if he wants her to peel him an apple and slice it real fine and bring it to him tomorrow. He grunts back a thousand times, No.

As Dad manages to eat better, Mother gets more excited about how well he is progressing, as if food intake is the only criterion for his getting out of the hospital. One evening after he eats most of his dinner with the assistance of a nurse's aide, he seems especially relaxed until suddenly he has a siege of 'flying feces' like I've never seen before, even in the worst of baby diapers. He messes everything in his bed. Barbara, his nurse, gets him up and to the bathroom; and with great difficulty finally gets him cleaned up, changes his bed, settles him on a potty chair and cleans up the bathroom. As soon as she gets him from the potty chair back into bed, he repeats the whole process--and this time, perhaps due to his weakness and the urgency, she asks me to help her steady him and get him to the bathroom. He is agitated by this whole process, but Barbara is firm, controlled and professional. She has definitely earned the "purple-brown heart-shaped stain smeared across the front of her uniform.

During the remainder of this same evening, Dad does his fecalistic flying flatulent number three more times. Though his speech has been slurred for days, each time he has no trouble with a loud "God-damn." The third time in the bathroom he plops down with a mushy splat on the toilet seat, looks down around himself and clearly states, "Oh shit! God-damned shit!"

Barbara and I looked at each other as we steady him from each side of the toilet and simultaneously echo, "Yes, God-damned shit!" All three of us laugh. Laughter eases the tension for Dad, too, and he tries harder to cooperate and let Barbara wash him and to struggle back to bed with her help.

God, I know You understand our desperation, and even our disrespectful tone. I do thank You for the Barbaras of the world. Please help us all to understand and to do what needs to be done at this time.

Later as Mother and I return to 516 and she is unlocking the front door, she pauses and turns to me, "I just couldn't have done what you and Barbara did tonight. I guess Dad *will* have to be moved to the nursing home--at least for a while."

Almighty God, thank you for another purple tulip.

CHAPTER 41

Oh, God, Why Don't You Take Him?

"MOM, I'M SORRY it was such a horrible time at the hospital tonight, but I'm glad you're trying to understand."

Mother returns to the task of opening the door, and we enter the dimly lit living room. As I close the front door, Mother startles me as she barks, "What's that? What's in that big bag? Who's moving my things out of here?" She tugs at the knot tied in the top of a bulging garbage bag in the middle of living room.

"Mother, Mother, wait, don't open that. That's a bag of garbage Rolf and I didn't get out to the dumpster today."

"That's not garbage. You guys are loading up my things and moving them out."

"Mom, no, listen--it's filled with your used Depends and all those old papers that were on the floor beside your bed and wet with urine. It's part of the cleaning Rolf and I have been doing. We just didn't get the bag out to the dumpster."

"Well, I've got ceramic things missing, and I don't want them thrown out. Let me see what's in this bag?" She jerks on the plastic knot making it tighter..

"Mother, please don't open it. It really is used Depends and old newspapers soaked with urine."

"Who pissed on newspapers? I certainly didn't do that!" She claws at the side of the bag. "I want to see what's in this bag!"

"Mom, I took those newspapers out of your bedroom and since Dad is in the hospital and no one else is here. I guess you're the one who peed in them."

Without looking up Mother shouts, "Well, I'll have you know I did no such thing. I never have done that!"

"Mother, it's not like you did it purposefully. You probably just stood up when you got up in the morning, and you couldn't get to the bathroom in time."

"I never did any such thing. I didn't do that. Rolf must have done that."

"Mother, please, spare me. Rolf has problems, but he doesn't have that one. I packed this bag myself.

"Okay, okay, Mom, I give up. Here, let me help you." I twist and pick until I loosen the knotted slick black plastic. "Do I have to empty it all out here in your living room?"

Mother gropes the content of the bag, and the stench puffs up at us. "Well, no, but I didn't piss on any newspapers!"

"No, I guess you didn't." I gather the top of the plastic bag muttering under my breath, "Actually, you're right. No matter where you're standing the urine usually misses the newspaper and the plastic protective runners, too." I look up at her, "Have you seen enough?"

"Yes. My god, we need to get this nasty mess out of here before it stinks up the whole house!"

I twist the top of the bag and re-tie the knot as the doorbell rings. Rolf's voice calls through the closed wicket, "Hey, it's me. What's going on in there?"

I unlock the door and continue my mumbling. "Keep laughing, Betty! Irregular! Irregular! Irregular! They're all irregular! *I'm* irregular!"

Rolf enters the living room with both Mother and me blabbing out bits and pieces of the garbage bag episode. He laughs heartily as he hoists the huge, awkward black plastic blob to his shoulder. As I open the front door for him, he shrugs, "See, Sis, you're just like me. Welcome to the club."

I grit my teeth to squelch a surge of denial at my likeness to him, as well as fend against the cold, ripping wind sucking through the open door. I grab a couple of shopping bags full of newspapers and kitchen garbage and follow Rolf into the cold darkness around the house to the alley whispering my mantra into the wind, "Irregular! Irregular! Irregular!"

When we return to the house, Mother has the eleven o'clock news on high volume. I negotiate with her for a wee bit lower volume, and then we all try to concentrate on the most recent news from the Middle East. Rolf becomes an echo to the newscaster. My silent irritation to his know-it-all attitude about everything from Saddam Hussein to racial violence and the Ku Klux Klan causes me to depart for The Sterling early. The cab of my truck becomes my private altar.

Dear God, I know I'm tired and frustrated, but please don't let me be just like Rolf. I continue to see him as part of the problem. I feel like I'm working as hard as I'm able to, but it's like I'm trying to catch a handle on a whirling merry-go-round. I see the handle. I grab. I miss. I get further and further behind. My achievements are limited and almost useless. God, I'm really trying to function according to Your will. Please forgive my shortcomings. All that I've done I've tried to do for my parents' best interest, and I know that I've been trustworthy and I've shown integrity. When I lay my head to the pillow, I sleep calmly in your care, and I'm thankful for that- -well, at least most times. On the other hand, maybe that's because I'm so damned tired half the time I fall asleep immediately anyway. Tonight is such a night--God, I'm so tired.

God, why? Why do you allow this situation? I can't do anything about it. We begin to die the day we're born, but it's so gradual. This is no longer gradual--it worsens day by day. I don't ever want to be eighty years old. Tonight the hospital seemed full of people like Dad who have been so vivacious in their living. Some of them I even knew when I was a child. Now they are lying in their beds covered in plastic diapers, bedsores, and soaked in their own urine and horrendous fecal messes. Why? Mother has been more tender toward Dad than I've known her to be for years. I know she hurts, senility or not. My own heart breaks for both of them. Oh, God, if Dad could roll the clock back ten years and see the future and the image of himself being diapered, washed in intimate places by a stranger, being disinfected for messy bedsores and babbling, groaning, and trying to feed himself and stringing green strained spinach through his beard making him look like a troll from under the bridge, he would walk to his bedroom, load his 30-06 and do a medication number on himself with lead. Oh, God, he was such a vibrant, physical, hard-working, talkative man. For his own dignity, he just wouldn't have endured the image that would have been forecast. Oh, God, why don't you take him?

CHAPTER 42

‒⊗⊗⊗‒

What Do You Want Me to Do Now?

MOTHER CONTINUES TO be vigilant in her hospital visits, but she often cries and is sad. In her own fragmented thinking, she must know Dad isn't any better; and no matter how much she says it, she knows she can't care for him ever again. It hurts so much to watch her gradually letting go, submitting to the agony of her own defeat. I wonder if senility prevents full recognition of defeat. Maybe those who are not senile suffer more because they understand what is happening? Or do they? What is all this for? My family and I are not alone in this dilemma. Hospitals are crowded with patients and families struggling with problems and decisions similar to ours.

In the next few days I find my roles as daughter and guardian in conflict. Malfaits have no funds for nursing home care. Dad has too much in assets to qualify for Medicaid, even though I have transferred all property to Mother's name. Nursing homes all want cash up front, and they don't care whose. More than once it is suggested that it be my cash. Hospitals don't want these deteriorating patients any longer than absolutely necessary for them to die, and my job as the guardian is to assure the best care possible to keep Dad alive. I have repeated my painful family history and the sequence of events leading to a court-appointed guardianship so many times I *am* a broken record. Each social worker type listens sympathetically and pledges their best effort to help me and my family, but nothing happens. Everyone wants cash, and no one seems to care that the only cash Malfaits have is not even enough for the first month in a nursing home--and even then using it for Dad would be taking food money away from Mother

The doctors remain adamant Dad is to be discharged and sent to a nursing home facility. As his guardian I refuse to sign the discharge papers, and my obstinacy causes me to be referred to an upper level hospital administrator for a conference. She is firm and emphatic, "Betty, it's your obligation to sign these discharge papers. That's what you have to do as your father's guardian. You have to figure out how this transfer to a nursing home is to be taken care of--how it is to be paid for. That's *your* responsibility. We've done everything we can for you. He needs to be in nursing home care, and we need the hospital bed space. He *must* be discharged tomorrow. We really can't help you any further."

I sit in silence, rub the dry skin on my forehead, and wipe away the crustiness around my eyes from earlier tears. Despite my blurred vision, I concentrate on a spot on the desk where the reddish swirls of mahogany meet the gold-plated name on Dr. Something-or-Other's desk pen set.

On the other side of the perfectly arranged desk, the hospital administrator closes my father's file and reflects her helplessness with pursed lips, wrinkled brow, and a slow wagging of her head. She introduced herself, but I can't recall her name. It's not the same as the name on the gold name-plate on the desk. I wonder if she's a doctor. I wonder if she's a daughter. I wonder if she's ever been a guardian.

I lift my head and our eyes meet. "Well, Ma'am--I suggest *you* call a special meeting of all the doctors who have waited on my father--brilliant as they are--and I suggest you gather all your hospital administrative colleagues. You all come down to his room and personally pick him up and chuck my emaciated, frail, senile, bed-sore-infected father--and his discharge papers--out the front door of this merciful, sanitized, Catholic hospital right under the statue of the Virgin Mary on your front lawn. Then, *I* will call the *Ridgeview Daily* and we can all sit down together and do a feature story on hospital and societal elder care, emphasizing the transitions from home and family to the hospital and then to the ultimate comfort zone--the nursing home."

The prim figure moves Dad's file to the side of her desk and wags her head a bit more vigorously. "No, no, no--we don't want to do that. We'll have to think on this some more. I'm sure we can work something out."

"Well, I'm not so sure. What will you all do tomorrow if I walk out of here and go home? You people can call the honorable Judge Fox of the Superior Court of this county, and you can determine who has the authority to admit Dad to a nursing home. Who will pay? And how much? You people can then all put your heads together and figure out who will be an effective guardian for Malfaits. I have done my very best for years now--and somehow it's just not enough!"

I push the heavy chair away from the imposing mahogany desk with its fancy gold name plate of Dr. Somebody-or-Other. I rise, turn away and silently leave the administrator's office.

Standing on the front steps outside the hospital, I suck in the cold, crisp December air. I am angry and frustrated beyond words, and yet words come. Even if my only recipient is the statue of the Virgin Mary on the lawn in front of me, I mutter aloud to her—and anyone else who may be in proximity. *"This whole mess is so complicated. It's totally impossible! I can't do this any more! Why do I have to? It's not really my problem.*

"Much of this hospital mess—nursing home care—who's responsible— much of it would not have had to be if Malfaits had done their legal business correctly. It's not just un-filed property deeds. If they had updated their wills more frequently and talked about their wishes for final care of themselves—if they had given copies of their wishes to appropriate people. They should have granted a Durable Power of Attorney years ago, or at least Mother should have done it after Dad had the stroke three years ago. Any transfer of property should have occurred at that time.

"Damn it, people should plan as well for their deaths as they do for events in life such as weddings, education, and births!

"Nobody listens to me—not Mom, Dad, Rolf—not hospital admin-istrators—not even you!" I shake my truck keys at the Virgin Mary.

I should probably be thankful there is no one else listening to me—at least not right now. There's a crispness in the air and huge, ominous, gray clouds bulging in the darkened sky. I move along the sidewalk to my truck, unlock the door and slide in across the cold, scratchy seat, clenching my teeth against further verbal expounding.

At my "sterling home" a hot shower and clean sheets offer minimal comfort. I pick up the Gideon Bible which I had been reading and left on the nightstand this morning. I pitch it into the nightstand drawer, "So much for useless Biblical platitudes!" I paw through some old magazines in the drawer, "I'd get as much help from one of these as I would from the Bible." I snatch up a tattered copy of the October issue of <u>Readers' Digest,</u> and take my frustration out on the already abused, ill-fitting nightstand drawer as it resists my slamming efforts. I flop onto the bed and begin reading the magazine front to back.

On page 124 is a story entitled "Miracle Comeback of Dave Dravecky," an incredibly touching story which concludes with a statement that, 'Life isn't always fair, at least in the short run, but the Bible taught us not to confuse life with God. When you're confronted with trouble, you don't ask, 'Why me?' You ask God, 'What do you want me to do in this situation?'.'

Okay, God, what do you want me to do in this situation? Gideon Bible or not, I guess you're going to talk to me, even when I'm angry with you, and even if it's through Readers' Digest. I do believe my faith in you is no longer just an intellectualization of Sunday School lessons and Bible stories. You have been real and warm and comforting. I have felt your presence whenever I've called out to you in several instances over the past few years. I do believe each person must confront adversity in the process of living, whether it's death, or war, or divorce, or Alzheimer's. If that person calls for your help, you always answer. I do not think I could have reached the level of human understanding and compassion that I have without each of the incidents that caused me to cry out and ask you for yet another Purple Tulip. Thank you, Oh, God, for each one of them.

What do you want me to do now?

No voice answers me back. No angels appear. I fall asleep.

In the loneliness of the less-than-sterling Sterling, I open the drapes the following morning to see four inches of clean stark white snow.

Hello, God, is that you? I still don't know which way to go or what to do, but I need another purple tulip--and since I now have the snows of December, I guess I can just open the door and start looking along the cracks of the sidewalk.

Perhaps Dad himself is the purple tulip, and I've been concentrating so much on my own inadequacies that I've missed your direction. Oh, God, I would like to get in my truck and go home today. Let Judge Fox or St. Mary's Hospital or whomever have a go at this guardianship. On the other hand, I know I'm in the short run of this whole game. There is a larger picture. God, you've never abandoned me before. Please be with me today.

By the time I get to the hospital, Dad is somehow miraculously qualified for Medicaid, despite the Whidbey property. Plans for moving him to the nursing home have been finalized and are in progress. No one in hospital administration summons me to any office. Only a social worker, one I have never met before, stops by his hospital room with the discharge papers for signing. And she asks me to keep a follow-up appointment at Department of Social and Health Services, an appointment she has made for this afternoon. Mother is sad, but she's already talking about how those nice folks at the hospital have been able to get Dad into the nursing home located right here behind the hospital. She can walk or ride the bus to see him every day until he gets home.

I know in my head and in my heart Dad will never return to 516.

The clouds which have been accumulating over Ridgeview for the past two days release a bounty of snow throughout the day. When I get to the DSHS offices I am told the appointment is canceled due to the snow. Their next available time is Christmas Eve at 3:00 PM. They are sorry my drive is three hours and fifteen minutes and it's the day before a holiday, but this interview must be done as soon as possible, and that is their earliest available appointment time. I have no choice. I have to accept the appointment.

A few days later, although highway conditions are treacherous, I arrive at DSHS offices on time. Sparse, powdery snowflakes tease the cold air, occasionally sticking to my eyelashes, as I labor across the parking lot with my two briefcases tugging at my aching shoulders. I brought every possible court document, bill, check book, and bank statement which I thought might be at all helpful.

The DSHS waiting room is occupied by only a couple of people. A man in a tattered red and black-checkered flannel shirt hunches over on a gray metal folding chair, hands clasped in his lap, staring at the client counter and tapping one foot. A woman sits stiffly on a brown metal folding chair on the opposite side of the room. She clutches a baby bundled in a plaid car blanket close to her over-sized blue and gold baseball letterman jacket. Before I can settle into a bronze-colored metal chair in the middle of the row between the two of them, a door to the right bearing large black letters 'Private" opens, and a woman steps out and calls my name. She's a small, harsh looking woman--no make-up, short mouse-brown hair which she keeps pushing behind her ear on one side. She's wearing a heavy, drab, olive green wool sweater, blue jeans and snow boots with a border of fur around the boot tops. She calls my name again before I even have time to pick up my two brief cases. I don't think she wants to be here any more than I do.

Once in her office the DSHS person gets immediately into inquiry of Malfait money matters. "First off, give me all your mom and dad's bank statements from December 1st of last year. Include the most recent one of December 1st of this year. I need their property tax statements, too."

I begin extracting the requested statements from one of my briefcases.

"Right now let me see your current checkbook for them."

I leave the first briefcase search for the bank statements and rummage through my purse for their checkbook.

"Do you keep a budget book?"

"Yes."

"Let me see that, too."

I hand the checkbook across the desk and open the other briefcase and look for the budget book.

The interviewer thumbs though the checkbook, stops and squints down at a particular item. "What was this purchase for in August of last year? Indian fish?"

I begin an explanation about purchase of fresh fish from an Indian boat on the river near my home. Before I can finish she asks, "What's the current balance of this checkbook?"

I leave my open briefcases and piles of the requested bank statements on the floor and turn to her desk with the statements from the past year and the budget book. I point out the last figure in the checkbook and indicate it as the current balance, wondering why she couldn't do that herself. I place the pile of a year's bank statements and the budget book on her desk.

"Now you're sure this checkbook balance is current?"

"Yes, as of a couple of days ago."

She begins opening envelopes containing bank statements, barely glancing at any one of them. Abruptly she turns to a file folder on her desk and extracts a single sheet. "What's with the cars parked on the Malfait property? Do they own them?"

"Yes."

"Do you have any paper work with you that shows they own them?"

"Well, no, but those cars have been parked in the front yard for years. Malfaits no longer drive, and neither the cars nor Mom and Dad have had licenses for a long time. I don't know how many years that would be."

"We have to have a true and fair value for those cars. You've said here on this form you filled out for us that those cars are only worth fifty dollars apiece."

"That's what I think is their fair value based on conversations I've had with a number of car people. Both cars are all rusted out, but they may have some value in their parts. Really, they're an eyesore and the city has served abatement notices on them because of neighbors' complaints. They're both junkers, and I've made several calls recently to junkyards about them. The people there say they're worth about fifty bucks apiece, but then they want to charge $50.00 apiece to haul them away--which really means they're worth nothing. I haven't found anyone who is interested in buying them to part them out, and so far no one will haul them off for free."

The DSHS interviewer pulls out a little book from her desk drawer. "Let me see here--this blue book lists Buick sedans in the 50's and 60's at between $3,000 and $16,000. Hmmm, they're probably classic cars."

"That's not possible! I've called several junk dealers and described the years and models. They don't want them. It's going to cost me to have them hauled away!"

The interviewer continues perusing her booklet. "Yes, and this is a very common way people use to try to hide their assets." She looks up at me, "I can't decide anything further until we have an expert of our choosing look at those cars and evaluate them." She shuts the little book and drops it into her desk drawer, making a little smacking sound with her lips and sucking air through her front teeth.

My hot tears spill. I slump further into my chair clutching briefcase number one containing Malfait's financial records. All these people in federal, state and county agencies, whether it's DSHS, hospitals, or Social Security, must take lessons in how to intimidate clients and reduce them to tearful, blubbering idiocy. Next comes the predictable consoling step. It's so rote I want to rip her hand away, when she comes around the desk, scrapes a tissue box in my direction, and pats me on the arm, "It's going to be fine. I need to make some copies. You can put your papers away now."

My DSHS interview has extended over two grueling hours. I leave the building and walk into a raging snowstorm. The icy prickles against my face feel good, somehow validating that I am alive and maybe I'm something more than an inept, helpless, evil, financial sleeze-bag. I can't distinguish my truck from any of the other white automotive lumps in the parking lot, but I tromp toward a largest lump in the second row. When I finally slip and slide up next to the window, I brush the snow away and glance in. My gray travel bag is sitting like a DSHS orphan on the far side of the cab. I struggle with an iced over keyhole and finally get the door open. I heave the two briefcases across the truck seat, each slapping against the travel bag with a cold thud. I grasp the steering wheel and pull myself up onto the truck seat. The four of us, my travel bag, my two briefcases, and I, begin the journey home.

My normal three hour and fifteen minute trip today takes me six hours, much of it in first gear and leaning close to the windshield in order to see the tail-lights of the vehicle ahead and stay in its tire track marks.

Oh well, I'm used to traveling blind and being in one raging storm after another. I haven't really known where I was or where I was headed for years now!

CHAPTER 43

— ∞∞ —

Happy New Year - Bah! Humbug!

JANUARY, 1991. EVERYONE about me is making New Year's Resolutions, most of them aimed at self-improvement. Most of them destined to fail. I resolve to survive and to keep my sanity. *Bah! Humbug!*

Mother shows some signs of improvement. She is devoted to a routine of getting up, dressing, having breakfast at the corner cafe, and visiting Dad at the nursing home. She is more consistent with the Depends, though she often says, "I sure hope this old time of the month will get over soon." Sally, the owner-operator of the cafe, says Mother's spirits are improved. She comes almost every day for breakfast. She *always* studies the menu, then orders bacon and eggs, two pieces of white toast and coffee. She's very chatty with everyone in the cafe. In fact, she's quite sharp lately about people and what's going on in the world. When she's almost finished with breakfast, she usually orders a treat like cheesecake or a milkshake to take to the nursing home for Papa, and sometimes something for Carl, Dad's roommate.

During January Mother's purses show Rolf is staying out of them, and she's spending about $7.00 per day. She and I have a scheme in which I take cash from her monthly pension money and mail some back to her each week throughout the month. This routine seems helpful. She adds her expenses on paper and usually comes up pretty close to her budgeted amount for the week. She is delighted when it matches perfectly.

At the end of January Mother is a little frustrated with the budget system when I arrive for my visit. "Oh, gosh, Betty, I just can't account for my money this time."

"How far off are you?"

"Well, I'm missing fifty-two cents."

"Gee, Mom, that's a lot better than I do on my monthly food budget. You're doing great with your money. I guess our new system of mailing some cash weekly is working out."

"Oh, yes, I like getting the money that way, and I like just getting the mail. You always tape the money inside those pretty cards. It's like I keep getting Christmas cards."

"That's good, Mom. Say, how's that new Christmas microwave? Are you following those directions we taped up on the cabinet and using it?"

"Oh, Betty, the silly thing scares me to death! But did you know you can have the most wonderful baked potato in just five or six minutes?"

I don't know if that means *I can* or *she has been* having a wonderful baked potato. "So are you using it pretty often then?"

"Well, no, not really. It's not worth a damn on those little cartons of soup you got for me! My, God, the sparks fly all over the kitchen!"

"Geez, Mom, the lids on those have a little metal rim. Remember, it says right here on your paper *No Metal in the microwave. Take soup lids off.*"

"Well, I'll just use it for baked potatoes. I can fix me a can of soup a lot better on the regular stove."

"Oh, keep trying, Mom. You'll get better at using it. You can't hurt anything." To myself I mumble, I hope you can't hurt anything. Who knows, it only took two years for the Depends lessons.

The two of us bundle up against the January cold and get on our way doing errands. Mother seems more energetic than usual about our tasks. Her daily walks to the nursing home have been good exercise for her.

When our last stop at the Thrift Bakery is completed and I am pulling the truck into traffic to head for home, Mother speaks up with some urgency, "Wait, I need to get to a hardware store."

"What do you need there?"

"I'd like to have a door key made for you. You know, when you come down you should go in the house if I'm not there. I don't think you should be sleeping in your truck on my driveway anymore. Besides, it's awful cold now in January, and you could get sick doing that. You should go on in the house and sleep in my bed."

"Mother, how thoughtful of you. I would appreciate having a key." Without saying so, I think I'll pass on sleeping in her bed, but the key--WOW! I haven't had one of those since the summer I got married and she asked me to return my door-key--she and Dad guessed I wouldn't be needing it anymore. That's almost thirty years ago. I've been making these weekend helping trips to their home for over five years. Maybe I've earned a key. Some part of Mother's brain and her emotional trust level has been rekindled, and that's more important to me than the key.

After the key purchase, we stop by the nursing home to visit Dad. It's late afternoon and he's asleep, but as soon as we are beside his bed his thin, wrinkled eyelids open and his faded blue eyes take on a momentary sparkle. His mouth forms a ragged uneven smile like a man recuperating from a numbing experience with the dentist. His head stretches toward Mother for a hello kiss, and his irregularly pursed lips make a slobbery smack. I, in turn, get the same affectionate greeting, and then his head falls back to the pillow. I place my hand in his. He squeezes gently and rolls his head in slow, sleight, side to side motion, "Ohhhh, Betty..." The faded blue orbs disappear behind drooping eyelids. His head drops to one side, and his fingers release from my hand. I don't know if he's sad or exhausted--or if he just died.

Mother steps forward and interrupts my concerned musing, "Dad, Dad--look here. I brought you a piece of coconut cream pie."

Dad's wrinkly eyelids flick open, and he twists and presses his head and shoulders as much as he is able to in Mother's direction. His lips begin to work in small preparatory smacking motions causing bits of drool to release at the corners of his mouth. His eyes seek Mother's, "Oh, Mama--you are--such--a blessing."

She laughs. "Yes, a blessing in disguise." She dips the plastic spoon into the creamy mixture and slips a generous spoonful of the pie between the eager lips which now hang in slack-jawed readiness.

The lips close, fitting their irregular margins mostly together. Dad closes his eyes, releases his head and shoulders and flops back against the pillow.

Mother cajoles, "Dad, Dad--open wide. Here we go." Dad pulls toward her again, and she introduces another spoonful.

With repeated encouragement from Mother and strained effort followed by short rests, Dad consumes almost all of the piece of pie. Finally his eyes close and his lips squeeze in defense of the spoon. Mother eats the last couple of bites herself.

I lean close to Dad and stroke his hand. "I'm glad you ate the pie, Dad. Mother said that was one of your favorites. She comes every day and brings you tasty goodies like that which aren't on the menu here. She's helping you get better."

Dad's head rolls away from me. "Ummmm."

Mother steps over and kisses Dad's cheek. "Good night, Dad. I'll see you tomorrow." She turns to me, "Come on, Betty. He'll sleep the whole time now until tomorrow morning. There's no use of our sitting here with him. He'll just sleep. Tomorrow we'll come earlier. He'll be much more talkative. I think I'll bring him some of those beautiful sweet seedless grapes we got today. He loves green grapes."

The next day we make our visit mid-morning. Dad is again dozing when we enter the room, but his eyes flick open much faster than when we visited last evening. Mother leans close, "Look what I've got for you." She dangles a large cluster of lush greenness back and forth in front of his eyes. His eyes struggle to follow the waving motion. The rubbery lips go into their anticipatory irregular smacking. Like a hungry baby bird, his head and shoulders strain to the full extent of his ability as he turns toward Mother. The rest of his body and his arms remain motionless against the whiteness of his bleached hospital nest. Mother plucks a grape from the bunch and rolls it through the eager, rubbery lips into his mouth.

Dad's anticipated savoring comes to a dramatic halt. The rubbery lips pucker and his head falls back onto the pillow, "Oh--shit--Honey. A man--can't eat--those!"

"Why, Dad, these aren't a bit sour." Mother smiles and winks at me, somehow pleased with Dad's alertness and improved speech. She breaks off a smaller cluster from the big bunch. "You must have just had some milk or something." She begins alternately plucking one for him and one for her, gently tucking one grape at a time into his eager lips, until the two of them finish the entire bunch of grapes.

I hope this won't create a whole new Depend problem for either one of them, but for the moment the affectionate sharing of this simple treat is well worth any fecal folderol later. Dad's eyes finally close and he begins to drift.

"Well, Mom, I guess it's his nap time again. Maybe I better get on the road."

"That's fine, Betty. I'll stay awhile. It's a sunny day. I can walk home."

As I pull on my coat Dad's eyes pop open. His body remains still, but he shakes his head side to side with strained vigor, "No--no, kid. You--just--got here."

"I know, Dad, but I have a long drive home, and I have to work to-morrow. I'll see you again in two weeks."

"Oh, kid--two weeks--is--too long. My problems--are heavy."

"I know, and I'm sorry about that. But you're being well cared for here, and Mother is able to come twice a day to help take care of you. You'll be fine."

Tears well, but they do not veil the sadness in his old blue eyes, "Give--me--a kiss." He puckers his distorted mouth and makes a loud smacking noise against my lips. The three of us laugh. "I--like--that."

"I like that, too, Dad. Goodbye."

The next weekend is not a scheduled Ridgeview trip. It's El's birthday. Don and I go to visit both Nick and El at West Pacific College, especially to have a family birthday celebration for her.

It's late afternoon February 2, 1991, when I receive a call from Campus Police.

Understanding of life's paradoxes floods over me, as I stand amid the cake and ice cream celebration of El's 19th birthday and receive the phone call informing me of Dad's death.

I call Mother immediately. She answers on the first ring and is clear for a few words but becomes hysterical—sobbing, wailing, and beating on the back kitchen door. I have never experienced hysteria with my mother nor anyone else. And definitely not long-distance. In fact, over the years Mother has almost never even cried about anything.

"Mother, Mother—please, talk to me. I need to know what happened. Mother, I need your help. What happened?"

After several repetitions, my fumbling words sink in, "Oh, Betty, I was feeding him a blueberry muffin, and he didn't want any more. He said he was tired, and he rolled over like he was going to sleep just like he always does, but I couldn't wake him up. I called the nurse, and she came in to check him. She asked me to step out for a moment. While she was in with Dad, Rolf arrived. He had come to visit Dad. Then the nurse came out and told us both Mr. Malfait was expiring now. I went back in and held his hand. His hand was warm, and he squeezed my hand so hard it hurt. Then he just let go and went to sleep…Oh, my God, I don't know what I'm going to do without him! I never thought he'd go first!"

I tighten my grip on the phone and bow my head.

Thank you, God, for the blessing of a quiet, clean death for my father! Please be with all of us now.

From West Pacific College campus my journey to Ridgeview takes four and a half hours. I stop along the Interstate every hour and call Mother as I promised I would. Each time she promptly answers the phone in a clear voice and then breaks into uncontrollable sobbing and unintelligible blubbering about blueberry muffins, Rolf being at the nursing home, the nurse checking Dad, and Mr. Malfait's expiring. Each call quiets down to the concluding phrase, "Oh, my God, I don't know what I'm ever going to do without him. I never thought he'd go first."

That's my cue to begin my own repetitive mantra, "I know, Mother. Let's both be thankful his death was quiet and peaceful."

"Oh, Betty, his hand was so warm, and he squeezed my hand so hard it hurt. Then he just went to sleep."

"I know, Mother. And let's be thankful his death was quiet and peaceful. Now, Mom, I want you to look over at the stove clock and tell me what time it is." We compare times, and I tell her when to expect my next call.

CHAPTER 44

Do Funerals Always Bring
Out Love and Hate?

THE WEEK OF the funeral is busy. Each day my ever-present things-to-do-list gets pared down, and the next morning I make an even longer list. This week I learn firsthand why my mother always took food to people's houses when someone died. It's a practical way of unspoken care by the person doing it. It's a way for the family of the deceased to be on automatic pilot and occasionally talk about something other than the deceased, and hopefully to be nourished at a time when food and fixing food is not a very high priority. In addition to food, there are cards, money, and visitors. All the expressions of sympathy are appreciated, although I can't help wondering where some of these loving friends have been the past few years. Why does it take a funeral to bring them out?

Even simple funerals are expensive. Dad's costs $4,445.87, not including the cemetery plots which Malfaits purchased years ago. I hope this bill will be covered by insurance money from policies I have yet to locate. The funeral home director isn't worried about that, but I am. I have no idea where those policies are. I know where in the house they were kept for thirty years or more. But not too long ago when I uncovered that particular bureau drawer while searching for the Whidbey deed, they weren't there, and I haven't had time to look further.

Rolf and I work amicably on some funeral arrangements: times, flowers, clothes, casket and headstone. But for the most part, we keep our distance from one another.

Aunt Mavis arrives without Mother questioning how she got there or when or who picked her up in Portland. Her presence is comforting to Mother, who has since the day of Dad's death been subject to frequent outbreaks of hysterical sobbing wherever she is. Her walking has become unsteady and she collapses easily with little or no warning.

The three of us are supposed to go to the funeral home for a viewing, but Mother's unpredictable behavior makes both Mavis and me hesitant. "Mother, it was you who said we had to allow time for a viewing this week. The funeral home called this morning and said things are all ready. Do you want to view Dad's body or be with people who come to pay their respects?"

"No, I don't want to look at any dead body. Oh my God, I don't know what I'm ever going to do without Dad. I never thought he'd go first..."

My own mantra is becoming less soothing. "But, Mother, he did go first. And right now we have to deal with that. Do you want to go to the funeral home and stay a while for the visitation in case people come by-- or do you not want to go?"

"Oh my God, I don't know what I'm ever going to do without him..."

Mavis tries. "Francine, Betty and I need to know if you want to go with us to the funeral home."

"Oh my God, Mavis, I don't know what I'm ever going to do without Dad. I guess I'll just go home with you."

"Well, Francine, you can come for a visit with me sometime, but this time I'm flying on a special reduced rate airline ticket, which means I can only fly at certain times. I can't possibly get you a ticket to travel with me, and I'm not going anyplace today. Listen, we can talk about you visiting me another time. Right now, do you want to go to the funeral home with Betty and me?"

Aunt Mavis' question is met with another tearful outburst. She and I look at each other and shrug, returning to the kitchen and coffee cups that have already been refilled too many times.

Mother follows us a moment later. Groping the backs of the chairs around the kitchen, she makes her way to the back door and yanks off a paper towel from the roll under the kitchen cabinet, blows her nose mightily, and says to Mavis, "I'd like to go to the funeral home with you and Betty now." She turns and hobbles from the kitchen. By the time Aunt Mavis and I catch up with her, she has her coat on, is harnessed with her overloaded shoulder strap purse, and is opening the front door.

Mother jerks to a halt. "Oh, here's the mailman."

He hands her a stack of mail, and she begins ripping open cards as she stands in the entryway. Her weeping starts anew. "Oh, Mavis, I don't know what I'm ever going to do without Dad. I've just got to go home with you. Couldn't you please let me come home with you?"

Mavis is firm. "Francine, you've got to pull yourself together! They wouldn't even let you on an airplane like this! Of course, you can come and visit me. There's plenty of time for that next summer. You can stay a couple of months if you like."

I try to support Mavis' trip idea from a practical viewpoint and my newly established guardianship role, "You know, Mother, you really can't afford to buy an airline ticket today anyway. You don't have that kind of cash. Next summer is a much better time. Between now and then you could easily save enough for a ticket." In my own mind I don't know how that can possibly happen, but I'll figure that out later.

Mother looks at me with a wrinkled brow and questioning eyes. Her volume shoots up, "I should have plenty of money for an airplane ticket if I want to go home with Mavis *now!* Dad and I worked hard all these years, and we never got to take that trip again!" She turns to Mavis with the same volume, "I want to go home with you, Mavis! Why won't you let me go home with you?"

Mavis comes back at the same volume, "Francine, I've told you, you can come for a visit, but we're not going right now!"

I share the raised volume, "Mom, please, Mavis and I are both trying to say that you *will* be able to make that trip, just not *today*! We have to deal with Dad's funeral--with the viewing--right now--*today!*"

The front door is still ajar from Mother's mail pickup when Rolf suddenly pushes it wide open, "Hey, what's up?"

Mavis tries for a cheery tone, "Francine, look who's here."

Rolf steps through our stalled family group and flops down on the couch, "Yeah, I'm here, what little's left of me. I started out about 4:30 this morning. I got in three good loads today. We're haulin' some really nice logs from up near the mountain and bringin' 'em down here to Ridgeview. They go from here straight to Japan. Man, someone's makin' big bucks on these foreign log deals, and it sure ain't me. I'm workin' my butt off for chicken feed. It's hotter than hell in that truck cab all day. I'm beat!"

I bite my tongue at Rolf's *poor-me fanfare.* I would like to lash out at him about why we're stalled here in the doorway shouting at one another about Mother's lack of trip money.

Dear God, my faith and forgiveness are in short supply at this moment. Please help me control my emotions.

Rolf interrupts my contemplation as he pulls himself up off the couch and steps in front of me. He draws an old grocery store plastic produce bag from his jacket pocket. "You know, a while back when things really began gettin' goofy around here, I rescued some paperwork, which I guess might be important about now. These are paid-up insurance policies. When things was really bad here, I figured I'd better rescue these. They'd be important at a future time." He hands me the bag.

I remove the content and thumb through the policy titles, "Did you also rescue some wills?"

"Nope, I never seen no wills. I thought you'd get copies of their wills from that guardianship lawyer."

I return the insurance policies to the plastic produce bag, "There should have been copies of their wills here, too, since Mom and Dad kept their wills with these insurance policies. For over thirty years all of those papers were in that back bedroom in the top bureau drawer locked up in that little black metal box."

Rolf jerks his head in a quick sideways motion. "Nope, I never seen no wills and no black metal box."

"Rolf, I have to tell you I'm pissed about your taking this stuff from the house. You were here the day after Dad died when I got back from picking up Aunt Mavis at the airport. You knew then I had searched that bedroom, and you knew Mavis and I searched it all over again. You knew we were looking for the life insurance policies. We spent six hours going through all the drawers and closets in the back bedroom, and moving your boxes and junk around so we could get to the dresser drawers. I had a wretched allergy headache all evening as a result. That bedroom is filled floor to the ceiling with boxes of books, clothes, boots, boat machinery, guns, and all kinds of stuff--none of which belongs to Malfaits. Rolf, you had these policies *then*. You made us both go through all that useless work, and you didn't have a right to take them from the house in the first place."

Rolf shrugs, "Well, that's the paperwork you wanted, and it's here now." He turns away from me with a pleasurable smirk on his face. "I gotta get goin'. I got some people to see." No one says anything as he opens the front door and departs.

I hate Rolf. I know I am hurt and upset, but I HATE him! This is not how Mother or Dad would want us to behave. Neither of them would have ever done something like this, especially when death was stressing an already delicate situation. In fact, I recall a time where they helped after a friend died and her only daughter was living on the East Coast. They cleared out an entire house. They were totally supportive, impeccably honest, intent only on making life easier for the daughter. What is the matter with Rolf? We didn't grow up this way. Is there a gene for this kind of orneriness or jealousy? Is it anger because his financial scheming has been found out and exposed? That's probable, but if time moved backwards and decisions were to be made again, I would still seek the guardianship without him, and with better reason now than I had then. I feel I have acted prudently. I have been respectful and much too patient. I have been prayerful. I have sought professional guidance legally, religiously, from community agencies and counselors.

Attendance at the scheduled viewing does not take place. None of us resumes talk of the viewing nor taking trips. The afternoon blurs into evening, and I busy myself with ever-present tasks in the kitchen and the accumulation of casseroles and other food items. Mavis and Mother alternate the sobbing routine with watching TV news. After dinner, Mavis and I leave Mother at 516 and return to The Sterling where the two of us study the insurance policies. There's some sense of relief at having this information and knowing the funeral expenses are covered and some funds remaining--perhaps enough for some home repairs and maybe even for a trip to West Virginia But the missing will is worrisome.

Dear God, I'm sorry. I don't really hate Rolf. I hate what he has done! I feel as if anything I have done has been too little too late. Dad didn't live long enough, at least not in clear enough mental capacity, to understand and appreciate what I was trying to do. Mother is declining before my very eyes, and only you know what Dad's death will do to her. I feel awful for getting her hopes up about a trip to West Virginia, because I don't think that will ever be a viable consideration. It's not just the money--I don't think she could physically make the trip. Oh, God, I truly would like to be able to share with my brother at this time and have some sense of the love and enjoyment we had in our growing up years. What I have now instead of a brother is an ingenious, slobby, scum-bag crook! I feel sometimes over the years what my family may have excused as "unique" behaviors in Rolf may have been the advent of deviant, destructive mental behavior, and Malfaits' unconditional love for him began to be expressed monetarily long before I was aware of it. They were classic enablers for his behavior for years--and ultimately enablers to this despicable living family tragedy. Please, God, get me through this, and then get me away from Rolf!

CHAPTER 45

The Funeral

THE NEXT MORNING, the day of Dad's funeral, Rolf knocks loudly on the door of the room Mavis and I are sharing at The Sterling. It's 7:15 am.

Aunt Mavis jumps up to answer.

Even before she has the door completely opened, Rolf's voice barks, "Hey, did you guys take Mom to the funeral home yesterday to that viewing?"

Mavis rubs her eyes. "Well, good morning, Rolf. No, we didn't. She cried all afternoon and again after you left. She'd just get quieted down, and we'd ask about going over there, and she would break down again. We finally decided going to a viewing may not be in her best interest. We're planning to go early today and try to take her to view before the service."

"Well, I think you better get at it, because Mom needs to do that."

I pull up my covers and bite my tongue as a jumble of thoughts flit through my mind about Rolf knowing what Mom needs.

"Rolf, we were about to get up anyway. We'll get things done. Don't worry about us. You need to go on and get yourself ready for the funeral."

Rolf leans back from the doorway and stares down his nose, "I *am* ready."

Aunt Mavis blinks in disbelief at his old black and red plaid truck-driver shirt, his frayed blue jeans, and his stained canvas hunting vest lined with spaces meant to hold shotgun shells. "Is that what you're going to wear?"

"Yep! This *is* me! I ain't gonna put on no airs just for this day. Gettin' shock value from folks today is nothin' new. This is just me."

I pull my covers higher and mutter. "Yeah, that's you, Rolf. Today, however, I have the feeling you're using your appearance for some kind of showmanship."

Aunt Mavis persists. "Well, you could have washed that vest, couldn't you?"

"Nah, that's just how it is."

"Well, I'm glad you don't have it full of shells."

Rolf chuckles, "Oh, by the way, I was talkin' to the reverend yesterday, and I let him know I would be havin' a few things to say about Dad's life and all."

Mavis releases an embarrassed raspy half-chuckle and scowls, "Isn't that the preacher's job?"

"Yeah, yeah, I guess it is, but I just told him there were a few things that needed to be said, and I would be having some time."

"Remember, Rolf, they pay the preacher to do that part."

"Yeah, yeah--he already told me about the time and all, but he can just wait."

"Where are you going now so early?"

"Well, you know, we've got this pall-bearers' breakfast out at Bonnie and Clyde's Restaurant. That'll probably be a couple of hours. I'll be back over to the funeral home in plenty of time."

Mavis brow wrinkles. "I never heard anything about a pall-bearers' breakfast. In fact, I don't think I've ever heard of such a thing."

Rolf turns and walks away calling over his shoulder, "Well, that's where I'm going."

Mavis closes the door and crawls back into bed grumbling about pall-bearers' breakfasts and stained hunting vests.

A short while later Mavis and I both get up, as further sleep is not going to happen. We dress for the day and go to pick up Mother, hoping to take her to the funeral home for a visitation. When we arrive at 516 we find her refreshed and she wants to join us. We respond to her positive mood and get all of us back into the car immediately.

At the funeral home we make our way to the chapel where we are greeted by a floral display extending all across the front along the steps on both sides and by the walls down to the family pew.

Mother stops in her tracks. "My goodness, there's more flowers in here than around the whole house at 516. How wonderful that people remembered Dad and me like this. Betty, read all these tags to me."

At each arrangement I read the tag, and Mother explains to Mavis the relationship and significance of the sender. She seems comforted by the beauty and thoughtfulness of friends and neighbors who sent all the beautiful flowers.

We move on to the front of the chapel where Dad's body lies in a casket open for viewing of the upper torso. Mother pulls out the tag from an arrangement draped over the casket. "Who sent this big old ring thing?"

"That's a family piece--you know--from all of us."

"Well, I don't remember ordering that."

Before either of us can respond, Mother leans over and looks into the casket. "Dad sure does look better with that beard off!"

Mavis asks, "Do you want to touch him, Francine?"

Mother looks up at Mavis. "Oh, God, no!"

"Do you want to just sit by him for a while?"

"No."

I offer another option. "Mother, would you like to say any kind of prayer?"

"No, I've already done all the praying I'm going to do. Betty would you read me the cards on all the flowers, please?"

Though I had already done that, we again circle the room, pausing, admiring, and reading the tags on each floral arrangement. At the last one, a potted Benjamin fig from relatives in West Virginia, Mother says, "Dad will sure like that one. He'll probably plant it outside...Betty, I need some coffee."

"Well, Mom, they don't have coffee here. We can go out for some. There's a restaurant just three blocks over."

"That would be fine."

Mavis asks, "Are you sure you wouldn't like to stay here? It won't be long until people begin to show up, and you won't have any more private visitation time. One of us could run out and get the coffee."

"No, I don't want to hang around here, and I don't need any more private visitation. I want to go to coffee--and I'm hungry."

We sign the guest book and leave.

As I pull into the restaurant parking lot, Mother puts her face in her hands and breaks into wrenching sobs, "I just don't know what I'm going to do. I never thought Dad would go first..."

I am gentle but firm, "Mother, I will take you home or to a park to sit for a while, or I'll go through a drive-through and get your coffee, but Mavis and I cannot take you into a restaurant like this. Other people have a right to eat and not be stressed by your grief. It's okay for you to cry, but we can't impose on others in public places."

She stops as quickly as she started. She rubs her nose with an already well rubbed tissue she had been clutching. "I'm fine. I want to go into the restaurant."

We do that, and her 'coffee' order is an egg, two pieces of bacon, two pieces of white toast and coffee. We get through breakfast pleasantly and return to the funeral home.

We barely seat ourselves at the front of the chapel when people begin to arrive. By 11:30 the place is pretty well filled. Promptly at that time the funeral director walks down the center aisle accompanied by Rolf. Both men stop at the family pew, and the director gestures, "Here's where you should sit, Rolf."

I am seated nearest to the aisle, but there's ample room for Rolf. He squints down the pew at each of us. Mother is seated between Mavis and me. Next is El, then Nick, and furthermost down the bench by the wall is Don. Rolf makes no sign of recognition nor greeting. He turns away, scanning all the rows of the chapel in the softened light.

The funeral director leans closer to him and whispers, "Rolf, I really do need you to be seated here on the family pew by your sister, because I do the music and sound system from behind that curtain on the stage. When it gets to be time for you to speak, I can signal from back there. You'll be able to see my hand signal, and I won't have to call out to you and disturb the service. There's no way you can see me if you're further back in the room. You really need to sit here with the family."

Rolf reluctantly sits down as close to the aisle end of the bench as he can, leaving a wide space between the two of us. I sense his wrathful vibes, and I feel bad knowing I am a contributor to them.

Mother leans over toward Rolf and me and loudly cuts through the silent, frozen furor of the bench, "They, lookit up there. That's Pastor Ted up there behind Dad's casket. What's he doing up there? Why, he's gained so much weight I hardly recognize him."

I reach out and pat her hand. "Shhh, Mother. Remember, he's going to do the sermon part. You're the one who asked for him."

There are a few chuckles from the pew behind us as Mother continues, "Well, Lord God A-Mighty, he looks awful. He looks older than anybody here, including Dad. He looks like he should the one in the box up there." There are more chuckles.

God, what do I do now? Please be with us in this place.

The strains of "How Great Thou Art" fill the air. Mother leans over to Rolf and me once again and comments, "That music is really shitty."

I don't dare turn around. This time the chuckles are muffled by the music extolling how great God *really* is!

From behind the screen a hand points to Rolf and then to the podium. Rolf pushes himself up from the pew and walks slowly forward. He labors up the two steps to the stage and moves close to the casket, pausing to look down at Dad's body. With his back to the audience, in a firm voice but to no one in particular he says, "He was a good dad. May he rest in peace."

Rolf turns and takes a bundle of yellow folded papers from his shirt pocket. As he crosses the stage he unfolds them and shakes them out to their full yellow legal pad size. At the pulpit he smoothes the papers out several times before extracting a pair of thick reading glasses from a pocket in his hunting vest. He adjusts the glasses on his face and looks out at the audience, letting his magnified eyes rove and finally come to a point of concentration on the family pew.

I stare back up at his enlarged eyes and wonder if he can actually see anyone through the thick glasses. His face is red and his brow is furrowed in deep lines. Beads of sweat sparkle on his bald head.

His gaze lifts back up toward the back of the chapel, "Roger Virgil Malfait was one of the real good guys. He was part of what this country is all about. He was a hard worker from the time he was a young boy and throughout his whole life. He came from good Southern stock, just like many of you. When he graduated high school, he married Mom, there." Rolf motions toward the front pew. "Times were hard. The Great Depression wasn't over. Mom and him began their life on a piece of land that Dad made into a farm; and you all know how hard that kind of work is. They had a son, Franklin, who was a joy to them, but before he was two he got sick with pneumonia. Back in them days there wasn't much treatment available, and Franklin didn't make it. But Mom and Dad faced the hurt of that loss, and they went on with their lives. Dad, he was always looking for a better way for him and Mom. And when he heard about the great timber industry developing out here in Washington State, he knew if he could just get out here he could make it. That's what he did. He come to a little place up here in the mountains called Randal, Washington. And being a willing worker to take on any job, he was hired right away. He worked and scrimped and saved a whole year, and then he brought Mom out to be with him. Not long after that he got a job down here in the mills in Ridgeview. The two of them rented themselves a little house, and Dad even got himself a Model T Ford. It wasn't long 'til I came along in 1936, and that made them a happy family again. Of course, the war was brewin' in Europe by then, and it wasn't too much longer before a lot of our men were goin' off to war. That's when Mom started working in the paper industry. Both Mom and Dad always worked hard, and when the war was over they bought two lots in Ridgeview, and they worked hard there, too. They worked together and built their own home. Dad did most of the construction work himself. He built that house just like he worked. If one stud was required, he put in two. If two nails was needed, he put in four. I mean that house was built to hold up. I'm sure any building inspector around here would tell you that house at 516 is one of the best-built houses in Ridgeview."

Is this is a eulogy to the house that Dad built or to Dad? And wasn't I born sometime in that time span?

"Dad was always there for me whether it was to teach me to drive a stick shift or to help me pack out a quarter of a deer or an elk. He taught me what real work was all about. And, you know..." Rolf looks down at the front pew moving his glance from Don to Nick to El to Aunt Mavis-- to me. "Well, you all know, just like I do, most young people today don't know what hard work is all about. They've had everything done for them." The bifocal glance becomes a sweaty glare, and Rolf's magnified concentration focuses squarely on me for several seconds. "Parents today generally give their kids everything their mouths fall open for."

I stare steadily back up into Rolf's eyes, at least as steadily into his eyes as can be through the thick reading lenses.

Rolf is first to release from our blurred eye contact. He lowers his eyes toward the pile of yellow papers on the lectern and wags his head slowly back and forth. When he raises his head, he does another bifocal scan of the audience. "Like I said, a lot of folks today just don't know what real work is. They've never really had to bear down and make a livin' by the sweat of their brow like Mom and Dad did--and like many of you did--and still are."

Rolf rearranges his yellow papers. When he has located his place in his notes, he looks out at the audience and continues, "Another thing I'd like to say about Roger Malfait is that he was always a man of his word. When the folks were buildin' that house, money was tight and so was buildin' materials. Sometimes they needed materials right then to do a certain job. And if they didn't have the money, they could go into the buildin' materials store over here on Main Street and get whatever they needed on credit. When Dad said, 'I'll be down here next week when I get paid and pay you for this,' that's just what he meant. His word was as good as cash. And he would--he'd go right down and pay on his next payday--and always in cash. Dad was a man of his word--to Mom, to me, to everyone."

I've been left out again. I guess I'm in the everyone group.

"Most folks nowadays just give their kids everything on a silver platter."

The front pew receives another bi-focal glare.

"Those young people don't know what real work is. People like that have just gotten above their upbringin'."

Maybe I wasn't left out. I'm must be one of most folks or maybe I've gotten above my upbringing.

Rolf pauses and removes his reading glasses and returns them to the pocket of the hunting vest. He gathers the long yellow sheets of legal paper and taps them against the lectern until they form an orderly grouping. "Well, I promised Reverend Ted here that I'd stick to the time limit, and I mean to do that. Let me summarize by just saying again--Roger Malfait was a good dad, a hard worker, and a man of his word."

Rolf clutches the thick sheaf of yellow papers and walks slowly from the podium across the stage to the center steps. He ignores the family pew and continues down the center aisle to the back of the chapel.

The chorus of "How Great Thou Art" starts softly and crescendos to normal volume. As the last phrase echoes through the stillness of the crowded chapel, Pastor Ted emerges from his seat to the left of the coffin. He lays his watch on the stand, arranges his Bible and notes, and looks out over the audience and smiles. "Today is not a sad day for Roger Virgil Malfait. It's a glorious day, a time of rejoicing, a time of..."

Old Parents and Purple Tulips

A chill shudders through my body, but I'm not cold. Pastor Ted's words are lost as my thoughts silently rehash Rolf's speech. From the beginning it was the antithesis of God's greatness. It was a rambling family history. Parts of it were good, but my birth was utterly omitted. I was not remembered as a significant family member at any time in Malfait history. But I think I was remembered and chastised for not knowing what hard work is, for handing every possible thing to my children on a silver platter, and for getting above my upbringing. I wasn't named specifically, but I know those words were for me. Thank God his spiel stayed within the time limits Pastor Ted set for him.

I glance toward the podium and tune back in to the familiar words Pastor Ted is reading, "through the valley of the shadow of death, I will fear no evil; for You are with me." My lips begin to silently mimic the reading. "Your rod and Your staff, they comfort me. You prepare a table before me in the presence of my enemies; You anoint my head with oil; my cup runs over. Surely goodness and mercy shall follow me all the days of my life; and I will dwell in the house of the Lord forever." Pastor Ted closes his Bible. "Shall we pray? Almighty God, hold each of us today in your comforting arms, help us to rejoice in the return of one of your own to be with you."

Pastor Ted's funeral message recalls times when Dad was an active member of his congregation, when he and Mother both repeatedly expressed Christian kindness to his family and others in the congregation. He extolled the virtue of Roger Malfait, a man of simple and constant faith, a man of God. I relax in the family pew and allow his words to soothe like a gentle rain.

After the closing prayer, Pastor Ted slips behind the screen, and the funeral director emerges and moves to the center of the platform where he busies himself rearranging flowers near the casket. He turns to the audience and announces, "Those of you who wish to do so may now come forward and file by the casket."

Mother asks aloud, "What are *we* supposed to do?"

I whisper back, "We have to sit here for a minute until all the people go by."

Mafaits' friends and neighbors, mostly folks of seven or eight decades in age, file obediently by the open casket out of respect for the deceased, for the family, and out of the social habit of their generation. When the last person turns from the casket, the funeral director asks the pall bearers to go with him to help prepare the cars to move in a procession to the cemetery for the internment service. Don and Aunt Mavis walk Mother to the family limo. Nick and El depart to move our family car into the line behind the limousine. I don't know where Rolf is.

I approach Dad's casket by myself. I feel compelled to touch his cold hand and speak to his inert body, hopeful somewhere in the vastness of the universe his soul will hear me.

"Dad, I too believe you were a man of simple but constant faith, just as Pastor Ted said. I've always known that, ever since I was a small child listening to you say your prayers. I never doubted your relationship to Jesus as I heard each prayer end In Jesus' name, Amen. In these latter years your calling has been more like Oh, Jesus, kid--But somehow I think even those addresses were heard by the Almighty. I never doubted you loved Jesus, and I never doubted you loved and adored me. And if I did wrong, you probably would have had a hard time even believing it. I loved being your helper on all the various building projects. I loved going to the store with you. And from the time of that old mint green 1948 Buick on through an assortment of your hand-picked automotive treasures, I loved sitting on your lap and helping you drive. My special driver-training stretch of the street was from the Lutheran Church on the corner the whole three blocks down to 516. I've cherished all the work we've done together throughout my growing up years to make yards and gardens--in Don's and my first home on Lake Serenity, again in Woods View, and then on the Sylvan Way farm. You always wanted things to grow and be beautiful, and they surely did. I cherish the laughter, the squeals of delight, and the surprises shared between you and my children. They so adored you and your sense of humor. I regret we all were not able to share more of such moments in these last few years, but the children's love for you was never lessened by circumstances of our family problem, nor was Don's and mine. I love you for teaching me to love, and I often think that the stability of my relationship to Don and to my family is in great stead because that's how my relationship was to you. I could always count on you. Now that you're gone, I will continue to try to be a helper to Mother. Dad, I promise I'll be fair and honest in all things, and I will try to accomplish things that I know you would want done. With no further regrets, I celebrate your life *and* your death, and I will hold forever in my heart your promise that we will know *all* when we're on the other side.

I love you. Thanks, Dad!"

Author's youthful mother and father
at look-out over Columba River

Postscript

AFTER DAD'S DEATH, life goes on for Mother, Mavis, Rolf, and me and my family. Mother lives another four years. Care-taking and guardianship tasks do not become easier. It's still hard with only one.

Dear God, you are so good!

Find resources and resolve in the sequel to this book:
Discombobulated Purple Tulips: Continuing To Love An Aging Parent

CPSIA information can be obtained
at www.ICGtesting.com
Printed in the USA
FSOW02n0852150615
7962FS